JavaScript Step by Step, Second Edition

Steve Suehring

Published with the authorization of Microsoft Corporation by:
O'Reilly Media, Inc.
1005 Gravenstein Highway North
Sebastopol, California 95472

Printed and bound in the United States of America.

1 2 3 4 5 6 7 8 9   M   5 4 3 2 1 0

Microsoft Press titles may be purchased for educational, business or sales promotional use. Online editions are also available for most titles (*http://my.safaribooksonline.com*). For more information, contact our corporate/institutional sales department: (800) 998-9938 or *corporate@oreilly.com*. Visit our website at *microsoftpress.oreilly.com*. Send comments to *mspinput@microsoft.com*.

Acquisitions and Development Editor: Russell Jones
Production Editor: Holly Bauer
Production Services: Online Training Solutions, Inc.
Technical Reviewer: Michael Bazarewsky
Indexing: Potomac Indexing, LLC
Cover: Karen Montgomery
Illustrator: Robert Romano

978-0-735-64552-3

To Chris

—Steve Suehring

Contents at a Glance

Table of Contents

Part I JavaWhat? The Where, Why, and How of JavaScript

What do you think of this book? We want to hear from you!

Microsoft is interested in hearing your feedback so we can continually improve our books and learning resources for you. To participate in a brief online survey, please visit:

www.microsoft.com/learning/booksurvey/

Part II **Applying JavaScript**

What do you think of this book? We want to hear from you!

Microsoft is interested in hearing your feedback so we can continually improve our books and learning resources for you. To participate in a brief online survey, please visit:

www.microsoft.com/learning/booksurvey/

Acknowledgements

Every time I write a book, I get mired in a futile attempt to thank everyone who has helped make it possible. I originally thought that I should thank everyone and their respective families in case I never wrote a book again. But now that I've written several books, some of them twice, there seems to be less urgency to thank everyone. It's not that people need to be thanked less or that I did this all myself—far from it. But inevitably I always forget to thank someone, and though they may not be offended (who cares, it's just a technology book), I still feel bad.

And yet as I sit here and write these acknowledgements, I still want to thank some people. As always, this is in no particular order and the list is incomplete. Obviously, thank you to Rebecca and Jakob and my family, who support the 16 to 20 hour days involved in getting a book written in a short time. Thanks to Russell Jones at O'Reilly for his editing and encouragement throughout, and thanks to Neil Salkind at Studio B as well. Thanks to Chris Tuescher, John Hein, Jeremy Guthrie, and Jim Leu, Andy Berkvam, Dan Noah, Justin Hoerter, and Mark Little. All those individuals told me that when I thank them in a book they feel compelled to buy a copy. (If it worked like that for everyone, I'd go get the phone book.) While I'm fishing for people to thank, I should thank Jason, Kelly, John, and Jeff as well as the web team and all my coworkers.

Thanks to brother Bob for helping me choose music to write by. Thanks as well to Jim Oliva and John Eckendorf. More than one Saturday morning was spent listening to the radio while writing, and it made working on a Saturday morning less painful. Thank you to Tim and Rob at Partners, Pat Dunn, and Dave Marie as well. Thank you to Jeff Currier for putting a door on my office.

Thank you also to the readers who sent feedback for the first edition of the book. That helped in shaping some of the areas to highlight in this second edition.

After rereading these acknowledgements, I realize I should have just thanked everyone using first names. That would give plausible deniability: "Yes, when I thanked John, I really meant you and not the other one." I think there was someone else that I promised to thank, too, but I can't recall who, but thank you, too.

Introducing *JavaScript Step by Step, Second Edition*

Much has changed since the first edition of *JavaScript Step by Step* was written in 2007. The underlying JavaScript specification received a major update; Microsoft released Windows Internet Explorer 8—and now 9 (which is about to be released as I write this); JavaScript development frameworks have matured and are now ubiquitous; and browsers other than Internet Explorer and Firefox, such as Safari, Chrome, and mobile browsers, became much more popular.

This second edition of *JavaScript Step by Step* builds on the foundation laid down by the first edition. The underlying architecture of the JavaScript language is largely the same, but its use has become pervasive, increasing hugely even in just the last three years. With that in mind, the layout and coverage of the book have also remained largely the same, with two notable exceptions: this edition places a much greater emphasis on JavaScript event handling, and it includes an entirely new section covering JavaScript libraries. Specifically, the book focuses on jQuery, which can help simplify JavaScript development, especially on large projects.

Throughout the book, you'll find highlights and additions for the new features in the latest version of JavaScript. Also, the examples used in the book received greater scrutiny, in multiple browsers, to reflect the reality of today's web landscape. Reader feedback from the first edition is reflected in the content and was the impetus for adding jQuery and emphasizing event handling.

The introduction to the first edition is still relevant and applicable, and so I've included it here.

JavaScript is an integral language for web application development, regardless of whether you're adding interactivity to a web page or creating an entire application. Today's web wouldn't be the same without JavaScript.

JavaScript is a standards-based language with a formal specification; however, as any web developer will tell you, almost every web browser interprets that specification differently, which makes web developers' jobs more difficult. Fortunately, most web browsers are converging in their support and interpretation of JavaScript's core functions.

This book provides an introductory look at JavaScript, including some of its core functions as well as newer features and paradigms, such as Asynchronous JavaScript and XML (AJAX). Today's web users rely on many different platforms and many different browsers to view web content. This fact was central to development of every aspect of the book, so you'll see screenshots in multiple browsers and an emphasis on standards-based, rather than proprietary, JavaScript development.

The first part of the book examines JavaScript and helps you get started developing JavaScript applications. You don't need any specific tools for JavaScript development, so you see how to create JavaScript files in Microsoft Visual Studio, in Eclipse, and even in Notepad (or any text editor). Next, the book examines JavaScript's core language and functions, followed by an exploration of the relationship between JavaScript and the web browser. Finally, you see AJAX demonstrated and see how to build dynamic search forms.

The final part of the book highlights JavaScript frameworks and libraries, giving specific focus to jQuery and jQuery UI.

Who Should Read This Book?

This book is for beginning JavaScript programmers—people who are interested in learning the basics of modern JavaScript programming: the language syntax, how it works in browsers, what the common cross-browser problems are, and how to take advantage of AJAX and third-party libraries such as jQuery to add interactivity to your web pages.

Features and Conventions of This Book

This book takes you step by step through the process of learning the JavaScript programming language. Starting at the beginning of the book and following each of the examples and exercises provides the maximum benefit to help you to gain knowledge about the JavaScript programming language.

If you already have some familiarity with JavaScript, you might be tempted to skip the first chapter of this book. However, Chapter 1, "JavaScript Is More than You Might Think," details some of the background history of JavaScript as well as some of the underlying premise for this book, both of which might be helpful in framing the discussion for the remainder of the book. Chapter 2, "Developing in JavaScript," shows you how to get started with programming in JavaScript. If you're already familiar with web development, you might already have a web development program, and therefore you might be tempted to skip Chapter 2 as well. Nevertheless, you should become familiar with the pattern used in Chapter 2 to create JavaScript programs.

The book contains a Table of Contents that will help you to locate a specific section quickly. Each chapter contains a detailed list of the material that it covers.

In addition, you can download the source code for many of the examples shown throughout the book.

Convention	Meaning
Lists	Step-by-step exercises are denoted by procedural lists with steps beginning with 1.
See Also	These paragraphs point you to other sources of information about a specific topic.
Tip/Note/ Important	Tips and notes feature additional bits of information that might be helpful for a given subject.
Inline Code	Inline code—that is, code that appears within a paragraph—is shown in *italic* font.
`Code Blocks`	Code blocks are shown in a different font to highlight the code.

What's in the Companion Content

The downloadable companion content included with this book contains all the important source code from the examples and exercises shown throughout the book. The download consists of projects and files laid out on a per-chapter basis—one directory for each chapter. Each chapter directory contains the step-by-step exercises used within that chapter.

Because JavaScript is usually dependent on a surrounding web page, the source code for the step-by-step exercises has been split within the directories. This enables you to copy and paste much of the repetitive HTML and concentrate on entering the JavaScript into the example.

Each chapter directory also contains a CompletedCode subdirectory that contains the entire example. You can open the files in the CompletedCode folder to see the examples as laid out in the chapter.

Downloading the Companion Content

Most of the chapters in this book include exercises that let you interactively try out new material you learn in the main text. All the sample projects and files are available for download from the book's catalog page on the website for Microsoft's publishing partner, O'Reilly Media, at:

http://oreilly.com/catalog/9780735645523/

Click the Companion Content link on that page. Locate and download the file 9780735645523-files.zip. Unzip that file into a folder on your local drive.

Minimum System Requirements

The code will work on many platforms, including Microsoft Windows, Linux, and Mac.

- **Processor** A Pentium 133 megahertz (MHz) or greater. (Any computer capable of running a web browser with JavaScript support.)

- **Memory** 64 megabytes (MB) of RAM or any amount that can run a computer capable of using a web browser with JavaScript support.

- **Hard disk** 2 MB free hard disk space.

- **Operating System** Windows 98SE or later, most distributions of Linux, and versions of Mac OS X.

- **Display Monitor** with 640x480 or higher screen resolution and 16-bit or higher color depth.

- **Software** Any web browser capable of running JavaScript. Internet Explorer 6 or later, Mozilla Firefox 2.0 or later, Safari 2 or later, Opera 9, and Konqueror 3.5.2 or later are recommended.

Getting Help

Every effort has been made to ensure the accuracy of this book and the companion content. If you run into problems, please contact the appropriate source, listed in the following sections, for help and assistance.

Getting Help with This Book and the Companion Content

If you have questions or concerns about the content of this book or its companion content, please first search the online Microsoft Press Knowledge Base, which provides support information for known errors in or corrections to this book, at the following website:

www.microsoft.com/mspress/support/search.asp

If you do not find your answer in the online Knowledge Base, send your comments or questions to Microsoft Learning Technical Support at:

mspinput@microsoft.com

Part I

JavaWhat? The Where, Why, and How of JavaScript

Chapter 1

JavaScript Is More Than You Might Think

After reading this chapter, you'll be able to:

- Understand the history of JavaScript.

- Recognize the parts of a JavaScript program.

- Use the *javascript* pseudo-protocol.

- Understand where JavaScript fits within a webpage.

- Understand what JavaScript can and cannot do.

- Understand some of the changes in the latest standard related to JavaScript.

A Brief History of JavaScript

JavaScript isn't Java. There! With that clarification out of the way, you can move on to bigger, more important learning, like how to make cool drop-down menus. In all seriousness, JavaScript is one implementation of a specification known as ECMAScript. You'll learn more about ECMAScript later in this chapter.

Where did JavaScript come from? You might not know the rich and storied history of JavaScript—and you may not really care much about it, either. If that's the case, you might be tempted to jump ahead to the next chapter and begin coding JavaScript. Doing so, of course, would be a mistake—you'd miss all the wonderful information that follows in this chapter. And understanding a bit about the history of JavaScript is important to understanding how the language is implemented in various environments today.

JavaScript was originally developed by Brendan Eich at Netscape sometime in 1995–1996. Back then, the language was called LiveScript. That was a great name for a new language—and the story could have ended there. However, in an unfortunate decision, the folks in marketing had their way, and the language was renamed to JavaScript. Confusion soon ensued. You see, Java was the exciting new language at the time, and someone decided to try to capitalize on Java's popularity by using its name. As a result, JavaScript found itself associated with the Java language. This was a disadvantage for JavaScript, because Java, though popular in the sense that it was frequently used, was also unpopular because it had earned a fairly bad reputation—developers used Java in websites to present data or to add useless enhancements (such as annoying scrolling text). The user experience suffered because Java required a plug-in to load into the web browser, slowing down the browsing process and causing grief for visitors as well as accessibility problems. Only in recent years has JavaScript begun to separate from this negative Java association.

JavaScript is not a compiled language, which makes it look and feel like a language that lacks power. But programmers new to JavaScript soon came to realize its strengths and usefulness for both simulating and creating interactivity on the World Wide Web. Up until that realization, programmers developed many websites using only simple Hypertext Markup Language (HTML) and graphics that often lacked both visual appeal and the ability to interact with the site's content.

Early JavaScript concentrated on client-side form validation and working with images on webpages to provide rudimentary, though helpful, interactivity and feedback to the visitor. When a visitor to a website filled in a form, JavaScript instantly validated the contents of the web form rather than make a roundtrip to the server. Especially in the days before broadband was pervasive, preventing the roundtrip to the server was a great way to help applications seem a little quicker and more responsive—and it still is.

Enter Internet Explorer 3.0

With the release of Microsoft Internet Explorer 3.0 in 1996, Microsoft included support for core JavaScript, known in Internet Explorer as JScript, as well as support for another scripting language called Microsoft Visual Basic, Scripting Edition, or VBScript. Although JavaScript and JScript were similar, their implementations weren't exactly the same. Therefore, methods were developed to detect which browser the website visitor was using and respond with appropriate scripting. This process is known as *browser detection*, and is discussed in Chapter 11, "JavaScript Events and the Browser." Browser detection is still used, though it is considered undesirable for most applications.

And Then Came ECMAScript

In mid 1997, Microsoft and Netscape worked with the European Computer Manufacturers Association (ECMA) to release the first version of a language specification known as ECMAScript, more formally known as ECMA-262. Since that time, all browsers from Microsoft have implemented versions of the ECMAScript standard. Other popular browsers, such as Firefox, Safari, and Opera, have also implemented the ECMAScript standard.

ECMA-262 version 3 was released in 1999. The good news is that browsers such as Microsoft Internet Explorer 4.0 and Netscape 4.5 supported the version 3 standard, and that every major browser since then has supported the version of JavaScript formalized in the ECMA-262 version 3 standard. The bad news is that each browser applies this standard in a slightly different way, so incompatibilities still plague developers who use JavaScript.

The latest version of ECMAScript, as formalized in the standard known as ECMA-262, was released in late 2009 and is known as ECMA-262 version 5. Version 4 of the specification was skipped for a variety of reasons and to avoid confusion among competing proposals for the standard. ECMA-262 version 5 is becoming more widely supported as of this writing and will likely (I'm hopeful) be in versions of popular browsers such as Internet Explorer, Firefox, Opera, and Safari by the time you read this book.

It's important to note that as a developer who is incorporating JavaScript into web applications, you need to account for the differences among the versions of ECMA-262, as well as the many interpretations of JavaScript. Accounting for these differences might mean implementing a script in slightly different ways, and testing, testing, and testing again in various browsers and on various platforms. On today's Internet, users have little tolerance for poorly designed applications that work in only one browser.

> **Important** It is imperative that you test your websites in multiple browsers—including web applications that you don't think will be used in a browser other than Internet Explorer. Even if you're sure that your application will be used only in Internet Explorer or that's all you officially support, you still should test in other browsers. This is important not only for security, but because it shows that you're a thorough developer who understands today's Internet technologies.

So Many Standards...

If you think the standards of JavaScript programming are loosely defined, you're right. Each browser supports JavaScript slightly differently, making your job—and my job—that much more difficult. Trying to write about all these nuances is more challenging than writing about a language that is implemented by a single, specific entity, like a certain version of Microsoft Visual Basic or Perl. Your job (and mine) is to keep track of these differences and account for them as necessary, and to try to find common ground among them as much as possible.

The DOM

Another evolving standard relevant to the JavaScript programmer is the *Document Object Model (DOM)* standard developed by the World Wide Web Consortium (W3C). The W3C defines the DOM as "a platform- and language-neutral interface that allows programs and scripts to dynamically access and update the content, structure, and style of documents." What this means for you is that you can work with a specification to which web browsers adhere to develop a webpage in a dynamic manner. The DOM creates a tree structure for HTML and Extensible Markup Language (XML) documents and enables scripting of those objects. JavaScript interacts heavily with the DOM for many important functions.

Like JavaScript, the DOM is interpreted differently by every browser, making life for a JavaScript programmer more interesting. Internet Explorer 4.0 and previous versions of Netscape included support for an early DOM, known as Level 0. If you use the Level 0 DOM, you can be pretty sure that you'll find support for the DOM in those browsers and in all the browsers that came after.

Microsoft Internet Explorer 5.0 and 5.5 included some support for Level 1 DOM, whereas Windows Internet Explorer 6.0 and later versions include some support for the Level 2 DOM. The latest versions of Firefox, Safari, and Opera support the Level 2 DOM. Safari provides a representation of the Webkit rendering engine. The Webkit rendering engine is used as the basis for the browser on devices such as the iPhone and iPad as well as on Android-based devices.

If there's one lesson that you should take away while learning about JavaScript standards and the related DOM standards, it's that you need to pay particular attention to the code that you write (no surprise there) and the syntax used to implement that code. If you don't, JavaScript can fail miserably and prevent your page from rendering in a given browser. Chapter 10, "The Document Object Model," covers the DOM in much greater detail.

> **Tip** The W3C has an application that can test your web browser for its support of the various DOM levels. This application can be found at *http://www.w3.org/2003/02/06-dom-support.html*.

What's in a JavaScript Program?

A JavaScript program consists of *statements* formed from *tokens*, *operators*, and *identifiers* placed together in an order that is meaningful to a JavaScript interpreter, which is contained in most web browsers. That sentence is a mouthful, but these statements are really not all that complicated to anyone who has programmed in just about any other language. A statement might be:

```
var smallNumber = 4;
```

In that statement, a token, or reserved word—*var*—is followed by other tokens, such as an identifier (*smallNumber*), an operator (=), and a literal (*4*). (You learn more about these elements throughout the rest of the book.) The purpose of this statement is to set the variable named *smallNumber* equal to the integer *4*.

Like any programming language, statements get put together in an order that makes a program perform one or more functions. JavaScript defines functions in its own way, which you read much more about in Chapter 7, "Working with Functions." JavaScript defines several built-in functions that you can use in your programs.

Using the *javascript* pseudo-protocol and a function

1. Open a web browser such as Internet Explorer or Firefox.

2. In the address bar, type the following code and press Enter:

   ```
   javascript:alert("Hello World");
   ```

   After you press Enter, you see a dialog box similar to this one:

Congratulations! You just programmed your first (albeit not very useful) bit of JavaScript code. With just this little bit of code, however, are two important items that you are likely to use in your JavaScript programming endeavors: the *javascript* pseudo-protocol identifier in a browser, and more importantly, the *alert* function. You examine these items in more detail in later chapters; for now, it suffices that you learned something you'll use in the future!

JavaScript is also *event-driven*, meaning that it can respond to certain events or "things that happen," such as a mouse click or text change within a form field. Connecting JavaScript to an event is central to many common uses of JavaScript. In Chapter 11, you see how to respond to events by using JavaScript.

JavaScript Placement on Your Webpage

If you're new to HTML, all you need to know about it for now is that it delineates elements in a webpage using a pair of matching tags enclosed in brackets. The closing tag begins with a slash character (/). Elements can be nested within each other. JavaScript fits within *<script>* tags inside the *<head> </head>* and/or *<body> </body>* tags of a webpage, as in this example:

```
<html>
<head>
<title>A Web Page Title</title>
<script type="text/javascript">
// JavaScript Goes Here
</script>
</head>
<body>
<script type="text/javascript">
// JavaScript can go here too
```

```
</script>
</body>
</html>
```

JavaScript placed within the *<body>* tags executes as it is encountered by the browser, which is helpful when you need to write to the document by using a JavaScript function, as follows (the function calls are shown in boldface type):

```
<head>
<title>A Web Page Title</title>
<script type="text/javascript">
// JavaScript Goes Here
</script>
</head>
<body>
<script type="text/javascript">
document.write("hello");
document.write(" world");
</script>
</body>
</html>
```

Because of the way browsers load JavaScript, the current best practice for placing JavaScript in your HTML is to position the *<script>* tags at the end of the *<body>* element rather than in the *<head>* element. Doing so helps to ensure that the content of the page is loaded if the browser blocks input while the JavaScript files are being loaded.

When you're using JavaScript on an Extensible Hypertext Markup Language (XHTML) page, the less-than sign (*<*) and the ampersand character (&) are interpreted as XML, which can cause problems for JavaScript. To get around this, use the following syntax in an XHTML page:

```
<script type="text/javascript">
<![CDATA[
    // JavaScript Goes Here
]]>
</script>
```

Browsers that aren't XHTML-compliant don't interpret the CDATA section correctly. You can work around that problem by placing the CDATA section inside a JavaScript comment—a line or set of lines prefaced by two forward slashes (*//*), as shown here:

```
<script type="text/javascript">
//<![CDATA[
    // JavaScript Goes Here
//]]>
</script>
```

Yes, the code really is that ugly. However, there's an easy fix for this: use external JavaScript files. In Chapter 2, "Developing in JavaScript," you learn exactly how to accomplish this simple task.

Document Types

If you've been programming for the web for any length of time, you're probably familiar with Document Type declarations, or DOCTYPE declarations, as they're sometimes called. One of the most important tasks you can do when designing your webpages is to include an accurate and syntactically correct DOCTYPE declaration section at the top of the page. The DOCTYPE declaration, frequently abbreviated as DTD, lets the browser (or other parsing program) know the rules that will be followed when parsing the elements of the document.

An example of a DOCTYPE declaration for HTML 4.01 looks like this:

```
<!DOCTYPE html PUBLIC "-//W3C//DTD HTML 4.01//EN"
   "http://www.w3.org/TR/html4/strict.dtd">
```

If you're using Microsoft Visual Studio 2005 or a later version to create a web project, each page is automatically given a DOCTYPE declaration for the XHTML 1.0 standard, like this:

```
<!DOCTYPE html PUBLIC "-//W3C//DTD XHTML 1.0 Transitional//EN" "http://www.w3.org/TR
/xhtml1/DTD/xhtml1-transitional.dtd">
```

HTML version 5 uses a much simpler DOCTYPE:

```
<!DOCTYPE html>
```

If you fail to declare a DOCTYPE, the browser interprets the page using a mode known as *Quirks Mode*. Falling back to Quirks Mode means that the document might end up looking different from your intention, especially when viewed through several browsers.

If you do declare a DOCTYPE, making sure that the resulting HTML, cascading style sheet (also known as CSS), and JavaScript also adhere to web standards is important so that the document can be viewed as intended by the widest possible audience, no matter which interface or browser is used. HTML and CSS validation is discussed more in this book in Chapter 15, "JavaScript and CSS." The W3C makes available an online validator at *http://validator.w3.org/*, which you can use to validate any publicly available webpage.

 Tip Use the Markup Validator regularly until you're comfortable with coding to standards, and always check for validity before releasing your web project to the public.

What JavaScript Can Do

JavaScript is largely a complementary language, meaning that it's uncommon for an entire application to be written solely in JavaScript without the aid of other languages like HTML and without presentation in a web browser. Some Adobe products support JavaScript, but JavaScript is primarily used for web-related programming.

JavaScript is also the J in the acronym AJAX (Asynchronous JavaScript and XML), the darling of the Web 2.0 phenomenon. Beyond that, though, JavaScript is an everyday language providing the interactivity expected, maybe even demanded, by today's web visitors.

JavaScript can perform many tasks on the client side of the application. For example, it can add the needed interactivity to a website by creating drop-down menus, transforming the text on a page, adding dynamic elements to a page, and helping with form entry.

Before learning about what JavaScript can do—the focus of this book—you need to understand what JavaScript can't do, but note that neither discussion is comprehensive.

What JavaScript Can't Do

Many of the operations JavaScript can't perform are the result of JavaScript's usage being somewhat limited to a web browser environment. This section examines some of the tasks JavaScript can't perform and some that JavaScript shouldn't.

JavaScript Can't Be Forced on a Client

JavaScript relies on another interface or host program for its functionality. This host program is usually the client's web browser, also known as a *user agent*. Because JavaScript is a client-side language, it can do only what the client allows it to do.

Some people are still using older browsers that don't support JavaScript at all. Others won't be able to support many of JavaScript's fancy features because of accessibility programs, text readers, and other add-on software that assists the browsing experience. And some people might just choose to disable JavaScript because they can, because of security concerns (whether perceived or real), or because of the poor reputation JavaScript has as a result of certain annoyances like pop-up ads.

Regardless of the reason, you need to perform some extra work to ensure that the website you're designing is available to those individuals who don't have JavaScript. I can hear your protests already: "But this feature is really [insert your own superlative here: cool, sweet, essential, nice, fantastic]." Regardless of how nice your feature may be, the chances are you will benefit from better interoperability and more site visitors. In the "Tips for Using JavaScript" section later in this chapter, I offer some pointers you can follow for using JavaScript appropriately on your website.

It may be helpful to think of this issue another way. When you build a web application that gets served from Microsoft Internet Information Services (IIS) 6.0, you can assume that the application will usually work when served from an IIS 6.0 server anywhere. Likewise, when you build an application for Apache 2, you can be pretty sure that it will work on other Apache 2 installations. The same assumption cannot be made for JavaScript, however. When you write an application that works fine on your desktop, you can't guarantee it will work on somebody else's. You can't control how your application will work once it gets sent to the client.

JavaScript Can't Guarantee Data Security

Because JavaScript is run wholly on the client, the developer must learn to let go. As you might expect, letting go of control over your program has serious implications. Once the program is on the client's computer, the client can do many nasty things to the data before sending it back to the server. As with any other web programming, you should never trust any data coming back from the client. Even if you've used JavaScript functions to validate the contents of forms, you still must validate this input again when it gets to the server. A client with JavaScript disabled might send back garbage data through a web form. If you believe, innocently enough, that your client-side JavaScript function has already checked the data to ensure that it is valid, you may find that invalid data gets back to the server, causing unforeseen and possibly dangerous consequences.

> **Important** Remember that JavaScript can be disabled on your visitor's computer. You cannot rely on cute tricks to be successful, such as using JavaScript to disable right-clicks or to prevent visitors from viewing the page source, and you shouldn't use them as security measures.

JavaScript Can't Cross Domains

The JavaScript developer also must be aware of the *Same-Origin Policy*, which dictates that scripts running from within one domain do not have access to the properties from another Internet domain, nor can they affect the scripts and data from another domain. For example, JavaScript can be used to open a new browser window, but the contents of that window are somewhat restricted to the calling script. When a page from my website (*braingia.org*) contains JavaScript, that page can't access any JavaScript executed from a different domain, such as *microsoft.com*. This is the essence of the Same-Origin Policy: JavaScript has to be executed in or originate from the same location.

The Same-Origin Policy is frequently a restriction to contend with in the context of frames and AJAX's *XMLHttpRequest* object, where multiple JavaScript requests might be sent to different web servers. With the introduction of Windows Internet Explorer 8, Microsoft introduced support for the *XDomainRequest* object, which allows limited access to data from other domains. I discuss some workarounds and more complete approaches to cross-domain requests in Chapter 19, "A Touch of AJAX." For now, be aware that JavaScript is limited to performing tasks in your own browser window.

JavaScript Doesn't Do Servers

When developing server-side code such as Visual Basic .NET or PHP (PHP is a recursive acronym that stands for *PHP: Hypertext Preprocessor*), you can be fairly certain that the server will implement certain functions, such as talking to a database or giving access to modules necessary for the web application. JavaScript doesn't have access to server-side variables. For example, JavaScript cannot access databases that are located on the server. JavaScript code is limited to what can be done inside the platform on which the script is running, which is typically the browser.

Another shift you need to make in your thinking, if you're familiar with server-side programming, is that with JavaScript, you have to test the code on many different clients to know what a particular client is capable of. When you're programming server-side, if the server doesn't implement a given function, you know it right away because the server-side script fails when you test it. Naughty administrators aside, the back-end server code implementation shouldn't change on a whim, and thus, you more easily know what you can and cannot code. But you can't anticipate JavaScript code that is intended to run on clients, because these clients are completely out of your control.

Tips for Using JavaScript

Several factors go into good web design, and really, who arbitrates what is and is not considered good anyway? One visitor to a site might call the site an ugly hodgepodge of colors and text created as if those elements were put in a sack and shaken until they fell out onto the page; the next visitor might love the design and color scheme.

Because you're reading this book, I assume that you're looking for some help with using JavaScript to enhance your website. I also assume that you want to use this programming language to help people use your site and to make your site look, feel, and work better.

The design of a website is not and will never be an entirely objective process. The goal of one website might be informational, which would dictate one design approach, whereas the goal of another website might be to connect to an application, thus requiring specialized design and functionality. That said, many popular and seemingly well-designed sites have certain aspects in common. I try to break down those aspects here, although I ask you to remember that I didn't create a comprehensive list and the items reflect one person's opinions.

A well-designed website does the following:

- **Emphasizes function over form**   When a user visits a website, he or she usually wants to obtain information or perform a task. The more difficult your site is to browse, the more likely the user is to move to another site with better browsing.

  Animations and blinking bits come and go, but what remain are sites that have basic information presented in a professional, easily accessible manner. Using the latest cool animation software or web technology makes me think of the days of the HTML *<blink>* tag. The *<blink>* tag, for those who never saw it in action, caused the text within it to disappear and reappear on the screen. Nearly all web developers seem to hate the *<blink>* tag and what it does to a webpage. Those same developers would be wise to keep in mind that today's exciting feature or special effect on a webpage will be tomorrow's *<blink>*. Successful websites stick to the basics and use these types of bits only when the content requires them.

  Use elements like a site map, alt tags, and simple navigation tools, and don't require special software or plug-ins for viewing the site's main content. Too often, I visit a website, only to be stopped because I need a plug-in or the latest version of this or that player (which I don't have) to browse it.

  Although site maps, alt tags, and simple navigation may seem quaint, they are indispensable items for accessibility. Text readers and other such technologies that enable sites to be read aloud or browsed by individuals with disabilities use these assistive features and frequently have problems with complex JavaScript.

- **Follows standards**   Web standards exist to be followed, so ignore them at your own peril. Using a correct DOCTYPE declaration and well-formed HTML helps ensure that your site will display correctly to your visitors. Validation using the W3C's Markup Validator tool is highly recommended. If your site is broken, fix it!

- **Renders correctly in multiple browsers**   Even when Internet Explorer had 90 percent market share, it was never a good idea for programmers to ignore other browsers. Doing so usually meant that accessibility was also ignored, so people with text readers or other add-ons couldn't use the site. People using operating systems other than Microsoft Windows might also be out of luck visiting those sites.

  Though Internet Explorer is still the leader among web visitors, there's a great chance that at least 3 or 4 of every 10 visitors might be using a different browser. Of course, this variance depends largely on the subject matter. The more technical the audience, the more you need to accommodate browsers other than Internet Explorer. Therefore, if your site appeals to a technical audience, you might need your site to work in Firefox, Safari, or even Lynx.

  Regardless of the website's subject matter, you never want to turn away visitors because of their browser choice. Imagine the shopkeeper who turned away 3 of every 10 potential customers just because of their shoes. That shop wouldn't be in business too long— or at the very least, it wouldn't be as successful.

If you strive to follow web standards, chances are that you're already doing most of what you need to do to support multiple browsers. Avoiding the use of proprietary plug-ins for your website is another way to ensure that your site renders correctly. You need to look only as far as the Apple iPad to see a device that is popular but whose use is restricted because it doesn't natively support Flash or Java. For this reason, creating sites that follow standards and avoid proprietary plug-ins ensures that your site is viewable by the widest possible audience.

- **Uses appropriate technologies at appropriate times** Speaking of plug-ins, a well-designed website doesn't overuse or misuse technology. On a video site, playing videos is appropriate. Likewise, on a music site, playing background music is appropriate. On other sites, these features might not be so appropriate. If you feel as though your site needs to play background music, go back to the drawing board and examine why you want a website in the first place! I still shudder when I think of an attorney's website that I once visited. The site started playing the firm's jingle in the background, without my intervention. Friends don't let friends use background music on their sites, unless your friend is from the band Rush and you are working on the band's website.

Where JavaScript Fits

Today's web is still evolving. One of the more popular movements over the past year is known as *unobtrusive scripting*. The unobtrusive scripting paradigm is part of the larger movement called behavioral separation. *Behavioral separation* calls for structure to be separated from style, and both of these to be separated from behavior. In this model, HTML or XHTML provides the structure whereas the CSS provides the style and JavaScript provides the behavior. The JavaScript is unobtrusive; it doesn't get in the way. If JavaScript isn't available in the browser, the website still works because the visitor can use the website in some other way.

When applied properly, unobtrusive scripting means that JavaScript is not assumed to be available and that JavaScript will fail in a graceful manner. Graceful degradation helps the page function without JavaScript or uses proper approaches to make JavaScript available when it's required for the site. One such approach is covered in Chapter 11.

I'm a proponent of unobtrusive scripting, because it means that standards are followed and the resulting site adheres to the four recommendations I shared in the previous section. Unfortunately, this isn't always the case. You could separate the HTML, CSS, and JavaScript and still end up using proprietary tags, but when you program in an unobtrusive manner, you tend to pay closer attention to detail and care much more about the end result being compliant with standards.

Throughout this book, I strive to show you not only the basics of JavaScript, but also the best way to use JavaScript effectively and, as much as possible, unobtrusively.

A Note on JScript and JavaScript and This Book

This book covers JavaScript as defined by the ECMA standard, in versions all the way through the latest version 5. In some sections, I highlight information related to JScript and JScript .NET. For an additional reference on only JScript, I recommend the following site:

JScript (Windows Script Technologies) http://msdn.microsoft.com/en-us/library /hbxc2t98.aspx

Which Browsers Should the Site Support?

Downward compatibility has been an issue for the web developer for a long time. Choosing which browser versions to support becomes a trade-off between using the latest functionality available in the newest browsers and the compatible functionality required for older browsers. There is no hard and fast rule for which browsers you should support on your website,
so the answer is: it depends.

Your decision depends on what you'd like to do with your site and whether you value visits by people using older hardware and software more than you value the added functionality available in later browser versions. Some browsers are just too old to support because they can't render CSS correctly, much less JavaScript. A key to supporting multiple browser versions is to test within them.

Obtaining an MSDN account from Microsoft will give you access to legacy products, including older versions of Internet Explorer, so that you can see how your site reacts to a visit from Internet Explorer 4.0. Additional resources are the Application Compatibility Virtual PC Images, available for free from Microsoft. These allow you to use a time-limited version of Microsoft Windows containing browsers such as Internet Explorer 6.0 and Windows Internet Explorer 7. For more information, see: *http://www.microsoft.com/downloads /details.aspx?FamilyId=21EABB90-958F-4B64-B5F1-73D0A413C8EF&displaylang=en*.

Many web designs and JavaScript functions don't require newer versions of web browsers. As already explained, however, verifying that your site renders correctly in various browsers is always a good idea. See *http://browsers.evolt.org/* for links to archives of many historical versions of web browsers. Even if you can't conduct extensive testing in multiple browsers, you can design the site so that it fails in a graceful manner. You want the site to render appropriately regardless of the browser being used.

What's New in ECMAScript Version 5?

Several enhancements were made to the ECMAScript 262 standard when version 5 was introduced in 2009. This section looks at some of the enhancements and changes. Most of these changes are not downward-compatible with older versions of web browsers. However, as new versions of web browsers are released, the changes introduced with ECMAScript 262 version 5 will begin to show up and become available for use in cross-browser web applications.

New Array Methods

ECMA-262 version 5 introduced several new methods for use with arrays. These include a *foreach* method to iterate through the elements of an array, as well as a *map* method, a *filter* method, and other methods that determine the index and reduce the size of an array. Chapter 8, "Objects in JavaScript," examines arrays and includes some discussion of these new methods.

New Controls on Object Properties

Object properties, discussed in Chapter 8, have increased flexibility. ECMA-262 version 5 introduced *get* and *set* functions, which are called when a property is retrieved or assigned a value, respectively. You can control access to properties through the *writable*, *configurable*, and *enumerable* attributes. For example, a property might have a value that you can configure to be nonenumerable, meaning that the property wouldn't be returned on object iteration. Consider this code:

```
{
    value: "testvalue",
    enumerable: false
}
```

The value won't be returned if passed through a *for* loop. Don't be discouraged if this syntax doesn't quite make sense yet. The chapters that follow examine the creation and iteration of objects in detail.

New JSON Object

JavaScript Object Notation (JSON) is an approach to exchanging data, frequently between a client application such as a web browser that is running JavaScript, and a server. JSON is much less cumbersome than XML for data exchange, especially within JavaScript applications, and is therefore often used as an alternative data format for AJAX applications.

ECMA-262 version 5 added a native JSON object to the language specification. This book discusses JSON primarily in Part IV, "AJAX and Server-Side Integration."

Changes to the Date Object

ECMA-262 version 5 added new methods to the *Date* object that parse and produce dates in ISO format. The *toISOString()* method generates output in ISO-8601 format, as shown here:

2011-03-12T18:51:50.000Z

A New Strict Mode

ECMA-262 version 5 introduces a new mode for code execution, called *strict mode*. In strict mode, the JavaScript engine uses a more rigid set of syntax checks that can help catch issues within the code, such as a coding error or an undeclared variable.

Browser Support

ECMA-262 version 5 and introduces numerous changes and enhancements, affecting how developers program with JavaScript. Unfortunately, these changes won't be supported in legacy browsers and—in the short term—will have limited support in Internet Explorer. You can find a compatibility table containing many popular browsers and their support for some of the features included in ECMA-262 version 5 at *http://kangax.github.com/es5-compat-table/*.

To work around the lack of support for ECMA-262 version 5 in legacy browsers, you need either to write code that takes into them into account, or use a JavaScript library such as jQuery. This book covers various JavaScript libraries in Chapter 21, "An Introduction to JavaScript Libraries and Frameworks."

Exercises

1. True or False: JavaScript is defined by a standards body and is supported on all web browsers.

2. True or False: When a visitor whose machine has JavaScript disabled comes to your website, you should block her or his access to the site because there's no valid reason to have JavaScript disabled.

3. Create a JavaScript definition block that would typically appear on an HTML page within the *<head>* or *<body>* block.

4. True or False: It's important to declare the version of JavaScript being used within the DOCTYPE definition block.

5. True or False: JavaScript can appear in both the *<head>* block and within the *<body>* text of an HTML page.

Chapter 2
Developing in JavaScript

After reading this chapter, you'll be able to:

- Understand the options available for developing in JavaScript.
- Configure your computer for JavaScript development.
- Use Microsoft Visual Studio 2010 to create and deploy a JavaScript application.
- Use Eclipse to create and deploy a JavaScript application.
- Use Notepad (or another editor) to create a JavaScript application.
- Understand options for debugging JavaScript.

JavaScript Development Options

Because JavaScript isn't a compiled language, you don't need any special tools or development environments to write and deploy JavaScript applications. Likewise, you don't need special server software to run the applications. Therefore, your options for creating JavaScript programs are virtually limitless.

You can write JavaScript code in any text editor; in whatever program you use to write your Hypertext Markup Language (HTML) and cascading style sheet (CSS) files; or in powerful integrated development environments (IDEs) such as Visual Studio. You might even use all three approaches. You might initially develop a web application with Visual Studio but then find it convenient to use a simple text editor such as Notepad to touch up a bit of JavaScript. Ultimately, use whatever tool you're most comfortable with.

This book primarily discusses how to develop in JavaScript using Visual Studio, but at times I may just recommend (and show) the use of a text editor, such as Notepad or Vim (which you can obtain here: *http://www.vim.org*). At other times, you'll be able to type JavaScript code into the Location or address bar of your web browser by using the *javascript:* pseudo-protocol identifier, as you saw in Chapter 1, "JavaScript Is More Than You Might Think."

After you've been developing JavaScript for a while, you'll notice that you do some of the same things on every webpage. In such cases, you can simply copy and paste the repeated code into the webpage that you're developing. Better still, you can create an external file containing common functions that you can then use throughout the sites you develop. Chapter 10, "The Document Object Model" has more information about functions, although you'll see functions used throughout the first 10 chapters.

Configuring Your Environment

This section looks at JavaScript development using a few different tools. You should be able to use whatever tool you feel most comfortable with for your JavaScript and website development, so don't consider this to be an exhaustive or prejudicial list of tools.

One useful JavaScript development tool is Visual Studio 2010. A simple web server—the ASP.NET Development Server—comes with the installation of Visual Studio 2010, which makes deploying and testing the applications in this book a little easier. This does not mean, however, that you should go out and purchase Visual Studio 2010 just for JavaScript development. If you choose to use Eclipse, the second tool discussed in this chapter, you can still test the JavaScript code that you write. Likewise, you can test the JavaScript code even if you don't use an IDE at all.

Another option for web development is Microsoft Visual Web Developer 2010 Express. This tool, available at *http://www.microsoft.com/express/Web/*, provides the Visual Studio interface as well with several tools and add-ons in a free package made just for web development.

You don't absolutely need a web server for most JavaScript development. The notable exception to this is when you're developing using Asynchronous JavaScript and XML (AJAX). AJAX cannot use the *file://* protocol, which in addition to the Same-Origin Policy covered in Chapter 1, prevents AJAX from working unless you use a web server. The bottom line is: if AJAX development is in your future, you need a web server.

AJAX notwithstanding, development does become a little easier if you have a web server handy. Any web server will work, because all you really want to do is serve HTML and JavaScript, and maybe a little CSS for fun. I've had great luck with Apache, available from *http://httpd.apache.org*. Apache runs on many platforms, including on the Microsoft Windows platform, and continues to be the most popular web server on the Internet.

Configuring Apache or any web server is beyond the scope of this book, and again, having a web server is not required. The Apache website has some good tutorials for installing Apache on Windows, and if you're using just about any version of Linux, Apache will likely be installed already, or is easily installed. Many of the examples used in the book will work whether you're using a web server or just viewing the example locally. However, a web server is necessary to take advantage of examples that use AJAX.

Writing JavaScript with Visual Studio 2010

Visual Studio 2010 lets developers quickly deploy web applications with JavaScript enhancements. When you first start Visual Studio 2010, you see options to select a certain style for your Visual Studio environment. The various styles result in differing Visual Studio 2010 views, each of which is designed to be most helpful for a particular development purpose or language. You can see an example of this dialog box in Figure 2-1.

FIGURE 2-1 Choosing the development environment style.

If you're using the General Development Settings collection, your Visual Studio environment is similar to that shown in Figure 2-2.

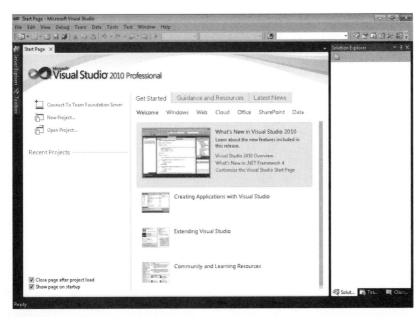

FIGURE 2-2 The General Development Settings collection provides an environment common to many programming tasks.

You can change Visual Studio 2010 so that it uses the Web Development Settings collection by selecting Import And Export Settings from the Tools menu, which opens the Import And Export Settings Wizard. Select Reset All Settings, as shown in Figure 2-3, and then click Next.

> **Note** Changing the development environment settings isn't required, but this book assumes that you selected Web Development Settings in Visual Studio 2010.

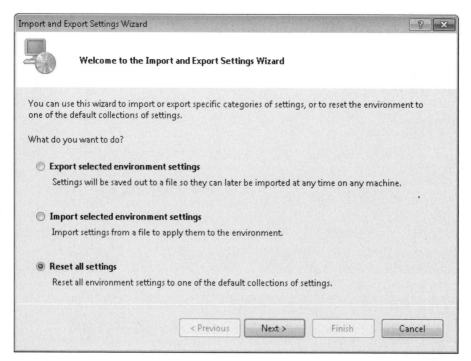

FIGURE 2-3 Preparing to change the settings in Visual Studio 2010 to Web Development Settings.

The Save Current Settings page of the wizard, shown in Figure 2-4, appears. If you have settings that you want to save, select Yes, Save My Current Settings. Otherwise, select No, Just Reset Settings, Overwriting My Current Settings. Click Next to continue.

The Choose A Default Collection Of Settings page of the wizard, shown in Figure 2-5, appears. Select Web Development settings, and then click Finish.

After a short time, you receive a Reset Complete message. Click Close to reset your environment to the Web Development settings.

With the Web Development settings, you have quick access to common tasks related to website development, not only with ASP.NET, but also with JavaScript, HTML, and CSS—the core languages of the web. For more information about settings in Visual Studio 2010, see *http://msdn.microsoft.com/en-us/library/zbhkx167.aspx*.

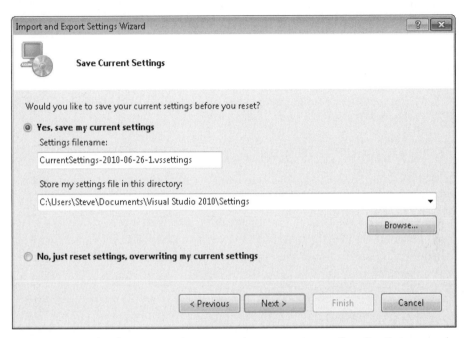

FIGURE 2-4 By saving the current settings, you can keep any custom configuration that you may have specified for your environment.

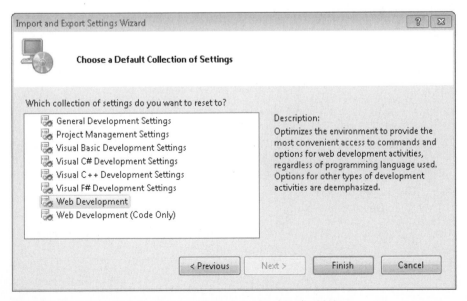

FIGURE 2-5 Selecting Web Development Settings in Visual Studio 2010.

Your First Web (and JavaScript) Project with Visual Studio 2010

Now you can create a web project and write a little JavaScript. If you're not using Visual Studio, skip ahead in this chapter to the section "Writing JavaScript with Eclipse" or the section "Writing JavaScript Without an IDE" for information about working in other development environments. I won't forget about you, I promise!

> **Note** You can download the code found in these examples and throughout the book. See this book's Introduction for directions about downloading the companion content.

Creating a web project with JavaScript in Visual Studio 2010

1. Within Visual Studio, using the Web Development Settings, select New Web Site from the File menu. This opens the New Web Site dialog box.

2. Select ASP.NET Web Site (the language selection—Visual Basic or Visual C#—is not important), as shown here. Change the name to **Chapter2**, with a path appropriate to your configuration. When the information is correct, click OK. Visual Studio creates a new project.

3. Visual Studio 2010 creates a new Default.aspx file for you and opens it in the editor. Close this Default.aspx file and create a new file by right-clicking the location within Solution Explorer (Solution Explorer is a pane usually found in the upper-right corner of the Visual Studio environment) and then selecting Add New Item. (You may also select New File from on the File menu.) The Add New Item dialog box opens, as shown in the following screen. Select HTML Page, change the name to **myfirstpage.htm**, and then click Add. Visual Studio opens the new file and automatically enters the DOCTYPE and other starting pieces of an HTML page for you.

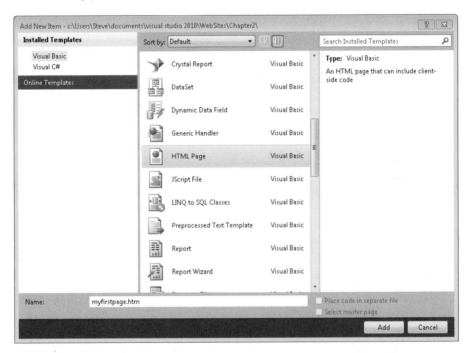

4. In the myfirstpage.htm page, place your cursor between the *<title>* and *</title>* tags and change the title to **My First Page**. Your environment should look like the one shown here.

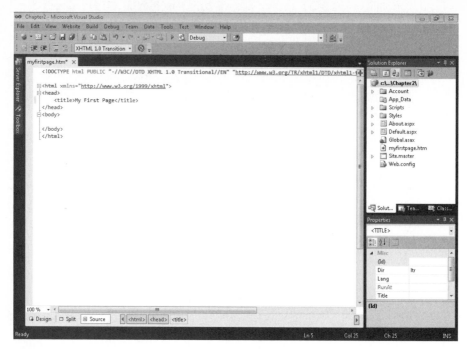

5. Between the *<head>* tag, after the closing *</title>* tag, add the following code:

```
<script type="text/javascript">
    function yetAnotherAlert(textToAlert) {
        alert(textToAlert);
    }
    yetAnotherAlert("This is Chapter 2");
</script>
```

6. Select Save All from the File menu. The finished script and page should resemble the screen here.

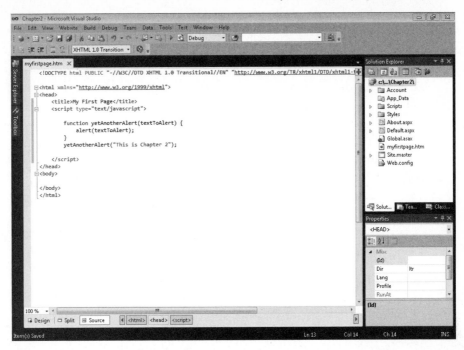

To view the page, select Start Without Debugging from the Debug menu. This starts the ASP
.NET Development Server (if it's not already started) and takes you to the page in your default
browser. You should receive a page with an alert, similar to Figure 2-6. Click OK, and then
close the browser.

The script works as follows. First, the script tag is opened and declared to be JavaScript, as
shown by this code:

```
<script type="text/javascript">
```

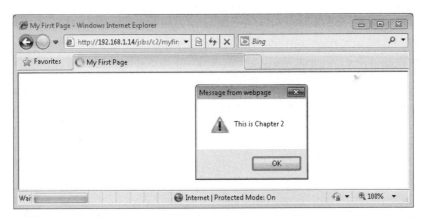

FIGURE 2-6 Running a JavaScript program courtesy of the ASP.NET Development Server.

> **Note** You can declare your script is JavaScript in other ways, but the approach you see here is the most widely supported.

Next, the script declares a function, *yetAnotherAlert,* which accepts one argument, *textToAlert,* as follows:

```
function yetAnotherAlert(textToAlert) {
```

The function has one task: to pop an alert into the browser window with whatever text has been supplied as the function argument, which the next line accomplishes:

```
    alert(textToAlert);
```

The end of the function is delineated by a closing brace (*}*). The next line of the script calls the function you just declared with a quoted string argument:

```
yetAnotherAlert("This is Chapter 2");
```

With this script, you're ready to develop JavaScript in Visual Studio 2010. But before you celebrate, consider sticking with me and learning about how to use external files to store your JavaScript code.

Using External JavaScript Files with Visual Studio 2010

JavaScript doesn't need to be contained wholly within the HTML files of your website. Instead, you can take advantage of the *src* attribute of the *<script>* tag. Attributes within tags help to further define, or provide more specifics, about the element. For example, a *<form>* element may have an *action* attribute that defines what action should happen when the form is submitted. Using the *src* attribute of the *<script>* tag, you can define the location of an external JavaScript file. The web browser then reads the JavaScript contained within the specified file when it loads the webpage. Using external JavaScript files means that you can maintain common JavaScript code in one place, as opposed to maintaining it within each individual page—which will save you a lot of work.

At this point, you should have a working webpage (built using Visual Studio) that displays an alert, thanks to some nifty JavaScript. The webpage you developed in the previous section contains the JavaScript code within the *<head>* tag portion of the page. In this section, I show you how to place JavaScript into an external file and then reference that code from within your HTML page.

Creating an external file for JavaScript using Visual Studio 2010

1. If the myfirstpage.htm file isn't open, open it by going into Visual Studio and selecting Open Project from the File menu. Select the project in which you saved the myfirstpage .htm file (available in the companion content) and open the file. Your environment should look something like the environment in step 6 in the previous example.

2. Create a new file to hold the JavaScript code by selecting New File from the File menu. The Add New Item dialog box appears. In the list of templates, select JScript File and change the name to **myscript.js**, as shown in the following screen, and then click Add. Note that your list may differ depending on your Visual Studio installation. You can find this source file, titled myscript.js, in the Chapter 2 sample code.

3. A new empty JavaScript (JScript) file opens and is added to your web project. You should see a tab for the new myscript.js file and another for the myfirstpage.htm file, as shown in the next screen. If the myfirstpage.htm file isn't opened in a tab, open it by double-clicking it in the Solution Explorer.

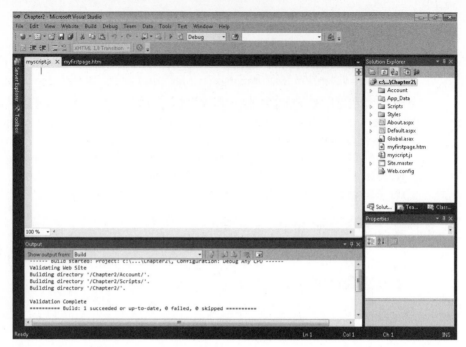

Note The colloquial extension for JavaScript and JScript is .js, but you are not required
to use it. I chose to use a JScript type of file in the preceding step 2 because this file type
automatically selects the correct file extension. You could just as easily have selected Text
Document from the Add New Item dialog box, and then named the file with a .js extension.

4. Click the myfirstpage.htm tab to make it active, and highlight the JavaScript code. Be
   sure to leave the actual JavaScript tags *<script>* and *</script>* intact and do not highlight them. (You don't need these tags right now, but you'll revisit this topic shortly.)
   You can also find this page, titled myfirstpage.htm, in the Chapter 2 sample code in the
   companion content.

5. Copy the highlighted code to the Clipboard by selecting Copy from the Edit menu.

6. Click the myscript.js tab, move the cursor below the first line, and select Paste from the
   Edit menu. The copied code is pasted at the cursor's location. Change the text of the
   yetAnotherAlert function call parameter so that it reads as follows: "This is the Second
   Example." The code is shown here:

```
function yetAnotherAlert(textToAlert) {
    alert(textToAlert);
}
yetAnotherAlert("This is the Second Example.");
```

7. Save the myscript.js file by selecting Save from the File menu. The file should look like this:

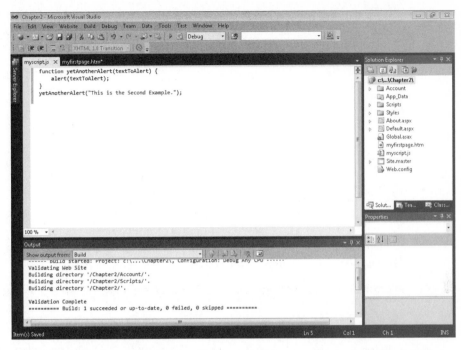

8. With the JavaScript code contained in its own file named myscript.js (you did save that file, right?), you can just delete the code from the myfirstpage.htm file, leaving the script tags, as follows:

```
<script type="text/javascript">
</script>
```

9. Now add the *src* attribute to the opening *<script>* tag:

```
<script type="text/javascript" src="myscript.js">
```

10. If desired, you can make the code look prettier by deleting the extra carriage return and placing the code on one line, like so:

```
<script type="text/javascript" src="myscript.js"></script>
```

The entire contents of myfirstpage.htm should now be the following:

```
<!DOCTYPE html PUBLIC "-//W3C//DTD XHTML 1.0 Transitional//EN" "http://www.w3.org/TR/
xhtml1/DTD/xhtml1-transitional.dtd">
<html xmlns="http://www.w3.org/1999/xhtml" >
<head>
    <title>My First Page</title>
    <script type="text/javascript" src="myscript.js"></script>
</head>
<body>

</body>
</html>
```

11. Save myfirstpage.htm.

12. View the page in a web browser by selecting Start Without Debugging from the Debug menu. The page will be served through the web server, and your browser window, if not already open, will open to the page. The result should be an alert with the text "This is the Second Example." An example of this is shown here:

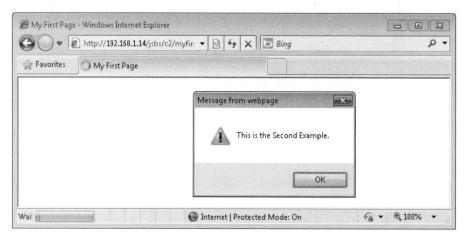

13. Click OK to close the alert dialog box. Now view the source to see the difference. In your web browser, select Source from the View menu. Note that the *<script>* tag now contains a reference to the external JavaScript file.

You've developed JavaScript with Visual Studio 2010. From here, you can skip ahead to the section on debugging or keep reading to learn about JavaScript development using other tools.

Writing JavaScript with Eclipse

Another popular IDE among web developers (and developers who use other languages) is Eclipse. Developers using Eclipse can install different frameworks to assist in specific development tasks. For example, web developers might use the Web Tools Platform or PHP (PHP Hypertext Preprocessor) development tools to create an environment that simplifies many common tasks for them. Discussion of the many potential Eclipse projects is beyond the scope of this book, but I discuss how to use the base Eclipse installation to develop JavaScript.

If you want to develop JavaScript with Eclipse, take a moment to download the software, and if necessary, the Java runtime environment. Details and download locations are available from the Eclipse website (*http://www.eclipse.org*). In this section of the book, I assume that you've never used Eclipse and are learning it for the first time. However, this section does not include a tutorial on installing Eclipse. I recommend you read the documentation included with Eclipse and available on the Eclipse website for the most up-to-date information.

Your First Web (and JavaScript) Project with Eclipse

It's now time to create a webpage with JavaScript using Eclipse. If you're not using Eclipse, this section isn't for you, and you can skip it. Later in the chapter, I show you how to develop without using any IDE, as well as some tips for debugging JavaScript.

> **Note** This section reviews how to the use the Eclipse IDE for JavaScript web developers. Your Eclipse environment might look a little different from the screenshots included in this section. The first time you open Eclipse, you are asked to select a workspace. Choose the default.

Creating a web project with JavaScript in Eclipse

1. Create a new project by selecting New, and then JavaScript, from the File menu. The New JavaScript Project dialog box appears. Type **Chapter2** in the Project name box and click Finish.

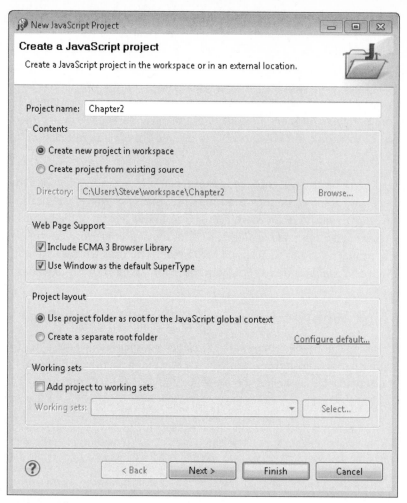

2. The Chapter2 folder opens in Project Explorer without files listed, as depicted here.

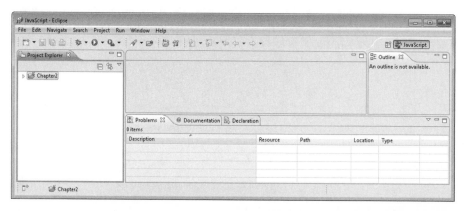

3. Right-click the Chapter2 folder, click New, and then click File. The New File dialog box opens. In the File Name text box, type **myfirstpage.htm**, as shown in the next screen, and click Finish. You can find this file, titled eclipse_myfirstpage.htm, in the Chapter 2 sample code. If you'd like to use this file, rename it to **myfirstpage.htm** for the remainder of this exercise.

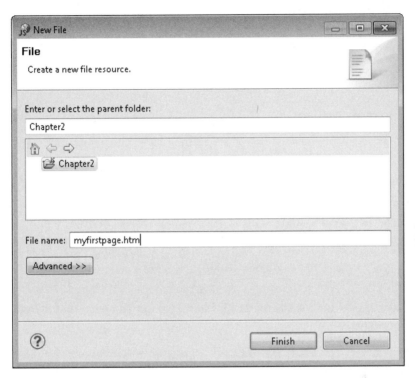

4. After you click Finish, Eclipse opens the page in its own web browser. However, you want to edit the page, not view it, so right-click myfirstpage.htm in Project Explorer and click Open. The page opens in an editor directly in Eclipse, as shown here:

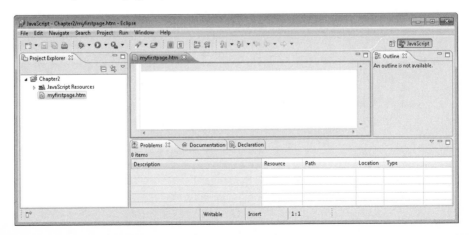

5. At last it's time to write some code! In the editor, type this code:

```
<!DOCTYPE html PUBLIC "-//W3C//DTD XHTML 1.0 Transitional//EN" "http://www.w3.org/TR/
xhtml1/DTD/xhtml1-transitional.dtd">
<html xmlns="http://www.w3.org/1999/xhtml" >
<head>
    <title>My First Page</title>
    <script type="text/javascript">

function yetAnotherAlert(textToAlert) {
    alert(textToAlert);
}
yetAnotherAlert("This is Chapter 2");

</script>
</head>
<body>

</body>
</html>
```

> **Note** For the purposes of this example, you can skip the DOCTYPE declaration if you
> don't want to type it, and just begin with an *<html>* tag on top. For real-world development
> outside the context of this book, you would definitely want to have a DOCTYPE declared.
> See Chapter 1 for more information about why this is important.

6. Select Save from the File menu. The finished script and page should resemble the one
shown here:

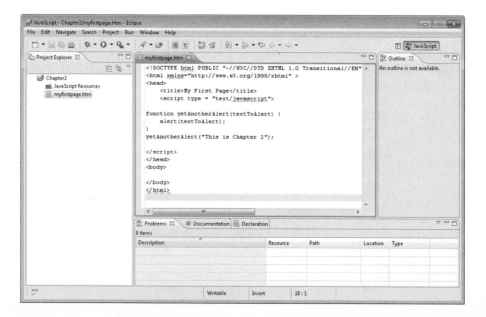

To view the page, right-click the file in Project Explorer, select Open With, and then click Web Browser. You will see the file locally through the Eclipse browser, and you should receive a page with an alert, similar to the one shown in Figure 2-7.

Alternatively, you can view the file through a different web browser on your computer, such as your system's default web browser. To do this, browse to the file (for example, my copy of the file is located in the C:\Users\Steve\workspace\Chapter2\folder), and then double-click the file.

> **Note** If you're using Windows Internet Explorer, you might receive an alert about viewing blocked content, depending on the security level set for your browser. The support article at *http://windows.microsoft.com/en-US/windows7/Internet-Explorer-Information-bar-frequently-asked-questions* has more information about this feature and how to disable it.

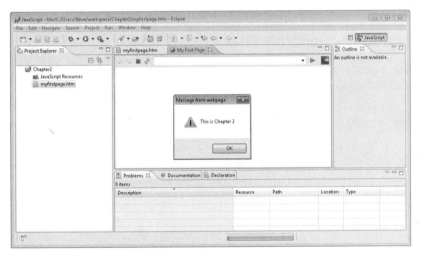

FIGURE 2-7 Viewing the file as developed in Eclipse.

In this example, you created a basic webpage with some embedded JavaScript. The JavaScript portion of the page contains just a few elements. First, the script tag is opened and declared to be JavaScript, as shown in this code:

```
<script type="text/javascript">
```

> **Note** You can declare that your script is JavaScript in other ways, but the approach you see here is the most widely supported.

Next, the script declares a function, *yetAnotherAlert*, which accepts one argument, *textToAlert*:

```
function yetAnotherAlert(textToAlert) {
```

The function has one task: to pop up an alert into the browser window with whatever text has been supplied as the function argument, which the next line accomplishes:

```
alert(textToAlert);
```

The function is delineated by a closing brace:

```
}
```

The script then calls the function you just declared with a quoted string argument, as follows:

```
yetAnotherAlert("This is Chapter 2");
```

In this brief example, you saw how to code JavaScript using Eclipse. The next section shows how to place the JavaScript in an external file, a common approach to using JavaScript.

Using External JavaScript Files with Eclipse

By the time you read this, you should have a working webpage (created with Eclipse) that displays an alert. The webpage you developed in the previous section contains the JavaScript code within the *<head>* tag portion of the page. In this section, I describe how to place JavaScript into an external file and then refer to that code from within your HTML page.

Creating an external file for JavaScript using Eclipse

1. If the myfirstpage.htm code isn't already open in Eclipse, open it. (You can find this file in the companion content.) Select the project in which you saved the myfirstpage.htm file, and open the file itself in an editor by right-clicking the file, selecting Open With, and then clicking Text Editor.

2. Create a new file to hold the JavaScript code by selecting New and then File from the File menu. The New File dialog box opens. Type **myscript.js** in the File Name text box, as shown here, and click Finish.

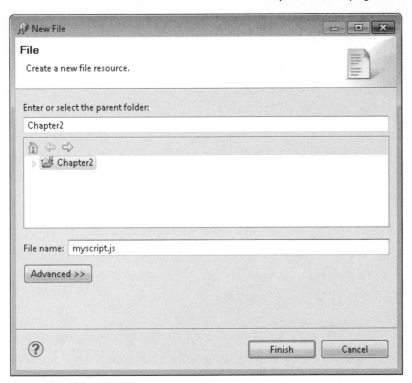

3. Eclipse adds a new empty JavaScript file to your project. If this file doesn't open automatically, right-click the myscript.js file in Project Explorer, select Open With, and then
click Text Editor. You should now see tabs for both the new myscript.js file and the
myfirstpage.htm file. You might also see the My First Page webpage.

> **Note** Although you are not required to use the colloquial extension for JavaScript, which is
> .js, doing so might help you more easily identify files later.

4. Click the myfirstpage.htm tab to make it active, and highlight the JavaScript code you
wrote earlier. Be sure to leave the actual JavaScript tags *<script>* and *</script>* intact
and do not highlight them. (You don't need those right now, but you'll revisit the topic
shortly.)

5. Copy the highlighted code to the Clipboard by selecting Copy from the Edit menu.

6. Click the myscript.js tab, and paste the code by selecting Paste from the Edit menu.
Change the text of the function call to "This is the Second Example." The code looks like
this:

```
function yetAnotherAlert(textToAlert) {
    alert(textToAlert);
}
yetAnotherAlert("This is the Second Example.");
```

7. Save the myscript.js file by selecting Save from the File menu. The file should look similar to the screen shown here:

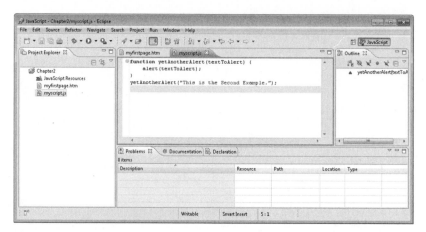

8. With the JavaScript code contained in its own file named myscript.js (you did save it, right?), you can safely delete the code from the myfirstpage.htm file. Just delete the code, leaving the script tags, like so:

```
<script type="text/javascript">
</script>
```

9. Add the *src* attribute to the opening *<script>* tag:

```
<script type="text/javascript" src="myscript.js">
```

10. If desired, to make the code look prettier, delete the extra carriage return to place the code on one line, like this:

```
<script type="text/javascript" src="myscript.js"></script>
```

The entire contents of myfirstpage.htm should now be the following:

```
<!DOCTYPE html PUBLIC "-//W3C//DTD XHTML 1.0 Transitional//EN" "http://www.w3.org/TR/
xhtml1/DTD/xhtml1-transitional.dtd">
<html xmlns="http://www.w3.org/1999/xhtml" >
<head>
    <title>My First Page</title>
    <script type="text/javascript" src="myscript.js"></script>
</head>
<body>

</body>
</html>
```

11. Save myfirstpage.htm.

12. View the page in a web browser by right-clicking myfirstpage.htm in Project Explorer, pointing to Open With, and then clicking Web Browser. The page is served locally, and a browser window opens to the page. The result should be an alert with the text "This is the Second Example." It looks like this:

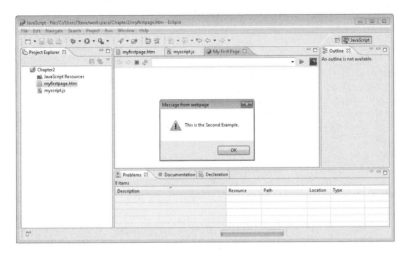

This basic primer about JavaScript development with Eclipse is complete. There's much more to it, though, and I recommend visiting the Eclipse website for more information about development with the Eclipse platform.

Writing JavaScript Without an IDE

You can just as easily forgo the IDEs in favor of a simpler approach to JavaScript development. Any text editor like Notepad or Vim will work fine for JavaScript development. I recommend against using word processors such as Microsoft Office Word for JavaScript development though, because they can leave artifacts within the resulting file, which in turn can wreak havoc on the resulting website.

Your First Web (and JavaScript) Project with Notepad

This section shows an example of JavaScript development with Notepad.

Creating a webpage with JavaScript in Notepad

1. In Microsoft Windows 7 (and Microsoft Windows XP and Microsoft Windows Vista), you can open Notepad by clicking the Start button and then clicking All Programs, Accessories, and then Notepad. In the document, enter the following code:

```
<!DOCTYPE HTML PUBLIC "-//W3C//DTD HTML 4.01//EN"
"http://www.w3.org/TR/html4/strict.dtd">
<html>
<head>
    <title>My First Page</title>
    <script type="text/javascript">

function yetAnotherAlert(textToAlert) {
    alert(textToAlert);
}
yetAnotherAlert("This is Chapter 2");

</script>

</head>
<body>

</body>
</html>
```

 Note For the purposes of this example, you could skip the DOCTYPE declaration if you don't want to type it, and just begin with an *<html>* tag on top. For real-world development outside the context of this book, you would definitely want to have a DOCTYPE declared. See Chapter 1 for more information about why this is important.

2. Select Save from the File menu. You are presented with a Save As dialog box. By default, unfortunately, Notepad adds a .txt extension to the document name unless you use double quotation marks. Therefore, be sure to place double quotation marks around the filename—for example, *"myfirstpage.htm"*. If you omit the quotation marks, Notepad will add the .txt extension and save the file as "myfirstpage.htm.txt" instead. The following image shows an example of using double quotation marks around the filename. Be sure to note where you save this document.

3. To view the page, use the web browser of your choice to browse to the location where you saved the file. (If, as in the screen shown in the previous step, you saved the file to the Desktop, browse there.) The next image shows the file rendered in Firefox.

Note If you are using Internet Explorer, you might receive an alert about viewing blocked content, depending on the security level set for your browser. The support article at *http://windows.microsoft.com/en-US/windows7/Internet-Explorer-Information-bar-frequently-asked-questions* has more information about this feature and how to disable it.

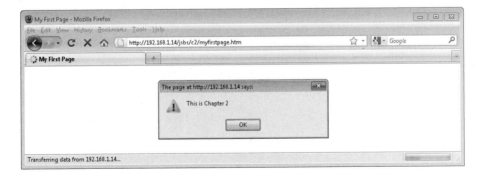

So far in this example, you created a basic webpage with some embedded JavaScript. The JavaScript portion of the page contains just a few elements. First, the script tag is opened and declared to be JavaScript, as shown by this code:

```
<script type="text/javascript">
```

> **Note** You can declare that your script is JavaScript in other ways, but the approach you see here is the most widely supported.

Next, the script declares a function, *yetAnotherAlert*, which accepts one argument, *textToAlert*:

```
function yetAnotherAlert(textToAlert) {
```

The function has one task: to pop up an alert in the browser window with whatever text has been supplied as the function argument, which the next line accomplishes:

```
    alert(textToAlert);
```

The function is delineated by a closing brace (*}*). The script then calls the function you just declared with a quoted string argument:

```
yetAnotherAlert("This is Chapter 2");
```

In this brief example, you've seen how to code JavaScript without an IDE. The next section shows how to place the JavaScript in an external file, a quite common approach to JavaScript usage.

Using External JavaScript Files Without an IDE

By the time you read this, you should have a working webpage (created in Notepad) that displays an *alert()* dialog box. The webpage you developed in the previous section contains the JavaScript code within the *<head>* tag portion of the page. This section shows how to place JavaScript into an external file and then refer to that code from within your HTML page.

Creating an external file for JavaScript using Notepad

1. If the myfirstpage.htm code isn't open, open it. If you're using Notepad, you might need to right-click the file and select Open With, and then select Notepad.

2. Highlight the JavaScript code. Be sure to leave the actual JavaScript tags *<script>* and *</script>* intact and do not highlight them. Copy the code to the Clipboard by highlighting it and selecting Copy from the Edit menu.

3. Create a new file to hold the JavaScript code by selecting New from the File menu. The new file opens. Paste the JavaScript code into the file by selecting Paste from the Edit

menu. Change the text of the parameter to the function call so that it reads "This is the Second Example." This code is shown here:

```
function yetAnotherAlert(textToAlert) {
    alert(textToAlert);
}
yetAnotherAlert("This is the Second Example.");
```

4. Save the file by selecting Save from the File menu. Type **myscript.js** in the File Name text box, and be sure to include double quotation marks again because the extension needs to be .js and not .txt.

> **Note** The colloquial extension for JavaScript files is .js, but you don't have to use it. However, doing so might help you identify files more easily later.

5. With the JavaScript code contained in its own file named myscript.js (you did save it, right?), you can safely delete the code from the myfirstpage.htm file. Open myfirst-page.htm again in Notepad. In myfirstpage.htm, just delete the JavaScript code that you pasted earlier, leaving the script tags:

```
<script type="text/javascript">
</script>
```

> **Tip** Be sure you're viewing All Files and not just Text Documents when trying to open files that don't have a .txt extension, such as the .htm or .js files that you just created. To do this, select All Files from the Files Of Type drop-down list in the Open dialog box.

6. Add the *src* attribute to the opening *<script>* tag, as follows:

```
<script type="text/javascript" src="myscript.js">
```

7. If desired, you can make the code look prettier by deleting the extra carriage return and placing the code on one line, like this:

```
<script type="text/javascript" src="myscript.js"></script>
```

The entire contents of myfirstpage.htm are now the following:

```
<!DOCTYPE HTML PUBLIC "-//W3C//DTD HTML 4.01//EN"
"http://www.w3.org/TR/html4/strict.dtd">
<html>
<head>
    <title>My First Page</title>
    <script type="text/javascript" src="myscript.js"></script>
</head>
<body>

</body>
</html>
```

8. Save myfirstpage.htm.

9. View the page in a web browser. The result, shown in the following screen, should be an alert with the text "This is the Second Example."

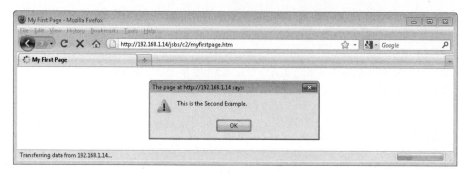

This primer on JavaScript development without an IDE is complete. Although this example used Notepad, several other editors might be more suited to basic development, including the aforementioned Vim, and Textpad from Helio Software Solutions, both of which are more powerful than Notepad.

Debugging JavaScript

Debugging JavaScript can be an alarming experience, especially in more complex applications. Some tools, such as Venkman (*http://www.mozilla.org/projects/venkman/*), can assist in JavaScript debugging, but the primary tool for debugging JavaScript is the web browser. Major web browsers include some JavaScript debugging capabilities. Among the programs you should consider using is Firebug, a notable add-on to Firefox. Firebug is available at *http://www.getfirebug.com/.*

I find Firebug to be virtually indispensable for web development, especially web development with JavaScript and AJAX. This software allows you to inspect all the elements of a webpage, and to see the results of AJAX calls as well as CSS, all in real time, which makes debugging much easier. Figure 2-8 shows an example of Firebug in action on my website's home page.

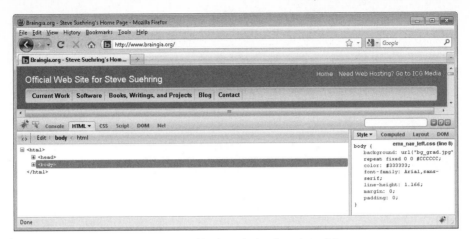

FIGURE 2-8 Firebug is an important tool in the web developer's toolkit.

I recommend using Firebug for developing JavaScript and debugging it. When debugging JavaScript, I find that the *alert()* function is quite useful. A few well-placed *alert()* functions can show you the values contained within variables and what your script is currently doing. Of course, because *alert()* causes a dialog box to open, if you place an *alert()* within a loop and then mistakenly cause that loop to repeat endlessly without exiting, you'll find that you need to exit the web browser uncleanly, maybe using Task Manager.

Exercises

1. Create a new webpage and call it mysecondpage.htm. Create a script in JavaScript within the *<body>* portion of the page and have that script display an *alert()* dialog box with your name. Try this script in at least two different web browsers.

2. Edit the webpage that you created in Exercise 1 and create a function within the *<head>* portion of the page and move the *alert()* dialog box that you currently have in the *<body>* script into your new function. Call the new function from the existing *<body>* script.

3. Move the function created in Exercise 2 to an external JavaScript file, and link or call this file from within your webpage.

Chapter 3
JavaScript Syntax and Statements

After reading this chapter, you'll be able to:

- Understand the basic rules of using the JavaScript programming language.

- Place JavaScript correctly within a webpage.

- Recognize a JavaScript statement.

- Recognize a reserved word in JavaScript.

A Bit of Housekeeping

The rest of the book looks more closely at specific aspects of JavaScript and how they relate to specific tasks. However, you must walk before you can run, so before examining JavaScript in more depth, you should learn some of its *lexical structure*—that is, the rules of the language, also known as *syntax rules*.

Case Sensitivity

JavaScript is case sensitive. You must be aware of this when naming variables and using the language keywords. A variable named *remote* is not the same as a variable named *Remote* or one named *REMOTE*. Similarly, the loop control keyword *while* is perfectly valid, but naming it *WHILE* or *While* will result in an error.

Keywords are lowercase, but variables can be any mix of case that you'd like. As long you are consistent with the case, you can create any combination you want. For example, all these examples are perfectly legal variable names in JavaScript:

```
buttonOne
txt1
a
C
```

 Tip You'll typically see JavaScript coded in lowercase except where necessary—for example, with function calls such as *isNaN()*, which determines whether a value is Not a Number (the *NaN* in the function name). You learn about this in Chapter 4, "Working with Variables and Data Types."

Chapter 4 provides much more information about variables and their naming conventions. For now, remember that you must pay attention to the case when you write a variable name in JavaScript.

White Space

For the most part, JavaScript ignores *white space*, which is the space between statements in JavaScript. You can use spaces, indenting, or whatever coding standards you prefer to make the JavaScript more readable. There are some exceptions to this rule, however. Some keywords, such as *return*, can be misinterpreted by the JavaScript interpreter when they're included on a line by themselves. You'll see an example of this problem a little later in this chapter.

Making programs more readable is a good enough reason to include white space. Consider the following code sample. It includes minimal white space and indenting.

```
function cubeme(incomingNum) {
if (incomingNum == 1) {
return "What are you doing?";
} else {
return Math.pow(incomingNum,3);
}
}
var theNum = 2;
var finalNum = cubeme(theNum);
if (isNaN(finalNum)) {
alert("You should know that 1 to any power is 1.");
} else {
alert("When cubed, " + theNum + " is " + finalNum);
}
```

Now consider the same code with indenting. (You can find this code, named example1.txt, in the Chapter 3 sample code in the companion content.)

```
function cubeme(incomingNum) {
    if (incomingNum == 1) {
        return "What are you doing?";
    } else {
        return Math.pow(incomingNum,3);
    }
}

var theNum = 2;
var finalNum = cubeme(theNum);

if (isNaN(finalNum)) {
    alert("You should know that 1 to any power is 1.");
} else {
    alert("When cubed, " + theNum + " is " + finalNum);
}
```

The second code sample performs just like the first, but it's easier to read and follow—at least it appears so to me! I find that it takes a short amount of time to actually write code, but several years to work with it. When I visit the code a year later, I'm much happier when I've made the code more readable and easier to follow.

Comments

Speaking of creating more readable code and maintaining that code over the long term, comments are your friends. Code that seems blatantly obvious now won't be nearly so obvious the next time you look at it, especially if a lot of time has passed since you wrote it. Comments can be placed into JavaScript code in two ways: multiline and single-line.

A multiline comment in JavaScript will look familiar to you if you've coded in the C programming language. A *multiline* comment begins and ends with /* and */ respectively, as this code example shows:

```
/*  This is a multiline comment in JavaScript
It is just like a C-style comment insofar as it can
span multiple lines before being closed.  */
```

A *single-line* comment begins with two front slashes (//) and has no end requirement, because it spans only a single line. An example is shown here:

```
// Here is a single line comment.
```

Using multiple single-line comments is perfectly valid, and I use them for short comment blocks rather than use the multiline comment style previously shown. For example, look at this block of code:

```
// Here is another comment block.
// This one uses multiple lines.
// Each line must be preceded with two slashes.
```

> **Tip** You may find it quicker to use the two-slash method for small comments that span one line or a few lines. For larger comments, such as those at the beginning of a program or script, the multiline comment style is a better choice because it makes adding or deleting information easier.

Semicolons

Semicolons are used to delineate expressions in JavaScript. Technically, semicolons are not required for most statements and expressions. However, the subtle problems that you can encounter when you don't use semicolons add unnecessary errors and hence unnecessary debugging time. In some instances, the JavaScript interpreter inserts a semicolon when you may not have wanted one at all. For example, consider this statement:

```
return
(varName);
```

In all likelihood, you wanted to write:

```
return(varName);
```

But JavaScript, acting on its own, inserts a semicolon after the *return* statement, making the code appear like this to the JavaScript interpreter:

```
return;
(varName);
```

This code won't work; the interpreter will misunderstand your intentions. If you used this code in a function, it would return *undefined* to the caller, which is unlikely to be what you want. This is an example where free use of white space is not allowed—you can't successfully use line breaks (explained in the next section) to separate the *return* keyword from the value that it's supposed to return.

You'll find programming in JavaScript much easier if you use semicolons as a rule rather than try to remember where you might not have to use them.

But you definitely shouldn't use semicolons in one instance: when using loops and conditionals. Consider this bit of code:

```
if (a == 4)
{
    // code goes here
}
```

In this case, you wouldn't use a semicolon at the end of the *if* statement. The reason is that the statement or block of statements in opening and closing braces that follows a conditional is part of the conditional statement, in this case, the *if* statement. A semicolon marks the end of the *if* statement, and if improperly placed, dissociates the first part of the *if* statement from the rest of it. For example, the following code is wrong (the code within the braces will execute regardless of whether *a* equals 4):

```
if (a == 4);
{
    // code goes here
}
```

Tip When opening a loop or function, skip the semicolons.

Line Breaks

Related closely to white space and even to semicolons in JavaScript are line breaks, sometimes called *carriage returns*. Known in the official ECMA-262 standard as "Line Terminators," these characters separate one line of code from the next. Like semicolons, the placement of line breaks matters. As you saw from the example in the previous section, placing a line break in the wrong position can result in unforeseen behavior or errors.

Not surprisingly, the most common use of line breaks is to separate individual lines of code for readability. You can also improve readability of particularly long lines of code by separating them with line breaks. However, when doing so, be aware of issues like the one illustrated by the *return* statement cited earlier, in which an extra line break can have unwanted effects on the meaning of the code.

Placing JavaScript Correctly

JavaScript can be placed in a couple of locations within a Hypertext Markup Language (HTML) page: in the *<head> </head>* section, or between the *<body>* and *</body>* tags. The most common location for JavaScript has traditionally been between the *<head>* and *</head>* tags near the top of the page. However, placing the *<script>* stanza within the *<body>* section is becoming more common. Be sure to declare what type of script you're using. Though other script types can be used, because this is a JavaScript book, I'll declare the following within the opening *<script>* tag:

```
<script type="text/javascript">
```

One important issue to note when you use JavaScript relates to pages declared as Extensible Hypertext Markup Language (XHTML). In such pages, the *<script>* tag must be declared within a CDATA section; if it is not, XHTML tries to parse the *<script>* tag as just another XML tag, and code within the section might not work as you expect. Therefore, JavaScript used within strict XHTML should be declared as follows:

```
<script type="text/javascript">
<![CDATA[

    //JavaScript goes here

]]>
</script>
```

Older browsers may not parse the CDATA section correctly. This problem can be worked around by placing the CDATA opening and closing lines within JavaScript comments, like this:

```
<script type="text/javascript">
//<![CDATA[

    //JavaScript goes here

//]]>
</script>
```

When you place the actual JavaScript code in a separate file (as you learned how to do in Chapter 2, "Developing in JavaScript"), you don't need to use this ugly CDATA section at all. You'll probably discover that for anything but the smallest scripts, defining your JavaScript in separate files—usually with the file extension .js—and then linking to those scripts within the page, is desirable. Chapter 2 showed this in full detail, but here's a reminder of how you link to a file using the *src* attribute of the *<script>* tag:

```
<script type="text/javascript" src="myscript.js">
```

Placing JavaScript in an external file has several advantages, including:

- **Separation of code from markup**   Keeping the JavaScript code in a separate file makes maintaining the HTML easier, and it preserves the structure of the HTML without you having to use a CDATA section for XHTML.

- **Easier maintenance**   With JavaScript as a separate file, you can make changes to the file without touching another file on the site.

- **Caching**   Using a separate file for JavaScript allows web browsers to cache the file, thus speeding up the webpage load for the user.

JavaScript Statements

Like programs written in other languages, JavaScript programs consist of statements put together that cause the JavaScript interpreter to perform one or more actions. And like statements in other languages, JavaScript statements can be simple or compound. This section briefly examines the form of JavaScript statements, with the assumption that you already saw several examples in the previous chapters and that you'll see others throughout the book.

What's in a Statement?

As covered in Chapter 1, "JavaScript Is More Than You Might Think," a JavaScript statement, or expression, is a collection of tokens, operators, and identifiers that are put together to create something that makes sense to the JavaScript interpreter. A statement usually ends with a semicolon, except in special cases like loop constructors such as *if*, *while*, and *for*, which are covered in Chapter 5, "Using Operators and Expressions."

Here are some examples of basic statements in JavaScript:

```
var x = 4;
var y = x * 4;
alert("Hello");
```

The Two Types of JavaScript Statements

JavaScript statements come in two basic forms, simple and compound. I won't spend a lot of time discussing statements because you don't really need to know much about them. However, you should know the difference between simple and compound statements. A *simple statement* is just what you'd expect—it's simple, like so:

```
x = 4;
```

A *compound statement* combines multiple levels of logic. An *if/then/else* decisional such as the one given here provides a good example of this:

```
if (something == 1) {
    // some code here
} else {
    // some other code here
}
```

Reserved Words in JavaScript

Certain words in JavaScript are *reserved*, which means you can't use them as variables, identifiers, or constant names within your program, because doing so will cause the code to have unexpected results, such as errors. For example, you've already seen the reserved word *var* in previous examples. Using the word *var* to do anything but declare a variable may cause an error or other unexpected behavior, depending on the browser. Consider this statement:

```
// Don't do this!

var var = 4;
```

The code example won't result in a direct error to a browser, but it also won't work as you intended, possibly causing confusion when a variable's value isn't what you expect.

The following list includes the words that are currently reserved by the ECMA-262 specification:

break	delete	if	this	while
case	do	in	throw	with
catch	else	instanceof	try	
continue	finally	new	typeof	
debugger	for	return	var	
default	function	switch	void	

Several other words (shown in the following list) are reserved for future use and therefore shouldn't be used in your programs:

class	enum	extends	super	
const	export	import		

The following list of words are reserved for the future when in strict mode:

implements	let	private	public	yield
interface	package	protected	static	

A Quick Look at Functions

You've already seen examples of functions in previous chapters. JavaScript has several *built-in functions*, or functions that are defined by the language itself. I discussed the *alert()* function already, but there are several others. Which built-in functions are available depends on the language version you're using. Some functions are available only in later versions of JavaScript, which might not be supported by all browsers. Detecting a browser's available functions (and objects) is an important way to determine whether a visitor's browser is capable of using the JavaScript that you created for your webpage. This topic is covered in Chapter 11, "JavaScript Events and the Browser."

> **Tip** You can find an excellent resource for compatibility on the QuirksMode website: *(http://www.quirksmode.org/compatibility.html)*.

JavaScript is similar to other programming languages in allowing user-defined functions. An earlier example in this chapter defined a function called *cubeme()*, which raised a given number to the power of 3. That code provides a good opportunity to show the use of JavaScript in both the *<head>* and *<body>* portions of a webpage.

Placing JavaScript with a user-defined function

1. Using Microsoft Visual Studio, Eclipse, or another editor, edit the file example1.htm in the Chapter 3 sample code.

2. Within the webpage, add the code in bold type, replacing the TODO comments:

```
<!DOCTYPE HTML PUBLIC "-//W3C//DTD HTML 4.01//EN"
"http://www.w3.org/TR/html4/strict.dtd">
<html>
<head>
<script type="text/javascript">
function cubeme(incomingNum) {
    if (incomingNum == 1) {
        return "What are you doing?";
    } else {
        return Math.pow(incomingNum,3);
    }
}
</script>
    <title>A Chapter 3 Example</title>
</head>

<body>
<script type="text/javascript">
var theNum = 2;
var finalNum = cubeme(theNum);

if (isNaN(finalNum)) {
    alert("You should know that 1 to any power is 1.");
} else {
    alert("When cubed, " + theNum + " is " + finalNum);
}
</script>

</body>
</html>
```

3. Save the page, and then run the code or view the webpage in a browser. You'll receive an alert like this:

The code in this example incorporates the code from the earlier example into a full HTML page, including a DOCTYPE declaration. The code declares a function, *cubeme()*, within the *<head>* of the document, like this:

```
function cubeme(incomingNum) {
    if (incomingNum == 1) {
        return "What are you doing?";
    } else {
        return Math.pow(incomingNum,3);
    }
}
```

This code accepts an argument called *incomingNum* within the function. An *if/then* decisional statement is the heart of the function. When the incoming number equals *1*, the function returns the text string, "What are you doing?" When, on the other hand, the incoming number is not equal to 1, the *Math.pow* method is called, passing the *incomingNum* variable and the integer 3 as arguments. The call to *Math.pow* raises the incoming number to the power of 3, and this value is then returned to the calling function. This call is shown again in Chapter 4.

All the previous code was placed within the *<head>* of the document so it can be called by other code, which is just what we're going to do. The browser then renders the *<body>* of the document, which includes another bit of JavaScript code. This next bit of code sets a variable, *theNum*, equal to the integer 2:

```
var theNum = 2;
```

The code then calls the previously defined *cubeme()* function using the *theNum* variable as an argument. You'll notice that the variable *finalNum* is set to receive the output from the call to the *cubeme()* function, as follows:

```
var finalNum = cubeme(theNum);
```

The final bit of JavaScript on the page is another *if/then* decisional set. This code checks to determine whether the returned value, now contained in the *finalNum* variable, is a number. It does this by using the *isNaN()* function. If the value is not a number, an alert is displayed reflecting the fact that *1* was used as the argument. (Of course, there could be other reasons this isn't a number, but bear with me here and follow along with my example.) If the return value is indeed a number, the number is displayed, as you saw in the *alert()* dialog box shown in the preceding step 3.

JavaScript's New Strict Mode

ECMA-262 version 5 introduced a strict variant, commonly referred to as *strict mode*, which adds enhanced error checking and security. For example, to help fight against mistyped variable names, variable declarations require the use of the *var* keyword. Additionally, changes to the *eval()* function and other areas help JavaScript programmers to improve their code.

Strict mode is enabled with the following syntax, which is very similar to syntax used in Perl:

```
"use strict";
```

Strict mode is locally scoped, meaning that it can be enabled globally, by placing the *use strict* line at the beginning of the script; or it can be enabled only within a function, by placing the line within the function itself, like so:

```
function doSomething() {

    "use strict";

    // function's code goes here.

}
```

One strict mode enhancement that will help catch typographical errors is the prevention of undeclared variables. All variables in strict mode need to be instantiated prior to use. For example, consider this code:

```
"use strict";

x = 4;  // Produces a syntax error
```

The code would create an error condition because the variable *x* hasn't been declared with the *var* keyword, as it is here:

```
"use strict";

var x = 4;  // This syntax is ok
```

Of the notable security enhancements that strict mode provides is the change to how the *eval()* function is handled. In strict mode, *eval()* cannot instantiate a new variable or function that will be used outside of the *eval()* statement. For example:

```
"use strict";

eval("var testVar = 2;");

alert(testVar);  // Produces a syntax error.
```

In the code example, a syntax error would be produced because strict mode is enabled and the *testVar* variable isn't available outside of the *eval()* statement.

Strict mode also prevents the duplication of variable names within an object or function call:

```
"use strict";

var myObject = {

    testVar: 1,

    testVar: 2

};
```

The previous code would produce a syntax error in strict mode because *testVar* is set twice within the object's definition.

Like other aspects of ECMA-262 version 5, strict mode may not be available in all browsers and likely won't be available for older browsers. For more information about ECMA-262 version 5 as well as a full implementation, see *http://besen.sourceforge.net/*.

Exercises

1. Which of the following are valid JavaScript statements? (Choose all that apply.)

   a. if (var == 4) {   // Do something }

   b. var testVar = 10;

   c. if (a == b) {   // Do something }

   d. testVar = 10;

   e. var case = "Yes";

2. True or False: Semicolons are required to terminate every JavaScript statement.

3. Examine this bit of JavaScript. What is the likely result? (Assume that the JavaScript declaration has already taken place and that this code resides properly within the *<head>* section of the page.)

```
var orderTotal = 0;
function collectOrder(numOrdered) {
    if (numOrdered > 0) {
        alert("You ordered " + orderTotal);
        orderTotal = numOrdered * 5;
    }
    return orderTotal;
}
```

Chapter 4
Working with Variables and Data Types

After reading this chapter, you'll be able to:

- Understand the primitive data types used in JavaScript.
- Use functions associated with the data types.
- Create variables.
- Define objects and arrays.
- Understand the scope of variables.
- Debug JavaScript using Firebug.

Data Types in JavaScript

The *data types* of a language describe the basic elements that can be used within that language. You're probably already familiar with data types, such as strings or integers, from other languages. Depending on who you ask, JavaScript defines anywhere from three to six data types. (The answer depends largely on the definition of a data type.) You work with all these data types regularly, some more than others.

The six data types in JavaScript discussed in this chapter are as follows:

- Numbers
- Strings
- Booleans
- Null
- Undefined
- Objects

The first three data types—numbers, strings, and Booleans—should be fairly familiar to programmers in any language. The latter three—null, undefined, and objects—require some additional explanation. I examine each of the data types in turn and explain objects further in Chapter 8, "Objects in JavaScript."

Additionally, JavaScript has several reference data types, including the *Array*, *Date*, and *RegExp* types. The *Date* and *RegExp* types are discussed in this chapter, and the *Array* type is discussed in Chapter 8.

Working with Numbers

Numbers in JavaScript are just what you might expect them to be: numbers. What might be a surprise, however, for programmers who are familiar with data types in other languages like C, is that integers and floating point numbers do not have special or separate types. All these are perfectly valid numbers in JavaScript:

```
4
51.50
-14
0xd
```

The last example, *0xd*, is a hexadecimal number. Both hexadecimal and octal numbers are valid in JavaScript, and you won't be surprised to learn that JavaScript allows math to be performed using those number formats. Try the following exercise.

Performing hexadecimal math with JavaScript

1. Using Microsoft Visual Studio, Eclipse, or another editor, edit the file example1.htm in the Chapter04 sample files folder in the companion content.

2. Within the webpage, replace the TODO comment with the boldface code shown here (the new code can be found in the example1.txt file in the companion code):

```
<!DOCTYPE HTML PUBLIC "-//W3C//DTD HTML 4.01//EN"
"http://www.w3.org/TR/html4/strict.dtd">
<html>
<head>
<title>Hexadecimal Numbers</title>
<script type="text/javascript">
var h = 0xe;
var i = 0x2;
var j = h * i;
alert(j);
</script>
</head>
<body>
</body>
</html>
```

3. View the webpage in a browser. You should see a dialog box similar to this one:

This script defines two variables (you learn about defining variables later in this chapter) and sets them equal to two hexadecimal numbers, 0xe (14 in base 10 notation) and 0x2, respectively:

```
var h = 0xe;
var i = 0x2;
```

Then a new variable is created and set to the product of the previous two variables, as follows:

```
var j = h * i;
```

The resulting variable is then passed to the *alert()* function, which displays the dialog box in the preceding step 3. It's interesting to note that even though you multiplied two hexadecimal numbers, the output in the alert dialog box is in base 10 format.

Numeric Functions

JavaScript has some built-in functions (and objects too, which you learn about soon) for working with numeric values. The European Computer Manufacturers Association (ECMA) standard defines several of them. One more common numeric function is the *isNaN()* function. By *common*, I mean that *isNaN()* is a function that I use frequently in JavaScript programming. Your usage may vary, but an explanation follows nonetheless.

NaN is an abbreviation for *Not a Number,* and it represents an illegal number. You use the *isNaN()* function to determine whether a number is legal or valid according to the ECMA-262 specification. For example, a number divided by zero would be an illegal number in JavaScript. The string value "This is not a number" is obviously also not a number. Though people may have a different interpretation of what is and isn't a number, the string "four" is not a number to the *isNaN()* function, whereas the string "4" is. The *isNaN()* function requires some mental yoga at times because it attempts to prove a negative—that the value in a variable *is not* a number. Here are a couple of examples that you can try to test whether a number is illegal.

Testing the *isNaN()* function

1. Open your web browser, such as Windows Internet Explorer or Firefox.

2. In the address bar, type the following (also available the file called isnan.txt in the companion content):

    ```
    javascript:alert(isNaN("4"));
    ```

You receive an alert with the word False, as shown here:

The function *isNaN()* returns false from this expression because the integer value 4 *is* a number. Remember the meaning of this function is, "Is 4 Not a Number?" Well, 4 *is* a number, so the result is false.

Now consider this example:

1. Open your web browser, such as Internet Explorer or Firefox.

2. In the address bar, type:

    ```
    javascript:alert(isNaN("four"));
    ```

You receive an alert with the word true, like this:

In this case, because the numeral 4 is represented as a string of nonnumeric characters *four*, the function returns *true*: the string *four* is not a number. I purposefully used double quotation marks in each code example (that is, *"4"* and *"four"*) to show that the quotation marks don't matter for this function. Because JavaScript is smart enough to realize that *"4"* is a number, JavaScript does the type conversion for you. However, this conversion can sometimes be a disadvantage, such as when you're counting on a variable or value to be a certain type.

The *isNaN()* function is used frequently when validating input to determine whether something—maybe a form variable—was entered as a number or as text.

Numeric Constants

Other numeric constants are available in JavaScript, some of which are described in Table 4-1. These constants might or might not be useful to you in your JavaScript programming, but they exist if you need them.

TABLE 4-1 **Selected Numeric Constants**

Constant	Description
Infinity	Represents positive infinity
Number.MAX_VALUE	The largest number able to be represented in JavaScript
Number.MIN_VALUE	The smallest number able to be represented in JavaScript
Number.NEGATIVE_INFINITY	A value representing negative infinity
Number.POSITIVE_INFINITY	A value representing positive infinity

The *Math* Object

The *Math* object is a special built-in object used for working with numbers in JavaScript, and it has several properties that are helpful to the JavaScript programmer, including properties that return the value of pi, the square root of a number, a pseudo-random number, and an absolute value. Some properties are value properties, meaning they return a value, whereas others act like functions and return values based on the arguments sent into them. Consider this example of the *Math.PI* value property:

```
javascript:alert(Math.PI);
```

The result is shown in Figure 4-1.

FIGURE 4-1 Viewing the value of the *Math.PI property.*

Dot Notation

Dot notation is so named because a single period, or *dot*, is used to access the members of an object. The single dot (.) creates an easy visual delineator between elements. For example, to access a property that you might call the "length of a variable *room*," you would write *room.length*. The *dot* operator is used similarly in many programming languages.

Several other properties of the *Math* object may be helpful to your program. Some of them act as functions or methods on the object, several of which are listed in Table 4-2. You can obtain a complete list of properties for the *Math* object in the ECMA-262 specification at *http://www.ecma-international.org/publications/files/ECMA-ST/Ecma-262.pdf*.

TABLE 4-2 Select Properties of the *Math* Object

Property	Definition
Math.random()	Returns a pseudo-random number
Math.abs(x)	Returns the absolute value of *x*
Math.pow(x,y)	Returns x to the power of *y*
Math.round(x)	Rounds x to the nearest integral value

Working with Strings

Strings are another basic data type available in JavaScript. They consist of one or more characters surrounded by quotation marks. The following examples are strings:

- *"Hello world"*
- *"B"*
- *"This is 'another string'"*

The last example in the preceding list requires some explanation. Strings are surrounded by either single or double quotation marks. Strings enclosed in single quotation marks can contain double quotation marks. Likewise, a string enclosed in double quotation marks, like the ones you see in the preceding example, can contain single quotation marks. So basically, if the string is surrounded by one type of quotation mark, you can use the other type within it. Here are some more examples:

- *'The cow says "moo".'*
- *'The talking clock says the time is "Twelve Noon".'*
- *"'Everyone had a good time' was the official slogan."*

Escaping Quotation Marks

If you use the same style of quotation mark both within the string and to enclose the string, the quotation marks must be *escaped* so that they won't be interpreted by the JavaScript engine. A single backslash character (\) escapes the quotation mark, as in these examples:

- *'I\'m using single quotation marks both outside and within this example. They\'re neat.'*
- *"This is a \"great\" example of using \"double quotes\" within a string that's enclosed with \"double quotes\" too."*

Other Escape Characters

JavaScript enables other characters to be represented with specific escape sequences that can appear within a string. Table 4-3 shows those escape sequences.

TABLE 4-3 **Escape Sequences in JavaScript**

Escape Character	Sequence Value
\b	Backspace
\t	Tab
\n	Newline
\v	Vertical tab
\f	Form feed
\r	Carriage return
\\	Literal backslash

Here's an example of some escape sequences in action. (Let me be the first to apologize for the continued use of the *alert()* function. I promise to get into more complex ways to display output soon.)

Using escape sequences

1. Open your web browser, such as Internet Explorer or Firefox.

2. In the address bar, type the following (also found in the escapesequences.txt file in the companion content):

```
javascript:alert("hello\t\thello\ngoodbye");
```

The following dialog box appears. (If it does not appear, close and then reopen your browser.) Note that in some browsers, such as Chrome, the way the tab character is used in this example is not honored.

This rather contrived example shows escape sequences in action. In the code, the alert displays two words "hello" surrounding two tabs, represented by their escape sequence of \t, followed by a newline character represented by its escaped sequence of \n, finally followed by the word "goodbye".

String Methods and Properties

JavaScript defines several properties and methods for working with strings. These properties and methods are accessed using dot notation ("."), explained earlier in this chapter and familiar to many programmers.

> **Note** In the same way I describe in this book only some of the elements of JavaScript, I cover only a subset of the string properties and methods available in the ECMA-262 specification. Refer to the ECMA specification for more information.

The *length* property on a *string* object gives the length of a string, not including the enclosing quotation marks. The *length* property can be called directly on a string literal, as in this example:

```
alert("This is a string.".length);
```

However, it's much more common to call the *length* property on a variable, like this:

```
var x = "This is a string.";
alert(x.length);
```

Both examples give the same result, which you can see by following this next example.

Obtaining the length of a string

1. Open your web browser, such as Internet Explorer or Firefox.

2. In the address bar, type the following (also found in the stringlength.txt file in the companion content):

   ```
   javascript:alert("This is a string.".length);
   ```

The result is a dialog box showing 17, as shown here:

3.   Now try typing this code in the address bar:

```
javascript:var x = "This is a string."; alert(x.length);
```

The result is a dialog box showing 17, the same as in the previous example.

The *substring* method returns the characters from the first argument up to but not including the second argument, as shown in the following example:

```
alert(x.substring(0,3));
```

This next code would return the first through fifth characters of the string *x*. For example:

```
var x = "Steve Suehring";
alert(x.substring(0,5));
```

The result is a message box displaying the string *"Steve"*.

Odd Indexing

The indexes used for the *substring* method are a bit odd—or at least I think they are. The first character is represented by the integer 0. This is fine, because 0 is used numerous other places in programming to represent the first index. However, the last index of the *substring* method represents not the last character that you see, but one greater than the last character.

For example, you might think that with index values of *0* and *5* (as in the preceding example), the output would be the first six characters, *0* through *5* inclusive, resulting in a string of *"Steve "* with the additional space on the end. However, this is not the case. The output is really *"Steve"*—just the first five characters. So the key is to remember that the second index value of *substring* is really one greater than what you want; it's not inclusive.

Some commonly used *string* methods besides *substring* include *slice, substr, concat, toUpper-Case, toLowerCase,* and the pattern matching methods of *match, search,* and *replace.* I discuss each of these briefly.

Methods that change strings include *slice, substring, substr,* and *concat.* The *slice* and *substring* methods return string values based on another string. They accept two arguments: the beginning position and an optional end position. Here are some examples:

```
var myString = "This is a string.";
alert(myString.substring(3));  //Returns "s is a string."
alert(myString.substring(3,9));  //Returns "s is a"
alert(myString.slice(3)); //Returns "s is a string."
alert(myString.substring(3,9));  //Returns "s is a"
```

The *substr* method also accepts two arguments: the first is the beginning position to return and, in contrast to *substring/slice,* the second argument is the number of characters to return, not the stopping position. Therefore, the code examples for *substring/slice* work a little differently with *substr*:

```
var myString = "This is a string.";
alert(myString.substr(3));  //Returns "s is a string." (The same as substring/slice)
alert(myString.substr(3,9));  //Returns "s is a st" (Different from substring/slice)
```

The *concat* method concatenates two strings together:

```
var firstString = "Hello ";
var finalString = firstString.concat("World");
alert(finalString);   //Outputs "Hello World"
```

The *toUpperCase* and *toLowerCase* methods, and their brethren *toLocaleUpperCase* and *toLocaleLowerCase,* convert a string to all upper or all lowercase, respectively:

```
var myString = "this is a String";
alert(myString.toUpperCase());  // "THIS IS A STRING"
alert(myString.toLowerCase());  // "this is a string"
```

 Note The *toLocale* methods perform conversions in a locale-specific manner.

As I stated previously, numerous string properties and methods exist. The remainder of the book features other string properties and methods, and you can always find a complete list within the ECMA specification at *http://www.ecma-international.org/publications/files /ECMA-ST/Ecma-262.pdf.*

Booleans

Booleans are kind of a hidden, or passive, data type in JavaScript. By *hidden,* or passive, I mean that you don't work with Booleans in the same way that you work with strings and numbers; you can define and use a Boolean variable, but typically you simply use an expression that evaluates to a Boolean value. Booleans have only two values, *true* and *false*, and in practice you rarely set variables as such. Rather, you use Boolean expressions within tests such as an *if/then/else* statement.

Consider this statement:

```
If (myNumber > 18) {
    //do something
}
```

A Boolean expression is used within the *if* statement's condition to determine whether the code within the braces will be executed. If the content of the variable *myNumber* is greater than the integer 18, the Boolean expression evaluates to *true*; otherwise, the Boolean evaluates to *false*.

Null

Null is another special data type in JavaScript (as it is in most languages). *Null* is, simply, nothing. It represents and evaluates to *false*. When a value is *null*, it is nothing and contains nothing. Don't confuse this nothingness with being empty, however. An empty value or variable is still full of emptiness. Emptiness is different from *null*, which is just plain nothing. For example, defining a variable and setting its value to an empty string looks like this:

```
var myVariable = '';
```

The variable *myVariable* is empty, but it is not null.

Undefined

Undefined is a state, sometimes used like a value, to represent a variable that hasn't yet contained a value. This state is different from *null*, though both *null* and *undefined* can evaluate the same way. You'll learn how to distinguish between a null value and an undefined value in Chapter 5, "Using Operators and Expressions."

Objects

Like functions, objects are special enough to get their own chapter (Chapter 8, to be exact). But I still discuss objects here briefly. JavaScript is an object-based language, as opposed to a full-blown object-oriented language. JavaScript implements some functionality similar to object-oriented functionality, and for most basic usages of JavaScript, you won't notice the difference.

Objects in JavaScript are a collection of properties, each of which contains a primitive value. These properties—think of them as *keys*—enable access to values. Each value stored in the properties can be a value, another object, or even a function. You can define your own objects with JavaScript, or use the several built-in objects.

Objects are created with curly braces, so the following code creates an empty object called *myObject*:

```
var myObject = {};
```

Here's an object with several properties:

```
var dvdCatalog = {
    "identifier": "1",
    "name": "Coho Vineyard "
};
```

The preceding code example creates an object called *dvdCatalog*, which holds two properties: one called *identifier* and the other called *name*. The values contained in each property are *1* and "Coho Vineyard", respectively. You could access the name property of the *dvdCatalog* object like this:

```
alert(dvdCatalog.name);
```

Here's a more complete example of an object, which can also be found in the sample code in the file object.txt:

```
// Create a new object with curly braces
var star = {};
// Create named objects for each of four stars.
star["Polaris"] = new Object;
star["Deneb"] = new Object;
star["Vega"] = new Object;
star["Altair"] = new Object;
```

Examples later in the book show how to add properties to these objects as well as how to access properties. There's much more to objects and Chapter 8 gives that additional detail.

Arrays

You've seen in the previous example how to create an object with a name. You can also use unnamed objects that are accessed by a numbered index value. These are the traditional arrays, familiar to programmers in many languages. You just saw several objects, each named for a star. The following code creates an array of the same objects. This code can also be found in the book's sample code in a file named stararray.txt.

```
var star = new Array();
star[0] = "Polaris";
star[1] = "Deneb";
star[2] = "Vega";
star[3] = "Altair";
```

The same code can also be written like this, using the implicit array constructor, represented by square brackets:

```
var star = ["Polaris", "Deneb", "Vega", "Altair"];
```

Arrays can contain nested values, as in this example that combines the star name with the constellation in which it appears:

```
var star = [["Polaris", "Ursa Minor"],["Deneb","Cygnus"],["Vega","Lyra"],
["Altair","Aquila"]];
```

Finally, although less common, you can call the *Array()* constructor with arguments:

```
var star = new Array("Polaris", "Deneb", "Vega", "Altair");
```

> **Note** Calling the *Array()* constructor with a single numeric argument sets the length of the array rather than the value of the first element, which is what you might expect.

The new ECMA-262 version 5 specification added several new methods for iterating and working with arrays. Arrays, including methods that iterate through them and work with them, are covered in more detail in Chapter 8.

Defining and Using Variables

Variables should be familiar to programmers in just about any language. Variables store data that might change during the program's execution lifetime. You've seen several examples of declaring variables throughout the previous chapters of this book. This section formalizes the use of variables in JavaScript.

Declaring Variables

Variables are declared in JavaScript with the *var* keyword. You can find examples in the companion content for this book, in the variablenaming.txt file. The following are all valid variable declarations:

```
var x;
var myVar;
var counter1;
```

Variable names can contain uppercase and lowercase letters as well as numbers, but they cannot start with a number. Variables cannot contain spaces or other punctuation, with the exception of the underscore character (_). (In practice, though, I haven't seen very many underscore characters in JavaScript variables.) The following variable names are invalid:

```
var 1stCounter;
var new variable;
var new.variable;
var var;
```

Take a look at the preceding example. Whereas the other three variable names are invalid because characters are used that aren't valid at all (or aren't valid in that position, as is the case with the first example), the last variable name, *var,* is invalid because it uses a keyword. For more information about keywords or reserved words in JavaScript, refer to Chapter 2, "Developing in JavaScript."

You can declare multiple variables on the same line of code, as follows:

```
var x, y, zeta;
```

These can be initialized on the same line, too:

```
var x = 1, y = "hello", zeta = 14;
```

Variable Types

Variables in JavaScript are not strongly typed. It's not necessary to predeclare whether a given variable will hold an integer, a floating point number, or a string. You can also change the type of data being held within a variable through simple reassignment. Consider this example, where the variable *x* first holds an integer, but then through another assignment, it changes to hold a string:

```
var x = 4;
var x = "Now it's a string.";
```

Variable Scope

A variable's *scope* refers to the locations from which its value can be accessed. Variables are *globally scoped* when they are used outside a function. A globally scoped variable can be accessed throughout your JavaScript program. In the context of a webpage—or a document, as you might think of it—you can access and use a global variable throughout.

Variables defined within a function are scoped solely within that function. This effectively means that the values of those variables cannot be accessed outside the function. Function parameters are scoped locally to the function as well.

Here are some practical examples of scoping, which you can also find in the companion code in the scope1.txt file:

```
<script type="text/javascript">
var aNewVariable = "I'm Global.";
function doSomething(incomingBits) {
    alert(aNewVariable);
    alert(incomingBits);
}
doSomething("An argument");
</script>
```

The code defines two variables: a global variable called *aNewVariable;* and a variable called *incomingBits,* which is local to the *doSomething()* function. Both variables are passed to respective *alert()* functions within the *doSomething()* function. When the *doSomething()* function is called, the contents of both variables are sent successfully and displayed on the screen, as depicted in Figures 4-2 and 4-3.

FIGURE 4-2 The variable *aNewVariable* is globally scoped.

FIGURE 4-3 The variable *incomingBits* is locally scoped to the function.

Here's a more complex example for you to try.

Examining variable scope

1. Using Visual Studio, Eclipse, or another editor, edit the file scoping.htm in the Chapter04 sample files folder.

2. Within the page, replace the TODO comment with the boldface code shown here (the new code can be found in the scoping.txt file in the companion content):

```
<!DOCTYPE HTML PUBLIC "-//W3C//DTD HTML 4.01//EN"
"http://www.w3.org/TR/html4/strict.dtd">
<html>
<head>
    <title>Scoping Example</title>
    <script type="text/javascript">
    var aNewVariable = "is global.";
    function doSomething(incomingBits) {
        alert("Global variable within the function: " + aNewVariable);
        alert("Local variable within the function: " + incomingBits);
    }

    </script>

</head>
<body>
<script type="text/javascript">

    doSomething("is a local variable");
    alert("Global var outside the function: " + aNewVariable);
    alert("Local var outside the function: " + incomingBits);

</script>
</body>
</html>
```

The result is three alerts on the screen.

The first alert is this:

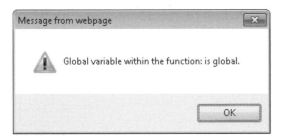

The second alert is this:

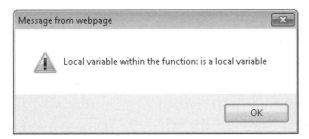

The third alert looks like this:

But wait a minute—examine the code. How many calls to the *alert()* function do you see? Hint: Two are in the *<head>* portion and another two are within the *<body>* portion, for a total of four calls to the *alert()* function. So why are there only three alerts on the screen when four calls are made to the *alert()* function in the script?

Because this is a section on variable scoping (and I already explained the answer), you may already have figured it out. But this example demonstrates well how to troubleshoot JavaScript problems when the result isn't what you expect.

The next procedure requires the use of the Firebug add-on to the Mozilla Firefox web browser. As a web developer, I'm going to assume that you have Firefox installed (see Chapter 1, "JavaScript Is More Than You Might Think," for reasons why you should). If you don't yet have Firefox, download it from *http://www.mozilla.com/firefox/.*

Installing Firebug

This first procedure walks you through installing Firebug in Firefox. Although Internet Explorer has a script debugger, and you could also use the Microsoft Script Debugger, Firebug is much more powerful and flexible.

1. With Firefox installed, it's time to get the Firebug add-on. Accomplish this task by going to *http://www.getfirebug.com/.* Once at the site, click the install link. (If you're installing Firebug for the first time, you may receive a warning that Firefox has prevented the site from installing software. Later versions of Firefox don't show this warning.)

2. When you click the install link, a Software Installation dialog box opens, as shown in the following screen. Click Install Now.

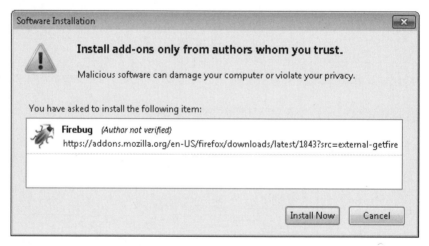

3. The Add-Ons dialog box opens (shown in the following screen), and the Firebug add-on downloads. The installation completes when you restart Firefox, so click Restart Firefox after the add-on finishes downloading.

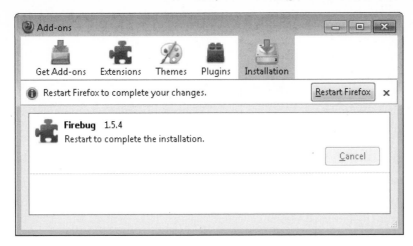

4. Firefox closes and opens again, showing the installed add-on. Close the Add-On dialog box, if it opens. Congratulations! Firebug is installed. Notice a small icon in the lower right corner of the Firefox browser window. Click this icon to open the Firebug console:

5. Firebug is disabled, but don't worry—the next procedure walks you through enabling and using it. Feel free to experiment with Firebug by enabling it for this site only or for all websites.

With Firebug installed, you can troubleshoot the earlier problem you encountered in the scoping example of only three of the four expected alerts being displayed.

Troubleshooting with Firebug

1. Open Firefox and select the scoping.htm example that was created earlier in this chapter. The JavaScript code again executes as before, showing the three alerts. Close all three alerts. You end up with a blank page loaded in Firefox.

2. Click the Firebug icon in the lower right corner of the Firefox browser window so that Firebug opens.

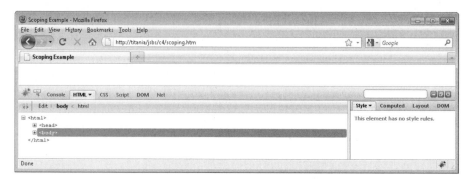

3. Click the Script tab to open the Script pane and note that it is disabled. You want to enable the Console pane so that you are informed of errors. The Script pane is activated when the Console pane is activated, so enable the Console panel. Click the Console tab, click the arrow/triangle next to the word Console, and click Enabled. You can see here that the JavaScript debugger is also activated:

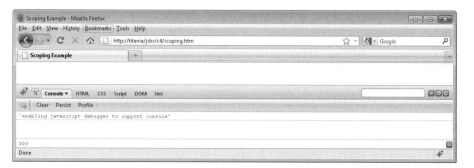

4. With both the Console and Script panes enabled, click the Reload button on the main Firefox toolbar or select Reload from the View menu. The page reloads, and the JavaScript executes again. All three alerts are displayed again, but notice now that Firebug has discovered an error, denoted by the red X and 1 Error indication in the lower right corner of the status bar, as shown here:

5. If the Console pane isn't open, click the Console tab in the Firebug portion of the window to reveal the error, which is that the variable *incomingBits* isn't defined. This window also shows the line number at which the problem occurred. Note, however, that because of the way the document is parsed, the line number in your original source code might not always be accurate. Regardless, you can see that *incomingBits* is not defined within the *<body>* of the webpage because its scope is limited to the *doSomething()* function.

This procedure demonstrated not only the use of Firebug but also the effect of local versus global scoping of variables. Firebug is an integral part of JavaScript (and webpage) debugging. I invite you to spend some time with Firebug on just about any site to see how JavaScript, CSS, and HTML all interact.

In this procedure, the fix would be to define the variable *incomingBits* so that it gets instantiated outside the of the function call. (This new line of code follows and is in the file scoping-fixed.htm in the Chapter04 folder in the companion content.) Because this variable was defined only as part of the function definition, the variable didn't exist outside of the function's scope.

```
<!DOCTYPE HTML PUBLIC "-//W3C//DTD HTML 4.01//EN"
"http://www.w3.org/TR/html4/strict.dtd">
<html>
<head>
    <title>Scoping Example</title>
    <script type="text/javascript">
    var aNewVariable = "is global.";
    function doSomething(incomingBits) {
        alert("Global variable within the function: " + aNewVariable);
        alert("Local variable within the function: " + incomingBits);
    }

    </script>

</head>
<body>
<script type="text/javascript">
    var incomingBits = " must be defined if necessary.";
```

```
        doSomething("is a local variable");
        alert("Global var outside the function: " + aNewVariable);
        alert("Local var outside the function: " + incomingBits);

    </script>
    </body>
    </html>
```

You can find more information about functions in Chapter 7, "Working with Functions."

The Date Object

The *Date* object includes many methods that are helpful when working with dates in JavaScript—too many, in fact, to examine in any depth in a beginner-level book such as this—but I do show you some examples that you might incorporate in your projects.

One of the unfortunate aspects of the *Date* object in JavaScript is that the implementation of its methods varies greatly depending on the browser and the operating system. For example, consider this code to return a date for the current time, adjusted for the local time zone and formatted automatically by the *toLocaleDateString()* method:

```
var myDate = new Date();
alert(myDate.toLocaleDateString());
```

When run in Internet Explorer 8 on a computer running Windows 7, the code results in a date like that shown in Figure 4-4.

FIGURE 4-4 The *toLocaleString()* method of the *Date* object in Internet Explorer 8.

Figure 4-5 shows what happens when that same code is executed in Firefox 3.6 on Linux.

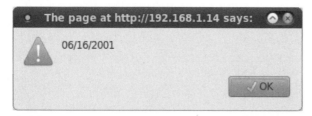

FIGURE 4-5 The *toLocateString()* method of the *Date* object displays the message differently in Firefox on Linux.

The difference between these two dialog boxes may seem trivial, but if you were expecting to use the day of the week in your code (Monday, in the examples), you'd be in for a surprise. And don't be fooled into thinking that the implementation issues are merely cross-operating system problems. Differences in the implementation of the *Date* object and its methods exist in browsers on products running Microsoft Windows as well.

The *getYear()* method of the *Date* object provides another example of differing JavaScript implementations, this time between two computers running the same version of Windows 7. Consider this code:

```
var myDate = new Date();
alert(myDate.getYear());
```

When called in Internet Explorer 8, this code produces the output as shown in Figure 4-6.

FIGURE 4-6 The output from the *getYear()* method in Internet Explorer 8 shows the full year.

When called in Firefox 3.6 on a computer running Windows, the code produces the output shown in Figure 4-7.

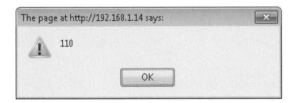

FIGURE 4-7 The output from the *getYear()* method in Firefox shows the year minus 1900.

The Firefox version returned the current year minus 1900, leaving 110 as the output. Which one is correct? The Firefox version is the correct output according to the ECMA-262 specification. The third and final step listed for the *getYear()* method specification (Section B.2.4) is "Return YearFromTime(LocalTime(t)) – 1900."

Fortunately, this difference in implementations has an easy (and recommended) workaround. The ECMA-262 specification provides the *getFullYear()* method, which returns the full year—2010 in the example shown.

The only way to resolve these and other implementation differences in your JavaScript application is to perform both cross-browser and cross-platform tests. Doing so adds time to the application development cycle, but finding and fixing a problem during development is probably less costly than finding and fixing the problem after users discover it in a production environment.

What Date?

Notice the date in Figures 4-4 and 4-5: Saturday, June 16, 2001. You may be questioning whether the book was written in 2001. It wasn't. But using a previous year illustrates an issue with JavaScript and dates. The date returned by any JavaScript function reflects the date on the computer that is executing the JavaScript.

It just so happens that I changed the date on my computer to June 16, 2001, to illustrate this point. Whenever you use any of the *Date* object's methods, remember that they reflect the time on the visitor's computer. (Incidentally, June 16, 2001, is my wedding date, and now I have an easy place to find it as a reference in case I forget. Not that I ever would, of course...)

The *Date* object can be handed a number of arguments ranging from zero arguments up to seven arguments. When the *Date* object constructor is passed a single string argument, the string is assumed to contain the date. When it is passed a number type of argument, the argument is assumed to be the date in milliseconds since January 1, 1970, and when it is passed seven arguments, they're assumed to be the following:

```
new Date(year, month, day, hours, minutes, seconds, milliseconds)
```

> **Note** Only *year* and *month* are required arguments; the others are optional.

Remember the following points when using a *Date* object:

- The year should be given with four digits unless you want to specify a year between the year 1900 and the year 2000, in which case you'd just send in the two-digit year, 0 through 99, which is then added to 1900. So, 2008 equals the year 2008, but 98 is turned into 1998.

- The month is represented by an integer 0 through 11, with 0 being January and 11 being December.

- The day is an integer from 1 to 31.

- Hours are represented by 0 through 23, where 23 represents 11 PM.

- Minutes and seconds are both integers ranging from 0 to 59.

- Milliseconds are an integer from 0 to 999.

Although the following procedure uses some items that won't be covered until later chapters, you're looking at the *Date* object now, so it's a good time learn how to write the date and time to a webpage—a popular operation.

Writing the date and time to a webpage

1. Using Visual Studio, Eclipse, or another editor, edit the file writingthedate.htm in the Chapter04 sample files folder in the companion content.

2. Within the page, add the code in boldface type shown here:

```
<!DOCTYPE HTML PUBLIC "-//W3C//DTD HTML 4.01//EN"
"http://www.w3.org/TR/html4/strict.dtd">
<html>
<head>
    <title>the date</title>
</head>
<body>
    <p id="dateField"> </p>
    <script type="text/javascript">

    var myDate = new Date();
    var dateString = myDate.toLocaleDateString() + " " + myDate.toLocaleTimeString();
    var dateLoc = document.getElementById("dateField");
    dateLoc.innerHTML = "Hello - Page Rendered on " + dateString;
    </script>

</body>
</html>
```

3. When saved and viewed in a web browser, you should receive a page like this (though the date you see will be different from what's shown here):

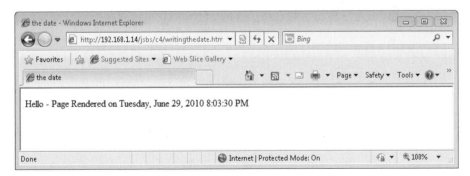

The relevant JavaScript from the preceding steps is repeated here:

```
var myDate = new Date();
var dateString = myDate.toLocaleDateString() + " " + myDate.toLocaleTimeString();
var dateLoc = document.getElementById("dateField");
dateLoc.innerHTML = "Hello - Page Rendered on " + dateString;
```

The JavaScript related to the *Date* object is rather simple. It takes advantage of the *toLocale-DateString()* method, which you've already seen, and its cousin, *toLocaleTimeString()*, which returns the local time. These two methods are concatenated together with a single space and placed into the *dateString* variable, like this:

```
var dateString = myDate.toLocaleDateString() + " " + myDate.toLocaleTimeString();
```

The remainder of the code writes the contents of the *dateString* variable to the webpage. More information about that aspect of JavaScript is described in Chapter 10, "The Document Object Model."

Counting down to a certain date in the future

1. Using Visual Studio, Eclipse, or another editor, edit the file countdown.htm in the Chapter04 sample files folder, which you can find in the companion content.

2. Add the following code shown in boldface type to the page:

```
<!DOCTYPE HTML PUBLIC "-//W3C//DTD HTML 4.01//EN"
"http://www.w3.org/TR/html4/strict.dtd">
<html>
<head>
    <title>the date</title>
</head>
<body>
    <p id="dateField"> </p>
    <script type="text/javascript">
    var today = new Date();
    var then = new Date();
    // January 1, 2012
    then.setFullYear(2012,0,1);
    var diff = then.getTime() - today.getTime();
    diff = Math.floor(diff / (1000 * 60 * 60 * 24));
    var dateLoc = document.getElementById("dateField");
    dateLoc.innerHTML = "There are " + diff + " days until 1/1/2012";
    </script>

</body>
</html>
```

3. Save the page and view it in a web browser. Depending on the date on your computer, the number of days represented will be different, but the general appearance of the page should look like this:

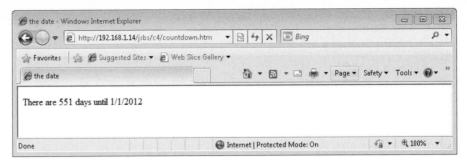

 Tip Be careful when using JavaScript dates for anything other than displaying them. Because the dates are dependent on the visitor's time, don't rely on them when an accurate time might be important, for example, in an ordering process.

The exercise you just completed used some additional functions of both the *Math* and *Date* objects, namely *floor()* and *getTime()*. While this book does cover a lot of ground, it's not a complete JavaScript language reference. For that and even more information, refer to the ECMA-262 standard at *http://www.ecma-international.org/publications/standards /Ecma-262.htm*.

The next procedure shows how to calculate (or better yet, roughly estimate) the time it takes for a webpage to load in a person's browser.

 Note The next procedure isn't accurate because it doesn't take into consideration the time required for the loading and rendering of images (or other multimedia items), which are external to the text of the webpage. A few more bits load after the script is finished running. I've seen a widget used on several websites to calculate dates, which you might find useful.

Calculating render time

1. Using Visual Studio, Eclipse, or another editor, edit the file render.htm in the Chapter04 sample files folder, which you can find in the companion content.

2. Add the following code shown in boldface type to the page:

```
<!DOCTYPE html PUBLIC "-//W3C//DTD XHTML 1.0 Transitional//EN"
"http://www.w3.org/TR/xhtml1/DTD/xhtml1-transitional.dtd">
<html>
<head>
    <title>the date</title>
    <script type="text/javascript">
    var started = new Date();
    var now = started.getTime();
    </script>
</head>
```

```
<body>
    <p id="dateField"> </p>
    <script type="text/javascript">
    var bottom = new Date();
    var diff = (bottom.getTime() - now)/1000;
    var finaltime = diff.toPrecision(5);
    var dateLoc = document.getElementById("dateField");
    dateLoc.innerHTML = "Page rendered in " + finaltime + " seconds.";
    </script>

</body>
</html>
```

3. Save the page and view it in a web browser. Depending on the speed of your computer, web server, and network connection, you might receive a page that indicates only 0 seconds for the page load time, like this:

4. If your page takes 0.0000 seconds, as mine did, you can introduce a delay into the page so that you can test it. (I'd never recommend doing this on a live site, however, because I can't think of a reason you'd want to slow down the rendering of your page! But introducing a delay can come in handy for testing purposes.) Using a *for* loop is a cheap and easy way to slow down the JavaScript execution:

```
for (var i = 0; i < 1000000; i++) {
    //delay
)
```

The value I chose, 1000000, is arbitrary. You may need to choose a larger or smaller number to cause the desired delay. The final code looks like this:

```
<!DOCTYPE html PUBLIC "-//W3C//DTD XHTML 1.0 Transitional//EN"
"http://www.w3.org/TR/xhtml1/DTD/xhtml1-transitional.dtd">
<html xmlns="http://www.w3.org/1999/xhtml">
<head>
    <title>the date</title>
    <script type="text/javascript">
    var started = new Date();
    var now = started.getTime();
    for (var i = 0; i < 1000000; i++) {
        //delay
```

```
    }
    </script>
</head>
<body>
    <p id="dateField"> </p>
    <script type="text/javascript">
    var bottom = new Date();
    var diff = (bottom.getTime() - now)/1000;
    var finaltime = diff.toPrecision(5);
    var dateLoc = document.getElementById("dateField");
    dateLoc.innerHTML = "Page rendered in " + finaltime + " seconds.";
    </script>

</body>
</html>
```

5. Save the page and view it again in a web browser. You should see some delay in the page load, which causes the value to be a positive number:

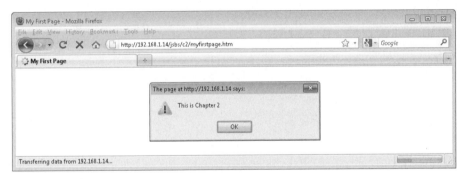

When using this or similar functions to determine the page load times, to calculate the most accurate value, place the initial variable near the top of the page or script, and then place another one near the bottom of the page.

It's important to note that the *now()* method of the *Date()* object can also be used as a substitute for *getTime()*.

You just learned about a few of the more than 40 methods of the *Date* object. Many of these methods have UTC (Coordinated Universal Time) counterparts, meaning that they can get or set the date and time in UTC rather than local time. Table 4-4 lists the methods that return dates. With the exception of *getTime()* and *getTimezoneOffset()*, all these methods have UTC counterparts that are called using the format *getUTCDate()*, *getUTCDay()*, and so on.

TABLE 4-4 The *get* Methods of a *Date* Object

Method	Description
getDate()	Returns the day of the month
getDay()	Returns the day of the week
getFullYear()	Returns the four-digit year and is recommended in most circumstances over the *getYear()* method
getHours()	Returns the hours of a date
getMilliseconds()	Returns the milliseconds of a date
getMinutes()	Returns the minutes of a date
getMonth()	Returns the month of a date
getSeconds()	Returns the seconds of a date
getTime()	Returns the milliseconds since January 1, 1970
getTimezoneOffset()	Returns the number of minutes calculated as the difference between UTC and local time

Many of the *get...()* methods have siblings prefixed with *set*, as shown in Table 4-5. And like their *get* brethren, most of the *set...()* methods have UTC counterparts, except for *setTime()*.

TABLE 4-5 The *set* Methods of a *Date* Object

Method	Description
setDate()	Sets the day of the month of a date
setFullYear()	Sets the four-digit year of a date. Also accepts the month and day-of-month integers
setHours()	Sets the hour of a date
setMilliseconds()	Sets the milliseconds of a date
setMinutes()	Sets the minutes of a date
setMonth()	Sets the month as an integer of a date
setSeconds()	Sets the seconds of a date
setTime()	Sets the time using milliseconds since January 1, 1970

The *Date* object also has several methods for converting the date to a string in a different format. You already reviewed some of these methods such as *toLocaleDateString()*. Other similar methods include *toLocaleString()*, *toGMTString()*, *toLocaleTimeString()*, *toString()*, *toISOString()*, *toDateString()*, *toUTCString()*, and *toTimeString()*. Feel free to experiment with these, noting that *toISOString()* is a new method in the ECMA-262 version 5 specification and support for it may not be available in all browsers. (It's notably missing from most versions of Internet Explorer.) The following simple code examples will get you started experimenting. Try typing them in the address bar of your browser:

```
javascript:var myDate = new Date(); alert(myDate.toLocaleDateString());

javascript:var myDate = new Date(); alert(myDate.toLocaleString());

javascript:var myDate = new Date(); alert(myDate.toGMTString());

javascript:var myDate = new Date(); alert(myDate.toLocaleTimeString());

javascript:var myDate = new Date(); alert(myDate.toString());

javascript:var myDate = new Date(); alert(myDate.toISOString());

javascript:var myDate = new Date(); alert(myDate.toDateString());

javascript:var myDate = new Date(); alert(myDate.toUTCString());

javascript:var myDate = new Date(); alert(myDate.toTimeString());
```

You can also write these code samples without creating the *myDate* variable, like so:

```
javascript: alert(new Date().toUTCString());
```

Using the RegExp Object

Regular expressions are the syntax you use to match and manipulate strings. If you've worked with a command prompt in Microsoft Windows, or the shell in Linux/Unix, you may have looked for files by trying to match all files using an asterisk, or star (*) character, as in:

```
dir *.*
```

or:

```
dir *.txt
```

If you've used a wildcard character such as the asterisk, you've used an element akin to a regular expression. In fact, the asterisk is also a character used in regular expressions.

Regular expressions, through use of the *RegExp* object and regular expression literals in JavaScript, provide a powerful way to work with strings of text or alphanumerics. The ECMA-262 implementation of regular expressions is largely borrowed from the Perl 5 regular expression parser. Here's a regular expression to match the word JavaScript:

var myRegex = /JavaScript/;

The regular expression shown would match the string JavaScript anywhere that it appeared within another string. For example, the regular expression would match in the sentence "This is a book about JavaScript," and it would match in the string "ThisIsAJavaScriptBook," but it would not match "This is a book about javascript," because regular expressions are case sensitive. (You can change this, as you'll see later in this chapter.)

The Syntax of Regular Expressions

Because of string parsing, regular expressions have a terse—and some would argue cryptic—syntax. But don't let terse syntax scare you away from regular expressions, because in that syntax is power. For example, the following regular expression looks for digits and then performs a substitution to reformat an entire Internet Protocol (IP) address block (in the format 192.168.0/24) by using grouping. What this example does is not really relevant to our discussion beyond showing an example of a more complex regular expression. (It was part of a Perl script that parses an Asia Pacific Network Information Centre (APNIC) network list on a firewall, if you must know.)

```
s/([0-9]+)\.([0-9]+)(\/[0-9]+)/$1\.$2\.0$3/;
```

The same regular expression can be written in JavaScript using the *replace* method of the *String* object, like so:

```
var theIP = "192.168.0/28";
alert(theIP.replace(/([0-9]+)\.([0-9]+)(\/[0-9]+)/,"$1\.$2\.0$3"));
```

The syntax of regular expressions includes several characters that have special meaning, including characters that anchor the match to the beginning or end of a string, a wildcard, and grouping characters, among others. Table 4-6 shows several of the special characters

TABLE 4-6 Common Special Characters in JavaScript Regular Expressions

Character	Description
^	Sets an anchor to the beginning of the input.
$	Sets an anchor to the end of the input.
.	Matches any)character.
*	Matches the previous character zero or more times. Think of this as a wildcard.
+	Matches the previous character one or more times.
?	Matches the previous character zero or one time.
( )	Places the match inside of the parentheses into a group, which can be used later.
{n, }	Matches the previous character at least n times.
{n,m}	Matches the previous character at least n but no more than m times.
[ ]	Defines a character class to match any of the characters contained in the brackets. This character can use a range like 0–9 to match any number or a–z to match any letter.
[^]	The use of a caret within a character class negates that character class, meaning that the characters in that class cannot appear in the match.
\	Typically used as an escape character, and meaning that whatever follows the backslash is treated as a literal character instead of as having its special meaning. Can also be used to define special character sets, which are shown in Table 4-7.

In addition to the special characters, several sequences exist to match groups of characters or nonalphanumeric characters. Some of these sequences are shown in Table 4-7.

TABLE 4-7 **Common Character Sequences in JavaScript Regular Expressions**

Character	Match
\b	Word boundary.
\B	Nonword boundary.
\c	Control character when used in conjunction with another character. For example, \cA is the escape sequence for Control-A.
\d	Digit.
\D	Nondigit.
\n	Newline.
\r	Carriage return.
\s	Single whitespace character such as a space or tab.
\S	Single nonwhitespace character.
\t	Tab.
\w	Any alphanumeric character, whether number or letter.
\W	Any nonalphanumeric character.

In addition to the characters in Table 4-7, you can use two modifiers, *i* and *g*, to specify that the regular expression should be parsed in a case-insensitive manner and that the regular expression matching should continue after the first match, sometimes called *global* or *greedy* (thus the *g*).

The *RegExp* object has its own methods, including *exec* and *test*, the latter of which tests a regular expression against a string and returns *true* or *false* based on whether the regular expression matches that string. However, when working with regular expressions, using methods native to the *String* type, such as *match*, *search*, *replace*, and *her from the bank*, is just as common.

The *exec()* method of the *RegExp* object is used to parse the regular expression against a string and return the result. For example, parsing a simple URL and extracting the domain might look like this:

```
var myString = "http://www.braingia.org";
var myRegex = /http:\/\/\w+\.(.*)/;
var results = myRegex.exec(myString);
alert(results[1]);
```

The output from this code is an alert showing the domain portion of the address, as shown in Figure 4-8.

FIGURE 4-8 Parsing a typical web URL using a regular expression.

A breakdown of this code is helpful. First you have the string declaration:

```
var myString = "http://www.braingia.org";
```

This is followed by the regular expression declaration and then a call to the *exec()* method, which parses the regular expression against the string found in *myString* and places the results into a variable called *results*.

```
var myRegex = /http:\/\/\w+\.(.*)/;
var results = myRegex.exec(myString);
```

The regular expression contains several important elements. It begins by looking for the literal string *http:*. The two forward slashes follow, but because forward slashes (/) are special characters in regular expressions, you must escape them using backslashes (\),making the regular expression *http:\/\/* so far.

The next part of the regular expression, *\w*, looks for any single alphanumeric character. Web addresses are typically *www*, so don't be confused into thinking that the expression is looking for three literal w's—the host in this example could be called *web*, *host1*, *myhost*, or *www*, as shown in the code you're examining. Because *\w* matches any single character, and web hosts typically have three characters (*www*), the regular expression adds a special character + to indicate that the regular expression must find an alphanumeric character at least once and possibly more than once. So now the code has *http:\/\/\w+*, which matches the address *http://www* right up to *.braingia.org* portion.

You need to account for the dot character between the host name (*www*) and the domain name (*braingia.org*). You accomplish this by adding a dot character (.), but because the dot is also a special character, you need to escape it with *\.*. You now have *http:\/\/\w+\.*, which matches all the elements of a typical address right up to the domain name.

Finally, you need to capture the domain and use it later, so place the domain inside parentheses. Because you don't care what the domain is or what follows it, you can use two special characters: the dot, to match any character; and the asterisk, to match any and all of the previous characters, which is any character in this example. You're left with the final regular expression, which is used by the *exec()* method. The result is placed into the results variable.

If a match is found, the output from the *exec()* method is an array containing the entire string and an index for each captured portion of the expression. The second index (*1*) is sent to an alert, which produces the output shown in Figure 4-8.

```
alert(results[1]);
```

That's a lot to digest, and I admit this regular expression could be vastly improved with the addition of other characters to anchor the match, and to account for characters after the domain as well as nonalphanumerics in the host name portion. However, in the interest of keeping the example somewhat simpler, the less-strict match is shown.

The *String* object type contains three methods for both matching and working with strings, and uses regular expressions to do so. The *match*, *replace*, and *search* methods all use regular expression pattern matching. Because you've learned about regular expressions, it's time to introduce these methods.

The *match* method returns an array with the same information as the *Regexp* data type's *exec* method. Here's an example:

```
var emailAddr = "suehring@braingia.com";
var myRegex = /\.com/;
var checkMatch = emailAddr.match(myRegex);
alert(checkMatch[0]);  //Returns .com
```

This can be used in a conditional to determine whether a given email address contains the string *.com*:

```
var emailAddr = "suehring@braingia.com";
var myRegex = /\.com/;
var checkMatch = emailAddr.match(myRegex);
if (checkMatch !== null) {
    alert(checkMatch[0]);  //Returns .com
}
```

The *search* method works in much the same way as the *match* method but only sends back the index (position) of the first match, as shown here:

```
var emailAddr = "suehring@braingia.com";
var myRegex = /\.com/;
var searchResult = emailAddr.search(myRegex);
alert(searchResult);  //Returns 17
```

If no match is found, the *search* method returns *-1*.

The *replace* method does just what its name implies—it replaces one string with another when a match is found. Assume in the email address example that I want to change any .com email address to .net email address. You can accomplish this by using the *replace* method, like so:

```
var emailAddr = "suehring@braingia.com";
var myRegex = /\.com$/;
var replaceWith = ".net";
var result = emailAddr.replace(myRegex,replaceWith);
alert(result);  //Returns suehring@braingia.net
```

If the pattern doesn't match, the original string is placed into the *result* variable; if it does, the new value is returned.

> **Note** You can use several special characters to help with substitutions. Please see the ECMA-262 specification for more information about these methods.

Later chapters show more examples of *string* methods related to regular expressions. Feel free to use this chapter as a reference for the special characters used in regular expressions.

References and Garbage Collection

Some types of variables or the values they contain are primitive, whereas others are reference types. The implications of this might not mean much to you at first glance—you might not even think you'll ever care about this. But you'll change your mind the first time you encounter odd behavior with a variable that you just copied.

First, some explanation: objects, arrays, and functions operate as *reference types*, whereas numbers, Booleans, *null*, and *undefined* are known as *primitive types*. According to the ECMA-262 specification, other primitive types exist such as *Numbers* and *Strings*, but *Strings* aren't relevant to this discussion.

When a number is copied, the behavior is what you'd expect: The original and the copy both get the same value. If you change the original, however, the copy is unaffected. Here's an example:

```
// Set the value of myNum to 20.
var myNum = 20;
// Create a new variable, anotherNum, and copy the contents of myNum to it.
// Both anotherNum and myNum are now 20.
var anotherNum = myNum;
// Change the value of myNum to 1000.
myNum = 1000;
// Display the contents of both variables.
// Note that the contents of anotherNum haven't changed.
alert(myNum);
alert(anotherNum);
```

The alerts display *1000* and *20*, respectively. Once the variable *anotherNum* gets a copy of *myNum*'s contents, it holds on to the contents no matter what happens to the variable *myNum* after that. The variable does this because numbers are primitive types in JavaScript.

Contrast that example with a variable type that's a reference type, as in this example:

```
// Create an array of three numbers in a variable named myNumbers.
var myNumbers = [20, 21, 22];
// Make a copy of myNumbers in a newly created variable named copyNumbers.
var copyNumbers = myNumbers;
// Change the first index value of myNumbers to the integer 1000.
myNumbers[0] = 1000;
// Alert both.
alert(myNumbers);
alert(copyNumbers);
```

In this case, because arrays are reference types, both alerts display *1000,21,22*, even though only *myNumbers* was directly changed in the code. The moral of this story is to be aware that object, array, and function variable types are reference types, so any change to the original changes all copies.

Loosely related to this discussion of differences between primitive types and reference types is the subject of garbage collection. *Garbage collection* refers to the destruction of unused variables by the JavaScript interpreter to save memory. When a variable is no longer used within a program, the interpreter frees up the memory for reuse. It also does this for you if you're using Java Virtual machine or .NET Common Language Runtime.

This automatic freeing of memory in JavaScript is different from the way in which other languages such as C++ deal with unused variables. In those languages, the programmer must perform the garbage collection task manually. This is all you really need to know about garbage collection.

Learning About Type Conversions

Before finishing the discussion on data types and variables, you should know a bit about *type conversions*, or converting between data types. JavaScript usually performs implicit type conversion for you, but in many cases, you can explicitly cast, or convert, a variable from one type to another.

Number Conversions

You've already seen a conversion between two number formats, hexadecimal to base 10, in the example discussed in the section "Data Types in JavaScript" earlier in this chapter. However, you can convert numbers to strings as well. JavaScript implicitly converts a number to a string when the number is used in a string context.

To explicitly convert a number to a string, cast the number as a string, as in this example:

```
// Convert myNumString as a string with value of 100
var myNumString = String(100);
```

String Conversions

In the same way that you can convert numbers into strings, you can convert strings into numbers. You do this by casting the string as a number. (You can find this example in the companion content, in the stringconversion.txt file.)

```
var myNumString = "100";
var myNum = Number(myNumString);
```

> **Tip** JavaScript converts strings to numbers automatically when those strings are used in a numeric context. However, in practice, I've had hit-or-miss luck with this implicit conversion, so I usually just convert to a number whenever I want to use a number. The downside of doing this is that you have to execute some extra code, but doing that is better than the uncertainty inherent in leaving it up to a JavaScript interpreter.

Boolean Conversions

Booleans are converted to numbers automatically when used in a numeric context. The value of *true* becomes *1*, and the value of *false* becomes *0*. When used in a string context, *true* becomes "true", and *false* becomes "false". The *Boolean()* function exists if you need to explicitly convert a number or string to a Boolean value.

Exercises

1. Declare three variables—one number and two strings. The number should be *120*, and the strings should be "5150" and "Two Hundred Thirty".

2. Create a new array with three numbers and two strings or words.

3. Use the *alert() function* to display the following string, properly escaped: Steve's response was "Cool!".

4. Use Firebug to examine three of your favorite websites. Look closely for any JavaScript errors that Firebug reports. Bonus: Use Internet Explorer to view those same three websites and debug the errors using Internet Explorer tools and other related tools.

Chapter 5
Using Operators and Expressions

After reading this chapter, you'll be able to:

- Understand the operators available in JavaScript.

- Use JavaScript operators to perform math, equality tests, relational tests, and assignments.

- Use the *void* operator to open a new window by using a link.

Meet the Operators

The ECMA-262 specification defines assorted operators of various forms. These include:

- Additive operators

- Multiplicative operators

- Bitwise operators

- Equality operators

- Relational operators

- Unary operators

- Assignment operators

Operators can be used on both literal values, such as on the numeral 10, and on variables and other objects in JavaScript.

Additive Operators

The term *additive operators* includes both addition and subtraction operators, which seems like a misnomer, really. But as my fifth-grade math teacher would remind me, subtraction is just addition with a negative number. As you might guess, the operators for addition and subtraction are + and –, respectively. Here are some examples of how they are used.

 Note You can find these examples in the file additiveops.txt in the companion content.

```
4 + 5;  // This would be 9.
x + y;  // Adds x and y together.
5 - 1;  // Results in 4.
```

The addition operator operates in different ways depending on the types of the values being added. When adding two strings, the addition operator concatenates the left and right arguments. When the types being added differ, you can get odd results, because JavaScript must convert one of the types before performing the addition (or any math operation). For example, you won't get the expected results when you think you have a numeric variable but the JavaScript interpreter thinks you have a string. Here are some specific examples:

```
var aNum = 947;
var aStr= "Rush";
var anotherNum = 53;
var aStrNum = "43";
var result1 = aNum + aStr;    // result1 will be the string "947Rush";
var result2 = aNum + anotherNum;  // result2 will be the number 1000;
var result3 = aNum + aStrNum;  // result3 will be 94743;
```

As discussed in Chapter 4, "Working with Variables and Data Types," in many cases, you can explicitly change or convert one type to another in JavaScript. Take a look at the *result3* variable in the previous example. You probably want *result3* to hold the result of the mathematical expression 947+43. But because the second value, represented by *aStrNum*, is a string, the expression concatenates the two values rather than adds them mathematically as numbers. However, using the *ToNumber()* function instead converts *aStrNum* to a number so that you can use it as expected in a mathematical expression, such as addition. Here's the relevant code, corrected to do what you might think it would:

```
var aNum = 947;
var aStrNum = ToNumber("43");
var result3 = aNum + aStrNum;  // result3 will be 990;
```

Multiplicative Operators

Like additive operators, multiplicative operators behave just as you might expect; they perform multiplication and division. The multiplication operator (*) multiplies two numbers, whereas the division operator (/) divides numbers. Here's a multiplication example and its output:

```
javascript:alert(2 * 2);
```

The multiplicative operators include the modulo operator, which is indicated by the percent sign (%). The modulo operator yields the remainder of the division of two numbers. For example, the modulo of 4 divided by 3 is 1, as shown in the next bit of code.

> **Note** These examples can be found in the file multiplicativeops.txt in the companion content.

```
javascript:alert(4 % 3);
```

The result is shown here:

Bitwise Operators

Bitwise operators include **AND**, **OR**, **XOR**, **NOT**, **Shift Left**, **Shift Right With Sign**, and **Shift Right With Zero Fill**. Each operator is represented by one or more characters, as shown in Table 5-1.

TABLE 5-1 Bitwise Operators

Operator	Meaning
&	AND
|	OR
^	XOR
~	NOT
<<	Shift Left
>>	Shift Right With Sign
>>>	Shift Right With Zero Fill

In-depth coverage of the bitwise operators is beyond the scope of this book, though I mention them in later chapters. You can find more information about bitwise operators in the ECMA-262 specification.

Equality Operators

You use equality operators to test whether two expressions are the same or different. These operators always return Boolean types: either *true* or *false*. Table 5-2 lists JavaScript's equality operators.

TABLE 5-2 Equality Operators

Operator	Meaning
==	Equal
!=	Not equal
===	Equal using stricter methods
!==	Not equal using stricter methods

As you can see from Table 5-2, you can test for equality and inequality in two different ways. These approaches differ in their strictness—that is, in the degree of equality they require to determine whether two values are truly equal. The stricter of the two, represented by a triple equals sign (===), requires not only that the values of a given expression are equal, but also that the types are identical. The strict test would determine that a string with the value "42" is not equal to a number with the value of *42*, whereas the less strict equality test would find them to be equal. The example that follows is helpful for understanding this.

Testing the equality operators

1. Using Microsoft Visual Studio, Eclipse, or another editor, edit the file equality.htm in the Chapter05 sample files folder in the companion content.

2. In the webpage, replace the TO DO comment with the boldface code shown here. (This code can be found in equality.txt.)

```
<!DOCTYPE HTML PUBLIC "-//W3C//DTD HTML 4.01//EN"
"http://www.w3.org/TR/html4/strict.dtd">

<html>
<head>
    <title>Equality</title>
    <script type="text/javascript">
    var x = 42;
    var y = "42";
    if (x == y) {
        alert("x is equal to y with a simple test.");
    } else {
        alert("x is not equal to y");
    }
    </script>
</head>
<body>

</body>
</html>
```

3. Point your web browser to the newly created page. The code is fairly straightforward. It defines two variables, *x* and y. The variable *x* is set to the number value *42*, and *y* is set to the string value of *"42"* (notice the double quotation marks). The simple test for equality is next, using ==. This type of equality test measures only the values and ignores whether the variable types are the same. The *if* block calls the appropriate *alert()* function based on the result. You should receive an alert like this:

4. Change the equality test so that it uses the strict test. To do this, first change the equality test to use the stricter of the two equality tests (that is, ===), and then change the alert to read *strict* instead of *simple*. The full code should look like this (the changed lines are shown in boldface type and are in the file equality2.txt in the companion content):

```
<!DOCTYPE HTML PUBLIC "-//W3C//DTD HTML 4.01//EN"
"http://www.w3.org/TR/html4/strict.dtd">

<html>
<head>
    <title>Equality</title>
    <script type="text/javascript">
    var x = 42;
    var y = "42";
    if (x === y) {
        alert("x is equal to y with a strict test.");
    } else {
        alert("x is not equal to y");
    }
    </script>
</head>
<body>

</body>
</html>
```

5. Point your web browser to the page again. The test for equality now uses the stricter test, ===. The stricter test is like the simpler equality test in that it examines the values, but it is different in that it also tests variable types. Because variable *x* is a number and variable *y* is a string, the preceding equality test fails. The appropriate *alert()* function is called based on the result. This time the alert looks like this:

Relational Operators

Relational operators test expressions to find out whether they are greater than or less than each other, or whether a given value is in a list or is an instance of a certain type. Table 5-3 lists the relational operators in JavaScript.

TABLE 5-3 Relational Operators

Operator	Meaning
>	Greater than
<	Less than
>=	Greater than or equal to
<=	Less than or equal to
in	Contained within an expression or object
instanceof	Is an instance of an object

You are probably familiar with the first four relational operators in Table 5-3, but here are some quick examples nonetheless. Take a look at the following code, which you can find in the companion content in the file relational.txt:

```
if (3 > 4) {
    // do something
}
```

The integer 3 is never greater than the integer 4, so this code will never evaluate to *true*, and the code inside the *if* block will never be executed. In a similar way, the following code tests whether the variable *x* is less than *y*:

```
if (x < y) {
    // do something
}
```

The *in* Operator

The *in* operator is most commonly used to evaluate whether a given property is contained within an object. Be aware that the *in* operator searches for the existence of a property and not the value of that property. Therefore, the following code (which you can find in the companion content in the inop.txt file) will work because a property called "star" is in the *myObj* object:

```
var myObj = {
    star: "Algol",
    constellation: "Perseus"
};

if ("star" in myObj) {
        alert("There is a property called star in this object");
}
```

The *in* operator is commonly used to iterate through an object. You see an example of this usage in Chapter 8, "Objects in JavaScript."

The *instanceof* Operator

The *instanceof* operator tests whether a given expression, usually a variable, is an instance of the object that is included as part of the statement. Yes, that's awkward. Rather than fumble around some more trying to explain it, I'll just skip ahead to an example, and then it will all make sense:

```
var myDate = new Date();
if (myDate instanceof Date) {
        //do something
}
```

Because the variable *myDate* is an instance of the built-in *Date* object, the *instanceof* evaluation returns *true*. The *instanceof* operator affects user-defined objects as well as on built-in objects, as shown in the previous example.

Unary Operators

Unary operators have a single operand or work with a single expression in JavaScript. Table 5-4 lists the JavaScript unary operators.

TABLE 5-4 Unary Operators

Operator	Meaning
delete	Removes a property
void	Returns undefined
typeof	Returns a string representing the data type
++	Increments a number
--	Decrements a number
+	Converts the operand to a number
-	Negates the operand
~	Bitwise NOT
!	Logical NOT

Because the way you use unary operators isn't obvious, I explain them a little more in this chapter.

Incrementing and Decrementing

You use the ++ and -- operators to increment and decrement a number, respectively, as shown in the following code (you can find this code in the file incrementing.txt in the companion code):

```
var aNum = 4;
aNum++;
++aNum;
```

The placement of the operator in relation to the operand to which it is applied determines the value returned by the code. When appended to the variable (referred to as *postfixed*), as in the second line of code in the previous example, the operator returns the value *before* it is incremented (or decremented, as the case may be). When prefixed, as in the last line of code from the previous example, the operator returns the value after it is incremented (or decremented).

Here are a couple of examples showing the difference between prefixing and postfixing in code. The first example is postfixing:

```
var aNum = 4;
var y = aNum++;   // y now has the value 4, but aNum then has the value 5
```

The second example is prefixing:

```
var aNum = 4;
var y = ++aNum;   // y now has the value 5, as does aNum
```

In practice, you use the postfix increment operator more often than the prefix increment operator or the decrement operator because it is a convenient counter within a loop structure. You learn about looping in JavaScript in Chapter 6, "Controlling Flow with Conditionals and Loops."

Converting to a Number with the Plus Sign

The plus sign (+) is supposed to convert a value to a number. In practice, however, I find it to be somewhat unreliable—or at least not reliable enough to use in production code. When I need to convert something to a number, I use the *ToNumber()* function explicitly. You can, however, use the plus sign as a unary operator to attempt conversion, as follows (also shown in the converting.txt file in the companion code):

```
var x = +"43";
```

This code results in the string "43" being converted to a number by JavaScript and the numeric value 43 being stored in the variable *x*.

Creating a Negative Number with the Minus Sign

It may come as no surprise that when you use a minus sign (-) in front of a number, the number is converted to its negative counterpart, as in this code (also shown in the file creating.txt in the companion code):

```
var y = "754";
var negat = -y;
alert(negat);
```

Negating with *bitwise not* and *logical not*

The tilde (~) character is a **bitwise not**, and the exclamation point (!) is a **logical not**. These operators negate their counterparts. In the case of a **bitwise not**, its bit complement is given, so a 0 changes to a -1 and a -1 to a 0. A logical not, which is the negation you use most frequently in JavaScript programming, negates the expression. If the expression is *true,* the **logical not** operator makes it *false.*

For more information about Bitwise operations, see http://en.wikipedia.org/wiki /Bitwise_operation.

Using the *delete* Operator

The *delete* operator takes a property of an object or the index of an array and removes it, or causes it to become undefined. Here's a simple example using an array:

```
var myArray = ("The RCMP", "The Police", "State Patrol");
delete myArray[0];  // myArray now contains only "The Police" and "State Patrol"
```

The preceding code creates an array called *myArray* and then promptly deletes the value at the first index. The *delete* operator works with objects too, as you can see in this next example.

Using the *delete* operator with objects

1. Using Visual Studio, Eclipse, or another editor, edit the file deleteop1.htm in the Chapter05 sample files folder in the companion content.

2. Create the contents for a base page from which you use the *delete* operator in a later step. In the page, replace the TO DO comments with the following code shown in bold-face. (The code can also be found in deleteop1.txt file in the companion content.)

```
<!DOCTYPE HTML PUBLIC "-//W3C//DTD HTML 4.01//EN"
"http://www.w3.org/TR/html4/strict.dtd">

<html>
<head>
    <title>The Delete Operator</title>
    <script type="text/javascript">

    var star = {};

    star["Polaris"] = new Object;
    star["Mizar"] = new Object;
    star["Aldebaran"] = new Object;
    star["Rigel"] = new Object;

    star["Polaris"].constellation = "Ursa Minor";
    star["Mizar"].constellation = "Ursa Major";
    star["Aldebaran"].constellation = "Taurus";
    star["Rigel"].constellation = "Orion";

    </script>
</head>
<body id="mainbody">
<script type="text/javascript">

    for (starName in star) {
        var para = document.createElement('p');
        para.id = starName;
```

```
        para.appendChild(document.createTextNode(starName +
            ": " + star[starName].constellation));
        document.getElementsByTagName("body")[0].appendChild(para);
    }

</script>

</body>
</html>
```

In the *<head>* portion of the code, you created an empty *star* object and several additional *star* objects, each named *star["starname"]*. Then you gave the objects a *constellation* property that has the value of the star's constellation. Within the *<body>* portion
of the code, a *for* loop executes to iterate through each of the stars in the star object.
This code uses the Document Object Model (DOM), which is covered in Chapter 10,
"The Document Object Model." For now, don't concern yourself too much with what
the code inside the *for* loop is doing.

3. Save the file and view it in your web browser. The output is shown here:

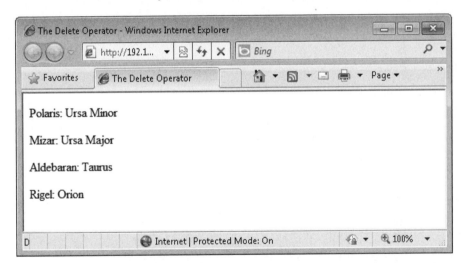

4. Add the *delete* operator above the *for* loop in the code to remove the constellation
from Polaris. The code (available in the file deleteop2.txt in the companion content)
looks like this:

```
<!DOCTYPE HTML PUBLIC "-//W3C//DTD HTML 4.01//EN"
"http://www.w3.org/TR/html4/strict.dtd">

<html>
<head>
    <title>The Delete Operator</title>
    <script type="text/javascript">

    var star = {};
```

```
                star["Polaris"] = new Object;
                star["Mizar"] = new Object;
                star["Aldebaran"] = new Object;
                star["Rigel"] = new Object;

                star["Polaris"].constellation = "Ursa Minor";
                star["Mizar"].constellation = "Ursa Major";
                star["Aldebaran"].constellation = "Taurus";
                star["Rigel"].constellation = "Orion";

            </script>
    </head>
    <body id="mainbody">
    <script type="text/javascript">

        delete(star["Polaris"].constellation);

        for (starName in star) {
            var para = document.createElement('p');
            para.id = starName;
            para.appendChild(document.createTextNode(starName +
                ": " + star[starName].constellation));
            document.getElementsByTagName("body")[0].appendChild(para);
        }

    </script>

    </body>
    </html>
```

Notice the addition of the *delete* operator in the *<script>* tag in the document's body (shown in boldface type).

5. Save the file and view it in a web browser. The output looks like this:

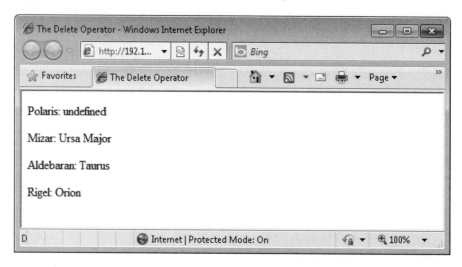

Using the *delete* operator causes the constellation for Polaris to become undefined. You can also delete the entire Polaris object like this:

```
delete(star["Polaris"]);
```

Returning Variable Types with the *typeof* Operator

As you might expect, the *typeof* operator returns the variable type of the given operand. Using *typeof*, you can determine, for example, whether a given variable was created and is being used as a string, a number, or a Boolean; or whether that variable is a certain type of object or function. Consider this code:

```
var star= {};
if (typeof(star) == "object") {
        alert("star is an object");
}
```

The *typeof* operator returns "number" if a number is evaluated, "string" if a string type is evaluated, and (as you saw from the example), "object" if an object is evaluated. When you use properties, JavaScript smartly assumes that you want to know the type of variable that the property is, rather than the type of object, so it returns that property's *value* type. Here's an example that borrows a little code from earlier in the chapter.

Using the *typeof* operator

1. Using Visual Studio, Eclipse, or another editor, edit the file typeof.htm in the Chapter05 sample files folder in the companion content.

2. Within the webpage, add the following code shown in boldface (available in the file typeof.txt in the companion content):

```
<!DOCTYPE HTML PUBLIC "-//W3C//DTD HTML 4.01//EN"
"http://www.w3.org/TR/html4/strict.dtd">
<html>
<head>
    <title>The Typeof Example</title>

    <script type="text/javascript">
        var star = {};

        star["Polaris"] = new Object;
        star["Polaris"].constellation = "Ursa Minor";

        alert(typeof star["Polaris"].constellation);
```

```
        </script>

    </head>
    <body>

    </body>
    </html>
```

3. The code within the *<script>* tags creates a new object for the star Polaris and sets its *constellation* property to the string *"Ursa Minor"*. It then calls an alert dialog box using the *typeof* operator to show that the type of the *star*["Polaris"].constellation property is a string.

4. Save the file and view it in a web browser. You get an alert like this:

Using the *typeof* operator, you can also see the difference between *null* and *undefined*.

The *void* Operator

If you've examined any source code in JavaScript, you've likely seen the *void* operator. The *void* operator returns *undefined* after evaluating its argument. This means that the *void* operator enables the web developer to call a function without the results being shown in the browser. Even though this operator and the *javascript:* pseudo-protocol exist JavaScript code, avoid using it in any new code. This book's coverage of the *void* operator and the *javascript:* pseudo-protocol is included so that you understand what the operator is doing when debugging existing JavaScript code.

A common use of the *void* operator is to submit a form or to open a new window. The following example shows the *void* operator in use:

```
void(window.open());
```

More commonly, you'd place *javascript:void* code inside a link on a webpage to open a new window, as follows:

```
<a href="javascript:void(window.open())">Open a new window by clicking here.</a>
```

> **Note** The *void* operator, or more specifically, the use of the *javascript:* pseudo-protocol within an *href*, is generally not recommended.

Assignment Operators

You already reviewed assignments in this chapter, and you've seen them throughout the book. The primary (or most frequently used) assignment operator is the equal sign (=). This type of operator is known as a *simple assignment*. JavaScript has many more assignment operators, including those listed in Table 5-5.

TABLE 5-5: COMPOUND ASSIGNMENT OPERATORS

Operator	Meaning
*=	Multiplies the left operand by the right operand
/=	Divides the left operand by the right operand
%=	Provides the division remainder (modulus) of the left and right operand
+=	Adds the right operand to the left operand
-=	Subtracts the right operand from the left operand
<<=	Bitwise left shift
>>=	Bitwise right shift
>>>=	Bitwise unsigned right shift
&=	Bitwise *AND*
^=	Bitwise *XOR*
|=	Bitwise *OR*

Compound assignment operators provide shortcuts that save a few keystrokes and bytes. For example, you can add or subtract from a number using += and -=, respectively, as in this example:

```
var myNum = 10;
alert(myNum);
myNum += 30;
alert(myNum);
```

The first alert, just after the variable has been defined and set equal to 10, is:

The next alert, after using a compound addition assignment, is:

> ## The Importance of Byte Conservation (a.k.a. Minification)
>
> Conserving bytes is an important topic for every JavaScript programmer. Byte conservation refers to programming with shortcuts so that the resulting program in JavaScript (or any other language, for that matter) consumes less memory and bandwidth. Each time you can take advantage of features to save bytes, such as compound assignment statements, the better off the program will be.
>
> Fewer bytes means smaller scripts for users to download. Quantifying how many bytes you can save, or how much that can assist you, is difficult. Some programmers might argue that the effect is negligible—and for smaller scripts that's probably true, especially because users increasingly have broadband or faster connections. But the positive effect smart shortcuts can have is very real for larger scripts, especially when those scripts have to be downloaded using a dial-up or other slow type of connection.
>
> One common approach to saving bytes during downloads is through minification of JavaScript. *Minification* refers to the removal of all nonessential elements from a JavaScript file on a live or production website. The nonessential elements include not only comments, but also spaces and carriage returns. The resulting minified files are fairly unreadable unless you reintroduce some spaces and carriage returns.

The Comma Operator

The comma operator separates expressions and executes them in order. Commonly, the comma is used to separate variable declarations, which enables multiple variables to be declared on one line:

```
var num1, num2, num3;
```

Alternatively, values can also be set:

```
var num1=3, num2=7, num3=10;
```

Exercises

1. Use the addition operator (+) to send three *alert()* dialog boxes to the screen (you can use three separate programs). The first alert should add two numbers. The second should add a number and a string. The third should add two strings. All should be represented by variables.

2. Use the postfix increment operator (++) to increment a number stored in a variable. Display the value of the variable before, while, and after incrementing. Use the prefix increment operator to increment the number and display its results before, while, and after incrementing by using an alert.

3. Use the *typeof* operator to check the type of variables you created in Exercise 1.

4. True or False: Unary operators don't appear in JavaScript very often.

5. True or False: It's always best to save bytes (using JavaScript shortcuts whenever possible), rather than use returns and indenting, which can slow down page loading.

Part II
Applying JavaScript

Chapter 6: Controlling Flow with Conditionals and Loops

Chapter 7: Working with Functions

Chapter 8: Objects in JavaScript

Chapter 9: The Browser Object Model

Chapter 6
Controlling Flow with Conditionals and Loops

After reading this chapter, you'll be able to:

- Understand the different types of conditional statements in JavaScript.

- Use the *if else* conditional statement to control code execution.

- Use the *switch* statement.

- Understand the different types of loop control structures in JavaScript.

- Use a *while* loop and a *do...while* loop to execute code repeatedly.

- Use different types of *for* loops to iterate through ranges of values.

If (and How)

The *if* statement evaluates an expression and, based on the results, determines which code executes within a program More complex *if* statements can control which code executes based on multiple conditions. If you've booked a flight on the Internet, you know about making decisions. You might want to go on a quick weekend getaway, for example, so when pricing the ticket, you would say, "If the ticket costs less than $350, I'll book the flight, otherwise I'll find a different getaway spot." Suppose I want to take out the trash. Should I take the garbage to the curb tonight or wait until the morning? If the weather forecast is windy overnight, the trash might get blown all over the neighbor's lawn, but if I wait until morning, I might miss the garbage truck. (A third option would be to tell my wife that it's her turn to take out the garbage, but that's never worked in the past.)

Although JavaScript won't help you make these real-life decisions, it can be a great help by making decisions like these—that is, it can control how a program acts depending on whether a variable contains a certain value or a form field is filled in correctly. This section reviews the syntax of the *if* statement in JavaScript.

Syntax for *if* Statements

The syntax for the *if* statement might be familiar to you if you've programmed in other languages, including Perl or PHP. The basic structure of an *if* statement is this:

```
if (some condition) {
    // do something here
}
```

> **Note** The *if* statement is sometimes called the *if* conditional. I use these terms interchangeably within this and other chapters to get you comfortable with both terms. But don't confuse the *if* conditional (the entire *if* statement) with the *if* condition, which is the Boolean expression that the *if* statement evaluates.

The *if* statement examines the validity, or truthfulness, of a condition to determine whether the code within the conditional (inside the braces) is to be executed. The condition is a Boolean expression that, when evaluated to *true*, causes the *if* statement to execute the code in the conditional. (You can negate an expression in the condition to cause the code to run if the expression evaluates to *false*.) Recall the use of Boolean and unary operators from Chapter 5, "Using Operators and Expressions." Here's an example:

```
if (! some condition) {
    // do something here
}
```

In this case, the condition starts with the negation operator, which means that the condition would need to evaluate to *false* for the code inside the conditional to execute.

The real-world airline cost example from earlier in the chapter might look like this in pseudocode:

```
if (flightCost < 350) {
    bookFlight();
}
```

If the flight costs less than $350, the code within the conditional executes. The garbage example might look like this:

```
if (forecast != "windy") {
    takeGarbageOut();
}
```

Later in this chapter, I show you how to use an *else* statement to cause other code to execute when the condition is *true*.

You use *if* statement with many of the operators you learned about in Chapter 5, especially relational operators that test whether one value is greater than or less than another value and equality operators that test whether two values are equal to each other. Take a look at these examples:

```
var x = 4;
var y = 3;
// Equality test
if (x == y) {
    // do something
}
```

Because the value in the variable *x* (4), does not equal the value in variable *y* (3), the code within the *if* conditional (inside the braces) doesn't execute. Here's an example with a relational operator:

```
var x = 4;
var y = 3;
// Relational test
if (x > y) {
    // do something
}
```

In this case, because the value in variable *x* (4) is greater than the value in variable *y* (3), the code within the braces executes.

The next section shows an example that you can perform yourself. This example takes advantage of the *prompt()* function to get input from a visitor through a simple interface.

The *prompt()* Function in Internet Explorer

With the introduction of Windows Internet Explorer 7, the *prompt()* function is no longer enabled by default. If you attempt to use the *prompt()* function with Internet Explorer, you receive a security warning like the one shown in Figure 6-1, or possibly a page with the word *null*, like the warning in Figure 6-2.

FIGURE 6-1 A security warning caused by the *prompt()* function in Internet Explorer.

FIGURE 6-2 When using the *javascript:* pseudo-protocol with the *prompt()* function, you can sometimes receive a page with the word *null*.

You can reliably get around this feature by clicking the information bar (shown in Figure 6-1) and selecting an option to allow scripts, or by changing the security settings. You can change security settings in Internet Explorer, for example, by selecting Internet Options from the Tools menu, clicking the Security tab, clicking Custom Level, and enabling the Allow Web Sites To Prompt For Information Using Scripted Windows option within the Scripting section.

However, you can't rely on your visitors doing the same with their Internet Explorer settings. Therefore, the *prompt()* function is no longer as useful as it was before Internet Explorer 7 was introduced. Some programmers might argue that the *prompt()* function was annoying (and I agree that it created problems sometimes), but it did have its advantages, and disabling it does very little to enhance security. But sometime it's useful for test purposes, such as in the following exercise.

Using *if* to make decisions about program flow

1. Using Microsoft Visual Studio, Eclipse, or another editor, edit the ifexample.htm file in the Chapter06 sample files folder, which you can find in the companion content.

2. In the page, replace the TO DO comment with the following code shown in boldface type, (this code is also in the ifexample.txt file in the companion content):

```
<!DOCTYPE HTML PUBLIC "-//W3C//DTD HTML 4.01//EN"
"http://www.w3.org/TR/html4/strict.dtd">
<html>
<head>
    <title>An If Example</title>
</head>
<body>

<script type="text/javascript">
var inputNum = prompt("Please enter a number below 100:");

if (inputNum > 99) {
    alert("That number, " + inputNum + ", is not below 100.");
}

</script>

<p>This is an example from Chapter 6.</p>

</body>
</html>
```

3. Save the page and view it in a web browser. If you attempt to view the page in Internet Explorer and receive a security warning, you need to change your security settings as described previously. You can also use Firefox or another browser instead.

4. When you view the page, you see a prompt asking for a number below 100. Internet Explorer typically fills in the text box with undefined in the dialog box. Type a number and click OK. I typed , as you can see here:

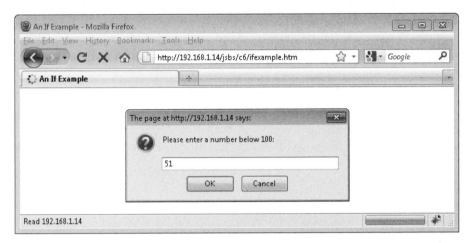

5. Click OK. You see a page like the one here:

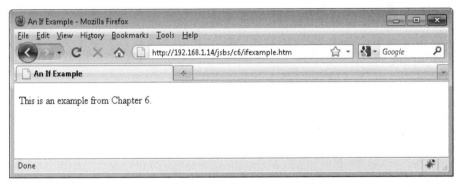

6. Reload the page in the browser, and this time, when prompted, type a number greater than 100. You receive an alert like this one:

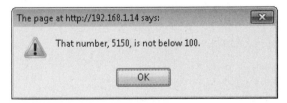

Aside from the Hypertext Markup Language (HTML) and opening script tags, which you've seen in previous examples, the code works as follows:

The first line within the body's *<script>* tag establishes a variable, *inputNum*, and then sets it equal to the result from the *prompt()* function:

```
var inputNum = prompt("Please enter a number below 100:");
```

The next lines of code use an *if* statement to examine the value in the *inputNum* variable. If the value is greater than 99, an alert is shown:

```
if (inputNum > 99) {
    alert("That number, " + inputNum + ", is not below 100.");
}
```

This example needs improvements in many areas, and later examples show how to improve the code, taking advantage of what you've already learned and using some new techniques you learn later on in this chapter.

Compound Conditions

Many times, you need to test for more than one condition within the same *if* statement. Consider the previous example. Suppose you wanted to have the visitor enter a number between 51 and 99 inclusive. You could combine those tests within one *if* statement like this:

```
if ((inputNum < 51 ) || (inputNum > 99)) {
    alert("That number, " + inputNum + ", is not between 50 and 100.");
}
```

Note You could also write that *if* statement without the extra parentheses around each evaluation on the first line; however, I find that adding them improves readability.

You can see the full code from the earlier example, with a compound *if* statement shown in boldface, in Listing 6-1. (You can find this code in the companion content as listing6-1.htm.)

LISTING 6-1 A compound *if* statement.

```
<!DOCTYPE HTML PUBLIC "-//W3C//DTD HTML 4.01//EN"
"http://www.w3.org/TR/html4/strict.dtd">
<html>
<head>
    <title>An If Example</title>

</head>
<body>

<script type="text/javascript">
var inputNum = prompt("Please enter a number between 50 and 100:");
```

```
if ((inputNum < 51) || (inputNum > 99)) {
    alert("That number, " + inputNum + ", is not between 50 and 100.");
}

</script>

<p>This is an example from Chapter 6.</p>

</body>
</html>
```

The statement in Listing 6-1 uses the logical *OR* operator and reads, "If *inputNum* is greater than 99 or *inputNum* is less than 51, do this."

Consider again the example we've been using for much of this chapter. If you enter a number greater than 99 or less than 51, you receive an alert. But what if the input is not a number at all? What if you entered the word *boo*? You wouldn't receive the alert because the condition being used checks only whether the variable is above or below specified numbers.

Therefore, the code should check whether the value contained in the variable is a number. You can accomplish this task with the help of the *isNaN()* function and by nesting the decision, like this:

```
if (isNaN(inputNum) || ((inputNum > 99) || (inputNum < 51))) {
    alert("That number, " + inputNum + ", is not between 50 and 100.");
}
```

The conditional is now evaluated to first check whether the value in the *inputNum* variable is a number. If this initial check proves true (the user did not enter a number), no further processing is done, preventing the rest of the statement from being evaluated. If the user did enter a number, the *isNaN* check fails, and the *if* statement performs the checks for the range of numbers, which are nested together between parentheses, creating their own conditional set. The result, when run with the input value of *boo*, is shown in Figure 6-3.

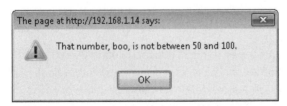

FIGURE 6-3 Running the example with the isNaN() function in a nested conditional.

The full code is shown in Listing 6-2 (in the listing6-2.htm file in the companion content). The nested condition is shown in boldface.

LISTING 6-2 A nested *if* statement.

```
<!DOCTYPE HTML PUBLIC "-//W3C//DTD HTML 4.01//EN"
"http://www.w3.org/TR/html4/strict.dtd">
<html>
<head>
    <title>An If Example</title>

</head  >
<body>

<script type="text/javascript">
var inputNum = prompt("Please enter a number between 50 and 100:");

if (isNaN(inputNum) || ((inputNum > 99) || (inputNum < 51))) {
    alert("That number, " + inputNum + ", is not between 50 and 100.");
}

</script>

<p>This is an example.</p>

</body>
</html>
```

Using *else if* and *else* Statements

The next problem with the code example used so far is that the alert dialog box text in Figure 6-3 always indicates that a number was entered. That obviously isn't always the case—I entered the word *boo*. What you really need is a way to perform multiple separate conditional checks. How can you do this? Here's where *else if* and *else* become useful.

> ### *Else if*
>
> Most modern programming languages have the *if/else if/else* conditional constructs, but they differ in how they use those constructs, especially the way they spell or construct the *else if* statement. Some languages define it as *elsif*, all one word (and misspelled). Others define it as *elseif*—all one word but spelled correctly. Remembering these different constructs is a challenge, and this discussion hasn't even considered the different ways that languages use braces to define the code to be executed. In JavaScript programming, you use *else if*—two words, both spelled correctly.

Using *else if* and *else,* you can create multiple levels of conditions, each of which is tested in turn. The code within the first matching condition is executed. If nothing matches, the code inside the *else* condition, if present, is executed. Listing 6-3 (listing6-3.htm in the companion content) shows code that first checks to see if the *inputNum* variable contains a number. If the value is indeed a number, the *else if* statement performs the checks to make sure the input value is within the appropriate range. The code calls an appropriate *alert()* function based on the matching condition. If you've entered a number, then the *else* condition fires and displays an alert showing the number.

LISTING 6-3 Using an *else if* and *else* condition.

```
<!DOCTYPE HTML PUBLIC "-//W3C//DTD HTML 4.01//EN"
"http://www.w3.org/TR/html4/strict.dtd">
<html>
<head>
    <title>An If Example</title>

</head>
<body>

<script type="text/javascript">
var inputNum = prompt("Please enter a number between 50 and 100:");

if (isNaN(inputNum)) {
    alert(inputNum + " doesn't appear to be a number.");
}
else if ((inputNum > 99) || (inputNum < 51)) {
    alert("That number, " + inputNum + ", is not between 50 and 100.");
}
else {
    alert("You entered a number: " + inputNum);
}

</script>

<p>This is an example from Chapter 6.</p>

</body>
</html>
```

In the same way you can use *else if* and *else* to test several conditions, you can (sometimes even must) use multiple levels of conditions. For example, you can test for a certain condition, and when successful, execute additional conditions. Here's an example that takes advantage of the *match()* function and a regular expression. For more information about regular expressions, see Chapter 4, "Working with Variables and Data Types."

Using multiple levels of conditionals and a regular expression

1. Open an editor and—if you followed the earlier procedure in this chapter—open the file you updated, ifexample.htm (in the companion content).

   The file should have the following code. (If you didn't follow the earlier example, just create an empty file, paste in the following code, and go on to the next step.)

   ```
   <!DOCTYPE HTML PUBLIC "-//W3C//DTD HTML 4.01//EN"
   "http://www.w3.org/TR/html4/strict.dtd">
   <html>
   <head>
       <title>An If Example</title>
   </head>
   <body>

   <script type="text/javascript">
   var inputNum = prompt("Please enter a number below 100:");

   if (inputNum > 99) {
       alert("That number, " + inputNum + ", is not below 100.");
   }

   </script>

   <p>This is an example from Chapter 6.</p>

   </body>
   </html>
   ```

2. Save the file with a different file name.

3. In the newly saved file, enter the following code shown in boldface. Note that I've included the changes from the earlier example in boldface:

   ```
   <!DOCTYPE HTML PUBLIC "-//W3C//DTD HTML 4.01//EN"
   "http://www.w3.org/TR/html4/strict.dtd">
   <html>
   <head>
       <title>A Multi-Level Example</title>

   </head>
   <body>
   ```

```
<script type="text/javascript">
var inputNum = prompt("Please enter a number between 50 and 100:");

if (isNaN(inputNum)) {
    if (inputNum.match(/one|two|three|four|five|six|seven|eight|nine|ten/)) {
        alert("While this is a number, it's not really a number to me.");
    } else {
        alert(inputNum + " doesn't appear to be a number.");
    }
}
else if ((inputNum > 99) || (inputNum < 51)) {
    alert("That number, " + inputNum + ", is not between 50 and 100.");
}

</script>

<p>This is an example from Chapter 6.</p>

</body>
</html>
```

4. Test all these conditions. Start by visiting the page in a web browser. You are prompted to enter a number. For this first test, type the word , as follows:

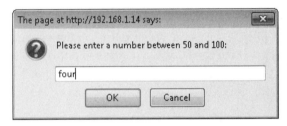

5. Click OK. The first *if* condition matches and then the nested *if* examines the input. The input matches the string "four", resulting in this dialog box:

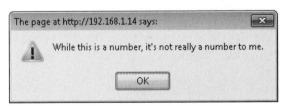

6. Click OK to close the dialog box. Reload the page. Now type the phrase:

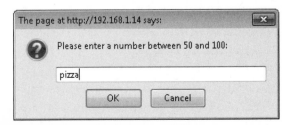

7. Click OK. As with the previous load of the page, the first condition (*isNaN()*) matches. However, because the inner *if* test doesn't match the phrase *pizza*, the *else* condition of the nested *if* will match, resulting in this dialog box:

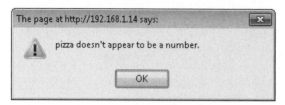

8. Click OK to close the dialog box, and once again, reload the page. This time, type the numeral *4* into the text box, as follows:

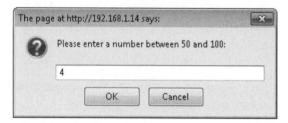

9. Click OK. Now the first *if* condition fails because the number 4 really is a number. Therefore, the *else if* condition is evaluated. Because the number 4 is less than 51 and not greater than 99, the *else if* condition is a match and displays this alert:

10. Good testing practices dictate that you also test a number above 99. Feel free to do so. When you're ready, just click OK to close the dialog box and reload the page once more. This time, type the number , like this:

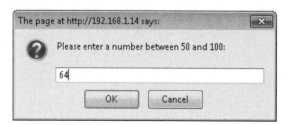

11. When you click OK, you won't receive any alerts, because the number 64 is between 50 and 100 and so doesn't match any of the test conditions.

I explained the code you're reviewing in this procedure and in previous procedures, but did not address the regular expression contained in the nested *if*. That statement was:

```
if (inputNum.match(/one|two|three|four|five|six|seven|eight|nine|ten/) {
```

The regular expression is used with the *match()* function (or property) of the *inputNum* variable. The *match()* function accepts a regular expression as its argument. In this case, the argument is this:

```
/one|two|three|four|five|six|seven|eight|nine|ten/
```

The expression is delineated with two forward slashes (/), one on each end. After that, the regular expression looks for any one of the strings *one*, *two*, *three*, *four*, *five*, *six*, *seven*, *eight*, *nine*, or *ten*. The pipe character (|) between each string indicates a logical *OR*, meaning that this regular expression will match any one of those strings, but not more than one.

Interestingly, although this regular expression is very simple, it's also very flawed. For this regular expression to be better, it would need to mark, or anchor, the position of the matching strings. As the code is written now, the string *sixty* would match just as the word *six* matches now.

My intention here wasn't to show a perfect regular expression, but rather to expose you to one so that when you need to work with them, you don't run away screaming!

Working with Ternary Conditionals

Another style of conditional construct is called a *ternary conditional*. This type of conditional uses the question mark (*?*) operator to create a compact *if/else* construct. The basic structure of a ternary conditional expression is quite simple

```
(name == "steve") ? "Hello Steve" : "Hello Unknown Person";
```

This statement might read as follows, "If name is steve, then "Hello Steve", else "Hello Unknown Person".

You might use a ternary expression in a statement like the following (this code is in the ternary.txt file in the companion content):

```
var greeting = (name == "steve") ? "Hello Steve" : "Hello Unknown Person";
alert(greeting);
```

This code sets the variable *greeting* to the value from the outcome of the ternary test. If the value of the *name* variable is "steve", the *greeting* variable gets the string value "Hello Steve"; otherwise, the *greeting* variable gets the string value "Hello Unknown Person". Here's that same code in the traditional *if/else* form:

```
if (name == "steve") {
    var greeting = "Hello Steve";
}
else {
    var greeting = "Hello Unknown Person";
}

alert(greeting);
```

The ternary construct can sometimes be confusing if you've never seen it before. There's no shame in sticking to the traditional *if/else* syntax if you think it will help the readability of your programs in the future—especially if the person reading them doesn't know about the ternary construction!

Testing with *switch*

The *switch* statement is an easy and efficient way to test a variable for several values and then execute code based on whichever case matches. Although you can accomplish the task by using *if/else if* statements, doing so can be cumbersome; the *switch* statement is more useful for this situation.

Consider the example of a website that needs to execute certain code based on the language that the user chooses. For this exercise, assume that the visitor has chosen his or her language through a form. (Chapter 11, "JavaScript Events and the Browser," examines a way to detect the default language of the visitor's browser.)

If this site needed to execute code for several languages, we could use a giant set of *if/else if/else* conditionals. Assuming a variable called *languageChoice* with the value of the chosen language, the code might look like this:

```
if (languageChoice == "en") {
    // Language is English, execute code for English.
}
else if (languageChoice == "de") {
    // Language is German, execute code for German.
}
else if (languageChoice == "pt") {
    // Language is Portuguese, execute code for Portuguese.
}
else {
    // Language not chosen, use Swedish.
}
```

This code works OK when only a few languages are selected, but imagine this scenario with 20 or more languages selected. Then add more code to be executed for each condition, and it quickly becomes a maze. Here's the same code within a *switch* (you can find the code in the switches.txt file in the companion content):

```
switch(languageChoice) {
    case "en":
        // Language is English, execute code for English.
        break;
    case "de":
        // Language is German, execute code for German.
        break;
    case "pt":
        // Language is Portuguese, execute code for Portuguese.
        break;
    default:
        // Language not chosen, use Swedish.
}
// Back to code outside the switch statement
```

The *switch* statement looks for each language case and then executes code for that case. The *break* statement indicates the end of the code that executes when a matching case is found. The *break* statement causes the code execution to break out of the *switch* statement entirely and continue executing after the closing brace of the *switch* statement.

For example, if the variable *languageChoice* was *de* and the *break* statement was missing, the code for German would be executed, but the switch statement would continue testing the rest of the code for the other languages until it encountered a *break* statement or reached the end of the *switch* statement.

You almost always use the *break* statement with each case in a *switch* statement. However, part of the elegance of the *switch* statement is apparent when you have multiple cases that *should* execute the same code. Consider an example where a visitor chooses which country or region he or she is from. On such a site, visitors from the United States, Australia, and Great Britain would probably want their page to be displayed in English, even though people in these three countries spell (and pronounce) many words differently. Here's an example *switch* statement (also in the switches.txt file in the companion content) for this:

```
switch(countryChoice) {
    case "US":
    case "Australia":
    case "Great Britain":
        // Language is English, execute code for English
        break;
    case "Germany":
        // Language is German, execute code for German.
        break;
    case "Portugal":
        // Language is Portuguese, execute code for Portuguese.
        break;
```

```
    default:
        // Locale not chosen, use Swedish.
}
// Back to code outside the loop
```

> **Note** As my friends from Montreal would point out and as I would recommend, visitors from any country should be able to choose another language that the site supports, such as French. Ignore that feature for this example, but take it into account when designing your site.

If the visitor chooses Australia as her country, the case for Australia will match, thus executing the code for English. Thanks to the *break* statement, JavaScript then breaks out of the *switch* statement and executes the first line of code following the *switch* statement.

Looping with *while*

The *while* statement creates a loop in which code is executed as long as some condition is true. This section examines the *while* statement and the related *do...while* statement.

The *while* Statement

A *while* loop executes the code contained within its braces until a condition is met. Here's an example (this code is in the while.txt file in the companion content):

```
var count = 0;
while (count < 10) {
    // Do something in here.
    // Multiple lines are fine.
    // Don't forget to increment the counter:
    count++;
}
```

Always keep in mind two important aspects of *while* loops, listed here and discussed in turn:

- The code contained within a *while* statement might never execute, depending on the starting value of the variable or condition being tested.

- The condition being tested by the *while* statement must be changed within the loop.

Making Sure the Code Executes at Least Once

In the preceding code example, the variable *count* is initially set to the number *0*. The *while* statement then runs as follows: the evaluation of the *while* statement examines the value of the *count* variable to see whether it is less than *10*. Because it is, the code within the braces executes. (However, if the value of the *count* variable was *not* less than *10*, the code within the *while* statement's braces would never execute—not even once.)

In JavaScript, the *do...while* loop executes code once, no matter what the initial condition is. The *do...while* loop is discussed a little later in this chapter.

Changing the Condition

As previously stated, the evaluation of the *while* statement in the example examines the variable to see whether it's less than *10*. If *count* is less than *10*, the code within the *while* loop executes.

One of the lines of code within the *while* loop increments the *count* variable using the ++ unary operator, as follows:

```
count++;
```

When the code in the *while* statement finishes executing, the evaluation repeats. Without the code to increment the *count* variable, *count* would always be less than 10, so you would have an endless loop on your hands—not what you want.

> **Tip** When you use a generic counter variable, as I did in the example, where you increment that variable is not important as long as you do it within the *while* statement's braces or within the *while* statement test. Here's an example: *while (i++ < 10)*. See Chapter 5 for more information about the postfix operator.

The moral of this story is to make sure that you increment or change whatever condition that you evaluate in the *while* statement.

The *do...while* Statement

Unlike the *while* statement, the *do...while* statement executes the code contained in its braces at least once. The *while* statement might read like this: "While the condition is met, run this code." On the other hand, the *do...while* statement might read like this: "Do (or run) this code while the condition is met." Consider this code (in the dowhile.htm file in the companion content):

```
<!DOCTYPE HTML PUBLIC "-//W3C//DTD HTML 4.01//EN"
"http://www.w3.org/TR/html4/strict.dtd">
<html>
<head>
    <title>Do While</title>
</head>
<body>
<script type="text/javascript">
var count = 0;
do {
    alert("Count is " + count);
    count++;
```

```
}
while (count < 3);

</script>
</body>
</html>
```

When this code executes, three dialog boxes appear. During the first run, the *count* variable holds a value of *0* because the variable is still set to the initial value, and the dialog box indicates that, as shown in Figure 6-4.

FIGURE 6-4 The count is zero during the first execution.

After running once, the *count* variable gets incremented. When the *while* statement is evaluated, *count* is still less than 3, so the code is executed again, resulting in the dialog box shown in Figure 6-5.

FIGURE 6-5 When running, the code increments the counter and shows the result of the next execution.

The same process occurs again. The *count* variable is incremented, and the *while* condition is evaluated. The value of *count* is still less than 3, so the code within the braces runs again, showing another dialog box that looks like Figure 6-6.

FIGURE 6-6 The count variable after another run.

Experiment with *while* and *do...while* statements until you're comfortable with the differences between them.

Using *for* Loops

A *for* loop is frequently used in the same way a *while* loop is, namely, to execute code a certain number of times. The *for* loop has two cousins in JavaScript: the *for...in* loop and the *for each...in* loop. This section examines both loop types.

The *for* Loop

You use a *for* loop to create a loop in which the conditions are initialized, evaluated, and changed in a compact form. Here's an example:

```
for (var count = 0; count < 10; count++) {
    // Execute code here
}
```

A *for* statement has three clauses in parentheses. The first clause sets the initial expression, as shown in the preceding example and also here:

```
var count = 0;
```

The next clause of a *for* statement specifies the test expression, represented by the following code from the example:

```
count < 10;
```

The final expression is usually used to increment the counter used for the test. In the code example, this expression is the final clause in the parentheses:

```
count++
```

Note The last expression in a *for* loop construct does not require a semicolon.

Here's an example that you can try. It uses a *for* loop to iterate over an array.

Using a *for* loop with an array

1. Using Visual Studio, Eclipse, or another editor, edit the forloop.htm file in the Chapter06 sample files folder in the companion content.

2. Within the page, replace the TO DO comment with the following boldface code (you can find the code in the forloop.txt file in the companion content):

```html
<!DOCTYPE HTML PUBLIC "-//W3C//DTD HTML 4.01//EN"
"http://www.w3.org/TR/html4/strict.dtd">
<html>
<head>
    <title>For Loop Example</title>
</head>
<body>
<script type="text/javascript">

var myArray = ["Vega","Deneb","Altair"];
var arrayLength = myArray.length;
for (var count = 0; count < arrayLength; count++ ) {
    alert(myArray[count]);
}

</script>
</body>
</html>
```

3. Save the page and view it in a web browser. You receive three successive *alert()* dialog boxes:

As you can see from the dialog boxes, the code iterates through each of the values within the *myArray* array. I'd like to highlight some of the code from this example. Recall from Chapter 4, in which you learned how to create an array, that arrays in JavaScript are indexed by integer values beginning at 0. (This knowledge will come in handy in a little while.) Here's the pertinent line from the preceding code example:

```
var myArray = ["Vega","Deneb","Altair"];
```

The code creates a variable called *arrayLength* and sets it to the length of the array. Obtaining the length of the *myArray* array illustrates the use of the array object property named *length*. (I explain objects in more depth in Chapter 8, "Objects in JavaScript.") Obtaining the length within a separate variable (*arrayLength* in this case, as shown in the following code) rather than by using the *length* property within the *for* loop improves performance.

```
var arrayLength = myArray.length;
```

The *for* loop first creates and initializes the *count* variable, and next checks whether the *count* variable is less than the length of the *myArray* array as set in the *arrayLength* variable. Finally, it increments the value of the *count* variable. The code within the body of the *for* loop shows an alert, using the value of the *count* variable to iterate through the indexes of the *myArray* array. Here's the code:

```
for (var count = 0; count < arrayLength; count++ ) {
    alert(myArray[count]);
}
```

The *for...in* Loop

The *for...in* loop iterates through the properties of an object, returning the names of the properties themselves. Here's an example:

```
for (var myProp in myObject) {
    alert(myProp + " = " + myObject[myProp]);

}
```

In this code, the variable *myProp* gets set to a new property of *myObject* each time the loop is executed. Here's a more complete example that you can try.

Using a *for...in* loop

1. Using Visual Studio, Eclipse, or another editor, edit the forinloop.htm file in the Chapter06 sample files folder, which you can find in the companion content.

2. Within the page, replace the TO DO comments with the following code shown in bold-face (the code is in the forinloop.txt file in the companion content):

```
<!DOCTYPE HTML PUBLIC "-//W3C//DTD HTML 4.01//EN"
"http://www.w3.org/TR/html4/strict.dtd">
<html>
<head>
    <title>For In Loop Example</title>
</head>
<body>
<script type="text/javascript">
    var star = new Object;

    star.name = "Polaris";
    star.type = "Double/Cepheid";
    star.constellation = "Ursa Minor";

    for (var starProp in star) {
        alert(starProp + " = " + star[starProp]);
    }
</script>

</body>
</html>
```

3. Save the file and view it in a web browser. You receive three dialog boxes:

As you can see from the code in the example, the variable *starProp* receives the name of the property, whereas using *starProp* as the index of the *star* object yields the value of that property.

Tip You sometimes see *for...in* loops used to iterate through an array in much the same way you saw them used in the previous section. However, using *for...in* to iterate through an array can have mixed results. One of the more visible problems of this approach is that a *for...in* loop doesn't return the properties in any particular order. This behavior can be troublesome, especially when you want to write text to a webpage with JavaScript! The point here is that when you want to loop through a simple array, use the *for* loop rather than the *for...in* loop.

The *for each...in* Loop

A newer construct available in JavaScript is the *for each...in* loop. Because it's new, this construct is not yet supported in all browsers—notably, it's not supported in Internet Explorer 8 and earlier. It is supported in Firefox 2.0 and later, though.

Whereas the *for...in* construct returns the name of the property, the *for each...in* loop returns the value of the property. The syntax is essentially the same, but with the addition of the word *each*:

```
for each (var myValue in myObject) {
    alert(myValue " is in the object.");
}
```

Replacing the *for...in* loop from the earlier example with a *for each...in* loop results in the following code. The new code is in boldface. (The updated file is in the foreach.htm file in the companion content.)

```
<!DOCTYPE HTML PUBLIC "-//W3C//DTD HTML 4.01//EN" "http://www.w3.org/TR/html4/strict.dtd">
<html>
<head>
    <title>For Each In Loop Example</title>
</head>
<body>
<script type="text/javascript">


    var star = new Object;

    star.name = "Polaris";
    star.type = "Double/Cepheid";
    star.constellation = "Ursa Minor";

    for each (var starValue in star) {
        alert(starValue + " is in the star object.");
    }
</script>

</body>
</html>
```

When you view the page in Internet Explorer, you see an error screen (or maybe just a blank screen). Viewing the page in Firefox 3.0, however, reveals the correct behavior. Figure 6-7 shows one of the three dialog boxes that results.

FIGURE 6-7 Iterating through an object using the *for each...in* loop.

You may want to refrain from using the *for each...in* loops construction because it is not supported in earlier (and still widely used) versions of Internet Explorer.

Validating Forms with Conditionals

Earlier in this chapter, you used the *prompt()* function to obtain input from the user. Using the *prompt()* function is somewhat uncommon, and it's fast becoming even less common because Internet Explorer 7 blocks it. This section previews using web forms with JavaScript. All of Chapter 14, "Using JavaScript with Web Forms," is devoted to this subject.

Using an *if else … if else* conditional to validate input is a common task, so let's do that.

Validating input with a conditional statement

1. Open Visual Studio, Eclipse, or another editor and create a new webpage. Name this one form1example.htm.

2. Within the page, enter the following markup and add the code shown in boldface, replacing the TO DO comment (you can find the new code in the form1example.txt file in the companion content):

```
<!DOCTYPE HTML PUBLIC "-//W3C//DTD HTML 4.01//EN"
"http://www.w3.org/TR/html4/strict.dtd">
<html>
<head>

    <title>Just Your Basic Form</title>
    <script type="text/javascript">
    function alertName() {
        var name = document.forms[0].nametext.value;
        if (name == "steve") {
            alert("Hello Steve.  Welcome to Machine");
        }
        else if (name == "nancy") {
            alert("Hello Tim.");
        }
        else {
            alert("Hello " + name);
        }
        return true;
    } //end function

    </script>
</head>
<body>
<form id="myform" action="#" onsubmit="return alertName();">
<p>Username: <input id="nametext" name="username" type="text" /></p>
<p><input type="submit" /></p>
</form>
</body>
</html>
```

3. Save the page and view it in a web browser. You should see a page like this:

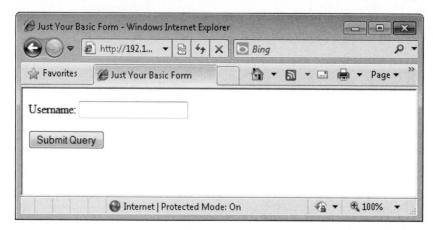

4. In the form, type the name **steve**, without the quotation marks, being sure to use lowercase letters. Click Submit Query, and you receive a dialog box like this:

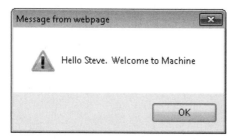

5. Click OK, and now type in the name , again without the quotation marks and in lowercase letters. When you click Submit Query, you receive a dialog box like this:

In case you're wondering, Tim's nickname is Nancy, so this dialog box actually does make sense. It's also correct per the code in the example.

6. Click OK to close the dialog box. Type the name and click Submit Query. You receive this dialog box:

7. Click OK to close this dialog box.

You created a basic web form, accessed that form using JavaScript, and used a conditional to take an action based on user input. Don't worry if everything used in this example doesn't quite make sense yet. The main goal of the example was just to give some context for the conditionals you learned about in this chapter.

Chapter 7, "Working with Functions," examines using functions within JavaScript. The first example in Chapter 14 shows how to write JavaScript validation code to ensure that required fields are filled in.

Exercises

1. Use a *prompt()* function to collect a person's name. Use a *switch* statement to execute a dialog box displaying the phrase "Welcome *<the entered name>*" if the name entered is yours, "Go Away" if the name entered is *Steve*, and "Please Come Back Later *<the entered name>*" for all other cases.

2. Use a *prompt()* function to collect the current temperature as input by the visitor. If the temperature entered is above *100*, tell the visitor to cool down. If the temperature is below *20*, tell the visitor to warm up.

3. Use a ternary statement to accomplish the same task as in Exercise 2.

4. Use a *for* loop to count from *1* to *100*. When the number is at *99*, display an alert dialog box.

5. Use a *while* loop to accomplish the same task described in Exercise 4.

Chapter 7

Working with Functions

After reading this chapter, you'll be able to:

- Understand the purpose of functions in JavaScript.

- Define your own functions.

- Call functions and receive data back from them.

- Understand some of the built-in functions in JavaScript.

What's in a Function?

A JavaScript function is a collection of statements, either named or unnamed (anonymous), that can be called from elsewhere within a JavaScript program. Functions can accept arguments, which are input values passed into the function. Within a function, those arguments passed into the function can be acted upon and the results returned to the caller of the function via a *return* value.

Functions are perfect when you have something that needs to happen multiple times within a program. Rather than defining the same code multiple times, you can use a function (which is really just like a miniprogram inside a program) to perform that action. Even if you have bits of code that are very similar—but not identical—throughout the program, you might be able to abstract them into a single function.

A good example of abstracting similar code is using a function to verify that required form fields have been filled in. You could write JavaScript code to verify each individual named field in the form, or you could use a function. Chapter 14, "Using JavaScript with Web Forms," shows an example of building a specific function and then abstracting it.

You've already seen functions at work through examples in earlier chapters. A function is defined with the keyword *function*, usually followed by the name of the function, and then by parentheses that contain optional arguments or parameters to be used. Use braces to surround the statements to be executed as part of the function:

```
function functionName() {
    // Statements go here;
}
```

> **Tip**   It's important to note that when a function is defined (you can see this in the preceding basic function definition), the code isn't actually executed until the function is invoked, or called. You see how to call a function later in this chapter.

Function Arguments

Place arguments passed to a function within the parentheses of the function definition. Here's a brief example of using function arguments:

```
function myFunction(argument1, argument2, ..., argumentN) {

}
```

Here's an example with two arguments

```
function myFunction(argument1, argument2) {
    // Do something

}
```

Calling, or invoking, the function is as simple as:

```
myFunction(val1,val2);
```

One of the differences between JavaScript (the ECMA-262 specification) and other languages is that in JavaScript, you don't need to specify the number of arguments being passed into a function, nor do the number of arguments being passed in need to match those that are defined in the function definition. When invoked, the function is given an object (that acts like an array) named *arguments. Arguments* holds the arguments sent into the function, which can be helpful when you don't know the number of arguments being sent in. Here's an example of how this works (you can find this code in the functionbasics.txt file in the companion content):

```
function myFunction() {
    var firstArg = arguments[0];
    var secondArg = arguments[1];
}
```

Better still, you could get the length of the *arguments* object and loop through each argument, as follows (also in the functionbasics.txt file in the companion content):

```
function myFunction() {

    var argLength = arguments.length;
    for (var i = 0; i < argLength; i++) {
    // Do something with each argument (i)
    }
}
```

Here's a more complete example showing the results from a simple use of the *arguments* object (also in the functionexample.htm file):

```
<!DOCTYPE HTML PUBLIC "-//W3C//DTD HTML 4.01//EN" "http://www.w3.org/TR/html4/strict.dtd">
<html>
<head>
    <title>Arguments Array</title>
</head>
<body>
<script type="text/javascript">
function myFunction() {
    var firstArg = arguments[0];
    var secondArg = arguments[1];
    alert("firstArg is: " + firstArg);
    alert("secondArg is: " + secondArg);
}
myFunction("hello","world");
</script>
</body>
</html>
```

When the code executes, it displays two alerts, as depicted in Figures 7-1 and 7-2.

FIGURE 7-1 Using the *arguments* object within a function to access the first argument.

FIGURE 7-2 Using the *arguments* object within a function to access the second argument.

Using the *arguments* object in this way, you can extrapolate to any number of arguments, not only to the two shown in this example.

Variable Scoping Revisited

Function arguments are frequently variable names and shouldn't be named the same as the variables that are used to invoke the functions. I purposefully use "shouldn't" rather than "don't," because you *could* use the same name for the variables in the function and the variables in the function invocation, but doing that could create some confusing code and confusing scoping, as you'll learn.

Chapter 4, "Working with Variables and Data Types," contains a section about variable scoping, including an exercise dealing with scoping inside and outside functions. The relevant code from one of the variable scoping examples in Chapter 4 (and repeated in the scoping revisit.txt file in the companion content) looks like this:

```
<head>
    <title>Scoping Example</title>
    <script type="text/javascript">
    var aNewVariable = "is global.";
    function doSomething(incomingBits) {
        alert("Global variable within the function: " + aNewVariable);
        alert("Local variable within the function: " + incomingBits);
    }

    </script>

</head>
<body>
<script type="text/javascript">

    doSomething("is a local variable");
    alert("Global var outside the function: " + aNewVariable);
    alert("Local var outside the function: " + incomingBits);

</script>
</body>
```

This example shows how you can globally and locally declare and scope variables from inside and outside a function. However, the example keeps the variables logically separate, in that it doesn't use the same variable name, and then changes the variable's value. Here's an example in which using the same variable name might cause confusion. I find that the code I wrote years ago is confusing enough without introducing weird scoping issues, so try to avoid code like this:

```
function addNumbers() {
    firstNum = 4;
    secondNum = 8;
    result = firstNum + secondNum;
    return result;
}
result = 0;
sum = addNumbers();
```

You might already have spotted the problem with this code. The *var* keyword is missing everywhere. Even though the code explicitly initializes the *result* variable to *0* outside the function, the variable gets modified by the call to the *addNumbers()* function. This in turn modifies the *result* variable to *12*, the result of adding *4* and *8* inside the function.

If you added an alert to display the *result* variable right after the initialization of the *result* variable, the alert would show *0*. And if you added another alert to display the *result* variable after the call to the *addNumbers()* function, the result would show *12*. I leave it to you in an exercise later to add these alerts in the right places.

The bottom line is that your life is easier when you use different names for variables inside and outside functions, and always use the *var* keyword to initialize variables. Depending on the code contained in the function, the function may or may not have a return value. That *return* value is passed back to the caller, as you see in the next section.

Return Values

When a function finishes executing its code, it can return a value to the caller by using the *return* keyword. Take a look at Listing 7-1 (in the listing7-1.txt file in the companion content).

LISTING 7-1 A simple *return* value example.

```
function multiplyNums(x) {
    return x * 2;
}
var theNumber = 10;
var result = multiplyNums(theNumber);
alert(result);
```

Listing 7-1 creates a function called *multiplyNums* with an intended input value, which will be assigned to the variable *x*. The function performs one task: it returns its argument multiplied by *2*, as follows:

```
function multiplyNums(x) {
    return x * 2;
}
```

The code then creates a variable called *theNumber,* as follows:

```
var theNumber = 10;
```

Next, the code creates another variable called *result*. This variable holds the result of the call to the *multiplyNums* function. The *multiplyNum* function uses the variable *theNumber* as an argument:

```
var result = multiplyNums(theNumber);
```

When run, the code results in a dialog box, like the one shown in Figure 7-3.

FIGURE 7-3 This alert shows the return value from the function call.

You can place the return value anywhere within a function, not just at the end. Using a *return* within a conditional or after a loop is common, as shown here (you can find this in the morereturnexamples.txt file in the companion content):

```
function myFunction(x) {
    if (x == 1) {
        return true;
    } else {
        return false;
    }
}
```

Be careful where you place the *return* statement, though, because when the function execution gets to the *return* statement, the function returns immediately and won't execute any code after that. For example, code such as this (you can find this in the morereturnexamples.txt file in the companion content) probably won't do what you want:

```
function myFunction() {
    var count = 0;
    var firstNum = 48;
    return;
    var secondNum = 109;
}
```

This code never reaches the initialization of the variable *secondNum*.

More on Calling Functions

You nearly always invoke a function with some arguments, or with empty parentheses, like this:

```
var result = orderFruit();
```

If arguments were required for that function, the function might look like this:

```
var result = orderFruit(type,quantity);
```

Omitting the parentheses to call a function may result in actions that are entirely different from what you want. Calling a function without parentheses results in the function *name* being returned, rather than whatever the function was supposed to return. Just as important, the function isn't actually executed.

Here's an example. Listing 7-2 (which you can find in the listing7-2.htm file in the companion content) shows some basic JavaScript code.

LISTING 7-2 Invoking a function.

```
<!DOCTYPE html PUBLIC "-//W3C//DTD XHTML 1.0 Transitional//EN" "http://www.w3.org/TR/
xhtml1/DTD/xhtml1-transitional.dtd">
<html xmlns="http://www.w3.org/1999/xhtml" >
<head>
    <title>Order Fruit</title>
    <script type="text/javascript">
    function orderFruit() {
        var total = 0;
        // Call another function to place order
        return total;
    }
    </script>
</head>
<body>
<script type="text/javascript">
var result = orderFruit();
alert("The total is " + result);
</script>
</body>
</html>
```

When executed, this code invokes the *orderFruit()* function. The *orderFruit()* function invokes another function (not shown) to place an order. The total is then calculated and sent back to the caller. As written, the code works fine and results in a dialog box like that shown in Figure 7-4.

FIGURE 7-4 Invoking the *orderFruit()* function with parentheses yields the results you'd expect.

A slight modification to the code—specifically, changing the function call to remove the parentheses—changes the entire result:

```
var result = orderFruit;
```

The result is shown in Figure 7-5.

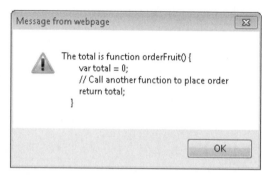

FIGURE 7-5 Calling *orderFruit* without parentheses probably doesn't turn out the way you want.

Regardless of whether a function returns a value or accepts any arguments, calling the function by using parentheses to execute its code is important.

Anonymous/Unnamed Functions (Function Literals)

The functions you've seen so far are formally defined. However, JavaScript doesn't require functions to be formally defined in this way. For example, with a function literal—also known as an unnamed, or anonymous function—the function is defined and tied to a variable, like this:

```
var divNums = function(firstNum,secondNum) { return firstNum / secondNum; };
```

You can easily test this functionality with the *javascript:* pseudo-protocol. Type the following code in the address bar of your browser:

```
javascript:var divNums = function(firstNum,secondNum) { return firstNum / secondNum; };
alert(divNums(8,2));
```

Anonymous functions are frequently used in object-oriented JavaScript and as handlers for events. You see an example of this usage in Chapter 8, "Objects in JavaScript," and in later chapters.

Closures

In JavaScript, nested functions have access to the outer function's variables. *Closures* refer to the existence of variables outside a function's normal execution context. Closures are frequently created by accident and can cause memory leak problems in Windows Internet Explorer if they're not handled properly. However, closures are one of the more powerful (and advanced) areas of JavaScript.

Here's an example of a closure:

```
function myFunction() {
    var myNum = 10;
    function showNum() {
        alert(myNum);
    }
    return showNum();
}
var callFunc = myFunction();
myFunction();
```

In this example, the function *showNum* has access to the variable *myNum* created in the outer (*myFunction*) function. The variable *callFunc* is created in the global context and contains a reference to the *showNum* function. When the *callFunc* variable is created, it immediately has access to the *myNum* variable.

Closures can be used to emulate private methods inside of objects, and have other uses, such as in event handlers. Closures are one of the more powerful and advanced concepts in JavaScript and as such aren't appropriate to discuss at length in an introductory book. You can find more information about closures at *http://msdn.microsoft.com/en-us/scriptjunkie /ff696765.aspx* and elsewhere on the Internet.

Methods

The easiest way to think about methods is that they are functions defined as part of an object. That's an oversimplification, but it suffices for now. You access a method of an object by using the dot operator ("."). Built-in objects, such as the *Math*, *Date*, and *String* objects, all have methods that you've seen (or will soon see) in this book. Functions such as the *alert()* function are actually just methods of the *window* object, and could be written as *window. alert()* rather than just *alert()*. Chapter 8 covers objects and methods in greater detail.

Note In much of the book, I use the term *method* and *function* interchangeably. I'll continue to do so just so that you better understand that the line between these two is blurry for most uses. When a function is used in an object-oriented manner, using the term *method* is often clearer. When not used directly in an object-oriented manner—for example, the way you use the *alert()* function— using the term *function* is acceptable.

Defining Your Own Functions vs. Using Built-in Functions

As you've seen throughout the book, JavaScript has numerous built-in functions, or methods. In addition to using these built-in functions, you will frequently find yourself defining your own functions. Except for trivial scripts, most scripts you write will involve your own functions.

In some cases, however, you might define a function and then later discover that JavaScript already has an equally good built-in function for that same purpose. If you find that a JavaScript built-in function performs the same task as your own function, using the JavaScript function is usually a better idea.

A Look at Dialog Functions

By now, you know all about the *alert()* function in JavaScript because you've seen many examples of it in previous chapters. You've also learned that the *alert()* function is just a method of the *window* object. This section looks at the everyday use of the *alert()* function in JavaScript, as well as two related functions of the *window* object.

More Info The *window* object is important enough to get some additional attention in Chapter 9, "The Browser Object Model." That chapter discusses numerous other methods of the *window* object.

Although the *window* object has several methods, for now, I'd just like to highlight these three (which I call functions): *alert()*, *confirm()*, and *prompt()*. Because you've already seen too many *alert()* dialog boxes in the book, I won't include another one here (thank me later). Chapter 6, "Controlling Flow with Conditionals and Loops," discussed the use of the *prompt()* function and how Internet Explorer 7 blocks it by default as a security measure. The *confirm()* function is still available in Internet Explorer, though.

The *confirm()* function displays a modal dialog box with two buttons, OK and Cancel, like the one shown in Figure 7-6. (A modal dialog box prevents other activity or clicks in the browser until the visitor closes the dialog box—in this case, by clicking OK or Cancel.)

FIGURE 7-6 The *confirm()* JavaScript function provides a dialog box for confirming user actions.

When you click OK, the *confirm()* function returns *true*. As you might guess, when you click Cancel, the *confirm()* function returns *false*.

Like *alert()* and *prompt()*, the *confirm()* function creates a modal dialog box on most platforms. This can get annoying if these functions are overused or used in the wrong place. But used properly, to provide important feedback and obtain vital information, these functions can be quite useful.

> **Tip** Don't use the *confirm()* function in place of a web form to obtain user input. The web form is much better for navigation and will keep your visitors happier.

The next exercise walks you through using the *confirm()* function to obtain input and make a decision based on that input.

Obtaining input with *confirm()*

1. Using Microsoft Visual Studio, Eclipse, or another editor, edit the file confirm.htm in the Chapter07 sample files folder in the companion content.

2. In the page, replace the TO DO comments with the following code shown in boldface (you can find this code is in the confirm.txt file in the companion content):

```
<!DOCTYPE HTML PUBLIC "-//W3C//DTD HTML 4.01//EN"
"http://www.w3.org/TR/html4/strict.dtd">
<html>
<head>
    <title>Confirming Something</title>

    <script type="text/javascript">

    function processConfirm(answer) {
        var result = "";
        if (answer) {
            result = "Excellent.  We'll play a nice game of chess.";
        } else {
            result = "Maybe later then.";
```

```
        }
        return result;
    }
    </script>
</head>
<body>
<script type="text/javascript">

var confirmAnswer = confirm("Shall we play a game?");
var theAnswer = processConfirm(confirmAnswer);
alert(theAnswer);
</script>
</body>
</html>
```

3. Save the page and view it in a web browser. You are presented with a dialog box that looks this:

4. Click OK. You see an *alert()* dialog box:

5. Click OK, and then reload the page.

6. You are again shown the original dialog box from the *confirm()* function, which asks if you'd like to play a game. This time click Cancel. You are presented with a different *alert()* dialog box:

7. Click OK to close the dialog box.

The code has two major areas to examine, one within the *<head>* portion and the other within the *<body>* portion. The function *processConfirm(answer)* is created in the *<head>* portion of the page:

```
function processConfirm(answer) {
    var result = "";
    if (answer) {
        result = "Excellent.  We'll play a nice game of chess";
    } else {
        result = "Maybe later then.";
    }
    return result;
}
```

This function evaluates the value contained in the argument held in the variable *answer*. If the value in the *answer* variable evaluates to *true,* as it does when the visitor clicks OK, the function creates the variable *result* and assigns to *result* a string value of "Excellent. We'll play a nice game of chess." But, if the value in the *answer* variable evaluates to *false,* as it does when the visitor clicks Cancel, the function still creates the *result* variable, but now assigns it the value of "Maybe later then." Regardless of what's held in the *answer* variable, *processConfirm* returns the *result* variable to the caller by using the *return* statement within the function. You could write this function more succinctly as:

```
function processConfirm(answer) {
    if (answer) {
        return "Excellent.  We'll play a nice game of chess.";
    } else {
        return "Maybe later then.";
    }
}
```

And even more succinctly:

```
function processConfirm(answer) {
    var result;
    (answer) ? result = "Excellent.  We'll play a nice game of chess." : result = "Maybe
later then.";
    return result;
}
```

> **Note** In all likelihood, I would use the last function example to perform this task. However, I've found many programmers who aren't comfortable with the ternary logic of the last example. So for readability, I'd choose the more explicit of the two:

```
function processConfirm(answer) {
    if (answer) {
        return "Excellent.  We'll play a nice game of chess.";
    } else {
        return "Maybe later then.";
    }
}
```

The JavaScript contained within the *<body>* section of the code creates the confirmation dialog box, calls the *processConfirm()* function, and displays the result:

```
var confirmAnswer = confirm("Shall we play a game?");
var theAnswer = processConfirm(confirmAnswer);
alert(theAnswer);
```

Like the *alert()* function, the *confirm()* function accepts a single argument, which is the message to be displayed in the dialog box. Though not necessary with the *alert()* function, with the *confirm()* function, phrasing your prompt in the form of a question or other statement that gives the visitor a choice is best. If the user really doesn't have a choice, use the *alert()* function instead. An even more succinct version combines all three lines, like this:

```
alert(processConfirm(confirm("Shall we play a game?")));
```

Exercises

1. Define a function that takes one numeric argument, increments that argument, and then returns it to the caller. Call the function from within the *<body>* of a page and display the result on the screen.

2. Define a function that accepts two numeric parameters. If the value of the first parameter is greater than the second, show an alert to the visitor. If the value of the first parameter is less than or equal to the second, return the sum of both parameters.

3. Add appropriate *alert()* functions to the following code so that you can see the value in the *result* variable both before and after the function call. Here's the code:

```
function addNumbers() {
    firstNum = 4;
    secondNum = 8;
    result = firstNum + secondNum;
    return result;
}
result = 0;
result = addNumbers();
```

4. Create an array with seven string values, initialized to the names of these stars: Polaris, Aldebaran, Deneb, Vega, Altair, Dubhe, and Regulus. Create an array with seven additional string values, initialized to the names of the constellations in which the stars are found: Ursa Minor, Taurus, Cygnus, Lyra, Aquila, Ursa Major, and Leo. Next, create a function that accepts a single string parameter. Within the function, iterate through the first array, searching for the star. When the star is found, return the value contained in that index within the second array. In other words, return the constellation name for that star. Within the *<body>* of the page, use a prompt to gather the name of the star from the visitor, and then call the function with that input. Don't forget to include code that executes when the star isn't found. Display the result on the screen.

Chapter 8
Objects in JavaScript

After reading this chapter, you'll be able to:

- Understand objects in JavaScript, including object properties, object methods, and classes.

- Create objects.

- Define properties and methods for objects.

- Understand arrays in JavaScript.

- Use several array methods.

Object-Oriented Development

For those who are new to object-oriented programming concepts or may need a refresher, read on. If you're already comfortable with object-oriented programming, skip ahead to the section called "Creating Objects."

A programming paradigm describes a methodology for solving the problems you encounter. More than 25 different programming paradigms exist, some of which might be challenging to find used in an actual program. You might have heard of others or even used them without knowing it. Among these paradigms are functional programming, event-driven programming, component-oriented programming, and structured programming.

Programming paradigms come and go. Object-oriented programming has been around for many years, however, and doesn't appear to be going away any time soon. This section can't do much more than give you an overview of this subject, but you need to be familiar with object-oriented techniques and terminology so that you're comfortable with the subset of those typically used by a JavaScript programmer.

Objects

Objects are things. In the real world—as opposed to the virtual and sometimes surreal world of computer programming—a ball, a desk, and a car are all objects. An object is something that has describable characteristics, you can affect, and behaves in a particular way. An object in the object-oriented programming paradigm is a combination of code and data that exhibits characteristics and behavior in a similar manner.

Properties

Objects have *properties*—defined as their attributes. Going back to the real world again, a ball has a color property—perhaps red, white, or multicolored. It also has a size property—perhaps it is small like a baseball or bigger like a basketball, or like something else entirely. These properties might be represented like this:

```
ball.color
ball.size
```

Methods

Just as objects can have properties, they can also have methods. *Methods* define the way an object behaves. A ball might have a *roll* method, which calculates how far the ball will roll. In theory, not all objects have methods, and not all objects have properties, though in practice most objects have at least one method or one property.

Remember from Chapter 7, "Working with Functions," that a method is just a function that belongs to an object. A method definition that uses a function *literal* for the *roll* method might look like this:

```
ball.roll = function() {
    var distance = this.size * this.forceApplied;
}
```

> ### What's *this*?
>
> The *ball.roll* example used something new—the keyword *this*, which refers to the object to which the current function or property belongs. In the context of objects, the keyword *this* refers to the calling object. The keyword *this* can be used to set properties of objects within a function call.
>
> The *this* keyword is a boon to JavaScript developers looking to validate web forms, which you learn in Chapter 14, "Using JavaScript with Web Forms."

Classes

In object-oriented programming, *classes* define sets of objects that share the same properties and methods. Classes simplify the creation of multiple objects of the same type. However, ECMA-262 has no concept of classes in its object interface. Therefore, to take advantage of the benefits of class-based programming, you have to use a pattern to create pseudo-classes.

Consider the star example, which I used in earlier chapters. Listing 8-1 (in the Listing8-1.txt file in the companion content) shows what you need for a comprehensive webpage that includes information about 14 important stars.

LISTING 8-1 Assembling a *star* object.

```
var star = {};

star["Polaris"] = new Object;
star["Mizar"] = new Object;
star["Aldebaran"] = new Object;
star["Rigel"] = new Object;
star["Castor"] = new Object;
star["Albireo"] = new Object;
star["Acrux"] = new Object;
star["Gemma"] = new Object;
star["Procyon"] = new Object;
star["Sirius"] = new Object;
star["Rigil Kentaurus"] = new Object;
star["Deneb"] = new Object;
star["Vega"] = new Object;
star["Altair"] = new Object;

star["Polaris"].constellation = "Ursa Minor";
star["Mizar"].constellation = "Ursa Major";
star["Aldebaran"].constellation = "Taurus";
star["Rigel"].constellation = "Orion";
star["Castor"].constellation = "Gemini";
star["Albireo"].constellation = "Cygnus";
star["Acrux"].constellation = "Crux";
star["Gemma"].constellation = "Corona Borealis";
star["Procyon"].constellation = "Canis Minor";
star["Sirius"].constellation = "Canis Major";
star["Rigil Kentaurus"].constellation = "Centaurus";
star["Deneb"].constellation = "Cygnus";
star["Vega"].constellation = "Lyra";
star["Altair"].constellation = "Aquila";

star["Polaris"].type = "Double/Cepheid";
star["Mizar"].type = "Spectroscopic Binary";
star["Aldebaran"].type = "Irregular Variable";
star["Rigel"].type = "Supergiant with Companion";
star["Castor"].type = "Multiple/Spectroscopic";
star["Albireo"].type = "Double";
star["Acrux"].type = "Double";
star["Gemma"].type = "Eclipsing Binary";
star["Procyon"].type = "Double";
star["Sirius"].type = "Double";
star["Rigil Kentaurus"].type = "Double";
star["Deneb"].type = "Supergiant";
star["Vega"].type = "White Dwarf";
```

```
star["Altair"].type = "White Dwarf";

star["Polaris"].spectralClass = "F7";
star["Mizar"].spectralClass = "A1 V";
star["Aldebaran"].spectralClass = "K5 III";
star["Rigel"].spectralClass = "B8 Ia";
star["Castor"].spectralClass = "A1 V";
star["Albireo"].spectralClass = "K3 II";
star["Acrux"].spectralClass = "B1 IV";
star["Gemma"].spectralClass = "A0 V";
star["Procyon"].spectralClass = "F5 IV";
star["Sirius"].spectralClass = "A1 V";
star["Rigil Kentaurus"].spectralClass = "G2 V";
star["Deneb"].spectralClass = "A2 Ia";
star["Vega"].spectralClass = "A0 V";
star["Altair"].spectralClass = "A7 V";

star["Polaris"].mag = 2.0;
star["Mizar"].mag = 2.3;
star["Aldebaran"].mag = 0.85;
star["Rigel"].mag = 0.12;
star["Castor"].mag = 1.58;
star["Albireo"].mag = 3.1;
star["Acrux"].mag = 0.8;
star["Gemma"].mag = 2.23;
star["Procyon"].mag = 0.38;
star["Sirius"].mag = -1.46;
star["Rigil Kentaurus"].mag = -0.01;
star["Deneb"].mag = 1.25;
star["Vega"].mag = 0.03;
star["Altair"].mag = 0.77;
```

As you can see, Listing 8-1 contains a lot of repeated code. Each star is defined and then given four properties: the constellation in which it appears; and the star's type, spectral class, and magnitude (represented by the word *mag* in the code listing).

Consider the code in Listing 8-2 (in the Listing8-2.txt file in the companion content). It accomplishes the same result as the code in Listing 8-1, but with the help of a constructor pattern to create a pseudo-class.

LISTING 8-2 Assembling a *star* object using a pseudo-class.

```
var star = {};

function Star(constell,type,specclass,magnitude) {
    this.constellation = constell;
    this.type = type;
    this.spectralClass = specclass;
    this.mag = magnitude;
}
```

```
star["Polaris"] = new Star("Ursa Minor","Double/Cepheid","F7",2.0);
star["Mizar"] = new Star("Ursa Major","Spectroscopic Binary","A1 V",2.3);
star["Aldebaran"] = new Star("Taurus","Irregular Variable","K5 III",0.85);
star["Rigel"] = new Star("Orion","Supergiant with Companion","B8 Ia",0.12);
star["Castor"] = new Star("Gemini","Multiple/Spectroscopic","A1 V",1.58);
star["Albireo"] = new Star("Cygnus","Double","K3 II",3.1);
star["Acrux"] = new Star("Crux","Double","B1 IV",0.8);
star["Gemma"] = new Star("Corona Borealis","Eclipsing Binary","A0 V",2.23);
star["Procyon"] = new Star("Canis Minor","Double","F5 IV",0.38);
star["Sirius"] = new Star("Canis Major","Double","A1 V",-1.46);
star["Rigil Kentaurus"] = new Star("Centaurus","Double","G2 V",-0.01);
star["Deneb"] = new Star("Cygnus","Supergiant","A2 Ia",1.25);
star["Vega"] = new Star("Lyra","White Dwarf","A0 V",0.03);
star["Altair"] = new Star("Aquila","White Dwarf","A7 V",0.77);
```

The *Star* function, shown in boldface in Listing 8-2, creates an interface for constructing *star* objects quickly.

When called, the function returns a new *star* object:

```
star["Polaris"] = new Star("Ursa Minor","Double/Cepheid","F7",2.0);
```

Even though the Listing 8-1 and Listing 8-2 are functionally equivalent, the code in Listing 8-2 is much shorter and easier to understand. Imagine an object that had nine properties instead of just the four shown here.

The creation of a class-like interface in this section used the constructor pattern. The constructor pattern is helpful but results in multiple instances of the same method being created each time the object is instantiated. A better, but more advanced, way to create multiple objects is to use a *prototype* pattern. For more information about creating objects using prototypes, see *http://msdn.microsoft.com/en-us/magazine/cc163419.aspx*.

Creating Objects

You can create an object in JavaScript in two ways:

- Using the new keyword, as shown here:

  ```
  var star = new Object;
  ```

- Using curly braces, as shown here:

  ```
  var star = {};
  ```

The version you use depends largely on personal preference; they both accomplish the same task.

Adding Properties to Objects

After creating an object, you can start assigning properties and methods to it. If you have just one *star* object, you could assign properties directly to it, like this:

```
star.name = "Polaris";
star.constellation = "Ursa Minor";
```

When you need to create multiple related objects, you can assign properties efficiently by following the example shown in the previous section.

Displaying Object Properties

With a *for...in* loop, you can loop through each of the properties in an object. Try it out.

Looping through object properties

1. Using Microsoft Visual Studio, Eclipse, or another editor, edit the file proploop.htm, which you can find in the Chapter08 sample files folder in the companion content.

2. In the page, replace the TO DO comment with the *for* loop shown here in boldface (you can find this code in the proploop.txt file in the companion content):

```
<!DOCTYPE HTML PUBLIC "-//W3C//DTD HTML 4.01//EN"
"http://www.w3.org/TR/html4/strict.dtd">
<html>
<head>
<title>Properties</title>

<script type="text/javascript">
    var star = {};

    function Star(constell,type,specclass,magnitude) {
        this.constellation = constell;
        this.type = type;
        this.spectralClass = specclass;
        this.mag  = magnitude;
    }

    star["Polaris"] = new Star("Ursa Minor","Double/Cepheid","F7",2.0);
    star["Mizar"] = new Star("Ursa Major","Spectroscopic Binary","A1 V",2.3);
    star["Aldebaran"] = new Star("Taurus","Irregular Variable","K5 III",0.85);
    star["Rigel"] = new Star("Orion","Supergiant with Companion","B8 Ia",0.12);
    star["Castor"] = new Star("Gemini","Multiple/Spectroscopic","A1 V",1.58);
    star["Albireo"] = new Star("Cygnus","Double","K3 II",3.1);
    star["Acrux"] = new Star("Crux","Double","B1 IV",0.8);
    star["Gemma"] = new Star("Corona Borealis","Eclipsing Binary","A0 V",2.23);
    star["Procyon"] = new Star("Canis Minor","Double","F5 IV",0.38);
    star["Sirius"] = new Star("Canis Major","Double","A1 V",-1.46);
    star["Rigil Kentaurus"] = new Star("Centaurus","Double","G2 V",-0.01);
    star["Deneb"] = new Star("Cygnus","Supergiant","A2 Ia",1.25);
    star["Vega"] = new Star("Lyra","White Dwarf","A0 V",0.03);
```

```
     star["Altair"] = new Star("Aquila","White Dwarf","A7 V",0.77);

</script>
</head>
<body>
<script type="text/javascript">

for (var propt in star) {
    alert(propt);
}

</script>
</body>
</html>
```

3. View this page in a web browser. You are presented with an *alert()* dialog box for each of the stars in the *star* object, for a total of 14. (Yes, it's a lot of clicking. Sorry about that.) Here's an example of the type of dialog box you see:

This step-by-step exercise builds on the earlier example of using pseudo-classes to define properties of objects. In this case, a *star* object was created with the following code:

```
var star = {};
```

That object was then given several properties of individual star names by using a call to create a new *Star* object (using the pseudo-class):

```
star["Polaris"] = new Star("Ursa Minor","Double/Cepheid","F7",2.0);
```

Each property of the original *star* object, in this case the name of each star, was then enumerated within the *<body>* of the code by using a *for...in* loop:

```
for (var propt in star) {
    alert(propt);
}
```

You might be wondering how to get to the actual properties of the stars, such as the constellations, magnitudes, types, and spectral class. Chapter 14 shows you how to enumerate through each of these.

Looking for a Property

Sometimes you don't want or need to loop through every property. Sometimes you just want to know whether a given property already exists within an object. You can use the *in* operator to test for the property, as in this pseudo-code:

```
if (property in object) {
    // do something here
}
```

Listing 8-3 shows a more complete example (available in the Listing8-3.txt file in the companion code). It examines the *star* object for one of the star names, "Polaris," and if found, adds a new property to it.

LISTING 8-3 Looking for a property.

```javascript
var star = {};

function Star(constell,type,specclass,magnitude) {
    this.constellation = constell;
    this.type = type;
    this.spectralClass = specclass;
    this.mag  = magnitude;
}

star["Polaris"] = new Star("Ursa Minor","Double/Cepheid","F7",2.0);
star["Mizar"] = new Star("Ursa Major","Spectroscopic Binary","A1 V",2.3);
star["Aldebaran"] = new Star("Taurus","Irregular Variable","K5 III",0.85);
star["Rigel"] = new Star("Orion","Supergiant with Companion","B8 Ia",0.12);
star["Castor"] = new Star("Gemini","Multiple/Spectroscopic","A1 V",1.58);
star["Albireo"] = new Star("Cygnus","Double","K3 II",3.1);
star["Acrux"] = new Star("Crux","Double","B1 IV",0.8);
star["Gemma"] = new Star("Corona Borealis","Eclipsing Binary","A0 V",2.23);
star["Procyon"] = new Star("Canis Minor","Double","F5 IV",0.38);
star["Sirius"] = new Star("Canis Major","Double","A1 V",-1.46);
star["Rigil Kentaurus"] = new Star("Centaurus","Double","G2 V",-0.01);
star["Deneb"] = new Star("Cygnus","Supergiant","A2 Ia",1.25);
star["Vega"] = new Star("Lyra","White Dwarf","A0 V",0.03);
star["Altair"] = new Star("Aquila","White Dwarf","A7 V",0.77);

if ("Polaris" in star) {
    star["Polaris"].aka = "The North Star";
    alert("Polaris found and is also known as " + star["Polaris"].aka);
}
```

Note There are other approaches for checking property existence that aren't covered in this book, such as the the *!==* operator.

Adding Methods to Objects

In the same way you can add properties to self-defined objects, you can add methods. For example, suppose you want to extend the *Star* class used in earlier examples to include a method called *show()*, which just presents an *alert()* dialog box. You could extend this method to do whatever you need it to do. For example, look at this code (from the adding-methods.txt file in the companion code):

```
function Star(constell,type,specclass,magnitude) {
    this.constellation = constell;
    this.type = type;
    this.spectralClass = specclass;
    this.mag  = magnitude;
    this.show = function() {
        alert("hello, this is a method.");
    }
}
```

To call the method, you write code that looks like this:

```
star["Polaris"].show();
```

Object-oriented programming in JavaScript doesn't end here. More advanced features of the object-oriented programming paradigm such as inheritance, superclassing, and prototypes are all possible with JavaScript, but they are beyond the scope of this book. MSDN Magazine published an article about some of the more advanced concepts, and you can find that article at http://msdn.microsoft.com/en-us/magazine/cc163419.aspx.

Finding Out More About Arrays

Chapter 4 introduced arrays and provided some examples of ways to define them. With arrays, you can group a set of values into an object and then access those values through a numbered index value. For example, you can use the *new Array( )* explicit constructor as follows (you can find this code in the morearrays.txt file in the companion content):

```
var star = new Array();
star[0] = "Polaris";
star[1] = "Deneb";
star[2] = "Vega";
star[3] = "Altair";
```

You also can perform the same task using the implicit array constructor (denoted by square brackets), like so:

```
var star = ["Polaris", "Deneb", "Vega", "Altair"];
```

The *length* Property

The *length* property of an array returns the number of elements in the array. There's an important distinction between how many elements the array contains and how many have been defined. Here's a simple example. Consider the implicit star array definition discussed previously. You can count four star names: Polaris, Deneb, Vega, and Altair. The *length* property returns the same result:

```
var numStars = star.length;   // star.length is 4.
```

Elements can be counted by the *length* property that have not yet been defined or initialized. Here's an example that creates an array with more elements than were assigned:

```
var myArray = new Array(5);
```

Array Methods

This section introduces you to some of the methods of the *array* object. You can find more information within the ECMA-262 specification at *http://www.ecma-international.org/publications /files/ECMA-ST/Ecma-262.pdf*.

Adding and Removing Elements

You can add elements to an array using a few different methods, by either *prepending* them to the front of the array or appending them to the end of it.

Using *concat()* to add elements   The *concat()* method appends elements to the end of the array on which it is invoked. To use it, you supply the *concat()* method with arguments containing the items to append. The method returns a new array, as follows (this code is in the morearray.txt file in the companion content):

```
var myArray = new Array();
myArray[0] = "first";
myArray[1] = "second";
var newArray = myArray.concat("third");
// newArray is now [first,second,third]
```

You can also concatenate one array to another, like this:

```
var myFirstArray = [51,67];
var mySecondArray = [18,"hello",125];
var newArray = myFirstArray.concat(mySecondArray)
// newArray is [51,67,18,"hello",125]
```

Adding elements with *concat()*

1. Using Visual Studio, Eclipse, or another editor, edit the concat.htm file in the Chapter08 sample files folder in the companion content.

2. Within the page, add the code shown in boldface type (the first part of the concat.txt file):

```
<!DOCTYPE HTML PUBLIC "-//W3C//DTD HTML 4.01//EN"
"http://www.w3.org/TR/html4/strict.dtd">
<html>
<head>
    <title>Concat</title>
    <script type="text/javascript">

    var star = ["Polaris", "Deneb", "Vega", "Altair"];

    for (var i = 0; i < star.length; i++) {
        alert(star[i]);
    }

    </script>
</head>
<body>

</body>
</html>
```

3. Save the page and view it in a web browser. You receive an *alert()* dialog box (like the one shown here) for each of the four star names defined in the star array.

4. Alter the code to concatenate some additional stars onto the star array. (Yes, I realize that you could just add them directly to the star array, but that's cheating.) Here's the code (the changes are shown in boldface and are in the second part of the concat.txt file):

```
<!DOCTYPE HTML PUBLIC "-//W3C//DTD HTML 4.01//EN"
"http://www.w3.org/TR/html4/strict.dtd">
<html>
<head>
    <title>Concat</title>
    <script type="text/javascript">
```

```
var star = ["Polaris", "Deneb", "Vega", "Altair"];

var newstars = ["Aldebaran", "Rigel"];
var morestars = star.concat(newstars);
var mStarLength = morestars.length;
for (var i = 0; i < mStarLength; i++) {
    alert(morestars[i]);
}

        </script>
    </head>
    <body>

    </body>
</html>
```

5. Save and view the page in a web browser. You receive six *alert()* dialog boxes (sorry!), one for each star, like this one for Aldebaran:

Joining and concatenating with *join*   The *join()* method converts all the elements of an array to a joined string. This method is unlike the *concat()* method, which concatenates but does not perform any type conversions. Here's the code:

```
var star = ["Polaris", "Deneb", "Vega", "Altair"];
var starString = star.join();
```

The *starString* variable contains Polaris,Deneb,Vega,Altair, as shown in Figure 8-1.

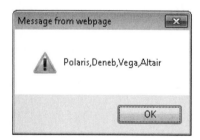

FIGURE 8-1 Using *join()* to join an array.

The *join()* method enables you to specify the join delimiter as well. Instead of just using a comma, you might want to use an asterisk, like this:

```
var star = ["Polaris", "Deneb", "Vega", "Altair"];
var starString = star.join("*");
```

The result would be Polaris*Deneb*Vega*Altair, as shown in Figure 8-2.

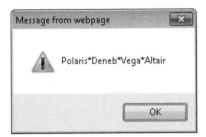

FIGURE 8-2 Joining with a different delimiter.

 Tip The *join()* method is a quick way to see the contents of an array without creating an entire *for* loop structure.

Using *push* and *pop* to add and remove elements   Whereas concat() returns the newly concatenated array, push() and pop() add and remove elements. The push() method returns the length of the new array, and *pop()* returns the removed element. The methods *push()* and *pop()* operate on the end of the array, as shown in the following code and in the evenmorearrays .txt file in the companion content:

```
var star = ["Polaris", "Deneb", "Vega", "Altair"];
star.push("Aldebaran");
```

Running the preceding code results in the *star* object containing five elements: Polaris, Deneb, Vega, Altair, and Aldebaran.

The *pop()* method removes the last element and returns the element that is removed:

```
var star = ["Polaris", "Deneb", "Vega", "Altair"];
var removedElement = star.pop();
```

The *removedElement* variable contains the string "Altair" because that was the last element of the array. The length of the array is also shortened (or decremented) by 1.

Using *shift* and *unshift* to add and remove elements   The *push()* and *pop()* methods operate on the end of the array. The *shift()* and *unshift()* methods perform the same functions as *push()* and *pop()*, except the former do it at the beginning of the array. In this code, the *unshift()* method adds an element to the beginning of an array:

```
var star = ["Polaris", "Deneb", "Vega", "Altair"];
star.unshift("Aldebaran");
```

The *star* array is:

```
["Aldebaran", "Polaris", "Deneb", "Vega", "Altair"]
```

Use *shift()* to remove an element from the beginning of an array. Note that *shift()* returns the removed element, just like *pop()*:

```
var star = ["Polaris", "Deneb", "Vega", "Altair"];
var removedElement = star.shift();
```

The *star* array now contains:

```
["Deneb", "Vega", "Altair"]
```

Using *slice* to return parts of an array The *slice()* method is useful when you need to return specific portions of an array, but you must be careful, because unless you make a copy of the array, *slice()* changes the original array. For instance, the following code returns and places into the *cutStars* variable the value *"Vega,Altair"*, because *Vega* and *Altair* are the third and fourth elements of the *star* array (remember that arrays start counting from zero).

```
var star = ["Polaris", "Deneb", "Vega", "Altair"];
var cutStars = star.slice(2,3);
```

Sorting elements with *sort* It's sometimes helpful to sort the elements of an array. Look at this code:

```
var star = ["Polaris", "Deneb", "Vega", "Altair"];
var sortedStars = star.sort();
```

The result is shown in Figure 8-3, and as you can see, the elements of the star array are sorted alphabetically, even though they weren't given alphabetically in the code. Note that both the original *star* array and the *sortedStars* variable contain sorted lists.

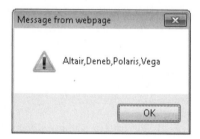

FIGURE 8-3 The result of a sorted array using the *sort()* method.

Be careful not to use the *sort()* method to sort numbers. Consider this code:

```
var nums = [11,543,22,111];
var sortedNums = nums.sort();
```

You might expect the *sortedNums* variable to contain 11,22,111,543, but instead it sorts the values alphabetically, as shown in Figure 8-4.

FIGURE 8-4 Attempting to sort numbers with *sort()* doesn't work—at least not if you want them sorted in numerical order.

Iterating through arrays   Two primary methods exist for iterating through array elements in JavaScript. As of this writing, the primary cross-browser method for doing so is the *for()* method, which you've seen throughout the book so far. Here's a quick reminder of its syntax:

```
var candies = ["chocolate","licorice","mints"];
for (var i = 0; i < candies.length; i++) {
    alert(candies[i]);
}
```

Introduced with ECMA-262 version 5 and supported in all browsers with the exception of Windows Internet Explorer 8 and earlier, the *forEach()* method walks through array elements as well. The syntax for *forEach()* is similar to that of a *for* loop:

```
var candies = ["chocolate","licorice","mints"];
candies.forEach(function(candy) {
    alert(candy);
}
```

> **Note** Use the *forEach()* method (and other new methods) with caution, because they aren't yet widely supported.

The array object has other methods that you should know about. Some that you might encounter are listed in Table 8-1, but you should refer to the ECMA-262 specification available at *http://www.ecma-international.org/publications/files/ECMA-ST/ECMA-262.pdf* for a full list. Methods that are new to the ECMA-262 version 5 standard are noted.

TABLE 8-1 Select Methods of the Array Object

Method	Description	New to ECMA-262 Edition 5
reverse()	Reverses the order of the elements.	No
map()	Executes a function on each array item and returns an array.	Yes
indexOf()	Returns the index of the first occurrence of the argument.	Yes
lastIndexOf()	Returns the last index of the argument in the array.	Yes
every()	Executes a function on each array item while the function continues to return *true*.	Yes
filter()	Executes a function on each array item and returns an array containing only the items for which the function returns *true*.	Yes
some()	Executes a function on each array item while the function returns *false*.	Yes
splice()	Inserts or removes elements from an array. Returns an array containing the deleted items.	No

Taking Advantage of Built-in Objects

The JavaScript language makes several useful objects available to assist with tasks common to the JavaScript program. You've already seen some of these, such as the *Date, Number,* and *Math* objects, which were covered in Chapter 4.

The Global Object

JavaScript has a global object that contains some of the methods already discussed, such as *isNaN()*. Another three commonly used global object methods are *encodeURI(), encodeURI-Component(),* and *eval(),* which are discussed in this section.

Making URIs Safe

The *encodeURI()* method takes a Uniform Resource Identifier (URI) that contains characters which are not allowed in a given URI scheme, and it encodes them so that they can be used according to the standard. For example, RFC (Request For Comments) 2396 defines a generic syntax for URIs. The *encodeURI()* method can be used to correct the following URI:

```
http://www.braingia.org/a uri with spaces.htm
```

The preceding URI contains spaces—which are not allowed in an HTTP URI—and therefore the URI needs to be encoded:

```
alert(encodeURI("http://www.braingia.org/a uri with spaces.htm"));
```

Figure 8-5 shows the result.

FIGURE 8-5 Using the *encodeURI()* method to properly encode a URI in JavaScript.

Whereas the *encodeURI()* method works on an entire URI, like the one shown in Figure 8-5, the *encodeURIComponent()* method works on only part of a URI, such as the */a uri with spaces .htm* portion of the example shown.

Both the *encodeURI()* and *encodeURIComponent()* methods have decoding counterparts, *decodeURI()* and *decodeURIComponent()*, respectively.

Using the *eval()* method

The *eval()* method is one of the most powerful and dangerous methods you can use in JavaScript. The *eval()* method takes a single argument that is interpreted and executed by the JavaScript engine, for example:

```
eval("alert('hello world')");
```

The *eval()* method executes the *alert* code, just as it would if the code were executed directly. Typically, you use the *eval()* method during Asynchronous JavaScript and XML (AJAX) calls, but doing so poses a security problem because the code returned from the AJAX call is executed just as if it were normal code, and that code could be malicious.

Exercises

1. Create code to loop through a simple array of four objects, shown here, and display those in an *alert()* dialog box, one for each element of the array:

```
var star = ["Polaris", "Deneb", "Vega", "Altair"];
```

2. Create an object to hold the names of three of your favorite songs. The objects should have properties containing the artist, the song length, and the title for each song.

3. The first step-by-step exercise in this chapter used a list of stars and a class to populate those objects, shown here:

```
function Star(constell,type,specclass,magnitude) {
    this.constellation = constell;
    this.type = type;
    this.spectralClass = specclass;
    this.mag  = magnitude;
}
star["Polaris"] = new Star("Ursa Minor","Double/Cepheid","F7",2.0);
star["Mizar"] = new Star("Ursa Major","Spectroscopic Binary","A1 V",2.3);
star["Aldebaran"] = new Star("Taurus","Irregular Variable","K5 III",0.85);
star["Rigel"] = new Star("Orion","Supergiant with Companion","B8 Ia",0.12);
star["Castor"] = new Star("Gemini","Multiple/Spectroscopic","A1 V",1.58);
star["Albireo"] = new Star("Cygnus","Double","K3 II",3.1);
star["Acrux"] = new Star("Crux","Double","B1 IV",0.8);
star["Gemma"] = new Star("Corona Borealis","Eclipsing Binary","A0 V",2.23);
star["Procyon"] = new Star("Canis Minor","Double","F5 IV",0.38);
star["Sirius"] = new Star("Canis Major","Double","A1 V",-1.46);
star["Rigil Kentaurus"] = new Star("Centaurus","Double","G2 V",-0.01);
star["Deneb"] = new Star("Cygnus","Supergiant","A2 Ia",1.25);
star["Vega"] = new Star("Lyra","White Dwarf","A0 V",0.03);
star["Altair"] = new Star("Aquila","White Dwarf","A7 V",0.77)
```

The code then used a simple *for* loop to move through each of the star objects and displayed the names of the stars, as shown here:

```
for (var propt in star) {
    alert(propt);
}
```

Your task is to modify this code to display one single dialog box containing all the star names rather than display one dialog box for each star.

Chapter 9
The Browser Object Model

After reading this chapter, you'll be able to:

- Understand the different objects available as part of the *window* object.

- Use the *navigator* object to view properties of the visitor's browser.

- Obtain information about the visitor's screen, including available height and width.

- Use JavaScript to detect whether Java is enabled in the browser.

- Parse the query string sent by the browser.

Introducing the Browser

Until this chapter in the book, you reviewed JavaScript mainly in the abstract. This chapter starts to examine JavaScript as you'd apply it in the real world.

I feel rather silly about writing this, but it's important, so I'm going to say it anyway: *the browser is central to JavaScript programming*. Projects like Rhino *(http://www.mozilla.org /rhino/)* want to change that, but understanding the environments that browsers provide is central to writing good JavaScript code that works well on multiple browsers running on multiple platforms. This section introduces you to the Browser Object Model.

The Browser Hierarchy

The Browser Object Model creates a tree-like hierarchy of objects, many of which provide properties and methods for the JavaScript programmer. The browser itself is represented by one object, called the *window* object. The *window* object is the parent of several child objects:

- *document*

- *frames*

- *history*

- *location*

- *navigator*

- *screen*

- *self/window/parent*

The *document* child of the *window* object is special because it has several child and even grandchild objects. The *window* object, its children, and their place in the browser hierarchy are illustrated in Figure 9-1.

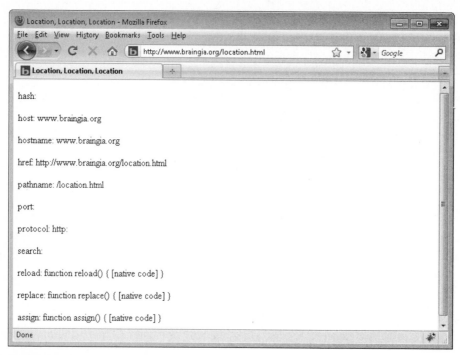

FIGURE 9-1 The *window* object and its children.

I discuss the *document* object in its own chapter—Chapter 10, "The Document Object Model." You learn about the other children of the *window* object in the remainder of this chapter.

Events

Events were briefly described in Chapter 1, "JavaScript Is More Than You Might Think." You use events in many areas of JavaScript programming, and quite a bit when working with web forms. Events are triggered when actions occur. The action can be initiated by users, when they click a button or link, or move the mouse into or out of an area; or by programmatic events, such as when a page loads. Chapter 11, "JavaScript Events and the Browser," goes into detail about events related to the *window* object; Chapter 14, "Using JavaScript with Web Forms," provides more information about web forms.

A Sense of *Self*

The *window* object is a global object that represents the currently open window in the browser. The *window* object has several properties, methods, and child objects. You already used some of these methods, such as *alert()* and *prompt()*. Because the *window* object is a global object, you don't need to preface its properties and methods with *window*. Instead, you can call them directly, as you already saw done in the examples that made calls to the *alert()* method.

Direct descendants of the *window* object don't require the *window* prefix, but when you deal with objects beyond the *window* object's direct descendants, you need to precede them with the *window* object name. For example, the *document* object is a direct descendant of the *window* object and therefore doesn't need the *window* prefix, but descendants of the *document* object do need it, as shown in the following example:

```
alert("something");  // note no window. prefix.
document.forms[0]  // note the document. prefix but still no window. prefix
```

The *window* object also has properties and methods. Among its properties is the *self* property, which refers to the *window* object (and gave me the idea for the title for this section). Table 9-1 lists some of the widely used properties of the *window* object. You examine many of these in examples throughout the book.

TABLE 9-1 Selected Properties of the *window* Object

Property	Description
closed	Set to *true* when the window has been closed
defaultStatus	Used to set the text that appears by default in the status bar of a browser
name	The name of the window as set when the window is first opened
opener	A reference to the window that created the window
parent	Frequently used with frames to refer to the window that created a particular window or is one level up from the frame
status	Frequently used to set the text in the status bar when a visitor hovers over an element such as a link
top	Refers to the highest or topmost parent window

Table 9-2 and Table 9-3 describe some of the *window* object's methods. You see examples of how to use many of these throughout the remainder of this book.

TABLE 9-2 Selected Methods of the *window* Object

Method	Description
addEventListener()	Cross-browser (except for Windows Internet Explorer) event handler method. See Chapter 11 for more information.
attachEvent()	The version of *addEventListener()* in Internet Explorer. See Chapter 11 for more information.
blur()	Changes the focus of keyboard input away from the browser window.
focus()	Changes the focus of keyboard input to the browser window.
close()	Closes the browser window.
detachEvent()	The version of *removeEventListener()* in Internet Explorer.
removeEventListener()	Cross-browser (except for Internet Explorer) event handler removal method.
open()	Opens a window.
print()	Causes the browser's print function to be invoked; behaves just as though someone clicked Print in the browser.

Some methods of the *window* object deal with moving and resizing the window and are described in Table 9-3.

TABLE 9-3 Selected Methods of the *window* Object for Moving and Resizing

Method	Description
moveBy()	Used to move the window to a relative location
moveTo()	Used to move the window to a specific location
resizeBy()	Used to change the size of the window by a relative amount
resizeTo()	Used to change the size of the window to a certain size

Timers are found in some JavaScript applications and are discussed in Chapter 11. The *window* object methods related to timers are the following:

- *clearInterval()*
- *clearTimeout()*
- *setInterval()*
- *setTimeout()*

The rest of the chapter looks more closely at some of the direct children of the *window* object.

Getting Information About the Screen

The *screen* object provides a way to obtain information about the visitor's screen. You might need this information to determine which images to display or how large the page can be. Regardless of whether you use the *screen* object, you need to create a good CSS-based design (CSS stands for Cascading Style Sheets) that gracefully handles screens of all sizes.

> **Note** You often see child objects of the *window* object referred to as properties of the *window* object—for example, the *screen* property rather than the *screen* object.

The available properties of the *screen* object are as follows:

- *availHeight*
- *availWidth*
- *colorDepth*
- *height*
- *width*

You might be wondering what the difference is between the *availHeight* and *availWidth* properties, and the *height* and *width* properties. The *availHeight* and *availWidth* properties return the available height and width (no kidding!) of the screen minus the space used by other controls, such as the taskbar in Microsoft Windows. The *height* and *width* properties return the gross height and width. This might make more sense with an example.

Determining a visitor's screen height and width

1. Using Microsoft Visual Studio, Eclipse, or another editor, edit the screen.htm file in the Chapter09 sample files folder in the companion content.

2. In the page, add the boldface code shown here (you can find this in the screen.txt file in the companion content):

```
<!DOCTYPE HTML PUBLIC "-//W3C//DTD HTML 4.01//EN"
"http://www.w3.org/TR/html4/strict.dtd">
<html>
<head>
    <title>Screen</title>

</head>
<body>
```

```
<script type="text/javascript">
    alert("Available Height: " + screen.availHeight);
    alert("Total Height: " + screen.height);
    alert("Available Width: " + screen.availWidth);
    alert("Total Width: " + screen.width);
</script>

</body>
</html>
```

3. Save and view the page in a web browser. You receive four *alert()* dialog boxes, one for each of the properties called. The sample screenshots shown here reflect a 1024 × 768 pixel display.

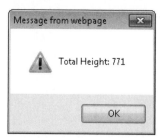

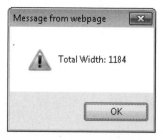

As you can see from these screenshots, the total width and height are 1184 pixels and 771 pixels, respectively. Notice that the available width remains 1184, whereas the available height is reduced to 731 from 771 because of the taskbar.

Using the *navigator* Object

The *navigator* object provides several properties that assist in the detection of various elements of the visitor's browser and environment. One of the most popular operations JavaScript can perform is detecting which browser the visitor is using. (Well, this section isn't about that—but it could be. See the sidebar "Problems with Browser Detection" for more information.)

Problems with Browser Detection

For a long time, websites used the *navigator* object to detect which browser the visitor was using. (Well, a long time in Internet years—which could be several years or as short as a few months, depending on the technology you're talking about.) Browser detection was used so that browser-specific JavaScript code could be executed. Although simple browser detection had its uses, some poorly designed sites used this technique as a means to lock out visitors who had particular browsers.

Little did they know that the information sent by a browser can be easily fooled. The User Agent Switcher add-on for Firefox is one such way to alter this information, thus rendering browser detection with the *navigator* object useless.

> **Tip** I've said it before in this book and I'll say it now (and probably will repeat it again later): never rely on anything sent from the visitor's browser to your website. Always verify. Assuming that the browser is Internet Explorer just because it says so is not sufficient. Chapter 11 shows a better method for detecting whether the browser is capable of handling the JavaScript on your website.

When you use the *navigator* object to detect the visitor's browser, you encounter another problem because there are so many browsers out there. A web developer can spend too much time keeping track of which browsers might support which functions and trying to account for all those browsers in the code. All is not lost for the *navigator* object though—it's still useful, as you will soon see.

In this exercise, you walk through the properties of the *navigator* object and their values.

Looking at the *navigator* object

1. Using Visual Studio, Eclipse, or another editor, edit the naviprops.htm file in the Chapter09 sample files folder in the companion content.

2. Within the page, replace the TODO comment with the boldface code shown here (this code is in the naviprops.txt file in the companion content):

```
<!DOCTYPE HTML PUBLIC "-//W3C//DTD HTML 4.01//EN"
"http://www.w3.org/TR/html4/strict.dtd">
<html>
<head>
    <title>The navigator Object</title>
</head>
<body>
    <script type="text/javascript">
            var body = document.getElementsByTagName("body")[0];
            for (var prop in navigator) {
                var elem = document.createElement("p");
                var text = document.createTextNode(prop + ": " + navigator[prop]);
                elem.appendChild(text);
                body.appendChild(elem);
            }
    </script>

</body>
</html>
```

3. Save and view the page in a web browser of your choice. If you chose Firefox, you see a page like this:

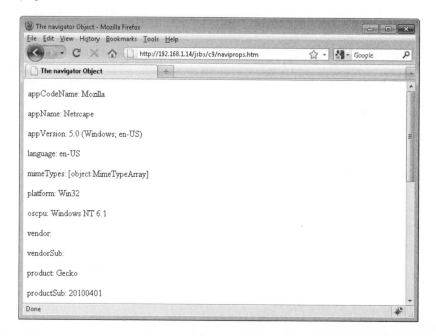

4. If you chose Internet Explorer, the page will look similar to this; however, note the difference in the available properties:

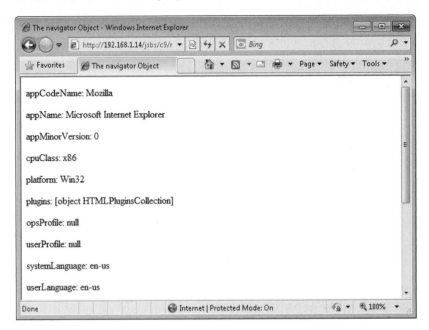

I just couldn't bring myself to use yet another *alert()* dialog box for this exercise, so I had to use some functions that I haven't yet introduced. Never fear, though—the elements in this example are introduced in Chapters 10 and 11.

The code for this exercise employs a function that uses the *Document* Object Model to create Hypertext Markup Language (HTML) elements within the webpage. A *for* loop is used to iterate through each of the properties presented by the *navigator* object:

```
function showProps() {
    var body = document.getElementsByTagName("body")[0];
    for (var prop in navigator) {
        var elem = document.createElement("p");
        var text = document.createTextNode(prop + ": " + navigator[prop]);
        elem.appendChild(text);
        body.appendChild(elem);
    }
}
```

If the JavaScript you're using doesn't work for a certain version of a web browser, you could detect the browser by implementing a workaround based on using the *navigator* object, but understand that this strategy isn't reliable and you really shouldn't use it as standard practice. But sometimes, you just need to use it.

If your site uses Java, you can use the *navigator* object to check whether Java is enabled. Here's how:

Using the *navigator* object to detect Java

1. Using Visual Studio, Eclipse, or another editor, edit the file javatest.htm in the Chapter09 sample files folder.

2. Within the page, replacing the TODO comment with the boldface the code shown here (also located in the javatest.txt file in the companion content):

```
<!DOCTYPE HTML PUBLIC "-//W3C//DTD HTML 4.01//EN"
"http://www.w3.org/TR/html4/strict.dtd">
<html>
<head>
    <title>Java Test</title>
    <script type="text/javascript">
        if (navigator.javaEnabled()) {
            alert("Java is enabled");
        } else {
            alert("Java is not enabled");
        }
    </script>
</head>

<body>

</body>
</html>
```

3. Save the page and view it in Internet Explorer (if you have it installed). By default, Java is enabled in Internet Explorer, so you should see a dialog box like this:

4. Switch to Firefox, if you have it available, and disable Java (in the Windows version of Firefox, you can do this by selecting Add-Ons from the Tools menu, clicking Plugin, and then clicking Disable For The Java Plugins.) When you disable Java and refresh the page, you see a dialog box like this:

The *location* Object

The *location* object gives you access to the currently loaded Uniform Resource Identifier (URI), including any information about the query string, the protocol in use, and other related components. For example, a URI might be:

http://www.braingia.org/location.html

If the webpage at that URI contains the JavaScript code to parse the URI that is presented in the next example, the output would look like that shown in Figure 9-2.

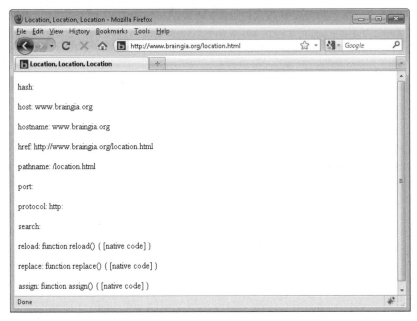

FIGURE 9-2 The *location* object being used to display the various properties.

The protocol in this case is *http:*, the host is *www.braingia.org* (as is the host name), and the pathname is *location.html*. Nothing was entered on the query string, so the search value remains empty. The port is the standard port for HTTP traffic, tcp/80, so that, too, is empty.

Here's an exercise that examines the query string.

Looking at the *location* object

1. Using Visual Studio, Eclipse, or another editor, edit the location1.htm file in the Chapter09 sample files folder in the companion content.

2. This first bit of HTML and JavaScript creates the page that you saw in Figure 9-2. (Actually, it steals the code from an earlier exercise that used the *navigator* object but with a slight modification for the *location* object.) We build upon that code for this exercise, so add the boldface code shown here to the location1.htm page:

```
<!DOCTYPE HTML PUBLIC "-//W3C//DTD HTML 4.01//EN"
"http://www.w3.org/TR/html4/strict.dtd">
<html>
<head>
    <title>Location, Location, Location</title>
</head>
<body>
    <script type="text/javascript">
            var body = document.getElementsByTagName("body")[0];
            for (var prop in location) {
                var elem = document.createElement("p");
                var text = document.createTextNode(prop + ": " + location[prop]);
                elem.appendChild(text);
                body.appendChild(elem);
            }
    </script>
</body>
</html>
```

3. View the page in a web browser. Your results will vary, depending on how you set up your web server. This example shows an Apache web server running on a local IP address: 192.168.1.14.

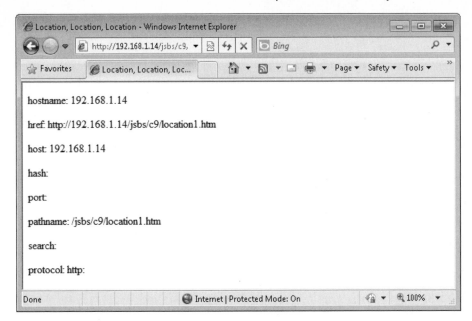

4. Modify the URI that you use to call the page by adding some query string parameter/value pairs. For example, the URI used for my local environment is *http://192.168.1.14/jsbs/c9/location1.htm*. (Your environment and the location from which you serve the file will likely be different from this.) I'm going to modify the URL and add two parameters, *name=Steve* and *country=US*. Feel free to change the value for the *name* parameter to your name and change the *country* value to your home country (if you're not from the United States, that is). The values you choose aren't all that important here—what matters is that you use more than one parameter/value pair. Here's my final URI: *http://localhost:1627/Chapter9/location1.htm?name=Steve&country=US*.

5. When you load the page with the parameters you added, the *search* property has a value, as shown here:

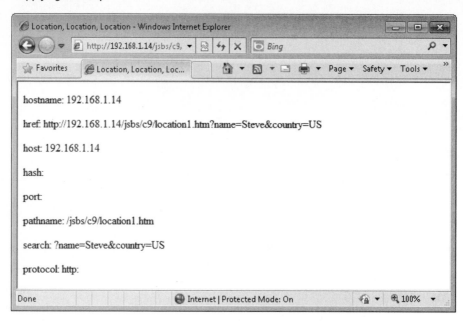

6. Open the location1.htm file again, and save it as **location2.htm**.

7. Alter the code in location2.htm so that it examines the *search* property, like this (the changes are shown in boldface type and are in the location2.txt file in the companion content):

```
<!DOCTYPE HTML PUBLIC "-//W3C//DTD HTML 4.01//EN"
"http://www.w3.org/TR/html4/strict.dtd">
<html>
<head>
    <title>Location, Location, Location</title>

</head>
<body>
    <script type="text/javascript">
            var body = document.getElementsByTagName("body")[0];
            for (var prop in location) {
                var elem = document.createElement("p");
                var text = document.createTextNode(prop + ": " + location[prop]);
                elem.appendChild(text);
                body.appendChild(elem);
            }
            if (location.search) {
                var querystring = location.search;
                var splits = querystring.split('&');
                for (var i = 0; i < splits.length; i++) {
                    var splitpair = splits[i].split('=');
                    var elem = document.createElement("p");
                    var text = document.createTextNode(splitpair[0] + ": " +
```

```
splitpair[1]);
                        elem.appendChild(text);
                        body.appendChild(elem);
                }
            }
    </script>
</body>
</html>
```

8. Execute this code by pointing your browser to *location2.htm?name=Steve&country=US* (alter the name and country as appropriate, unless your name is Steve and you live in the United States). You now receive a page that lists the normal properties that you saw earlier, but also lists (near the bottom) the parameter/value pairs parsed from the query string, like this:

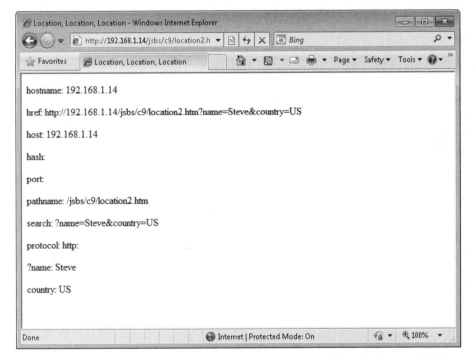

9. Notice, however, that the first parameter, *name*, contains the question mark (*?*) from the query string, which is not what you want. You can solve this problem in several ways. One of the simplest is to use the *substring()* method. Change the *querystring* variable definition line to read:

```
var querystring = location.search.substring(1);
```

The *substring()* method returns the string starting at the point specified. In this case, the first character of *location.search* (at index *0*) is the question mark; therefore, use *substring()* starting at index 1 to solve the problem. The final code (with the change shown in boldface type) looks like what follows. (You can find this in the location3.txt file in the companion content.):

```
<!DOCTYPE HTML PUBLIC "-//W3C//DTD HTML 4.01//EN"
"http://www.w3.org/TR/html4/strict.dtd">
<html>
<head>
    <title>Location, Location, Location</title>

</head>
<body>
    <script type="text/javascript">
            var body = document.getElementsByTagName("body")[0];
            for (var prop in location) {
                var elem = document.createElement("p");
                var text = document.createTextNode(prop + ": " + location[prop]);
                elem.appendChild(text);
                body.appendChild(elem);
            }
            if (location.search) {
                var querystring = location.search.substring(1);
                var splits = querystring.split('&');
                for (var i = 0; i < splits.length; i++) {
                    var splitpair = splits[i].split('=');
                    var elem = document.createElement("p");
                    var text = document.createTextNode(splitpair[0] + ": " +
splitpair[1]);
                    elem.appendChild(text);
                    body.appendChild(elem);
                }
            }
    </script>
</body>
</html>
```

10. Save this code as **location3.htm** and run it again. You see from the results that you've solved the problem of the question mark:

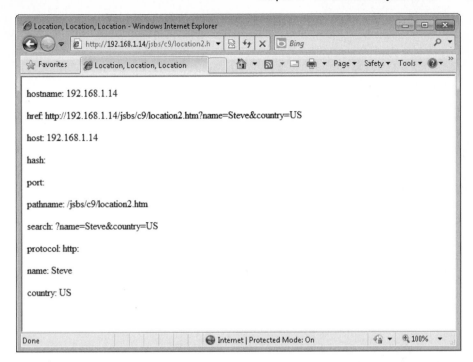

The location can also be set using JavaScript and the *location* object. Typically you accomplish this using the *assign()* method of the *location* object. For example, to redirect to my website (always a good idea), I might use this code:

```
location.assign("http://www.braingia.org");
```

Calling the *assign()* method is essentially the same as setting the *href* property:

```
location.href = "http://www.braingia.org";
```

You can also change other properties of the *location* object, such as the port, the query string, or the path. For example, to set the path to */blog,/*, you can do this:

```
location.pathname = "blog";
```

To set the query string to *?name=Steve*, do this:

```
location.search = "?name=Steve";
```

You can reload the page by calling the *reload()* method:

```
location.reload();
```

When you call *location.reload()*, the browser may load the page from its cache rather than re-request the page from the server; however, if you pass a Boolean *true* to the method, the browser reloads the page directly from the server:

```
location.reload(true);
```

> **Note** Be careful using the *reload()* method. Trying to reload the page within a script, as opposed to through a function call triggered by an event, is likely to cause a loop condition.

The *history* Object

The *history* object provides ways to move forward and backward through the visitor's browsing history. (However, for security reasons, JavaScript cannot access the URIs for sites that the browser visits.) Specifically, you can use the *back()*, *forward()*, and *go()* methods. It probably goes without saying, but *back()* and *forward()* move one page backward and forward, respectively. The *go()* method moves to the index value specified as the argument.

> **Note** If an application doesn't go to a different page or location in the address bar, the application won't be part of the browser's history and thus not accessible with these functions.

Here's some example code for moving backward and forward that can be adapted as needed. Examples in later chapters show more detail about how this kind of code might be used in the real world.

```
<!DOCTYPE HTML PUBLIC "-//W3C//DTD HTML 4.01//EN" "http://www.w3.org/TR/html4/strict.dtd">
<html>
<head>
    <title>History</title>
    <script type="text/javascript">
        function moveBack() {
            history.back();
        }
        function moveForward() {
            history.forward();
        }
    </script>
</head>
<body>
<p><a href="#" onclick="moveBack()">Click to go back</a></p>
<p><a href="#" onclick="moveForward()">Click to go forward</a></p>
</body>
</html>
```

Note This code uses an inline event handler (*onclick*), which is not recommended for use in unobtrusive JavaScript, because the event handler inserts behavior in the page markup. The use of *onclick* here is for illustrative purposes only, to avoid introducing the event handler concept, which gets its own chapter—Chapter 11.

Registering Handlers

HTML 5.0 introduced two new methods of the navigator object: *registerContentHandler()* and *registerProtocolHandler()*. Using these methods, a website can register a URI for handling certain types of information, such as an RSS feed. However, these methods are not yet widely supported, and therefore aren't covered in this book.

Exercises

1. Use the *availHeight* and *availWidth* methods to determine whether a screen is at least 768 pixels high and 1024 pixels wide. If it's not, display an *alert()* dialog box stating the size of the available screen.

2. Alter the step-by-step exercise that used the *location* object to display an *alert()* dialog box based on the values of the query string. Specifically, display the word "Obrigado" if the country is specified as Brazil, and display "Thank you" if the country is Great Britain. Test these conditions.

3. Install the User Agent Switcher add-on to Firefox or a similar add-on to Internet Explorer. Then use the code from the "Looking at the navigator object" exercise earlier in this chapter to experiment with the different values that you find. This exercise helps to show why using the *navigator* object as the sole means of determining compatibility is not recommended. Bonus: Define your own user agent.

Part III
Integrating JavaScript into Design

Chapter 10: The Document Object Model

Chapter 11: JavaScript Events and the Browser

Chapter 12: Creating and Consuming Cookies

Chapter 13: Working with Images in JavaScript

Chapter 14: Using JavaScript with Web Forms

Chapter 15: JavaScript and CSS

Chapter 16: JavaScript Error Handling

Chapter 10
The Document Object Model

After reading this chapter, you'll be able to:

- Use the Document Object Model (DOM) to retrieve elements from a document.

- Create new elements in a document.

- Make changes to elements in a document.

- Remove elements from a document.

The Document Object Model Defined

The Document Object Model provides a way to access and alter the contents of Hypertext Markup Language (HTML) documents. The DOM is a standard defined by the World Wide Web Consortium (W3C). Most Internet browsers implement the DOM in various forms—and with varying degrees of success.

Like many other standards, especially those related to web programming, the DOM has evolved over the years. It has three specifications, known as *levels* in DOM-speak, with a fourth specification on the way.

The DOM is much more powerful than this chapter or even this book can convey, and there's much more to it than I attempt to cover. You can use the DOM for more than just JavaScript programming. This book focuses on how you can use JavaScript to access and manipulate the DOM.

When I refer to the DOM in this chapter (and throughout this book), I emphasize how it relates to the current task rather than to the broader, relevant concepts or what might be possible with the DOM. For example, this book concentrates on how the DOM represents HTML documents as trees. The DOM does so for HTML and Extensible Markup Language (XML) alike, but because this is a book about JavaScript, it's most important that you understand the DOM's relation to HTML.

For more information about the DOM, refer to its specification at the W3C site: http://www.w3.org/DOM/.

> **Note** The examples in this chapter use the inline event handlers such as the onload event attached directly to the <body> tag, and the onclick event handler attached to various HTML tags. Use of inline event handlers is not best practice, and is used here for illustrative purposes only. Chapter 11, "JavaScript Events and the Browser," introduces a better approach for attaching events to HTML. DOM Level 0 is also known

DOM Level 0: The Legacy DOM

DOM Level 0 was implemented before other formal specifications of the DOM. After DOM Level 1 was specified, the previous technology related to document scripting was codified (though not really in any formal way by any standards body) as the legacy DOM Level 0. Today, every major browser supports DOM Level 0 components for downward compatibility. You don't want all those scripts you wrote back in 1998 to break!

The DOM Level 0 concentrated mainly on giving access to form elements, but it also incorporated providing access to links and images. Chapter 14, "Using JavaScript with Web Forms," covers forms and how you access them with the DOM. Rather than spend time on examples of DOM Level 0, I concentrate on DOM Levels 1 and 2, which you're more likely to use when you program in JavaScript.

DOM Levels 1 and 2

The W3C issued Level 1 of the DOM as a specification in 1998. Like the legacy DOM, Level 1 is supported, in various forms, by all the major browsers. Level 2 of the DOM was formally released in 2000. Support of Level 2 DOM varies more widely between browsers. Truthfully, support of all DOM levels varies from browser to browser and from version to version.

Versions of Windows Internet Explorer prior to version 9 claim to support the DOM, but they do so differently from other browsers. As a result, you need to be aware that the DOM feature or function you're using or attempting to use in your JavaScript code might not work in Internet Explorer or might work only in Internet Explorer and nowhere else (and no, that's not acceptable). Windows Internet Explorer Version 9 is a step in the right direction, but you still need to account for compatibility issues between browsers. Where applicable, I point out the places where browsers implement the DOM differently and some workarounds for such events.

The DOM as a Tree

The DOM represents HTML documents in a tree-like structure—or rather, an uprooted tree-like structure—because the root of the tree is on top. For example, consider the simple HTML document shown in Listing 10-1.

LISTING 10-1 A simple HTML document.

```
<html>
<head>
<title>Hello World</title>
</head>
<body>
<p>Here's some text.</p>
<p>Here's more text.</p>
<p>Link to the <a href="http://www.w3.org">W3</a></p>
</body>
</html>
```

Figure 10-1 shows the HTML from Listing 10-1 when viewed in the tree structure of the DOM.

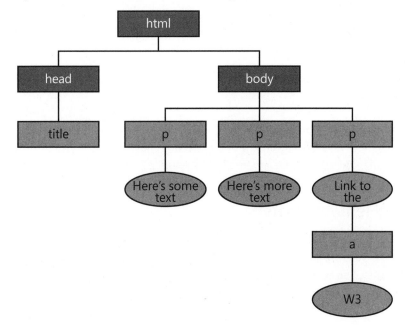

FIGURE 10-1 A simple document represented as a tree structure.

Many HTML elements can have attributes, such as the *href* attribute of the *<a>* element shown in Listing 10-1. You can both retrieve and set these attributes using the DOM, as you will see later in this chapter.

When working with the DOM, you should be aware of the distinction among retrieving elements, setting elements and items related to elements, and removing or deleting elements. The methods for working with DOM elements reflect this distinction.

Working with Nodes

The elements within the tree structure are sometimes referred to as *nodes* or *node objects*. Nodes at the level below a given node are known as *children*. For example, in the structure shown in Figure 10-1, the *body* node has three child nodes, all *p* elements, and one of the *p* elements has a child of its own, an *a* element. The *body* node is said to be a parent of the *p* nodes. Any nodes under a given node are known as *descendants* of that node. The three *p* nodes in Figure 10-1 are known as *siblings* because they're on the same level.

In the same way you use methods to work with elements of the DOM, you use methods to work with nodes that reflect the parent/child and sibling relationships. For example, you can use methods such as *appendChild()*, shown later in this chapter, to add nodes to an existing parent.

Retrieving Elements

Retrieving the elements of a document is an essential way you use the DOM when programming with JavaScript. This section examines two of the primary methods you use to retrieve elements: *getElementById()* and *getElementsByTagName()*.

Retrieving Elements by ID

The *getElementById()* method is a workhorse method of the DOM. It retrieves a specified element of the HTML document and returns a reference to it. To retrieve an element, it must have an *id* attribute. For example, you can modify the HTML from Listing 10-1 to add an *id* attribute to the *a* element, as shown in boldface here:

```
<html>
<head>
<title>Hello World</title>
<body>
<p>Here's some text.</p>
<p>Here's more text.</p>
<p>Link to the <a id="w3link" href="http://www.w3.org">W3</a></p>
</body>
</html>
```

Now that the *a* element has an *id*, you can retrieve it using the *getElementById()* method, as follows:

```
var a1 = document.getElementById("w3link");
```

The reference for the element with the ID *w3link* would be placed inside the JavaScript variable *a1*.

All HTML elements support *id* attributes, which makes them all retrievable by JavaScript. In this example, all the *p* elements get IDs, thus making them retrievable using the *getElementById()* method, too. Take a look at this code:

```
<html>
<head>
<title>Hello World</title>
<body>
<p id="sometext">Here's some text.</p>
<p id="moretext">Here's more text.</p>
<p id="linkp">Link to the <a id="w3link" href="http://www.w3.org">W3</a></p>
</body>
</html>
```

You can retrieve the *<p>* elements in the same way:

```
var p1 = document.getElementById("sometext");
var p2 = document.getElementById("moretext");
var plink = document.getElementById("linkp");
```

But what can you do with those elements after you retrieve them? For elements such as *a*, you can access their attributes by retrieving the value of the *href* attribute, as in this example. You can find this in the companion code in the getelement.htm file.

```
<html>
<head>
    <title>Get By Id</title>
    <script type="text/javascript">
    function checkhref() {
        var a1 = document.getElementById("w3link");
        alert(a1.href);
    }
    </script>
</head>
<body onload="checkhref()">
<p id="sometext">Here's some text.</p>
<p id="moretext">Here's more text.</p>
<p id="linkp">Link to the <a id="w3link" href="http://www.w3.org">W3</a></p>
</body>
</html>
```

The page containing this code displays a dialog box showing the *href* attribute from the *a* element, like the one in Figure 10-2.

FIGURE 10-2 The *href* attribute retrieved with the help of *getElementById()*.

Later in this chapter, you see how to change elements and attributes.

A Note on the *innerHTML* Property

One way to change the text of elements is to use the *innerHTML* property. The *inner HTML* property enables fast and simple access to the text in such elements as a *p* element. This property generally works well—so well, in fact, that although it wasn't well liked in many web programming circles for some time, I find it difficult to skip it entirely in this book. So I won't.

The problem with *innerHTML* is that it wasn't formally defined as a standard by the W3C, so it's not necessarily supported in all browsers in the way that other DOM-specified objects are. However, *innerHTML* will be a part of the HTML 5.0 specification, and with the sometimes unpredictable implementations of the actual DOM specification, *innerHTML* is still desirable. The major browsers support *innerHTML*—and they do so fairly consistently.

Take a look at this example, which you can find in the companion code in the inner html.htm file:

```
<!DOCTYPE HTML PUBLIC "-//W3C//DTD HTML 4.01//EN"
"http://www.w3.org/TR/html4/strict.dtd">
<html>
<head>
    <title>Get By Id</title>
    <script type="text/javascript">
    function changetext() {
        var p1 = document.getElementById("sometext");
        alert(p1.innerHTML);
        p1.innerHTML = "Changed Text";
    }
    </script>
</head>
<body onload="changetext()">
<p id="sometext">Here's some text.</p>
<p id="moretext">Here's more text.</p>
<p id="linkp">Link to the <a id="w3link" href="http://www.w3.org">W3</a></p>
</body>
</html>
```

The *changetext()* function retrieves the element with an ID of *sometext*, and places a reference to it in the variable *p1*, using this code:

```
var p1 = document.getElementById("sometext");
```

Next, it calls the *innerHTML* property, sending the result to an *alert()* dialog box.

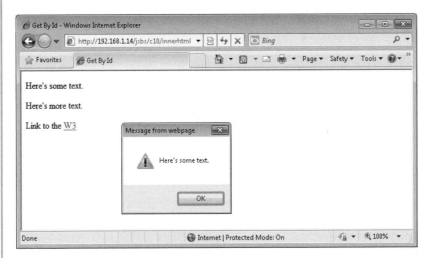

Notice not only the *alert()* dialog box, but also the text of the first line in the back-ground window: When the user clicks OK, the *alert()* dialog box disappears, and the next line of JavaScript executes, using the *innerHTML* property to change the text of the first *p* element to *"Changed Text"*. The result is shown here:

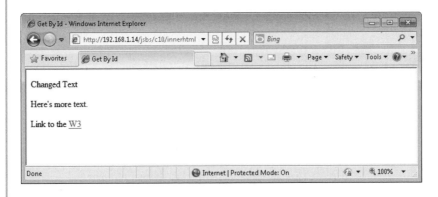

Retrieving by Tag Name

The *getElementById()* method works well when you're retrieving only one or just a few elements, but when you need to retrieve more than one element at a time, you might find the *getElementsByTagName()* method to be more appropriate.

The *getElementsByTagName()* method returns all the elements of the specified tag type in an array or in a list format. For example, to retrieve all the images (*<img>* tags) in a document, you write the following code:

```
var images = document.getElementsByTagName("img");
```

You could then examine the properties of the *img* elements stored in the *images* variable by looping through them.

Here's an example that modifies a table. This code changes the background color of each *td* element within the table when the user clicks the Click To Change Colors link. You can find this code in the companion content, in the file getbytagname.htm:

```
<!DOCTYPE HTML PUBLIC "-//W3C//DTD HTML 4.01//EN"
"http://www.w3.org/TR/html4/strict.dtd">
<html>
<head>
    <title>Tag Name</title>
    <script type="text/javascript">
    function changecolors() {
        var a1 = document.getElementsByTagName("td");

        var a1Length = a1.length;
        for (var i = 0; i < a1Length; i++) {
            a1[i].style.background = "#aaabba";
        }
    }

    </script>
</head>
<body>
<table id="mytable" border="1">
<tr><td id="lefttd0">Left column</td><td id="righttd0">Right column</td></tr>
<tr><td id="lefttd1">Left column</td><td id="righttd1">Right column</td></tr>
<tr><td id="lefttd2">Left column</td><td id="righttd2">Right column</td></tr>
</table>
<a href="#" onclick="return changecolors();">Click to Change Colors</a>
</body>
</html>
```

Figure 10-3 shows how this page looks when viewed in a web browser.

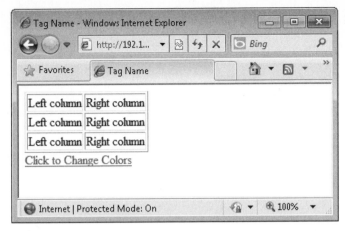

FIGURE 10-3 Using *getElementsByTagName()* to format elements from a table.

Clicking the link causes the table elements to change background color, which you can see in Figure 10-4.

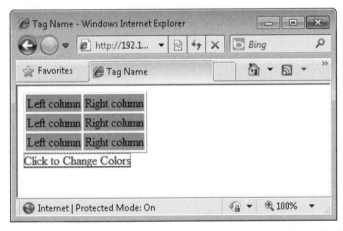

FIGURE 10-4 After a user clicks the link, the table elements change the background color.

Examining the code, you see that the JavaScript in the *<head>* portion of the page creates a function called *changecolors()*:

```
function changecolors() {
```

That function retrieves all the *td* elements by using the *getElementsByTagName()* method, placing them into the *a1* array:

```
var a1 = document.getElementsByTagName("td");
```

The code then enumerates this array using a *for* loop, starting at element *0*, and continuing to the end of the array. It uses the *a1Length* variable, which obtained the length of the *a1* array in the line preceding the *for* loop.

Within the *for* loop, one line of code changes the background style of each element to *#aaabba*, a shade of blue. It's normally better to change the actual style by applying it through CSS (Cascading Style Sheets) than to explicitly change an attribute, as shown in the example. However, until you read about CSS and JavaScript in Chapter 15, "JavaScript and CSS," this approach suffices:

```
for (var i = 0; i < a1Length; i++) {
    a1[i].style.background = "#aaabba";
}
```

The link calls the *changecolors()* function because of an *onclick* event:

```
<a href="#" onclick="return changecolors();">Click to Change Colors</a>
```

 Note The *onclick* event, along with *onload* and other events, are covered in detail in Chapter 11.

One common question concerns how to color or shade every other row within a table. You can do that easily with JavaScript and some CSS, as discussed in Chapter 15.

HTML Collections

A number of objects contain groups of elements from a document. These include:

- *document.anchors*   A group containing all the named *<a>* elements (in other words, those with a *name* attribute assigned to them).
- **document.forms**   A group containing all the *<form>* elements within a document.
- **document.images**   A group containing all the *<img>* elements.
- *document.links*   A group containing all the *<a>* elements that contain an *href* attribute.

Working with Siblings

JavaScript contains methods and properties for working with the parent/child and sibling relationship of an HTML document. For example, the *childNodes* property contains a group of nodes comprising the children of the given element. The group is similar to an array, though it's not a true *Array* type in JavaScript—for example, assume a *<div>* element with an ID of *mydiv* and several *<a>* anchor elements as its children. The following line of code retrieves the first child and places it into the *childOne* variable:

```
var childOne = document.getElementById("mydiv").childNodes[0];
```

Just as the parent node can have one or more children, each child can have a parent node, which you retrieve using its *parentNode* property. You can iterate through the children using the *nextSibling* and *previousSibling* properties. If there are no more siblings, the property returns *null*. For example, the *previousSibling* property returns *null* when used on the first child, and the *nextSibling* property returns *null* when used on the last child.

Finally, the *firstChild* and *lastChild* properties contain the first child (*childNodes[0]*) and last child of a given element, respectively. When an element contains no children, these properties are both *null*.

Working with Attributes

The attributes of elements are both gettable and settable through JavaScript. This section looks at both tasks.

Viewing Attributes

Sometimes, especially when first programming with JavaScript, you might not know what attributes are available for a given element. But you don't have to worry about that, because of a loop that calls the *getAttribute()* method. Here's a generic function that displays all the attributes of a given element:

```
function showattribs(e) {
    var e = document.getElementById("braingialink");
    var elemList = "";
    for (var element in e) {
        var attrib = e.getAttribute(element);
        elemList = elemList + element + ": " + attrib + "\n";
    }
    alert(elemList);
}
```

A little JavaScript with the *getElementById()* method is all you need to invoke this function, as you see in this exercise.

Retrieving element attributes

1. Using Microsoft Visual Studio, Eclipse, or another editor, edit the file showattribs.htm in the Chapter10 sample files folder.

2. Within the page, replace the TODO comment with the following code shown boldface type. (The code is in the showattribs.txt file in the companion content.)

```html
<!DOCTYPE HTML PUBLIC "-//W3C//DTD HTML 4.01//EN"
"http://www.w3.org/TR/html4/strict.dtd">
<html>
<head>
    <title>Show Attribs</title>
    <script type="text/javascript">
    function showattribs(e) {
        var e = document.getElementById("braingialink");
        var elemList = "";
        for (var element in e) {
            var attrib = e.getAttribute(element);
            elemList = elemList + element + ": " + attrib + "\n";
        }
        alert(elemList);
    }
    </script>
</head>
<body>
<a onclick="return showattribs();" href="http://www.braingia.org"
id="braingialink">Steve Suehring's
Web Site</a>
<script type="text/javascript">

</script>
</body>
</html>
```

3. Save the code and view it in a web browser. You see a page like this:

4. Click the link. The JavaScript function executes. The function retrieves the *a* element's attributes and loops through them, appending them to a variable. Finally, that variable displays in an *alert()* dialog box, like the partial one shown here:

Message from webpage

nextSibling: null
onresizeend: null
onrowenter: null
aria-haspopup: null
childNodes: null
ondragleave: null
canHaveHTML: null
onbeforepaste: null
ondragover: null
onbeforecopy: null
aria-disabled: null
onpage: null
recordNumber: null
previousSibling: null
nodeName: null
onbeforeactivate: null
accessKey: null
currentStyle: null
scrollLeft: null
onbeforeeditfocus: null
oncontrolselect: null
aria-hidden: null
onblur: null
hideFocus:
clientHeight: null
style: null
onbeforedeactivate: null
dir: null
aria-expanded: null
onkeydown: null
nodeType: null
ondragstart: null
onscroll: null
onpropertychange: null
ondragenter: null
id: braingialink
aria-level: null
onrowsinserted: null
scopeName: null
lang: null
onmouseup: null
aria-busy: null
oncontextmenu: null
language: null
scrollTop: null
offsetWidth: null
onbeforeupdate: null
onreadystatechange: null

Setting Attributes

You saw how the *getAttribute()* method retrieved the values in an attribute. You also can set attributes using the *setAttribute()* method.

The *setAttribute()* method takes two arguments or parameters: the attribute you want to change and the intended value for that attribute. Here's an example that changes the *href* attribute value, which you can also find in the companion code in the setattrib.htm file:

```
<!DOCTYPE HTML PUBLIC "-//W3C//DTD HTML 4.01//EN"
"http://www.w3.org/TR/html4/strict.dtd">
<html>
<head>
    <title>Set Attrib</title>

</head>
<body>
<a href="http://www.braingia.org" id="braingialink">Steve Suehring's Web Site</a>
<script type="text/javascript">
    var a1 = document.getElementById("braingialink");
    alert(a1.getAttribute("href"));
    a1.setAttribute("href","http://www.microsoft.com");
    alert(a1.getAttribute("href"));
</script>
</body>
</html>
```

When you view this page in a web browser, you see an *alert()* dialog box that displays the current value of the *href* attribute, as shown in Figure 10-5.

FIGURE 10-5 The initial value of the href attribute.

When the dialog box closes, the *setAttribute()* method executes and the *href* attribute changes, as shown in Figure 10-6.

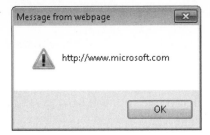

FIGURE 10-6 The new value of the *href* attribute.

The *setAttribute()* method doesn't work consistently in Internet Explorer prior to version 8.0, so a reliable way to set attributes is to use dot notation to access the element's properties. For example, you can set the *href* in the following code in the same way you used it in the previous code example:

```
a1.href = "http://www.braingia.org";
```

If your web application doesn't support earlier versions of Internet Explorer, using the *setAttribute()* and *getAttribute()* methods are preferable. Additionally, you can use the *removeAttribute()* method to remove an attribute entirely from an element. The same caution about support in earlier versions of Internet Explorer applies.

Creating Elements

You aren't limited to interacting with the elements that already exist on a page. You can add elements to a document using the DOM. This section examines some ways to do that.

Adding Text

In its most basic form, the *createElement()* method of the *document* object creates or adds an element to a document. Here's some example code:

```
var newelement = document.createElement("p");
```

The element within the variable *newelement* now has a reference to the new element. To make the element visible, you need to append the element to the document—though usually only after adding text to it. You add an element to a document using the *appendChild()* method, as follows:

```
document.body.appendChild(newelement);
```

But what good is a *p* element if it doesn't have any text? The *appendChild()* element can help there, too, in conjunction with the *createTextNode()* method, as follows:

```
newelement.appendChild(document.createTextNode("Hello World"));
```

You can use the three lines of code you've seen so far at any time after the body of the document has been declared. Here's the code in the context of a webpage. You can find this example in the companion code in the file create.htm:

```
<!DOCTYPE HTML PUBLIC "-//W3C//DTD HTML 4.01//EN"
"http://www.w3.org/TR/html4/strict.dtd">
<html>
<head>
    <title>Create</title>

</head>
<body>
    <script type="text/javascript">
    var newelement = document.createElement("p");
    document.body.appendChild(newelement);
    newelement.appendChild(document.createTextNode("Hello World"));
    </script>
</body>
</html>
```

When viewed in a browser, the result is a simple *p* element containing the text Hello World, as shown in Figure 10-7.

FIGURE 10-7 Using *createElement, createTextNode*, and *appendChild()* to create an element.

Adding an Element and Setting an ID

The previous example showed how to add an element. Usually you want to set some attributes, such as the *ID* for that element, as well. This code expands on the previous example to add an *id* attribute (you can find this code in the companion code in the file createid.htm):

```
<!DOCTYPE HTML PUBLIC "-//W3C//DTD HTML 4.01//EN"
"http://www.w3.org/TR/html4/strict.dtd">
<html>
<head>
    <title>Create</title>

</head>
<body>
    <script type="text/javascript">
    var newelement = document.createElement("p");
    newelement.setAttribute("id","newelement");
    document.body.appendChild(newelement);
    newelement.appendChild(document.createTextNode("Hello World"));
    </script>
</body>
</html>
```

Deleting Elements

You can remove nodes from a document using the *removeChild()* method. Recall the code from the previous section, which added an element. Expanding on that code by adding a few *p* elements simplifies your work with it:

```
<!DOCTYPE HTML PUBLIC "-//W3C//DTD HTML 4.01//EN"
"http://www.w3.org/TR/html4/strict.dtd">
<html>
<head>
    <title>Create</title>

</head>
<body>
    <script type="text/javascript">
    for (var i = 0; i < 3; i++) {
        var element = document.createElement("p");
        element.setAttribute("id","element" + i);
        document.body.appendChild(element);
        element.appendChild(document.createTextNode("Hello World, I'm Element " + i + "."));
    }
    </script>
</body>
</html>
```

When viewed in a web browser, the document creates a page that looks like the one in Figure 10-8.

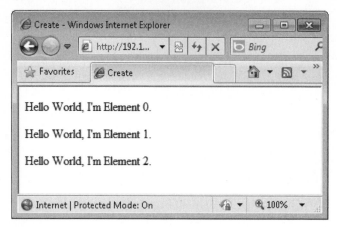

FIGURE 10-8 Creating and adding three elements using a *for* loop and the DOM.

You can add a few lines of code that remove one of the newly created elements. Using *removeChild()* remove any element from your documents, not just elements that you create. The two added lines of code are:

```
var removeel = document.getElementById("element1");
document.body.removeChild(removeel);
```

For this example, add the lines of code right after the code that creates the elements. In practice, you can place the call to *removeChild()* anywhere, as long as the element has already been created. The final code with the new lines shown in boldface type follows. You can find it in the companion code as removeel.htm:

```
<!DOCTYPE HTML PUBLIC "-//W3C//DTD HTML 4.01//EN"
"http://www.w3.org/TR/html4/strict.dtd">
<html>
<head>
    <title>Create</title>

</head>
<body>
    <script type="text/javascript">
    for (var i = 0; i < 3; i++) {
        var element = document.createElement("p");
        element.setAttribute("id","element" + i);
        document.body.appendChild(element);
        element.appendChild(document.createTextNode("Hello World, I'm Element " + i + "."));
    }
    var removeel = document.getElementById("element1");
    document.body.removeChild(removeel);
    </script>
</body>
</html>
```

Figure 10-9 shows the result. The *for* loop still creates three elements, but the code above in bold removes the middle one immediately.

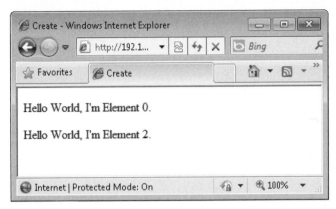

FIGURE 10-9 Using *removeChild()* to remove an element from a document.

Exercises

1. Create a document containing a paragraph of text that you create and append using the DOM. Create a link immediately after this paragraph that links to a site of your choice, also using the DOM. Make sure that all the elements have *id* attributes.

2. Create a document with any elements you like, or use an existing HTML document that contains *id* attributes in its elements. Retrieve two of those elements, make changes to them, and put them back into the document. The type of change you make depends on the type of element you choose. For example, if you choose an *a* element, you might change the *href*; if you choose a *p* element, you might change the text.

3. Create a document by using the DOM that contains a table with at least two columns and two rows. Add some text in the table cells.

Chapter 11
JavaScript Events and the Browser

After reading this chapter, you'll be able to:

- Understand the earlier event model.

- Understand the W3C JavaScript event model.

- Add event handlers to a webpage by using JavaScript.

- Open new windows by using JavaScript.

- Open new tabs in a web browser.

- Create a timer by using JavaScript.

Understanding Window Events

You've seen event handling used a few times in earlier chapters to respond to user actions or document events. To review, the *Window* object's events include *mouseover()* and *mouseout()*, and *load()* and *click()*. These events are fairly well standardized across all browsers, but other events and event handling are not as easy to implement. This section explores events and how you use them in JavaScript programming.

The Event Models

Your first challenge in understanding events is to understand the two distinct models: the model used by Windows Internet Explorer versions prior to 9, and the model defined by the World Wide Web Consortium (W3C). An older model—the earlier Document Object Model 0 (DOM 0)—includes the events you saw throughout earlier chapters. (You learned a little about DOM 0 in Chapter 1, "JavaScript Is More Than You Might Think.") DOM 0 is the most cross-browser compatible model and is supported by all JavaScript-capable browsers. In this discussion, I provide a brief overview of the DOM 0 event model, and then explore the competing W3C and Internet Explorer event models.

Using the DOM 0 Model

The DOM 0 event model is by far the easiest model to use (as you learned in previous chapters), and it is the most compatible one to use for event handling in JavaScript. (As mentioned earlier, it is supported in all major web browsers). So why not just use the DOM 0 event model everywhere? The reason is simple: it lacks the flexibility needed for complex event handling. For example, the DOM 0 model can't handle multiple event actions on the same element. Still, there's nothing wrong with using it for simple scripts, as shown throughout the book so far.

The DOM 0 event model includes several events that multiple Hypertext Markup Language (HTML) tags raise in response to various user actions or state changes. Table 11-1 describes each event.

TABLE 11-1 DOM 0 Events

Event Name	Description
onblur()	The element lost focus (that is, it is not selected by the user).
onchange()	The element has either changed (for example, a user typed into a text field) or lost focus.
onclick()	The mouse clicked an element.
ondblclick()	The mouse double-clicked an element.
onfocus()	The element got focus.
onkeydown()	A keyboard key is pressed (as opposed to released) while the element has focus.
onkeypress()	A keyboard key is pressed while the element has focus.
onkeyup()	A keyboard key is released while the element has focus.
onload()	The element is loaded (a document, a frameset, or an image).
onmousedown()	A mouse button is pressed.
onmousemove()	The mouse is moved.
onmouseout()	The mouse is moved off of or away from an element.
onmouseover()	The mouse is over an element.
onmouseup()	A mouse button is released.
onreset()	The form element is reset, such as when a user presses a form reset button.
onresize()	The window's size is changed.
onselect()	The text of a form element is selected.
onsubmit()	The form is submitted.
onunload()	The document or frameset is unloaded.

Newer Event Models: W3C and Internet Explorer

The W3C codified an event model that allows powerful event handling, and almost all later versions of major browsers support it with the notable exception of Internet Explorer prior to version 9, which uses a different model. Because the standard W3C event model and the earlier Internet Explorer event model differ, you must account for each in any JavaScript that uses either event handling approach rather than only the approach provided by the DOM 0 event model.

Conceptually, the process of event handling is similar in the W3C model and Internet Explorer models. In both models, you register the event first, associating a function with the event.

When a registered event gets triggered, the event's function gets called. However, the location at which the event occurs is one important difference between them.

To understand this difference, imagine a document with a *<body>* element and another element in the body, for example, an *<img>*. If a visitor moves the mouse over the image, should the *onmouseover()* event be handled first within the *<img>*, or within the *<body>*? The two models diverge in determining where the event should be processed.

The W3C model supports two forms for locating where the event should be handled: *Event Capture* and *Event Bubbling*. With *Event Capture*, the search for a handler begins at the top level (the document level) and proceeds downward through the DOM tree to more specific elements. If you used *Event Capture* in the example from the last paragraph, an event would be processed first by the *<body>* element and then by the *<img>* element. Processing occurs in exactly the reverse order for *Event Bubbling*; the element in which the event occurred gets searched for a handler first, and the search proceeds upward from there.

As previously stated, the W3C model—and therefore all browsers that adhere to it (in other words, all browsers except older versions of Internet Explorer)—can use both forms of event handling (you learn about this soon), whereas older versions of Internet Explorer use only *Event Bubbling*. With the W3C model, you register an event using the *addEventListener()* method. With the earlier Internet Explorer model, you use *attachEvent()*for the same purpose. In practical terms, this means that you need to use both methods in every script you write that handles events, choosing at runtime the one appropriate for the browser in which the script is running. The basic structure of the *addEventListener()* method is this:

```
addEventListener(event,function,capture/bubble);
```

The *capture/bubble* parameter is a Boolean value, where *true* indicates that the event should use top-down capturing and *false* indicates that the event should use bubbling. Here's a typical call to the *addEventListener()* method for a Submit button. The call registers the *submit* event, specifying a function named *myFunction()* (which would be defined elsewhere in the code), and uses top-down event capturing:

```
window.addEventListener("submit",myFunction(),true);
```

To register the same event using bubbling, you write this:

```
window.addEventListener("submit",myFunction(),false);
```

The *attachEvent()* method used in the earlier Internet Explorer model doesn't require the third argument, because you don't have to decide whether to use capturing or bubbling; the earlier Internet Explorer model offers only bubbling.

Here's an example of registering the *submit* event in earlier versions of Internet Explorer, associating it with *myFunction()* by calling *attachEvent()*:

```
window.attachEvent("onsubmit",myFunction());
```

You might have noticed a subtle difference in the name of the event to which the event handlers were added—*submit,* as opposed to *onsubmit* in the DOM Level 0 model. Many of the events in the DOM Level 2 changed names. Table 11-2 shows the names of several DOM Level 0 events and their W3C DOM Level 2 counterparts. Note that the DOM 2 events simply remove the word "on" from the event name. (The earlier Internet Explorer model uses the DOM 0 names.)

TABLE 11-2 DOM 0 and DOM Level 2 Events

DOM 0 Event	DOM 2 Event
onblur()	blur
onfocus()	focus
onchange()	change
onmouseover()	mouseover
onmouseout()	mouseout
onmousemove()	mousemove
onmousedown()	mousedown
onmouseup()	mouseup
onclick()	click
ondblclick()	dblclick
onkeydown()	keydown
onkeyup()	keyup
onkeypress()	keypress
onsubmit()	submit
onload()	load
onunload()	unload

Both the W3C and earlier Internet Explorer models include methods to remove event listeners. In the W3C model, the method is called *removeEventListener()* and takes the same three arguments as *addEventListener()*:

```
removeEventListener(event,function,capture/bubble)
```

The earlier Internet Explorer model uses *detachEvent()* for this same purpose:

```
detachEvent(event,function);
```

You might find it necessary to stop event handling from propagating upward or downward after the initial event handler is executed. The W3C model uses the *stopPropagation()* method for this purpose, whereas the earlier Internet Explorer model uses the *cancelBubble* property. I provide an example of this behavior in the "Opening, Closing, and Resizing Windows" section later in this chapter.

A Generic Event Handler

Adding event listeners for each event that you need to handle quickly can become too cumbersome. Instead, use a generic event handler for this purpose so that you can abstract the cross-browser incompatibilities. Listing 11-1 shows a generic event handler. You can find this code in the companion content, in the ehandler.js file in the Chapter11 folder.

LISTING 11-1 A generic event handler.

```javascript
var EHandler = {};
if (document.addEventListener) {
    EHandler.add = function(element, eType, eFunc) {
        if (eType == "load") {
            if (typeof window.onload == "function") {
                var existingOnload = window.onload;
                window.onload = function() {
                    existingOnload();
                    eFunc();
                } //end existing onload handler
            } else {
                window.onload = eFunc;
            }
        } else {
            element.addEventListener(eType, eFunc, false);
        }
    };

    EHandler.remove = function(element, eType, eFunc) {
        element.removeEventListener(eType, eFunc, false);
    };
}
else if (document.attachEvent) {
    EHandler.add = function(element, eType, eFunc) {
        if (eType == "load") {
            if (typeof window.onload == "function") {
                var existingOnload = window.onload;
                window.onload = function() {
                    existingOnload();
                    eFunc();
                } //end existing onload handler
            } else {
                window.onload = eFunc;
            }
        } else {
            element.attachEvent("on" + eType, eFunc);
        }
    };
    EHandler.remove = function(element, eType, eFunc) {
        element.detachEvent("on" + eType, eFunc);
    };
}
```

This generic event handler creates an object called *EHandler* (which stands for *event handler*), which then has two methods added to it, *add()* and *remove()*, both available in the W3C and the earlier Internet Explorer models. The *add* method in each model determines whether the event type is a load event, meaning that the function needs to be executed on page load. If the function does, the *add* handler needs to determine whether any existing *onload* functions are already defined. If they are, the handler must set the *onload* functions to run with the newly defined function.

For the purposes of this chapter and the remainder of the book, I expect you to save this file to an external JavaScript file called ehandler.js, and add the file into any JavaScript files in need of an event handler. As a reminder, you can add an external JavaScript file like this:

```
<script type="text/javascript" src="ehandler.js"></script>
```

Luckily, Windows Internet Explorer 9 uses the W3C compatible model; as that new browser version becomes more popular in the market, *attachEvent* will slowly be replaced. However, sites that support earlier browsers will still need to use the older Microsoft model for years to come.

You can improve on this event handler script so that it is more suitable for situations you might encounter when building more powerful JavaScript applications. (You can find more information about this topic at John Resig's website: *http://ejohn.org/blog/flexible-javascript-events/*.) However, a better solution is to use a JavaScript framework or library, such as jQuery, to abstract the event model even more.

> **More Information** I discuss in more depth jQuery and other JavaScript frameworks beginning with Chapter 19, "A Touch of AJAX." For now, the simple event handler script presented in this section suffices as an example in this book. For more advanced JavaScript programming using events, I recommend you use a library such as jQuery rather than the simple event handler shown here.

The remainder of this chapter applies knowledge you gained about events as well as about the Browser Object Model from Chapter 9, "The Browser Object Model"; the Document Object Model from Chapter 10, "The Document Object Model"; and the syntax from the Part I of the book, "JavaWhat? The Where, Why, and How of JavaScript."

Detecting Visitor Information

JavaScript programming often requires *browser detection*—that is, the detection of which browser a visitor to a website is using. For several years, browser detection was accomplished largely by using the *userAgent* property of the *navigator* object. The *userAgent* property is available through the *navigator* object and shows information about the user's browser. However, relying on the *userAgent* property is no longer recommended, because visitors can so easily forge it. In addition, maintaining accurate *userAgent* information for every version of every browser is incredibly difficult.

I personally use five different browsers of various versions. Maintaining an up-to-date list of which browser supports which feature for just my handful of browsers is even too cumbersome. Imagine what it would be like trying to maintain JavaScript code that accounted for *every* browser and *every* version of that browser! It would be virtually impossible. And that doesn't even take fake (either for malicious or other purposes) *userAgent* strings into account!

So I discuss the *userAgent* property only briefly and then move on to show the newer (and much better) methods for determining whether the JavaScript that you're using will work in the visitor's browser. This section also examines other properties of the *navigator* object that are helpful, if not 100 percent reliable.

A Brief Look at the *userAgent* Property

As mentioned, the *userAgent* string is a property of the *navigator* object. It contains information about the user's browser. To show the *userAgent* information, just type this in your browser:

```
javascript:alert(navigator.userAgent);
```

If you're using Windows Internet Explorer 7, you might see an alert like the one in Figure 11-1.

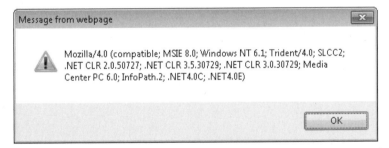

FIGURE 11-1 The *userAgent* property of the *navigator* object.

Other browsers report different information. For example, one version of Firefox reports itself as this:

```
Mozilla/5.0 (Windows; U; Windows NT 6.1; en-US; rv:1.9.2.3) Gecko/20100401 Firefox/3.6.3
```

This string usually changes as each new version of a browser is released. If you tried to track each released version of each browser, and then tried to track which version of each browser supported which feature of JavaScript, you'd be spending a lot of time (and possibly a lot of your employer's or client's time as well) maintaining that list.

A much better way to track what is and is not supported in the visitor's browser is a technique known as feature testing, discussed in the next section.

Feature Testing

Using *feature testing*, sometimes referred to as *object detection*, a JavaScript program attempts to detect whether the browser that is visiting the webpage supports a given feature.

Fortunately, you don't have to test whether *every* function and method you want to use are supported in the visitor's browser. The DOM Level 0 model and other earlier functions of JavaScript are so widely supported, and their cross-browser implementations are so close, that testing for particular features isn't necessary. However, you must still test whether JavaScript is available, because not all browsers support JavaScript, and not all visitors have the JavaScript support option turned on.

The *typeof* operator is the primary mechanism used to implement feature testing. In general terms, you use the operator as follows:

```
if (typeof featureName != "undefined") {
    // Do Something Fun With That Feature
}
```

Try an example. To test for the existence of the *getElementById()* method, which indicates that the browser supports the more advanced DOM interface, you might use this code:

```
if (typeof document.getElementById != "undefined") {
    alert("getelembyid is supported");
} else {
    alert("no getelembyid support");
}
```

You may be tempted to skip the use of *typeof* within the test, and you may see examples on the web where a feature test looks like this:

```
if (document.getElementById) { ... }
```

Unfortunately, this method of feature testing isn't as reliable as the *typeof* test. The problem is that the shorter syntax runs the method. When you omit *typeof*, the method or property being tested might return *0* or *false* by default, which makes the test fail; in other words, it appears that the browser doesn't support that method or property—when it actually does. Therefore, testing using *typeof* is safer and more reliable.

Another way to accomplish this task that looks a bit cleaner is to use the *ternary* operator to set a flag early in the code. Script that runs later on can use a standard *if* conditional to check the flag, as shown here:

```
// test for getElmementById, set getElem to the result
var getElem = (typeof document.getElementById == "function") ? true : false;

// now you can test getElem
if (getElem) {
    // We know getElementById is supported,
    // so let's use it.
}
```

Keeping JavaScript Away from Older Browsers

One of the most discouraging problems you face as a web programmer is dealing with the presence of older browsers. Writing webpages that have any sort of current look and feel and still display reasonably well in older browsers is becoming increasingly difficult. What defines an older browser? Ask three different web designers and you'll probably get three different answers. To me, an older browser is one that is more than three years old, though I lean toward saying two years rather than three.

By this definition, then, Firefox 1.0 is an older browser, even though most webpages display fine, and almost all the JavaScript code you write will probably work perfectly in that version of Firefox. A more general rule is that any version of Internet Explorer or Netscape earlier than version 5 tends to have many, many quirks that web designers must take into account.

Given the depressing fact that browsers even older than Microsoft Internet Explorer 5.0 are sometimes still in use, accepting that your code might fail in these browsers is a good idea. You can try to make your code fail gracefully; however, doing even that may not always be possible. I recently installed a copy of Netscape 3 (which, if I remember correctly, was released in 1997). The browser had trouble with most JavaScript, and also had problems displaying HTML and CSS (Cascading Style Sheets) on basic websites. This was to be expected, because that version of Netscape was released well before many of the standards in use today were codified. The point is that no matter how hard you try, your website is probably never going to fail gracefully in really old versions of browsers. I recommend that you choose a minimum browser level to support—and design for that target, keeping in mind that the later the minimum level, the more visitors you shut out of the site. The goal is to strike a balance between being a welcoming site and being a cutting-edge site.

There are two primary techniques for keeping JavaScript away from older browsers: inserting HTML-style comments into the JavaScript, and using the *<noscript> </noscript>* tags.

To use HTML comments in your JavaScript, you surround them within *<!--* and *-->* marks, as shown in this example:

```
<script type="text/javascript">
<!-- //Begin Comment
var helloelem = document.getElementById("hello");
alert(helloelem.innerHTML);
// End Comment-->
</script>
```

Unfortunately, not every browser obeys these HTML comments, so you still encounter errors sometimes. This style of commenting, or protection, is becoming less and less common. As the old browsers slowly get cycled out, this type of workaround isn't really necessary.

Whatever falls between the *<noscript> </noscript>* tag pairs is displayed only when the page detects no JavaScript support in the browser. Here's an example of *<noscript>*:

```
<noscript>
<p>This Web Page Requires JavaScript</p>
</noscript>
```

When visitors whose browsers don't accept JavaScript visit the webpage, they see whatever falls between the *<noscript> </noscript>* tag pair. In this example, they'd see the text "This Web Page Requires JavaScript." Note that using *<noscript>* doesn't halt execution or parsing of the remainder of the document, so other HTML within the page is displayed, but using it does provide you with a good opportunity to fail gracefully by offering a text-only page or a site map link.

I recommend keeping the use of *<noscript>* to a minimum, and using it only in those applications where JavaScript is an absolute necessity for functionality, rather than in applications where your JavaScript provides only behavioral aspects, such as rollovers. You can easily overuse JavaScript or use it incorrectly, hindering the user experience rather than enhancing it. There's nothing worse than to have visitors come to your site only to have their browsers crash, lock up, or become otherwise unresponsive because of some unnecessary JavaScript widget.

> **Tip** Remember that there are several legitimate reasons that a visitor might not have JavaScript capability, not the least of which is that she or he is using an accessible/assistive browser or text reader. You should strive to allow text capabilities on your site and provide a site map for usability.

Other *navigator* Properties and Methods

Although the *userAgent* string is falling out of favor, the *navigator* object does provide some helpful information that JavaScript programmers can retrieve. Chapter 9 explored the *navigator* object in detail, showing all the *navigator* object's properties as well as how to determine whether Java is enabled in the browser.

> **Note** Use the *navigator* object with caution. Sometimes the results might not be entirely accurate. Worse yet, the *navigator* object might not be available when JavaScript isn't supported on the visitor's browser. For example, relying on *navigator* object properties for the functionality of your page would definitely be a problem!

Opening, Closing, and Resizing Windows

One of the most maligned uses of JavaScript is its ability to open, close, and resize browser windows. The act of opening a browser window in response to or as part of the *onload* event was one of the most frequent and annoying operations that Internet advertisers employed (and still do). Mozilla Firefox, Opera, and others give their users the ability to block all these annoyances by default without sacrificing usability. Windows Internet Explorer 6.0 with Service Pack 2 and later has that capability as well.

I have yet to see an automatic pop-up window that actually enhances the usability of a website without being intrusive. If you believe that your site requires a component that opens a new window, I recommend rethinking the navigation before creating that component. Not only will your visitors thank you because your site has simplified navigation and is more intuitive, but your site will work better because it will rely less on JavaScript, which might be disabled.

Despite those annoying windows, your visitors sometimes might want to open new windows in response to events like a mouse click. For example, clicking a link might open a small side window that allows visitors to choose an option from a menu, or that displays Help text about the various options.

The *window* object contains several methods helpful for opening, closing, and resizing browser windows. The *open* method, as you might guess, is used to open a new browser window. The basic syntax of the *open()* method is this:

```
window.open(url, name, features)
```

The *url* parameter is a string representing the Uniform Resource Locator (URL) to load. If this parameter is left blank, the browser opens a default *about:blank* page. The *name* parameter is a string representing the name of the window to open. If a window with the same name is already open, the URL opens in that named window; otherwise, a new window opens.

The *features* parameter is a string of comma-separated options that represents various features you want the new window to have, such as the window's height and width, and a scrollbar. Table 11-3 lists some of the features available. This list is not comprehensive, because browsers support different features and feature names. See *http://msdn2.microsoft.com /en-us/library/ms536651.aspx* for information about Internet Explorer, and *https://developer .mozilla.org/en/DOM/window.open* for information about Firefox and the Mozilla family.

TABLE 11-3 Some Features Used in the *open()* Method of the *window* Object

Feature	Description
directories	Determines whether the personal toolbar or bookmarks toolbar displays in the new window. User-configurable in Firefox.
height	The height in pixels of the new window.
left	The location in pixels from the left edge of the screen where the new window is to be placed.
location	Determines whether the location bar will be displayed. This is always displayed in Internet Explorer 7 and later and can be changed to always be displayed in Firefox, so this option is slowly becoming obsolete.
menubar	Determines whether the menu bar appears in the new window.
resizable	Determines whether the window is resizable by the visitor. Firefox always allows the window to be resized for accessibility (and just general friendliness, too).
scrollbars	Determines whether scrollbars are displayed.
status	Determines whether the status bar is displayed in the new window. User-configurable in Firefox.
toolbar	Determines whether the toolbar appears in the new window.
top	The location in pixels from the top edge of the screen where the new window is to be placed.
width	The width in pixels of the new window.

Some browsers give users control over whether the options in Table 11-3 have any effect. For example, attempting to hide the location bar from a new window doesn't work in Internet Explorer or in Firefox (depending on how the user has configured Firefox).

The *close()* method of the *window* object has no parameters. To use *close()*, simply call it like this:

```
window.close()
```

This method doesn't always work reliably, so you should never assume that the window was actually closed. At best you can hope it was.

Window Opening Best Practices

Although you can open new windows using little more than the window frame, as shown in Figure 11-2, I recommend against doing so except in exceptional cases.

FIGURE 11-2 A window that does not have the menu bar or many other features users expect in browser windows.

Instead, include in any new open windows the menus, navigational elements, and the address bar. Firefox and increasingly Internet Explorer don't allow JavaScript to disable functionality such as resizing and interface components such as the status bar. Those elements are important for enabling the visitor to use the site and application in a way that works for her based on her needs rather than on the developer's needs. Including those options, and designing your pages and site so that the visitor isn't affected by those user interface elements, is the best approach.

You'll find *window.open()* increasingly unnecessary. With the advent of tabbed browsing, *window.open()* is near the end of its useful life. The next section moves outside the realm of a JavaScript book to show how you can open a new tab without any JavaScript.

Opening Tabs: No JavaScript Necessary?

Actually, you don't need any JavaScript to open a new tab, which is really what most developers are looking for anyway. Instead, you can open a new tab using the *target* attribute of anchor (*<a>*) elements. Using the *target* attribute is preferable, because it won't interfere with the visitor's experience in later browsers such as Firefox and Internet Explorer 7 or later.

Here's an example of the *target* attribute in action:

```
<a target="Microsoft" href="http://www.microsoft.com" id="mslink">Go To Microsoft</a>
```

Another example to open in a new unnamed tab:

```
<a target="_blank" href="http://www.microsoft.com" id="mslink">Go To Microsoft</a>
```

Resizing and Moving Windows

JavaScript also supports resizing the browser window. However, browsers like Firefox include an option to prevent window resizing by JavaScript. For this reason, I strongly recommend against resizing windows using JavaScript, and this book introduces you to the methods and properties for doing so only briefly. For more information about resizing or moving browser windows, refer to *http://support.microsoft.com/kb/287171*.

Chapter 9 included a section titled "Getting Information About the Screen," which showed properties of the window's *screen* object, including *availHeight* and *availWidth*. These properties are sometimes used to assist with changing the size of a browser window. Other helpful properties and methods in the *window* object related to resizing and moving windows are listed in Table 11-4.

TABLE 11-4 Selected Properties and Methods Related to Moving and Resizing Windows

Property/Method	Description
moveBy(x,y)	Move the window by the amount of x and y in pixels.
moveTo(x,y)	Move the window to the coordinates specified by x and y.
resizeBy(x,y)	Resize the window by the amount of x and y in pixels.
resizeTo(x,y)	Resize the window to the size specified by x and y.

Timers

JavaScript includes functions called *timers* that (as you might guess) time events or delay execution of code by a given interval.

Four global functions are involved in JavaScript timers:

- *setTimeout()*
- *clearTimeout()*
- *setInterval()*
- *clearInterval()*

At their most basic, the two timer-related functions for setting the timer—*setTimeout()* and *setInterval()*—expect two arguments: the function to be called or executed, and the interval. With *setTimeout()*, the specified function is called when the timer expires. With *setInterval()*, the specified function is called each time the timer interval has elapsed. The functions return an identifier that you can use to clear or stop the timer with the complementary *clearTimeout()* and *clearInterval()* functions.

Timer-related functions operate in milliseconds rather than in seconds. Keep this in mind when using the functions. There's nothing worse than setting an interval of 1, expecting it to execute every second, only to find that it tries to execute 1,000 times a second.

> **Tip** One second is 1,000 milliseconds.

Listing 11-2 (in the listing11-2.htm file in the companion content) shows an example of the *setTimeout()* function set to show an alert after 3 seconds.

LISTING 11-2 An example of *setTimeout()* .

```
<!DOCTYPE HTML PUBLIC "-//W3C//DTD HTML 4.01//EN"
"http://www.w3.org/TR/html4/strict.dtd">
<html>
<head>
<title>timer</title>
<script type="text/javascript" src="ehandler.js"></script>
</head>
<body id="mainBody">
<p>Hello</p>
<script type="text/javascript">
function sendAlert() {
    alert("Hello");
}
function startTimer() {
    var timerID = window.setTimeout(sendAlert,3000);
}
var mainBody = document.getElementById("mainBody");
EHandler.add(mainBody, "load", function() { startTimer(); });
</script>
</body>
</html>
```

The example in Listing 11-2 includes two functions, *sendAlert()* and *startTimer()*. The *onload* event of the page calls the *startTimer()* function, which has one line that calls the *setTimeout()* function. The *setTimeout()* function in this case calls another function called *sendAlert()* after 3 seconds (3,000 milliseconds).

The *timerID* variable contains an internal resource that points to the *setTimeout()* function call. You could use this *timerID* variable to cancel the timer, like this:

```
cancelTimeout(timerID);
```

The *setTimeout()* function can accept raw JavaScript code rather than a function call; however, using a function call is the recommended approach. Choosing to include raw JavaScript code rather than a function call can result in JavaScript errors in some browsers.

Exercises

1. Create a webpage that contains an *onclick* event handler connected to a link using a DOM 0 inline event. The event handler should display an alert stating "You Clicked Here".

2. Change the webpage created in Exercise 1 to use the newer style of event handling shown in ehandler.js (in the companion content) and connect the same *click/onclick* event to display the alert created in Exercise 1.

3. Create a webpage with a link to *http://www.microsoft.com*. Make that link open in a new tab.

Chapter 12
Creating and Consuming Cookies

After reading this chapter, you'll be able to:

- Understand HTTP cookies.

- Create cookies with JavaScript and send them to the browser.

- Understand how to make a cookie expire in the future.

- Understand how to set the path and domain for a cookie.

- Read cookies from the browser and parse their contents.

Understanding Cookies

Hypertext Transfer Protocol (HTTP) cookies are bits of data that are sent back and forth between a client (usually a browser) and a server. They are used to keep track of everything from the state of an application (such as where you are in the application), to session information, to information about your visit such as your user ID (though there are plenty of reasons why you shouldn't store user IDs or any other personal information in a cookie).

RFC 2965 describes HTTP cookies in some detail—perhaps even more than you want to know for now. You can see the RFC at http://www.rfc-editor.org/cgi-bin/rfcdoctype.pl?loc=RFC&letsgo=2965&type=ftp&file_format=txt.

Cookies and Privacy

Despite all the privacy problems that some may link to cookies, cookies themselves are quite harmless. At best, they reside in random access memory (RAM) only for the length of time that the visitor keeps the browser open. At worst, they sit as text files on the visitor's hard drive.

Cookies don't raise privacy issues except regarding the information stored in them. Yes, it's true that nothing stops a website operator from storing within a cookie data that shouldn't be there, but the website operator could also store that data in other unsafe ways that have nothing to do with cookies. Cookies aren't the problem—the problem is the people who misuse them to store private data. Everything you store in a cookie is only as secure as the computer on which it is stored. So, I would advise you never to store personally identifiable information within a cookie. Keep your visitors' data safe.

A cookie is typically just a text file—that's the easiest and most convenient way to think of it. A cookie can contain several different elements, but at heart it is a set of *name/value* pairs, many of which are set by the site operator or developer and are optional.

When visitors come to my website, *http://www.braingia.org/*, and go to the blog link, they might end up with a cookie on their computer. The contents of the cookie would be something like this:

```
Name: cookie4blog
Content: sess_id02934235
Domain: www.braingia.org
Path: /
Send For: Any type of connection
Expires: Never
```

The browser stores the cookie on the visitor's computer until the cookie expires, which in this case is never. When a repeat visitor returns to a site, the visitor's browser sends the cookie to the server. The server can then tell that the visitor was there before, and the server may use some personalized settings from the cookie to customize the visitor's experience.

One of the features of cookies is that they are sent only to servers on the domain for which they were set. So, the cookie shown in the preceding code is sent by the browser to a server only when the domain that the browser is trying to visit matches *www.braingia.org*. Also, a cookie can have its *secure* flag set (the one in the example does not). If the *secure* flag is set, the cookie can be sent only over a Secure Sockets Layer (SSL)–enabled session, such as over a Hypertext Transfer Protocol Secure (HTTPS) connection.

Note Third-party cookies and the subtle ways someone can work around the domain limitation are beyond the scope of this book.

JavaScript can both create and read cookies. The remainder of this chapter looks at both functions.

Creating Cookies with JavaScript

You can use JavaScript to create cookies by using the *document.cookie* property. This section discusses how to create cookies and send them to the site visitor's browser.

Tip When working with cookies, using simple string values is important. Avoid spaces, punctuation, and other nonalphanumeric characters, because they are not allowed. You can use these illegal characters in cookies, but not in their native form—you must escape them, otherwise, they might cause problems for the cookie, the page, and the browser. Like other problems with JavaScript and web programming in general, these problems might be subtle and generally difficult to troubleshoot. When in doubt, stick to alphanumeric characters.

Looking at a Simple Cookie

A cookie needs a name. This bit of JavaScript creates a cookie and then sends it to the browser:

```
var cookName = "testcookie";
var cookVal = "testvalue";
var myCookie = cookName + "=" + cookVal;
document.cookie = myCookie;
```

When you visit a page with the preceding JavaScript code, the code sets a cookie named *testcookie* in your browser. Assuming that you allow the cookie, the browser stores the cookie's data (*testvalue*) as well as other information about the cookie for future use.

When you set a cookie through JavaScript, the cookie gets appended to the end of any existing cookies. This process will make more sense when you start reading cookies. You should also understand that to specify attributes in a particular cookie, you must concatenate the attribute's *name/value* pair onto the cookie as you build it. The next example helps you to visualize this aspect of working with cookies in JavaScript.

Setting a Cookie's Expiration Date

The example shown earlier created a cookie by building a *name/value* pair, like so:

```
var myCookie = cookName + "=" + cookVal;
```

In essence, the code looks like this (this cookie has only the cookie name and cookie data set):

```
testcookie=testvalue;
```

To add an expiration date, you add an *expires* attribute, so the cookie becomes:

```
testcookie=testvalue; expires=Sat, 12 Mar 2011 17aad:51:50 GMT;
```

Adding an expiration date is just a matter of concatenating the expiration date onto the end of the cookie to be sent. The format of the expiration date is important. To get the date formatted correctly for the cookie, you need a few different JavaScript functions. In the following exercise, you practice creating a cookie with an expiration date.

Prior to beginning the exercise, it's a good idea to enable prompting for cookies in your browser. Doing so makes debugging much easier, because each time a server or some JavaScript code sends a cookie to your browser, you get prompted.

Unfortunately, enabling prompting in Windows Internet Explorer is unreliable, so you need to use Firefox for this exercise. In the Windows version of Firefox, click Tools and then Options (in the Linux version of Firefox, click Edit and then Preferences). In the Options dialog box, click the Privacy icon, and then select Use Custom Settings For History from the drop-down list. Now select Ask Me Every Time from the Keep Until drop-down list, as shown in Figure 12-1.

FIGURE 12-1 Changing cookie settings in Firefox.

 Tip Don't forget to change these settings back to your normal settings when you're finished testing cookie-related issues. The constant prompting can get quite annoying, because of the number of cookies that most websites set.

Adding an expiration date to a cookie

1. Using Microsoft Visual Studio, Eclipse, or another editor, edit the file cookie-expire.htm in the Chapter12 sample files folder in the companion content.

2. Within the webpage, add the code in boldface type, shown here (the code is in cookie-expire.txt, and the completed version in cookie.htm—both in the companion content):

```
<!DOCTYPE HTML PUBLIC "-//W3C//DTD HTML 4.01//EN"
"http://www.w3.org/TR/html4/strict.dtd">
<html>
<head>
```

```
<title>Hello Cookie</title>
<script type="text/javascript">
var cookName = "testcookie";
var cookVal = "testvalue";
var myCookie = cookName + "=" + cookVal;
document.cookie = myCookie;
</script>
</head>
<body>
<p>Hello</p>
</body>
</html>
```

3. Deploy this page to a server and view it in a web browser. You should receive a prompt like this:

Click Deny in Firefox to make sure this cookie does not get saved by the browser. If you accidentally accept the cookie, close your browser and reopen it. Because this was a session cookie, it'll be closed when you close the browser. Congratulations—you've used JavaScript code to send a cookie to the browser!

4. Modify the code to add lines for the date. This code should appear prior to the *myCookie* variable declaration, like this:

```
var date = new Date();
date.setTime(date.getTime()+604800000)
var expireDate = date.toGMTString();
```

5. Modify the *myCookie* variable declaration to include the new expiration elements:

```
var myCookie = cookName + "=" + cookVal + ";expires=" + expireDate;
```

6. The entire code should now look like this (the added lines are shown in boldface type):

```
<!DOCTYPE HTML PUBLIC "-//W3C//DTD HTML 4.01//EN"
"http://www.w3.org/TR/html4/strict.dtd">
<html>
<head>
<title>Hello Cookie</title>
<script type="text/javascript">
var cookName = "testcookie";
var cookVal = "testvalue";
var date = new Date();
date.setTime(date.getTime()+604800000)
var expireDate = date.toGMTString();
var myCookie = cookName + "=" + cookVal + ";expires=" + expireDate;
document.cookie = myCookie;
```

```
</script>
</head>
<body>
<p>Hello</p>
</body>
</html>
```

7. When viewed in a web browser, the JavaScript code on the page sends a cookie to the browser with an expiration date of exactly one week from the time of your visit. The dialog box you see looks like the following screenshot. Click the Show Details button to expand the dialog box so that it looks like this, if necessary:

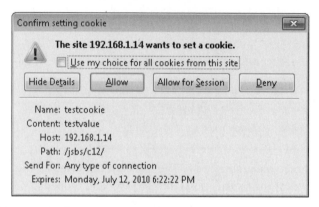

In this exercise, four lines were added or modified to allow the cookie to have an expiration date rather than exist only for the life of the active browser window. The first three lines set the date. The first line creates a new date and places it in the *date* variable. Next, the code sets the date using the *setTime()* method. The parameter for the *setTime()* method is an expression that includes a call to *getTime()*. The *getTime()* method retrieves the current date in milliseconds since 1/1/1970. The value returned by *getTime()* represents the current date, so for the cookie to expire at some point in the future (a week in this case), you calculate the number of seconds in a week (604,800 to be exact) and then multiply that by 1,000 to convert the time to milliseconds. Add the resulting number (604,800,000) to the value returned by *getTime()*. Then, you can convert this number to a Greenwich Mean Time (GMT) string with the help of the *date* object's *toGMTString()* method.

Finally, the code appends the *expires* attribute to the cookie. The final result looks like this:

```
testcookie=testvalue;expires=Mon, 12 Jul 2010 23:22:22 GMT
```

Setting the Cookie Path

In the examples shown so far, on my test machine, the browser sends the cookie to the server when the path for the HTTP request matches */jsbs/c12/*, because the server is where I've been serving the pages from for my environment. This path will probably be different in other cases, such as in your environment or on your test machine. You can change this path by adding another option onto the cookie when it's set. A more common scenario is just to set the path to a forward slash (/) so that the cookie is available for all requests from the originating domain.

Like the *expires* option, setting the path involves appending a *name/value* pair to the cookie.

Here's an example webpage like the ones shown so far in this chapter, which includes the previously added code to specify an expiration date and the new path option (shown in boldface type and in the cookie-path.htm file in the companion content):

```
<!DOCTYPE HTML PUBLIC "-//W3C//DTD HTML 4.01//EN"
"http://www.w3.org/TR/html4/strict.dtd">
<html>
<head>
<title>Hello Cookie</title>
<script type="text/javascript">
var cookName = "testcookie";
var cookVal = "testvalue";
var date = new Date();
date.setTime(date.getTime()+604800000)
var expireDate = date.toGMTString();
var path = ";path=/";
var myCookie = cookName + "=" + cookVal + ";expires=" + expireDate + path;
document.cookie = myCookie;
</script>
</head>
<body>
<p>Hello</p>
</body>
</html>
```

The preceding code added one line for the path functionality and changed the *myCookie* variable definition, adding the new path variable. With this new code, the resulting cookie now looks like this:

```
testcookie=testvalue;expires=Mon, 12 Jul 2010 23:22:22 GMT;path=/
```

View the page that creates this cookie, and you see the cookie dialog box similar to Figure 12-2.

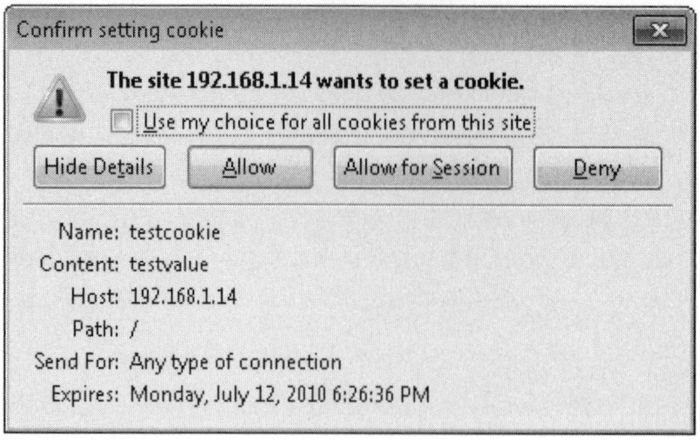

FIGURE 12-2 Setting the path within the cookie.

Setting the Cookie Domain

The examples shown so far haven't set a *domain* attribute; *domain* is by default set to the host and domain for the server that is sending the cookie to the browser (or for the server that sent the JavaScript code responsible for serving the cookie). In these examples, the domain has been *www.braingia.org*. However, many sites (including *braingia.org*) have multiple hosts from which HTTP content is served. For example, there might be an entirely separate server, maybe called *images.braingia.org*, that serves only the images on the pages in *braingia.org*. It would be convenient if you could simply set the domain to *braingia.org* so that the same cookies could be shared across the entire domain.

If you think that setting the domain for the cookie is just like setting the path, you're right. Appending the domain option to the cookie causes the domain to be set to a specific value. Here's an example webpage that integrates the path, expiration date, and now the domain. The new code to specify the domain and append the *domain* attribute to the *myCookie* variable is shown in boldface type (and is located in the cookie-domain.htm file in the companion content):

```
<!DOCTYPE HTML PUBLIC "-//W3C//DTD HTML 4.01//EN"
"http://www.w3.org/TR/html4/strict.dtd">
<html>
<head>
<title>Hello Cookie</title>
<script type="text/javascript">
var cookName = "testcookie";
var cookVal = "testvalue";
var date = new Date();
date.setTime(date.getTime()+604800000)
var expireDate = date.toGMTString();
var path = ";path=/";
var domain = ";domain=braingia.org";
var myCookie = cookName + "=" + cookVal + ";expires=" + expireDate + path + domain;
document.cookie = myCookie;
```

```
</script>
</head>
<body>
<p>Hello</p>
</body>
</html>
```

When you view the page in a browser, the dialog box, shown in Figure 12-3, appears.

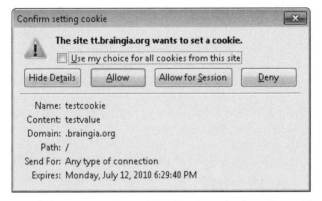

FIGURE 12-3 Setting the cookie's domain so that it can be read from anywhere in the *braingia.org* domain.

> **Tip** Just as you can make the domain less specific (as in this example), you can also make it *more* specific, which allows you to create cookies that might be read only by *images.braingia.org* or by *someotherspecificcomputer.braingia.org*. However, you cannot set a domain outside the domain from which the content is being served. For example, you can't change the domain value to *microsoft.com* for a cookie served from *braingia.org*. The browser will just ignore it.

Working with Secure Cookies

Setting the *secure* flag in a cookie indicates that the cookie will be sent only when the connection uses SSL, such as an HTTPS connection.

The code to add the *secure* flag onto the *myCookie* variable you've used throughout this chapter looks like this:

```
var myCookie = cookName + "=" + cookVal + ";expires=" + expireDate + path + domain +
";secure";
```

When you view this page in a browser, even over an unencrypted HTTP connection, the JavaScript code creates the cookie, as indicated in the dialog box shown in Figure 12-4. Notice that the Send For option value is now *"Encrypted connections only"*, whereas in all the previous screenshots in this chapter, the value was set to *"Any type of connection"*.

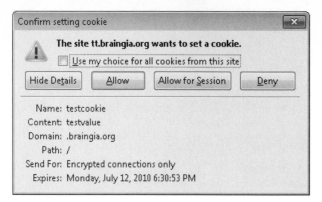

FIGURE 12-4 Setting a cookie's *secure* flag.

At this point, you know everything you need to know about setting cookies with JavaScript. It's finally time to learn how to read cookies with JavaScript.

Reading Cookies with JavaScript

Until now, you've looked at code that sends a cookie to the browser when you visit a webpage. When the browser subsequently visits a page whose domain and path match cookies stored on the client computer, the browser sends any matching cookies to the server along with the request for the webpage. The cookie is available to the JavaScript code in the page when the page is delivered to the browser.

Reading cookies with JavaScript involves taking the cookies from the *document.cookie* object and then splitting them into manageable pieces. A call to the *split* method of *document.cookie* takes care of it, because cookies are delimited by semicolons, similar to the way in which a cookie's attributes are delimited (as described in the previous section of the chapter). Here's an example:

```
var incCookies = document.cookie.split(";");
```

With this bit of JavaScript, all the cookies would be split up, waiting to be accessed. With the help of a *for* loop, you can loop through all the cookies available for the domain to find each cookie's name and data, as follows. (Note that this code does not examine the attributes of each cookie other than the cookie name and cookie data.)

```
<!DOCTYPE HTML PUBLIC "-//W3C//DTD HTML 4.01//EN"
"http://www.w3.org/TR/html4/strict.dtd">
<html>
<head>
<title>Reading Cookie</title>
<script type="text/javascript">
var incCookies = document.cookie.split(";");
var cookLength = incCookies.length;
```

```
for (var c = 0; c < cookLength; c++) {
    alert(incCookies[c]);
}
</script>
</head>
<body>
<p>Hello</p>
</body>
</html>
```

This code (available in readcookie.htm) reads the available cookies for the domain into a variable called *incCookies*. The cookies are split at their semicolon delimiters. For example, I set several cookies for the *braingia.org* domain, both through my normal use of the site and for the examples in this chapter. You can read all the cookies for the domain using the preceding code. Figure 12-5 and Figure 12-6 show two of the alerts.

FIGURE 12-5 The first cookie read by the loop.

FIGURE 12-6 The second cookie read by the loop.

Using the *for* loop, you can split the cookies along the equal sign (=) to further divide the cookie name from the cookie data, as shown in this code:

```
var incCookies = document.cookie.split(";");
var cookLength = incCookies.length
for (var c = 0; c < cookLength; c++) {
    var pairs = incCookies[c].split("=");
    var cookieName = pairs[0];
    var cookieValue = pairs[1];
    alert("Name: " + cookieName + " - " + "Value: " + cookieValue);
}
```

In this code (in the readcookie2.htm file in the companion content), each cookie, *incCookie[c]*, is split at the equal sign (=) and placed into a variable called *pairs*. The first index of the *pairs* variable is the name of the cookie; the second index is its data. Take a look at Figure 12-7 for an example of the output.

FIGURE 12-7 Splitting a *name/value* pair to separate the cookie name and cookie data.

Removing Cookies

There's no built-in method for removing or deleting cookies, either through JavaScript or by any other means. To remove a cookie, simply clear its value and set its expiration date to some time in the past.

A previous example used this code to create and set a cookie:

```
var cookName = "testcookie";
var cookVal = "testvalue";
var date = new Date();
date.setTime(date.getTime()+604800000)
var expireDate = date.toGMTString();
var path = ";path=/";
var domain = ";domain=braingia.org";
var myCookie = cookName + "=" + cookVal + ";expires=" + expireDate + path + domain;
document.cookie = myCookie;
```

You can delete this cookie by setting its expiration date to sometime in the past. Note that the components, such as *name, path,* and *domain,* must match for the cookie to be reset. In effect, you want to overwrite the existing cookie with a new one that expired in the past, as follows:

```
var cookName = "testcookie";
var cookVal = "";
var date = new Date();
date.setTime(date.getTime()-60)
var expireDate = date.toGMTString();
var path = ";path=/";
var domain = ";domain=braingia.org";
var myCookie = cookName + "=" + cookVal + ";expires=" + expireDate + path + domain;
document.cookie = myCookie;
```

This code (in the cookie-delete.htm file in the companion content) causes the *testcookie* data to be set to an empty value and the expiration date to be set in the past.

Note When this JavaScript executes, Firefox deletes the cookie immediately; however, other browsers may keep the cookie until the browser closes.

Exercises

1. Create a webpage that sends a cookie to the browser. Set the expiration date ahead one day. Verify that the JavaScript code sent the cookie to the browser by viewing it as it gets set or after it's been stored on the computer. You could accomplish this second part of the exercise; by using JavaScript or by viewing the cookies on the computer.

2. Create a webpage that sends a cookie with the cookie's expiration date set ahead one week, and set the *secure* flag. This page can be the same one you created for Exercise 1, but be sure to give the cookie a different name so that you've created two separate cookies, one for each exercise. Also, be sure to enable the *secure* flag for the cookie in this exercise, not for the cookie in Exercise 1.

3. Create a webpage that attempts to read the cookie with the *secure* flag set. Did you receive the cookie? If not, what would you need to do to receive it?

4. Create a webpage that reads the cookie you created in Exercise 1. Use a *for* loop and an *if* conditional to display an *alert()* dialog box when the cookie with the correct name is found within the loop. Don't display an *alert()* dialog box for any other cookies.

Chapter 13
Working with Images in JavaScript

After reading this chapter, you'll be able to:

- Understand both new and old methods for creating rollover images using JavaScript.

- Preload images using JavaScript.

- Create a slideshow of images.

- Enhance image maps using JavaScript.

Working with Image Rollovers

The term *image rollover* refers to changing an image when a user moves the mouse over it, to provide visual feedback about the mouse location on the screen. Although this technique has been largely supplanted by cascading style sheets–based solutions, because this is a JavaScript book, I show you only the JavaScript methods for creating rollovers. You can still benefit from learning how JavaScript-based rollovers work, even if you use cascading style sheets to create them.

Rollovers take advantage of certain events that relate to mouse movement on a computer, primarily *mouseover* and *mouseout*.

A Simple Rollover

Placing *mouseover* and *mouseout* event handlers within the *img* tag creates the rollover effect. The handlers display images that differ only slightly from each other. The following HTML creates a rollover effect using the old DOM event handling model:

```
<img id="home" name="img_home" src="box1.png" alt="Home"
mouseover="window.document.img_home.src='box2.png'"
mouseout="window.document.img_home.src='box1.png'">
```

The important parts of this *img* tag are its name (*img_home*); the *mouseover* and *mouseout* events; and code that runs when those events fire. The tag's name allows you to access the image easily through the *window.document* object call, and the *mouseover* and *mouseout* events make the action happen. When viewed in a web browser, the preceding code loads the image called box1.png, as shown in Figure 13-1.

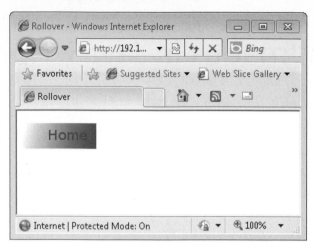

FIGURE 13-1 The initial load of the box1.png graphic through a webpage.

When you move the mouse over the graphic, the *mouseover* event fires, and the following code changes the source of the graphic to box2.png:

```
window.document.img_home.src='box2.png'
```

While the mouse is over the graphic, the image changes to the one shown in Figure 13-2, in which the direction of the gradient is reversed.

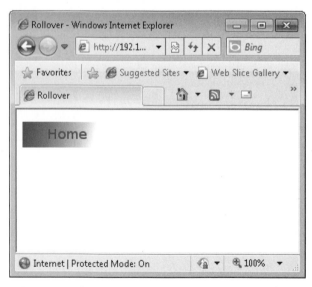

FIGURE 13-2 The graphic changes when the mouse moves over it.

When the mouse moves away from the graphic, the image changes back to box1.png, thanks to the *mouseout* event, which calls this JavaScript:

```
window.document.img_home.src='box1.png'
```

Modern Rollovers

A newer method for creating rollovers with JavaScript is to use the Document Object Model (DOM) and the *onload* event of the *window* object. (The *onload* event of the *window* object was covered in Chapter 11, "JavaScript Events and the Browser.") With the DOM in use, when the page calls the *onload* event, the *onload* handler calls a JavaScript function that populates the *mouseover* and *mouseout* events for all the images in the document.

> ## Using Modern Rollovers
>
> Although I call using the DOM with *onload* "Modern Rollovers," and it does accomplish the goal of unobtrusive scripting, it can be somewhat cumbersome. It can also be slightly less compatible when used across various browsers and platforms.
>
> The pragmatist in me wants to say that using the example that was just shown is acceptable, especially if your webpage has just a few graphics, but I feel like I'm teaching a bad practice if I tell you to use it. Therefore, I leave it up to you to choose which approach works best for you. If you have a lot of graphics that require the rollover effect, you'll find that this second, more current approach, which uses a generic function to handle the rollover events, is easier to maintain.

This page works exactly the same as the example in the preceding section, but uses different code, as shown in Listing 13-1 (see listing13-1.txt in the sample code).

LISTING 13-1 A different approach to rollovers

```
function rollover() {
    var images = document.getElementsByTagName("img");
    var imgLength = images.length;
    for (var i = 0; i < imgLength; i++) {
        images[i].mouseover = mouseOver;
        images[i].mouseout = mouseOut;
    }
}
function mouseOver() {
    this.src = "box2.png";
}

function mouseOut() {
    this.src = "box1.png";
}
```

This code, coupled with an *onload* event handler, creates a simple mouseover effect. By using the *EHandler* event creation object with the code created in Chapter 11 (ehandler.js), you can add the *onload* event to the *<body>* tag. First, include the ehandler.js script:

```
<script type="text/javascript" src="ehandler.js"></script>
```

Next, the *rollover* function gets called in response to the *onload* event. Again, you set this up using the *EHandler* object's *add* method. Add the following code to the end of the HTML:

```
<script type="text/javascript">
var bodyEl = document.getElementsByTagName('body')[0];
EHandler.add(bodyEl,"load",function() { rollover(); });
</script>
```

Even though the functionality is the same as the preceding example, the code in Listing 13-1 is not very portable. (You do some work to improve that soon.) Following is an explanation of the code from Listing 13-1.

The function retrieves all the *<img>* elements using the *getElementsByTagName()* method of the *document* object, and places them into a variable called *images*. Next, the code retrieves the number of elements contained in the *images* variable by using the *length* property, and stores the result in the *imgLength* variable. The code uses the value in *imgLength* to iterate through all the *images*. Within the loop, it sets the *mouseover* and *mouseout* events to their respective functions, called *mouseOver()* and *mouseOut()* in this code.

Up to this point, the code is remarkably portable, though it doesn't reflect best practice. The code gets a bit worse within the *mouseOver* and *mouseOut* event handlers, because the *src* attributes are hard-coded to the file names box1.png and box2.png. This is fine if all you have is one image and its accompanying rollover, as in this example. However, if you have a page full of images, as is more likely the case in the real world, this code breaks. In addition, the *this* keyword is quirky when it is called from another function related to event handling. Therefore, the script needs improving.

This example code does show the basic *theory* of how to implement rollovers. Loop through the images (or retrieve them by ID) and set their *mouseover* and *mouseout* events to specific functions, which in turn should set the *src* attribute to the name of the image to use for that event. Now it's your turn to make the function more portable so that you can use it in the future.

This exercise uses six images (three graphics, each of which has a default and a rollover image), but the code is written to support any number of images. I included the images used in this exercise with the downloadable code for this book, so you don't have to reinvent the wheel just to make this exercise work.

Creating portable rollovers

1. Using Microsoft Visual Studio, Eclipse, or another editor, edit the file rollover.htm in the Chapter13\rollover sample files folder in the companion content. This folder includes six images: home_default.png, home_over.png, about_default.png, about_over.png, blog_default.png, and blog_over.png. The file names containing *default* are the images to display initially; the file names containing *over* are the rollover images.

2. Within the webpage, add the boldface code shown here into rollover.txt (to replace the TODO comments):

```html
<!DOCTYPE HTML PUBLIC "-//W3C//DTD HTML 4.01//EN"
"http://www.w3.org/TR/html4/strict.dtd">
<html>
<head>
<title>Rollover</title>
<script type="text/javascript" src="ehandler.js"></script>
<script type="text/javascript">
function rollover() {
    var images = document.getElementsByTagName("img");
    var imgLength = images.length;
    for (var i = 0; i < imgLength; i++) {
        EHandler.add(images[i],"mouseover", function(i) {
            return function() {
                images[i].src = images[i].id + "_over.png";
            };
        }(i));
        EHandler.add(images[i],"mouseout", function(i) {
            return function() {
                images[i].src = images[i].id + "_default.png";
            };
        }(i));
    }
}
</script>
</head>
<body>
<p><img id="home" name="img_home" src="home_default.png" alt="Home"></p>
<p><img id="blog" name="img_blog" src="blog_default.png" alt="Blog"></p>
<p><img id="about" name="img_about" src="about_default.png" alt="About"></p>
<script type="text/javascript">
var bodyEl = document.getElementsByTagName("body")[0];
EHandler.add(bodyEl,"load", function() { rollover(); });
</script>
</body>
</html>
```

3. View the page in a browser. You should see a page similar to this screenshot. If you run into problems, make sure that each of the images is located in the current directory, because that's where the *<img>* tag is looking for them.

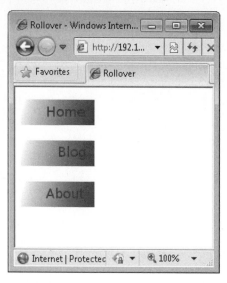

4. Roll the mouse over the buttons one at a time. Each image should change to its corre-
    sponding rollover image. Here's what the screen looks like when the mouse is over the
    Blog graphic:

This example shows a better rollover implementation. Like the previous example, this code
creates a function and then calls it using the *window.onload* event. Also, like the previous example, this code gathers all the images into a variable called *images* and then loops through
each one, adding an *mouseover* and *mouseout* event handler to each, as follows:

```
function rollover() {
    var images = document.getElementsByTagName("img");
    var imgLength = images.length;
    for (var i = 0; i < imgLength; i++) {
        EHandler.add(images[i],"mouseover", function(i) {
            return function() {
                images[i].src = images[i].id + "_over.png";
            };
        }(i));
        EHandler.add(images[i],"mouseout", function(i) {
            return function() {
                images[i].src = images[i].id + "_default.png";
            };
        }(i));
    }
}
```

Again, the example uses the *EHandler* event registration script developed in Chapter 11, calling the *EHandler add()* method to register a *mouseover* and *mouseout* event set for each image. The function used to register events is somewhat complex because of a problem with how Windows Internet Explorer handles the keyword *this* in event handling.

In other browsers such as Firefox, the *this* keyword refers to the actual element where the event fires—in this case, the *img* element. However, Internet Explorer doesn't register an event until it's used, so the element isn't registered during the event registration (inside of the *for* loop). Therefore, the code needs to jump through some hoops to pass a reference to the element for Internet Explorer. In this case, the index *i* is passed into the wrapper function, which then calls its own anonymous function.

This example differs from Listing 13-1 because it removes the definitions of the *mouseOver()* and *mouseOut()* functions. With this example, each image's ID is gathered with a call to *images[i].id* within an anonymous function. That name is then concatenated with the string *"_over.png"* and *"_default.png"* for their respective functions.

Making sure that the file names and the *<img>* tags' *id* attributes match is important. For example, here's one of the *<img>* tags from the example:

```
<p><img id="about" name="img_about" src="about_default.png" alt="About"></p>
```

Because these file names are generated in the *mouseover* and *mouseout* event handlers based on the element IDs, the file names for the About graphic must be about_default.png and about_over.png. Similarly, the image file names must be home_default.png and home_over.png for the Home graphic, and so on.

> **Note** Of course, you could use an entirely different naming convention—the important issue is that the naming convention you use for the rollover graphics files must match what you coded in the JavaScript.

The *rollover()* function shown in the example gathers all the images on the page. For real-world pages, that means there's a good chance that the *images* variable list contains graphics and images that don't have a rollover action. Therefore, a further improvement on this script is to create a conditional to check whether the graphic should be a rollover. One of the simplest solutions is to refine the naming convention for rollover graphics to include the word *rollover* in the *<img>* tag's *id* attribute, like this:

```
<p><img id="rollover_about" name="img_about" src="rollover_about_default.png" alt="About"></p>
```

The new code iteration uses a regular expression through the *match()* method to examine whether the *id* attribute contains the word *rollover*. If it does, the code continues the rollover action; otherwise, it simply returns. Figure 13-3 shows an example page with four images, three of which have rollover behavior.

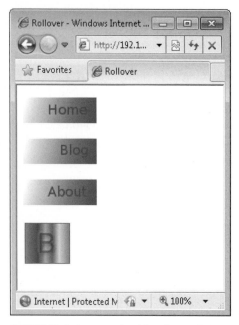

FIGURE 13-3 An example with only certain images being rollovers.

When you move the mouse over any of the top three images on the page, the rollover image loads. However, because the ID of the last image doesn't contain the word *rollover*, it doesn't get a *mouseover* or *mouseout* event handler. Here's the full code (but note that the script still needs a little more improvement before it's done). Note the new names of the image files. (This code is included in the companion content sample files in the \rolloverregexp folder.)

```
<!DOCTYPE HTML PUBLIC "-//W3C//DTD HTML 4.01//EN"
"http://www.w3.org/TR/html4/strict.dtd">
<html>
<head>
<title>Rollover</title>
<script type="text/javascript" src="ehandler.js"></script>
<script type="text/javascript">
function rollover() {
    var images = document.getElementsByTagName("img");
    var imgLength = images.length;
    for (var i = 0; i < imgLength; i++) {
        if (images[i].id.match(/rollover/)) {
            EHandler.add(images[i],"mouseover", function(i) {
                return function() {
                    images[i].src = images[i].id + "_over.png";
                };
            }(i));
            EHandler.add(images[i],"mouseout", function(i) {
                return function() {
                    images[i].src = images[i].id + "_default.png";
                };
            }(i));
        }
    }
}
</script>
</head>
<body>
<p><img id="rollover_home" name="img_home" src="rollover_home_default.png"
alt="Home"></p>
<p><img id="rollover_blog" name="img_blog" src="rollover_blog_default.png"
alt="Blog"></p>
<p><img id="rollover_about" name="img_about" src="rollover_about_default.png"
alt="About"></p>
<p><img id="logo" name="img_logo" src="logo.png" alt="Braingia Logo"></p>
<script type="text/javascript">
var bodyEl = document.getElementsByTagName("body")[0];
EHandler.add(bodyEl,"load", function() { rollover(); });
</script>
</body>
</html>
```

The differences between this code and the earlier code are slight and exist within the *rollover()* function and the *img* elements in the HTML. In the *rollover()* function, a regular expression is built directly within the *match()* method to look for the string *rollover* within the image's *id* attribute. If the string *rollover* appears within the ID, the rollover action is set, just as in the previous examples. If the string isn't found, the *for* loop continues.

Preloading Images

You may have noticed an issue when you first began working with the rollover examples in the previous section. When the rollover image is first loaded, it can take a second to render. This delay occurs because the image has to be loaded through the web server and network before it is displayed in the browser.

This isn't a huge issue; it's more of an annoyance when using the application across a super fast network connection. However, the lag is noticeable in real-world web applications, especially for users who may be running on slow dial-up connections. Luckily, you can preload the images using a little JavaScript. *Preloading* stores the images in the browser's cache, so they are available almost instantly when a visitor moves the mouse over an image.

The basic premise behind preloading an image is to create an *image* object and then call the *src()* method on that object, pointing to the image you'd like to preload. What you do with that object after you call the *src()* method isn't important. JavaScript makes the call to load the image asynchronously, so the rest of the script continues to execute while the image loads in the background.

The asynchronous nature of preloading does have an important implication when you're working with multiple images: you must create a new *image* object for each image that you need to preload. If you have a batch of rollover images, as is often the case, each image needs its own object and *src()* method call.

The final version of the rollover code incorporates preloading. Listing 13-2 shows the rollover script as well as the HTML page for context; the preload elements of the code are shown in boldface. This code is included in the companion content sample files in the rollover \regexp-preload folder.

LISTING 13-2 Preloading and rollovers.

```
<!DOCTYPE HTML PUBLIC "-//W3C//DTD HTML 4.01//EN" "http://www.w3.org/TR/html4/strict.
dtd">
<html>
<head>
<title>Rollover</title>
<script type="text/javascript" src="ehandler.js"></script>
<script type="text/javascript">
function rollover() {
    var images = document.getElementsByTagName("img");
    var imgLength = images.length;
    var preLoad = [];
    for (var i = 0; i < imgLength; i++) {
        if (images[i].id.match(/rollover/)) {
            preLoad[i] = new Image();
            preLoad[i].src = images[i].id + "_over.png";
            EHandler.add(images[i],"mouseover", function(i) {
```

```
                  return function() {
                        images[i].src = images[i].id + "_over.png";
                  };
            }(i));
            EHandler.add(images[i],"mouseout", function(i) {
                  return function() {
                        images[i].src = images[i].id + "_default.png";
                  };
            }(i));
      }
   }
}
</script>
</head>
<body>
<p><img id="rollover_home" name="img_home" src="rollover_home_default.png"
      alt="Home"></p>
<p><img id="rollover_about" name="img_about" src="rollover_about_default.png"
      alt="About"></p>
<p><img id="rollover_blog" name="img_blog" src="rollover_blog_default.png"
      alt="Blog"></p>
<p><img id="logo" name="img_logo" src="logo.png" alt="Braingia Logo"></p>
<script type="text/javascript">
var bodyEl = document.getElementsByTagName("body")[0];
EHandler.add(bodyEl,"load", function() { rollover(); });
</script>
</body>
</html>
```

To review, the code uses the image tag naming convention to construct the image names, so all the same warnings about synchronizing the *id* attributes with your JavaScript code discussed earlier in this chapter apply.

Working with Slideshows

You can use JavaScript to create a "slideshow" effect in which one image is swapped for another in the browser window. For the purposes of this chapter, you build a visitor-controlled slideshow—that is, one in which the visitor controls the image changes by clicking buttons to move forward and backward through them, as opposed to the timed slideshow, in which the application swaps the images automatically after a certain interval.

Creating a Slideshow

You can implement slideshow functionality through JavaScript in several ways. One approach might be to use a *for* loop to iterate through the images, but this section illustrates another, more straightforward slideshow variation.

Most slideshows are rather simple in design, though admittedly I've seen some overly complex ones. Listing 13-3, which I explain, shows the slideshow in its first version, with just forward capability.

LISTING 13-3 A basic (but slightly incomplete) slideshow.

```
<!DOCTYPE HTML PUBLIC "-//W3C//DTD HTML 4.01//EN"
"http://www.w3.org/TR/html4/strict.dtd">
<html>
<head>
<title>Slideshow</title>
<script type="text/javascript" src="ehandler.js"></script>
<script type="text/javascript">
var images = ['home_default.png','about_default.png','blog_default.png','logo.png'];
function nextImage() {
    var img = document.getElementById("slideimage");
    var imgname = img.name.split("_");
    var index = imgname[1];
    if (index == images.length - 1) {
        index = 0;
    } else {
        index++;
    }
    img.src = images[index];
    img.name = "image_" + index;
}

</script>
</head>
<body>
<p><img id="slideimage" name="image_0" src="home_default.png" alt="Home"></p>
<form name="slideform">
<input type="button" id="nextbtn" value="Next">
</form>
<script type="text/javascript">
var nextBtn = document.getElementById("nextbtn");
EHandler.add(nextBtn,"click",function() { nextImage(); });
</script>
</body>
</html>
```

I might as well discuss the HTML portion of this code, because it's short. Here it is:

```
<p><img id="slideimage" name="image_0" src="home_default.png" alt="Home"></p>
<form name="slideform">
<input type="button" id="nextbtn" value="Next">
</form>
```

This HTML code displays an image and sets its ID and name to specific values that will be used later by the JavaScript. Next, it creates a form button that has a value of *Next*. That's all there is to it.

The JavaScript portion of the code first links to the *EHandler* object script developed in Chapter 11:

```
<script type="text/javascript" src="ehandler.js"></script>
```

The heart of the code that moves forward through the slideshow is next:

```
var images = ['home_default.png','about_default.png','blog_default.png','logo.png'];
function nextImage() {
    var img = document.getElementById("slideimage");
    var imgname = img.name.split("_");
    var index = imgname[1];
    if (index == images.length - 1) {
        index = 0;
    } else {
        index++;
    }
    img.src = images[index];
    img.name = "image_" + index;
}
```

The JavaScript creates an array of images.

> **Note** This image array created in the preceding script contains only the file names, so the image files must be located in the same directory as the JavaScript being executed. Otherwise, the image file names within this array will also need to include the appropriate path(s).

Next, a script in the body of the document connects the *nextImage()* function to the *click* event of the Next button by using the *EHandler add()* method:

```
<script type="text/javascript">
var nextBtn = document.getElementById("nextbtn");
EHandler.add(nextBtn,"click",function() { nextImage(); });
</script>
```

At this point, when a user clicks the Next button, the script will call the *nextImage()* function. The *nextImage()* function retrieves the image object from the *<img>* HTML tag, using the *getElementById()* function. Next, it splits the *name* attribute of that image at the underscore character, so the function can obtain the number from the ending characters of the *name* attribute. It stores that number in the *index* variable.

The next portion of the code performs a conditional test that checks whether the *index* value equals the length of the *images* array minus 1. If this condition is true, the user has reached the end of the slideshow, so the script sets the *index* value back to *0* to start over. If the slideshow has not yet reached the end of the available images, the code increments the *index* value by 1.

The final two lines of JavaScript set the *src* attribute to the new image and set its name appropriately so that the next time the code goes through the function, the current index can be determined.

Moving Backward

You might think that adding a button to enable backward traversal through the slideshow should just be a matter of copying and pasting the code you just created, altering it slightly to implement the Previous button's functionality. In most instances, you'd be right. However, consider the special case of trying to go backward from the first image. Contending with that scenario makes using a Previous button a bit more challenging.

This next exercise reuses some of the graphics you've already seen in previous exercises and examples in this chapter. They may make the slideshow rather boring, so feel free to replace them with whatever other images you have handy. I didn't select four images for this example for any special reason, so you're welcome to use more. However, be sure to use at least three images so that you can fully test the backward and forward capabilities of the JavaScript.

Creating a Previous button

1. Using Visual Studio, Eclipse, or another editor, edit the file slideshow.htm in the Chapter13\slideshow sample files folder, which you can find in the companion content.

2. Within that page, replace the TODO comments in slideshow.txt with the boldface code shown here:

```
<!DOCTYPE HTML PUBLIC "-//W3C//DTD HTML 4.01//EN"
"http://www.w3.org/TR/html4/strict.dtd">
<html>
<head>
<title>Slideshow</title>
<script type="text/javascript" src="ehandler.js"></script>
<script type="text/javascript">
var images = ['home_default.png','about_default.png','blog_default.png','logo.png'];
function nextImage() {
    var img = document.getElementById("slideimage");
    var imgname = img.name.split("_");
    var index = imgname[1];
    if (index == images.length - 1) {
        index = 0;
```

```
    } else {
        index++;
    }
    img.src = images[index];
    img.name = "image_" + index;
}
</script>
</head>
<body>
<p><img id="slideimage" name="image_0" src="home_default.png" alt="Home"></p>
<form name="slideform">
<input type="button" id="nextbtn" value="Next">
</form>
<script type="text/javascript">
var nextBtn = document.getElementById("nextbtn");
EHandler.add(nextBtn,"click",function() { nextImage(); });
</script>
</body>
</html>
```

3. View the page in a web browser. You should see a page like this:

4. Click Next to scroll through all the images. Notice that the slideshow wraps back to the first image once the slideshow gets to its end.

5. Now alter the code to add a Previous button (the new code is shown in boldface):

```
<!DOCTYPE HTML PUBLIC "-//W3C//DTD HTML 4.01//EN"
"http://www.w3.org/TR/html4/strict.dtd">
<html>
<head>
<title>Slideshow</title>
<script type="text/javascript" src="ehandler.js"></script>
<script type="text/javascript">
var images = ['home_default.png','about_default.png','blog_default.png','logo.png'];
function nextImage() {
    var img = document.getElementById("slideimage");
    var imgname = img.name.split("_");
```

```
        var index = imgname[1];
        if (index == images.length - 1) {
            index = 0;
        } else {
            index++;
        }
        img.src = images[index];
        img.name = "image_" + index;
    }

    function prevImage() {
        var img = document.getElementById("slideimage");
        var imgname = img.name.split("_");
        var index = imgname[1];
        if (index == 0) {
            index = images.length - 1;
        } else {
            index--;
        }
        img.src = images[index];
        img.name = "image_" + index;
    }


    </script>
    </head>
    <body>
    <p><img id="slideimage" name="image_0" src="home_default.png" alt="Home"></p>
    <form name="slideform">
    <input type="button" id="prevbtn" value="Previous">
    <input type="button" id="nextbtn" value="Next">
    </form>
    <script type="text/javascript">
    var nextBtn = document.getElementById("nextbtn");
    var prevBtn = document.getElementById("prevbtn");
    EHandler.add(nextBtn,"click",function() { nextImage(); });
    EHandler.add(prevBtn,"click",function() { prevImage(); });
    </script>
    </body>
    </html>
```

   6. View the page in a browser again. You see that there's a Previous button.

7. Test the page's functionality by using both buttons in any combination to move backward and forward through the slideshow.

The code for this exercise added a new button within the HTML for the Previous function:

```
<input type="button" id="prevbtn" value="Previous">
```

In addition, the JavaScript added a new function called *prevImage()* to go backward through the images:

```
function prevImage() {
    var img = document.getElementById("slideimage");
    var imgname = img.name.split("_");
    var index = imgname[1];
    if (index == 0) {
        index = images.length - 1;
    } else {
        index--;
    }
    img.src = images[index];
    img.name = "image_" + index;
}
```

The code is strikingly similar to the *nextImage()* function, except for the conditional. If the index is *0*, the slideshow is at the first image, and therefore, the function needs to loop back to the last image. Otherwise, the code moves backward by one index, showing the previous image.

Working with Image Maps

Image maps are images that have particular areas defined to behave in specific ways, such as linking to another document. Image maps are frequently used in maps to pick out the country or region in which the visitor resides. They also are used within menus, though less so with the advent of cascading style sheets.

Unfortunately, I'm not nearly a good enough artist to draw a map of the Earth. Instead, I created a wildly out-of-scale representation of a small piece of the night sky facing north from 44.52 degrees North latitude, -89.58 degrees West longitude, during the summer months. This graphic is included within the sample code for this chapter (in the companion content) and is called nightsky_map_default.gif.

In the illustration shown in Figure 13-4 are four constellations: Ursa Minor, Cepheus, Draco, and Cassiopeia.

FIGURE 13-4 A small piece of the night sky as seen from Stevens Point, Wisconsin.

I made this graphic into an image map so that when visitors click any of the constellations, they're taken to the Wikipedia page about that constellation. The code for this image map is shown in Listing 13-4 (and is included in the sample files in the Chapter 13\nightsky folder in the companion content).

LISTING 13-4 An image map for the night sky graphic.

```
<!DOCTYPE HTML PUBLIC "-//W3C//DTD HTML 4.01//EN"
"http://www.w3.org/TR/html4/strict.dtd">
<html>
<head>
<title>Night Sky</title>
<script type="text/javascript">
</script>
</head>
<body>
<p><img id="nightsky" name="nightsky" src="nightsky_map_default.gif" isMap
useMap="#sky" alt="The Night Sky"></p>
<p><map name="sky">
<area coords="119,180,264,228" alt="Ursa Minor" shape="RECT"
 href="http://en.wikipedia.org/wiki/Ursa_Minor">
<area coords="66,68,193,170" alt="Draco" shape="RECT"
 href="http://en.wikipedia.org/wiki/Draco">
<area coords="36,170,115,246" alt="Draco" shape="RECT"
 href="http://en.wikipedia.org/wiki/Draco">
<area coords="118,249,174,328" alt="Draco" shape="RECT"
 href="http://en.wikipedia.org/wiki/Draco">
<area coords="201,47,298,175" alt="Draco" shape="RECT"
 href="http://en.wikipedia.org/wiki/Cepheus_(constellation)">
<area coords="334,95,389,204" alt="Cassiopeia" shape="RECT"
 href="http://en.wikipedia.org/wiki/Cassiopeia_(constellation)">
</map></p>
</body>
</html>
```

This code creates a simple image map using pixel coordinates that represent small rectangular shapes for each constellation, and three rectangles to account for the constellation Draco's shape and tail. This code alone is functional and creates a working image map, but you can enhance it with JavaScript.

The <area> tag of an image map supports *mouseover* and *mouseout* events. Using these events and some JavaScript, you can improve the usability of the image map. For example, when a visitor moves the mouse over one of the mapped areas, you could load a new image that highlights the constellation. The following code demonstrates using the *mouseover* and *mouseout* events in this manner. Listing 13-5 shows the code (which is also included in the sample files in the Chapter 13\nightsky folder in the companion content).

LISTING 13-5 An image map with JavaScript functionality.

```
<!DOCTYPE HTML PUBLIC "-//W3C//DTD HTML 4.01//EN"
"http://www.w3.org/TR/html4/strict.dtd">
<html>
<head>
<title>Night Sky</title>
<script type="text/javascript" src="ehandler.js"></script>
<script type="text/javascript">
function loadConst() {
    var areas = document.getElementsByTagName("area");
    var areaLength = areas.length;
    for (var i = 0; i < areaLength; i++) {
        EHandler.add(areas[i],"mouseover", function(i) {
                    return function() {
                        document.getElementById("nightsky").src = "nightsky_map_" +
                            areas[i].id + ".gif";
                    };
                }(i));
        EHandler.add(areas[i],"mouseout", function(i) {
                    return function() {
                        document.getElementById("nightsky").src =
                            "nightsky_map_default.gif";
                    };
                }(i));
    }  //end for loop
}  // end function loadConst
</script>
</head>
<body>
<p><img id="nightsky" name="nightsky" src="nightsky_map_default.gif" isMap
useMap="#sky"
alt="The Night Sky"></p>
<p><map name="sky">
<area id="ursaminor" coords="119,180,264,228" alt="Ursa Minor" shape="RECT"
 href="http://en.wikipedia.org/wiki/Ursa_Minor">
<area id="draco" coords="66,68,193,170" alt="Draco" shape="RECT"
 href="http://en.wikipedia.org/wiki/Draco">
<area id="draco" coords="36,170,115,246" alt="Draco" shape="RECT"
 href="http://en.wikipedia.org/wiki/Draco">
<area id="draco" coords="118,249,174,328" alt="Draco" shape="RECT"
 href="http://en.wikipedia.org/wiki/Draco">
<area id="cepheus" coords="201,47,298,175" alt="Draco" shape="RECT"
 href="http://en.wikipedia.org/wiki/Cepheus_(constellation)">
<area id="cassie" coords="334,95,389,204" alt="Cassiopeia" shape="RECT"
 href="http://en.wikipedia.org/wiki/Cassiopeia_(constellation)">
</map></p>
<script type="text/javascript">
var bodyEl = document.getElementsByTagName("body")[0];
EHandler.add(bodyEl,"load", function() { loadConst(); });
</script>
</body>
</html>
```

When you view the page in a web browser, as you move the mouse over each constellation, the constellation's outline appears, as shown in Figure 13-5. The JavaScript that enhances the image map is really just a variation of the rollover code you saw earlier in this chapter, although it retrieves *<area>* elements rather than *<img>* elements:

```
var areas = document.getElementsByTagName("area");
```

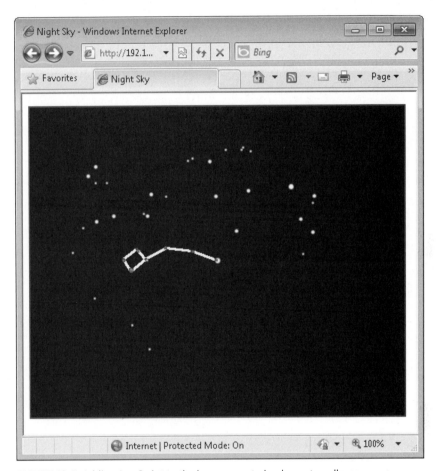

FIGURE 13-5 Adding JavaScript to the image map to implement a rollover.

An obvious improvement to this script would be to preload all the rollover images for the image map. (You do this later in one of the chapter exercises.)

Note The HTML used in this example isn't entirely valid according to the HTML 4.01 standard, because the *<area>* tags for the Draco constellation all use the same *id* value. To make this HTML valid, each tag would need its own *id* value. However, this would complicate the JavaScript because each ID would need to be split or otherwise parsed to make sure that Draco's outline is loaded; otherwise, you'd need to load three different images or find some other workaround.

Exercises

1. Create a preloaded rollover image, making sure to keep the JavaScript functions separate from the HTML.

2. Using the image map example from this chapter (or an image map of your own if you prefer), preload all the images used within the image map so that they don't need to be downloaded when the visitor moves the mouse over the different areas of the map.

Chapter 14
Using JavaScript with Web Forms

After reading this chapter, you'll be able to:

- Understand how to validate the input to a web form using JavaScript.

- Work with radio buttons, select boxes, and check boxes, both to get their values and set their state.

- Provide feedback based on validation, both through an *alert()* dialog box and inline within the document.

- Understand the limitations of JavaScript form validation, and see an example of validation gone wrong.

JavaScript and Web Forms

JavaScript has been used with web forms for a long time—typically, to quickly verify that a user has filled in form fields correctly before sending that form to the server, a process called *client-side validation*. Prior to JavaScript, a browser had to send the form and everything in it to the server to make sure that all the required fields were filled in, a process called *server-side validation*.

> **Important** When using JavaScript, you must perform server-side validation, just in case a user disabled JavaScript or is purposefully doing something malicious.

Remember the *alert()* function you examined in earlier chapters, which was used to illustrate simple examples? It's back. The *alert()* function is used often to provide user feedback during form validation, although newer techniques use the Document Object Model (DOM) to display friendlier feedback.

A webpage with a basic form might look like the one in Figure 14-1.

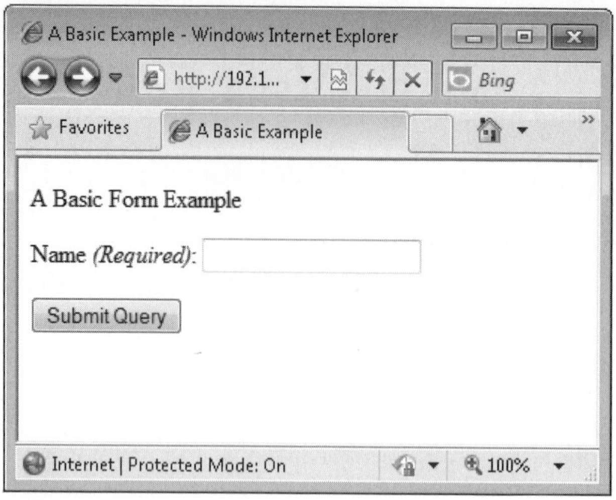

FIGURE 14-1 A basic web form.

When a user submits this form, the JavaScript code in the background checks to make sure that the Name text box was filled in. When filled out correctly, with the name *"Steve"*, for example, the page displays the entered name, as shown in Figure 14-2.

FIGURE 14-2 When the web form is filled out correctly, the Name text box displays a greeting.

If a user fails to enter any data in the Name text box, the script displays an *alert()* dialog box indicating that the field is required, as you can see in Figure 14-3.

FIGURE 14-3 The form displays an alert when the Name text box is empty.

The code that does all this follows. You can find it in the formvalid.htm file in the companion content. The file includes the Hypertext Markup Language (HTML) shown here:

```
<!DOCTYPE HTML PUBLIC "-//W3C//DTD HTML 4.01//EN"
"http://www.w3.org/TR/html4/strict.dtd">
<html>
<head>
<title>A Basic Example</title>
<script type="text/javascript" src="ehandler.js"></script>
<script type="text/javascript">
function formValid(eventObj) {
        if (document.forms[0].textname.value.length == 0) {
            alert("Name is required.");
            if (eventObj.preventDefault) {
                eventObj.preventDefault();
            } else {
                window.event.returnValue = false;
            }
            return false;
        } else {
            alert("Hello " + document.forms[0].textname.value);
            return true;
        }
}
</script>
</head>
<body>
<p>A Basic Form Example</p>
<form action="#">
<p>Name <em>(Required)</em>: <input id="textbox1" name="textname" type="text" /></p>
<p><input id="submitbutton1" type="submit" /></p>
<script type="text/javascript">
var formEl = document.getElementsByTagName("form")[0];
EHandler.add(formEl,"submit", function(eventObj) { formValid(eventObj); } );
</script>
</form>
</body>
</html>
```

The JavaScript within the *<head>* element first links to the event handler script ehandler.js, which was developed in Chapter 11, "JavaScript Events and the Browser." Next, it defines a function called *formValid()* to process the input from the simple form, as shown in this code:

```
function formValid(eventObj) {
        if (document.forms[0].textname.value.length == 0) {
            alert("Name is required.");
            if (eventObj.preventDefault) {
                eventObj.preventDefault();
            } else {
                window.event.returnValue = false;
            }
            return false;
```

```
        } else {
            alert("Hello " + document.forms[0].textname.value);
            return true;
        }
    }
```

Within the *formValid()* function, an *if* conditional test uses the *document.forms[]* array. By examining the first index value (*0*) of that array, the code finds the only form on this webpage. The conditional tests whether the length of the *textname.value* property on the form is *0*. If it is, the script indicates the error using an *alert()* dialog box. If it is not, it displays whatever is in the *textname.value* property.

The return value is important. When the *submit* or *click* event handlers are called and return *false*, the browser halts the form submission process. This is why returning *false* is important when validation fails. Without returning *false*, the default action is to continue and submit the form. You can stop the default action in most browsers by calling the *preventDefault()* method. However, *preventDefault()* is not available in Windows Internet Explorer prior to version 9, so the script executes a conditional test to see first whether the *preventDefault()* method is available. If it is, the script calls *preventDefault()*; otherwise, the script sets the *returnValue* property of the *window.event* object to *false* to account for Internet Explorer.

The next bit of JavaScript, which appears in the *<body>* HTML element, adds the *submit* event to the form by using the *EHandler* event handler script:

```
var formEl = document.getElementsByTagName("form")[0];
EHandler.add(formEl,"submit", function(eventObj) { formValid(eventObj); } );
```

Note that to retrieve the form, the *formValid()* function uses the first index value of the *document.forms[]* list, whereas the *var formEl* definition uses the *getElementsByTagName* method. Both of these approaches work fine when only one form is on the page. You'll also frequently see script that accesses the form through its name, as shown in the next section.

Obtaining Form Data

Before you can provide feedback based on the form data, you have to get access to it. The previous example showed how to access the form data using the *document.forms[]* array and the *getElementsByTagName* function. This section shows a different way to perform the same operation—using the form's *name* property instead of its index.

Like other elements of an HTML page, you can set the *id* attribute for a *form* element. Here's the previous example with an *id* attribute:

```
<form action="#" name="testform">
<p>Name <em>(Required)</em>: <input id="textbox1" name="textname" type="text" /></p>
<p><input id="submitbutton1" type="submit" /></p>
</form>
```

You can then access the form using its *name* rather than its index, as follows:

```
document.forms["testform"]
```

Using *name* is useful, because in some cases, you might not know the index value of the form you want to access, which happens sometimes when server-side or client-side code creates a form dynamically, and you have to figure out (or worse, guess) the index value of the specific form you need within the document. The most consistent way to ensure you can get a reference to the index value is to set the form's *id* and then access it through that *id*. You can also access the form directly in a nonstandard way, through the *document* object, but I wouldn't recommend it:

```
document.testform
```

This direct approach doesn't work consistently across browsers, and it's not that much more effort to type it correctly anyway, like this:

```
document.forms["testform"]
```

Working with Form Information

You can access all individual elements of web forms through the DOM. The exact method for accessing each element differs depending on the type of element. For text boxes and select boxes (also known as *drop-downs*), the *value* property holds the text that a visitor types in or selects. You use a somewhat different approach from *value* to determine the state of radio buttons and check boxes, though, which this section explains.

Working with Select Boxes

A select box holds groups of options. Here's an example of the HTML used to create a select box (which you can find in the selectbox.txt file in the companion content).

```
<form id="starform" action="">
Select A Constellation:
<select name="startype" id="starselect">
<option selected="selected"> </option>
<option value="Aquila">Aquila</option>
<option value="Centaurus">Centaurus</option>
<option value="Canis Major">Canis Major</option>
<option value="Canis Minor">Canis Minor</option>
<option value="Corona Borealis">Corona Borealis</option>
<option value="Crux">Crux</option>
<option value="Cygnus">Cygnus</option>
<option value="Gemini">Gemini</option>
<option value="Lyra">Lyra</option>
<option value="Orion">Orion</option>
<option value="Taurus">Taurus</option>
```

```
<option value="Ursa Major">Ursa Major</option>
<option value="Ursa Minor">Ursa Minor</option>
</select>
</form>
```

This code produces a select box like the one shown in Figure 14-4.

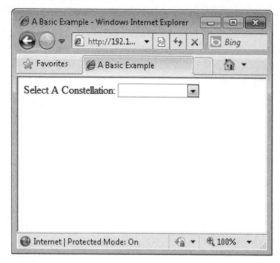

FIGURE 14-4 A select box based on the HTML example.

When a user selects an option, the select box's *value* property is set to the value of the particular option chosen. For this example, the select box named *startype* holds in its *value* property whatever the visitor selects. You can access this property as follows:

```
document.forms["starform"].startype.value
```

For this particular example, you need to connect an event handler to the *change* event of the select box, which you can do with the help of the *EHander* event handler script developed in Chapter 11. The *change* event triggers a function each time the selection in the select box changes, such as when the user selects an option using the drop-down menu. The page attaches the *change* event to the *<select>* box with the help of the code in Listing 14-1, which is added within the *<body>* section of the webpage.

> **Note** Don't forget to add the link to the *EHandler* script in the *<head>* element. See Chapter 11 for more information.

LISTING 14-1 Attaching a *change* event to a *<select>* element using the *EHandler* script from Chapter 11.

```
<script type="text/javascript">
var selEl = document.getElementById("starselect");
EHandler.add(selEl,"change", function() { displayValue();  } );
</script>
```

This code uses the *Ehandler.add()* method to add a function to the *change* event of the *<select>* element, which the code then retrieves through the *<select>* element's ID, *starselect*. In this case, the function added to the *change* event is a user-defined function called *displayValue()*, shown in Listing 14-2.

LISTING 14-2 The function called when the Form's *change* event is fired.

```
function displayValue(){
    var selected = document.forms["starform"].startype.value;
    alert("You selected " + selected);
}
```

This bit of JavaScript simply shows the value selected from the drop-down menu. For example, choosing Ursa Minor from the drop-down menu causes the *alert()* dialog box in Figure 14-5 to be shown.

FIGURE 14-5 Choosing a constellation through a form and then sending an *alert()* dialog box.

 Note The finished code for this example is in the sel.htm file, which is included with the Chapter 14 companion code.

The HTML for the select box includes an *attribute* named *selected*, which indicates which option is shown. The example selects an empty option so that the initial value of the select box is blank:

```
<option selected="selected"> </option>
```

It's also possible to select an option using JavaScript and the DOM. Programmatically selecting options is common on forms that have multiple inputs, where one choice automatically causes other options to be selected.

In the following exercise, you build a web form that a pizza company might use to take orders. The company makes just a few special pizzas: one with vegetables; one with a variety of meats; and one that is Hawaiian style, with ham and pineapple toppings. The company would like a webpage with three buttons to help their pizza makers keep track of the pizza types ordered. The buttons preselect the main topping on the pizza.

Selecting an option with JavaScript

1. Using Microsoft Visual Studio, Eclipse, or another editor, edit the file pizza.htm in the Chapter14 sample files folder (in the companion content).

2. Within the page, add the code shown here in boldface type (this is in pizza.txt in the companion content):

```
<!DOCTYPE HTML PUBLIC "-//W3C//DTD HTML 4.01//EN"
"http://www.w3.org/TR/html4/strict.dtd">
<html>
<head>
    <title>Pizza</title>
    <script type="text/javascript" src="ehandler.js"></script>
    <script type="text/javascript">
    function flip(pizzatype) {
        if (pizzatype.value == "Veggie Special") {
            document.forms["pizzaform"].topping.value = "veggies";
        } else if (pizzatype.value == "Meat Special") {
            document.forms["pizzaform"].topping.value = "meat";
        } else if (pizzatype.value == "Hawaiian") {
            document.forms["pizzaform"].topping.value = "hampineapple";
        }
    }
    </script>
</head>
<body>
<form id="pizzaform" action="#">
<p>
<input id="vegbutton" type="button" name="veggiespecial" value="Veggie Special">
<input id="meatbutton" type="button" name="meatspecial" value="Meat Special">
<input id="hawbutton" type="button" name="hawaiian" value="Hawaiian">
</p>
Main Topping: <select name="topping">
<option value="cheese" selected="selected">Cheese</option>
<option value="veggies">Veggies</option>
<option value="meat">Meat</option>
<option value="hampineapple">Ham & Pineapples</option>
</select>
</form>
<script type="text/javascript">
```

```
var vegEl = document.getElementById("vegbutton");
var meatEl = document.getElementById("meatbutton");
var hawEl = document.getElementById("hawbutton");
EHandler.add(vegEl,"click",function() { flip(vegEl); });
EHandler.add(meatEl,"click",function() { flip(meatEl); });
EHandler.add(hawEl,"click",function() { flip(hawEl); });
</script>
</body>
</html>
```

3. View the page within a web browser. You'll see a page like this:

4. Choose one of the buttons. (Notice that the select box for Main Topping changes accordingly.)

The heart of the example is the *flip()* function:

```
function flip(pizzatype) {
    if (pizzatype.value == "Veggie Special") {
        document.forms["pizzaform"].topping.value = "veggies";
    } else if (pizzatype.value == "Meat Special") {
        document.forms["pizzaform"].topping.value = "meat";
    } else if (pizzatype.value == "Hawaiian") {
        document.forms["pizzaform"].topping.value = "hampineapple";
    }
}
```

This function examines the value of the *pizzatype* variable that gets passed into the function, and then, using the conditional, changes the value of the select box called *topping* accordingly.

Again, the script in the *<head>* portion of the page links to the EHandler event handler script, and uses its *EHandler.add* method to attach *click* events to the buttons, in the same way the code you've seen throughout this and the previous three chapters does.

```
var vegEl = document.getElementById("vegbutton");
var meatEl = document.getElementById("meatbutton");
var hawEl = document.getElementById("hawbutton");
```

```
EHandler.add(vegEl,"click",function() { flip(vegEl); });
EHandler.add(meatEl,"click",function() { flip(meatEl); });
EHandler.add(hawEl,"click",function() { flip(hawEl); });
```

This example showed how to obtain information from a form and how to set information within a form. Although the form doesn't look like much, and the pizza company isn't making many pizzas right now, it's growing because of the popularity of its pizzas. Future examples in this chapter expand on this form.

Working with Check Boxes

The previous example showed select boxes, and you saw text boxes used earlier in this chapter, too. Another type of box—a check box—allows users to select multiple items. The pizza-ordering scenario introduced in the previous section serves as a good example for illustrating the check box.

Recall that in the initial pizza ordering system, when the pizza order taker selected one of three pizza types, the *"Main Topping"* select box changed to reflect the main ingredient of the pizza. However, allowing more flexibility, such as more pizza types, would be nice.

Figure 14-6 shows a new pizza prep form. The order taker can now select from a variety of ingredients, in any combination.

FIGURE 14-6 Changing the order prep form to include check boxes.

Selecting the various ingredients and clicking the Prep Pizza button displays the selected pizza toppings on the screen, as shown in Figure 14-7.

FIGURE 14-7 Ordering a pizza through the new form and adding elements by using the DOM.

The code for this functionality is shown in Listing 14-3 (listing14-3.htm in the companion content).

LISTING 14-3 Using check boxes with the order form.

```
<!DOCTYPE HTML PUBLIC "-//W3C//DTD HTML 4.01//EN"
"http://www.w3.org/TR/html4/strict.dtd">
<html>
<head>
    <title>Pizza</title>
    <script type="text/javascript" src="ehandler.js"></script>
    <script type="text/javascript">
    function prepza() {
        var checkboxes = document.forms["pizzaform"].toppingcheck.length;
        var newelement = document.createElement("p");
        newelement.setAttribute("id","orderheading");
        document.body.appendChild(newelement);
        newelement.appendChild(document.createTextNode("This pizza will have:"));

        for (var i = 0; i < checkboxes; i++) {
            if (document.forms["pizzaform"].toppingcheck[i].checked) {
```

```
                    var newelement = document.createElement("p");
                    newelement.setAttribute("id","newelement" + i);
                    document.body.appendChild(newelement);
                    newelement.appendChild(document.createTextNode(
                            document.forms["pizzaform"].toppingcheck[i].value));
                }
            }
        }
    </script>
</head>
<body>
<form id="pizzaform" action="#">
<p>Toppings:</p>
<input type="checkbox" id="topping1" value="Sausage"
    name="toppingcheck">Sausage<br>
<input type="checkbox" id="topping2" value="Pepperoni"
    name="toppingcheck">Pepperoni<br>
<input type="checkbox" id="topping3" value="Ham"
    name="toppingcheck">Ham<br>
<input type="checkbox" id="topping4" value="Green Peppers"
    name="toppingcheck">Green Peppers<br>
<input type="checkbox" id="topping5" value="Mushrooms"
    name="toppingcheck">Mushrooms<br>
<input type="checkbox" id="topping6" value="Onions"
    name="toppingcheck">Onions<br>
<input type="checkbox" id="topping7" value="Pineapple"
    name="toppingcheck">Pineapple<br>

<p><input type="button" id="prepBtn" name="prepBtn" value="Prep Pizza"></p>
</form>
<script type="text/javascript">
var prepBtn = document.getElementById("prepBtn");
EHandler.add(prepBtn,"click",function() { prepza(); });
</script>
</body>
</html>
```

The heart of the page is the function *prepza()*, which starts by gathering the number of check boxes contained within the form *pizzaform*. These are grouped together using the *name* attribute *toppingcheck*, as follows:

```
var checkboxes = document.forms["pizzaform"].toppingcheck.length;
```

After setting up a *<p>* element with a heading, the script uses a *for* loop to walk through the check boxes. Each check box is examined to see whether its *checked* property is set:

```
if (document.forms["pizzaform"].toppingcheck[i].checked) {
```

If the check box's *checked* property has indeed been set, the script creates a new *<p>* element and places it into the document. The result is the page you saw back in Figure 14-7. (You saw examples of how to create and append elements in Chapter 10, "The Document Object Model.")

Keep this example in mind, because one of the exercises at the end of the chapter asks you to combine it with functionality that automatically selects toppings when a user presses a button, as in the select box example you saw earlier.

The Prep Pizza button has a click event attached to it using the *EHandler.add()* method from Chapter 11.

Working with Radio Buttons

Radio buttons also create a group of options, but unlike check boxes, only one radio button from the group can be selected at any given time. In the context of the pizza restaurant example, visitors might use a radio button to select the type of crust for the pizza—thin, deep dish, or regular. Because a pizza can have only one kind of crust, using radio buttons for this selection type makes sense. Adding radio buttons to select a crust type results in a page like that shown in Figure 14-8.

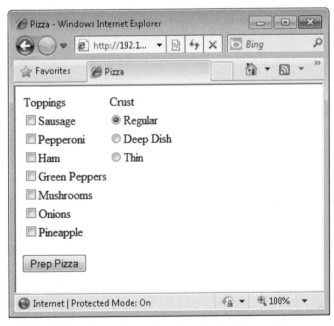

FIGURE 14-8 Adding radio buttons for selecting the crust type.

The HTML that adds these radio buttons and a simple table to hold them looks like this (also in the file radiobuttonhtml.txt in the companion content):

```
<table>
<tr><td>Toppings</td><td>Crust</td></tr>
<tr>
  <td><input type="checkbox" id="topping1" value="Sausage"
    name="toppingcheck">Sausage</td>
  <td><input type="radio" name="crust" value="Regular"
    checked="checked" id="radio1">Regular</td>
</tr>
<tr>
  <td><input type="checkbox" id="topping2" value="Pepperoni"
    name="toppingcheck">Pepperoni</td>
  <td><input type="radio" name="crust" value="Deep Dish"
    id="radio2" />Deep Dish</td>
</tr>
<tr>
  <td><input type="checkbox" id="topping3" value="Ham"
    name="toppingcheck">Ham</td>
  <td><input type="radio" name="crust" value="Thin" id="radio3">Thin</td>
</tr>
<tr>
  <td><input type="checkbox" id="topping4" value="Green Peppers"
    name="toppingcheck">Green Peppers</td>
  <td></td>
</tr>
<tr>
  <td><input type="checkbox" id="topping5" value="Mushrooms"
    name="toppingcheck">Mushrooms</td>
  <td></td>
</tr>
<tr>
  <td><input type="checkbox" id="topping6" value="Onions"
    name="toppingcheck">Onions</td>
  <td></td>
</tr>
<tr>
  <td><input type="checkbox" id="topping7" value="Pineapple"
    name="toppingcheck">Pineapple</td>
  <td></td>
</tr>
</table>
```

The code that processes the radio buttons is similar to the code you saw that processed the check boxes. The main difference is that radio buttons all share the same name and logical grouping, meaning that they are grouped together and only one can be checked at a time. The code for processing the radio buttons is added to the *prepza()* function, like this (in the radiobuttonjs.txt file in the companion content):

```
var crusttype = document.forms["pizzaform"].crust;
var crustlength = crusttype.length;
for (var c = 0; c < crustlength; c++) {
    if (crusttype[c].checked) {
        var newelement = document.createElement("p");
        newelement.setAttribute("id","crustelement" + i);
        document.body.appendChild(newelement);
        newelement.appendChild(document.createTextNode(crusttype[c].value + " Crust"));
    }
}
```

Prevalidating Form Data

JavaScript is frequently used to validate that a given form field is filled in correctly. You saw an example of this behavior earlier in this chapter, when a form asked you to fill in a name. If you didn't put anything in the field, an error alert appeared. JavaScript is good at prevalidating data to make sure that it resembles valid input. However, JavaScript is poor at actually validating the data that makes it to your server.

You should never, at any time, assume that what gets to the server is valid. I can't count the number of web developers whom I've heard say, "We have a JavaScript validation on the data, so we don't need to check it on the server." This assumption couldn't be further from the truth. People can and do have JavaScript disabled in their browsers; and people also can send POST-formatted and GET-formatted data to the server-side program without having to follow the navigation dictated by the browser interface. No matter how many client-side tricks you employ, they're just that—tricks. Someone will find a way around them.

The bottom line is that you can and should use JavaScript for prevalidation. Prevalidation is a small sanity check that may be helpful for providing quick feedback to users when your code notices something blatantly wrong with the input. But you *must* perform the actual validation of all input on the server side, after users have submitted their input completely.

This section looks at some ways to use JavaScript for prevalidation, but to frame that discussion, I first illustrate the dangers of using JavaScript as the sole validator for your site.

Hacking JavaScript Validation

This section uses a server-side program to create a catalog order system that has three simple elements: a product, a quantity, and a price. The items to be sold are blades of grass from my lawn. My area has had an extremely dry summer, so there's not much lawn left at this point—lots of weeds and sand, but not much of what I would call proper lawn. Because blades of grass from my lawn are so rare, orders are limited to three blades per household, and the price is high. I limit the order quantity by using some JavaScript code.

I created a page to sell the blades of grass. When viewed in a browser, the page looks like Figure 14-9.

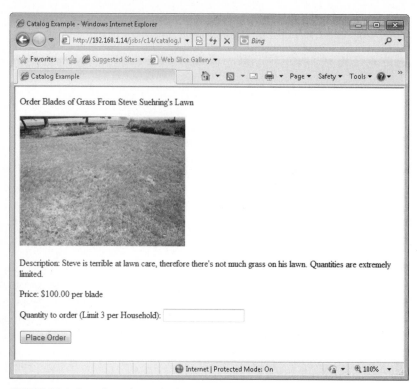

FIGURE 14-9 A small catalog order form.

Here's the HTML and JavaScript to produce the page (also present in the validate.htm sample file, in the companion content). Note the use of *document.forms* (shown in boldface type) to access the quantity filled in within the form. Note also that you won't be able to submit the form because the form action, catalog.php, doesn't actually exist. The action of the form isn't that important to this example.

```
<!DOCTYPE HTML PUBLIC "-//W3C//DTD HTML 4.01//EN"
"http://www.w3.org/TR/html4/strict.dtd">
<html>
<head>
<title>Catalog Example</title>
<script type="text/javascript" src="ehandler.js"></script>
<script type="text/javascript">
    function formValid(eventObj) {
        if (document.forms["catalogform"]["quantity"].value > 3) {
            alert("Limit 3 per Household.");
            if (eventObj.preventDefault) {
                eventObj.preventDefault();
            } else {
                window.event.returnValue = false;
            }
```

```
                return false;
        } else {
                return true;
        }
    }
</script>
</head>
<body>
<form name="catalogform" id="catalogform" action="catalog.php" method="POST">
<p>Order Blades of Grass From Steve Suehring's Lawn</p>
<div id="lawndiv"><img alt="steve suehring's lawn is dead" src="lawn.png"
id="lawnpic"><br></div>
<p>Description: Steve is terrible at lawn care, therefore there's not much
   grass on his lawn.  Quantities are extremely limited.</p>
<p>Price:  $100.00 per blade</p>
<p>Quantity to order (Limit 3 per Household): <input type="text" name="quantity"></p>
<p><input type="submit" value="Place Order"></p>
</form>
<script type="text/javascript">
var formEl = document.getElementsByTagName("form")[0];
EHandler.add(formEl,"submit", function(eventObj) { formValid(eventObj); } );
</script>
</body>
</html>
```

Note One improvement you could make to this validation would be to ensure that the visitor doesn't try to order fewer than one blade of grass, either!

With JavaScript enabled in my browser, the user's attempt to order a quantity of three or fewer blades of grass is acceptable, so the form gets submitted to the server-side script, which handles the request and returns an order total, shown in Figure 14-10.

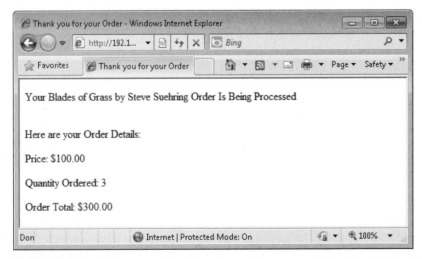

FIGURE 14-10 Ordering a quantity of three blades of grass or fewer gives the expected results, including an order total.

If the user goes back to the page, still with JavaScript enabled, and attempts to order a quantity of four blades of grass, he or she sees an *alert()* dialog box, like the one shown in Figure 14-11.

FIGURE 14-11 An error occurs through JavaScript when I attempt to order more than three blades.

So far, so good. Now imagine that I disabled JavaScript in my browser. There's no noticeable change in the page when I go to the order form, so the page looks exactly like the one in Figure 14-9. However, I'm now able to order a quantity of 1500. Simply entering 1500 into the quantity and clicking Place Order results in the server-side web form happily receiving and processing the order, as shown in Figure 14-12.

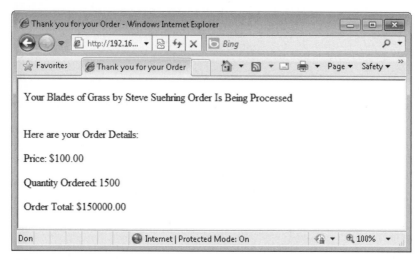

FIGURE 14-12 Because JavaScript is disabled, nothing validated this order before it hit the server.

Because no validation existed on the server side, this input was perfectly valid, and the order could be processed. The only problem is that I don't have 1500 blades of grass on my lawn (I counted), so I can't possibly fulfill this order.

You might be tempted to dismiss this scenario as contrived, but it represents an all-too-common occurrence in web applications. In fact, this example is relatively tame compared to some situations in which a site actually lets a visitor change the price of an item during the ordering process and never bothers to validate that input—because "no one will ever do that." Well, people have done that before, and they will again—if you don't stop them.

You might be tempted to try to solve the problem by requiring that all visitors have JavaScript enabled in their browsers before they can place an order—but that doesn't work. You can attempt to figure out if JavaScript is enabled, but you can never be 100 percent certain.

The only correct way to solve this issue is to validate, and enforce valid rules on the server side. The back-end script should check the business rule of the quantity limitation. Doing this won't be a problem the vast majority of the time, but it takes only that one time—and then I'd be outside trying to dig up 1500 blades of grass for my customers.

This section showed how easy it is to bypass JavaScript validation by simply turning off JavaScript in the browser. The next section shows you how to use JavaScript for prevalidation. JavaScript should be used only for prevalidation and never as the sole means of ensuring that input is valid.

Validating a Text Field

Back in the beginning of this chapter, you saw one example of how to validate a text field. If the field wasn't filled in, an *alert()* dialog box appeared. In this section, you see how to provide feedback inline, next to the form field, rather than use an *alert()* dialog box.

Here's the code to achieve this (you can find this code in the sample file catalog.htm in the companion content):

```
<!DOCTYPE HTML PUBLIC "-//W3C//DTD HTML 4.01//EN"
"http://www.w3.org/TR/html4/strict.dtd">
<html>
<head>
<title>Catalog Example</title>
<script type="text/javascript" src="ehandler.js"></script>
<script type="text/javascript">
    function formValid(eventObj) {
        if (document.forms["catalogform"]["quantity"].value > 3) {
            var submitbtn = document.forms["catalogform"]["submitbutton"];
            var quantityp = document.getElementById("quantityp");
            var errorel = document.createElement("span");
            errorel.appendChild(document.createTextNode(" Limit 3 per Household"));
            quantityp.appendChild(errorel);
            if (eventObj.preventDefault) {
                eventObj.preventDefault();
            } else {
                window.event.returnValue = false;
            }
            return false;
```

```
            } else {
                return true;
            }
        }
</script>
</head>
<body>
<form name="catalogform" id="catalogform" action="catalog.php" method="POST">
<p>Order Blades of Grass From Steve Suehring's Lawn</p>
<div id="lawndiv"><img alt="steve suehring's lawn is dead" src="lawn.png"
id="lawnpic"><br/></div>
<p>Description: Steve is terrible at lawn care, therefore there's not much
    grass on his lawn.  Quantities are extremely limited.</p>
<p>Price:  $100.00 per blade</p>
<p id="quantityp">Quantity to order (Limit 3 per Household): <input type="text"
    name="quantity"></p>
<p id="submitp"><input id="submitbutton" type="submit" value="Place Order"></p>
</form>
<script type="text/javascript">
var formEl = document.getElementsByTagName("form")[0];
EHandler.add(formEl,"submit", function(eventObj) { formValid(eventObj); } );
</script>
</body>
</html>
```

> **Tip** It's worth noting that the JavaScript validation in these last examples uses the *submit* event
> to trigger validation. The *submit* event of the entire form is preferred over the *click* event of the
> Submit button, because the form's *submit* event fires regardless of whether the visitor clicks the
> Submit button or presses the Enter key on the keyboard. Welcome to JavaScript programming!

Basically, this code doesn't do anything that you haven't already seen done. The code just
checks whether the form is valid. If the form is not valid, the code creates and appends an
HTML span element with the text *"Limit 3 per Household"*, as shown in Figure 14-13, rather
than shows an *alert()* dialog box.

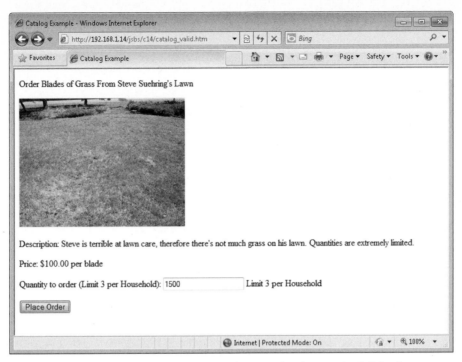

FIGURE 14-13 Providing inline feedback on a webpage rather than an *alert()* dialog box.

Exercises

1. Create a web form that displays an *alert()* dialog box based on a select box input type.

2. Add a set of radio buttons to the pizza form exercise seen earlier in this chapter to accept three pizza sizes: small, medium, and large. Display the results along with the result of the pizza order.

3. Redesign the pizza order system to add the buttons from the original pizza example, enabling the order taker to select the Veggie Special, Meat Special, or Hawaiian pizza types. These buttons should then select the correct topping check boxes for the particular type of pizza to be made. For the Veggie Special pizza, select Green Peppers, Mushrooms, and Onions. For the Meat Special pizza, select Sausage, Pepperoni, and Ham; and for the Hawaiian pizza, select Pineapple and Ham.

Chapter 15
JavaScript and CSS

After reading this chapter, you'll be able to:

- Understand the basics of Cascading Style Sheets (CSS).
- Understand the relationship between JavaScript and CSS.
- Use JavaScript to change the style of an individual element.
- Use JavaScript to change the style of a group of elements.
- Use JavaScript to provide visual feedback on a web form using CSS.

What Is CSS?

Using CSS, you can specify the look and feel of a webpage: You can apply color, fonts, and layout to the elements of a page.

Figure 15-1 shows a basic webpage. It's fairly boring—or at least the layout is.

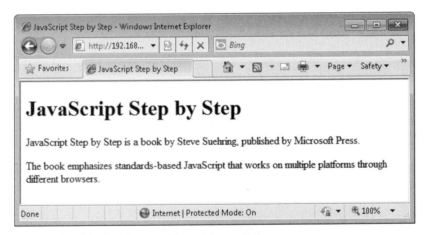

FIGURE 15-1 A basic webpage with no styles applied.

By using CSS, you can add styling that improves the look of the page in Figure 15-1 without altering the page's content, for example, change the font for the heading and emphasize a particular portion of the page using some boldface text markup, as shown in Figure 15-2.

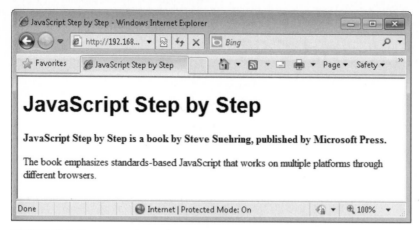

FIGURE 15-2 The same webpage from Figure 15-1 with CSS styles applied to it.

Using Properties and Selectors

The basic structure for CSS is to list a CSS ofproperty name followed by a colon, and then that property's value, for example:

```
property: value
```

The *style* property is one of many different properties you can set. In Figure 15-2, for example, the *font-weight* style property changed to boldface for the second line. You can find a full list of properties and their acceptable values on the World Wide Web Consortium (W3C) website at *http://www.w3.org/TR/CSS21/propidx.html*.

You can apply CSS style properties to a group of document elements based on the element type (*<p>*, *<h1>*, *<a>*, and so on), or to individual elements by specifying the *class* or *id* attribute values of the element. Collectively, these groupings are known as *selectors*.

A selector tells CSS to which element or elements the specified properties and values should be applied. The basic structure for CSS statements with a selector is this:

```
selector { property: value; }
```

For example, the code to apply the Arial font to all *<h1>* elements within the document looks like this (see the companion content file ex1.css in the sample code):

```
h1 { font-family: arial; }
```

Although applying a style to a whole element type is often useful, you will run across situations in which you want to style some elements of a certain type but not others, or you want to style elements of the same type in different ways. You do this more selective styling by using the *class* or *id* attributes of an element. These attributes enable granular control over the display of any elements within the document. For example, the document might have many *<p>* elements, but you want to give only certain *<p>* elements a boldface font. By using a *class* attribute with the appropriate CSS, you can give the *<p>* elements belonging to that class a specific style. For example, to apply a boldface font to all elements with a class of *boldParagraphs* you write the CSS like this:

```
.boldParagraphs { font-weight: bold; }
```

Note that class selectors start with a period. The boldface style is then applied to any HTML element that includes a class attribute with the *"boldParagraphs"* value:

```
class="boldParagraphs"
```

Here's a complete tag example:

```
<p class="boldParagraphs">This would be bold text.</p>
```

You can gain even more granular control with the *id* attribute, which enables you to select a specific element with its particular ID and apply a style to it, as was done in the example shown in Figure 15-2. Both the text *"JavaScript Step by Step is a book by Steve Suehring, published by Microsoft Press"* and the text *"The book emphasizes standards-based JavaScript that works on multiple platforms through different browsers"* are enclosed within *<p>* elements. However, the first sentence is given an ID of *tagline*, which allows it to be given a boldface font through a CSS.

Here's the Hypertext Markup Language (HTML):

```
<p id="tagline">JavaScript Step by Step is a book by Steve Suehring, published by Microsoft
Press.</p>
```

And the CSS (in the ex2.css file in the companion content):

```
#tagline { font-weight: bold; }
```

```
Note that individual ID selectors start with a hash symbol (#).
```

Applying CSS

Several approaches exist for applying styles to a document using CSS. You can:

- Apply a style directly to an HTML element within the element itself.

- Include a *<style>* element within the *<head>* portion of a document.

- Link to a CSS in an external file, in much the same way you link to JavaScript in external files.

By far the best approach is to use an external CSS file—just as the best practice with JavaScript is to use an external JavaScript file. Using a CSS promotes reusability and greatly simplifies ongoing maintenance of the site. Suppose that you manage a site with hundreds of pages, and your boss calls telling you that the new design for the company now requires the font to change for page headings. If the site uses a common external CSS file, the change is quick and easy, and you can make the change by modifying only a single file. If the CSS is contained in each document, such a change can be quite time-consuming.

There's much more to the subject of CSS than a JavaScript book can realistically cover. If you're unfamiliar with CSS and would like more information, you can find more information on the "CSS Overviews and Tutorials" page (*http://msdn2.microsoft.com/en-us/library /ms531212.aspx*) on the Microsoft website.

The Relationship Between JavaScript and CSS

You can use JavaScript to manipulate many document styles dynamically using the Document Object Model (DOM) 2 (which you encountered earlier in Chapter 11, "JavaScript Events and the Browser"). Using the DOM, you can retrieve an element by its tag name or ID and then set that element's *style* property.

For example, the heading text shown in Figure 15-1 is contained in an *<h1>* element. If you give that *<h1>* element a descriptive ID, such as *heading*, you can retrieve it using JavaScript's *getElementById()* method. You then use the *style* property of the element to retrieve a *style* object, which is JavaScript's way of altering the style of an element. Here's an example that changes the style to use a different font:

```
var heading = document.getElementById("heading");
heading.style.fontFamily = "arial";
```

Setting Element Styles by ID

Using *getElementById()* and the *style* object to set the style for an element, as you just saw, is an easy and effective way to change a style. You set styles individually using their JavaScript style name, which is usually similar to—but not always the same as—the corresponding CSS property. In JavaScript, the style property name is usually the same as the official CSS style name when the property is a single word, such as *margin*; however, when the CSS property is a hyphenated word, such as *text-align*, the property name becomes *textAlign*. Notice the hyphen was removed and an uppercase letter used to separate the main word from the subordinate words within name. Spelling a property name in this way is called *camelCase*.

Table 15-1 shows selected CSS properties and their JavaScript counterparts.

TABLE 15-1 **CSS and JavaScript Property Names Compared**

CSS Property	JavaScript Property
background	*background*
background-attachment	*backgroundAttachment*
background-color	*backgroundColor*
background-image	*backgroundImage*
background-repeat	*backgroundRepeat*
border	*border*
border-color	*borderColor*
color	*color*
font-family	*fontFamily*
font-size	*fontSize*
font-weight	*fontWeight*
height	*height*
left	*left*
list-style	*listStyle*
list-style-image	*listStyleImage*
margin	*margin*
margin-bottom	*marginBottom*
margin-left	*marginLeft*
margin-right	*marginRight*
margin-top	*marginTop*
padding	*padding*
padding-bottom	*paddingBottom*
padding-left	*paddingLeft*
padding-right	*paddingRight*
padding-top	*paddingTop*
position	*position*
float	*styleFloat* (in Windows Internet Explorer); *cssFloat* (in other browsers)
text-align	*textAlign*
top	*top*
visibility	*visibility*
width	*width*

One common use of JavaScript is to validate form entries. Using CSS with JavaScript can help you avoid using *alert()* dialogs and instead provide visual feedback directly in the page, right next to the area of the form that is filled out incorrectly. The next exercise shows you how to implement this feature.

Using CSS and JavaScript for form validation

1. Using Microsoft Visual Studio, Eclipse, or another editor, edit the file form.html in the Chapter15 sample files folder (in the companion content).

2. Within that page, replace the TODO comments with the boldface HTML shown here (you can find the code in the form.txt file in the companion content sample code):

```
<!DOCTYPE HTML PUBLIC "-//W3C//DTD HTML 4.01//EN"
"http://www.w3.org/TR/html4/strict.dtd">
<html>
<head>
<title>Form Validation</title>
</head>
<body>
<form name="formexample" id="formexample" action="#">
<div id="citydiv">City: <input id="city" name="city"></div>
<div><input id="submit" type="submit"></div>
</form>
</body>
</html>
```

3. View the page in a web browser. The page should look like this:

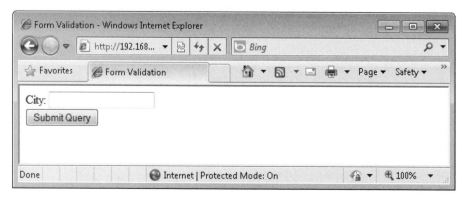

4. Create a JavaScript source file in the same folder where you saved the form.html file. Name this new JavaScript source file **form.js**.

5. Within form.js, place the following code. If you like, you can change the value against which *cityField* is being validated to a city other than Stevens Point (my hometown). Save the file.

```
function checkValid(eventObj) {
    var cityField = document.forms[0]["city"];
    if (cityField.value != "Stevens Point") {
        var cityDiv = document.getElementById("citydiv");
        cityDiv.style.fontWeight = "bold";
        cityDiv.style.border = "1px solid black";
        if (eventObj.preventDefault) {
            eventObj.preventDefault();
```

```
        } else {
            window.event.returnValue = false;
        }
        return false;
    } else {
        return true;
    }
}
```

6. Reopen form.html and alter it to add a reference to the external JavaScript file, and to add a *submit* event to the document. The form.html file should look like this (I high-lighted the changes in boldface):

```
<!DOCTYPE HTML PUBLIC "-//W3C//DTD HTML 4.01//EN"
"http://www.w3.org/TR/html4/strict.dtd">
<html>
<head>
<title>Form Validation</title>
<script type="text/javascript" src="ehandler.js"></script>
<script type="text/javascript" src="form.js"></script>
</head>
<body>
<form name="formexample" id="formexample" action="#">
<div id="citydiv">City: <input id="city" name="city"></div>
<div><input id="submit" type="submit"></div>
</form>
<script type="text/javascript">
var formEl = document.getElementsByTagName("form")[0];
EHandler.add(formEl,"submit", function(eventObj) { checkValid(eventObj); } );
</script>
</body>
</html>
```

7. Reload form.html in your browser. Within the *City* text field, type the word **test** and click Submit Query. You should immediately see the label City change to boldface and a border get added around the div.

8. Change the input for the *City* text field to **Stevens Point** (or whatever you used for the value in step 5) and click Submit Query. The background changes, and the field is empty. This is because the form continues along its submission path (in this case, the form doesn't do anything).

The code used in this example is merely a variation on code used earlier in the book with the addition of an external JavaScript file to perform the validation and provide the feedback through CSS. Inside the external JavaScript file is the validation code, which first retrieves the *text field* object from the form. Next, this field is examined to see whether its value matches *Stevens Point*. If the value isn't *Stevens Point*, the code changes the *font-weight* style property of the text field to boldface and adds a border property.

The problem with this approach is that the CSS styling for the element is now set within the JavaScript code. Maintenance is far easier when you keep markup, styles, and behavior separate. You can improve this example by setting a style with an element type selector, or by creating a common error class in the CSS and then applying that error class using the JavaScript code. The next sections examine each of these approaches in turn.

Setting Element Styles by Type

Although setting an element's style by ID as is a common approach to changing styles in JavaScript, you might also find it necessary to set properties on all the elements of a particular type.

Recall the screenshots shown earlier in this chapter, Figure 15-2 in particular. Listing 15-1 shows the HTML for that page.

LISTING 15-1 The HTML for Figure 15-2.

```html
<!DOCTYPE HTML PUBLIC "-//W3C//DTD HTML 4.01//EN"
"http://www.w3.org/TR/html4/strict.dtd">
<html>
<head>
<title>JavaScript Step by Step</title>
<style type="text/css">
h1 { font-family: arial; }
#tagline { font-weight: bold; }
</style>
</head>
<body>
<h1 id="heading">JavaScript Step by Step</h1>
<p id="tagline">JavaScript Step by Step is a book by Steve Suehring,
published by Microsoft Press.</p>
<p>The book emphasizes standards-based JavaScript that works on multiple
platforms through different browsers.</p>
</body>
</html>
```

Notice two *<p>* elements in Listing 15-1. The first *<p>* element has a style applied to it, *font-weight: bold*. You can use JavaScript to apply additional styles to all *<p>* elements. Consider the code in Listing 15-2, which adds some JavaScript code (shown in boldface type) to change the *<p>* element's font family.

LISTING 15-2 Using JavaScript plus HTML to change element style.

```
<!DOCTYPE HTML PUBLIC "-//W3C//DTD HTML 4.01//EN"
"http://www.w3.org/TR/html4/strict.dtd">
<html>
<head>
<title>JavaScript Step by Step</title>
<style type="text/css">
h1 { font-family: arial; }
#tagline { font-weight: bold; }
</style>
</head>
<body>
<h1 id="heading">JavaScript Step by Step</h1>
<p id="tagline">JavaScript Step by Step is a book by Steve Suehring, published by
Microsoft Press.</p>
<p>The book emphasizes standards-based JavaScript that works on multiple platforms
through different browsers.</p>
<script type="text/javascript">
var pElements = document.getElementsByTagName("p");
for (var i = 0; i < pElements.length; i++) {
    pElements[i].style.fontFamily = "arial";
}
</script>
</body>
</html>
```

When viewed in a web browser, the page shows that the two *<p>* elements are in the Arial font, as depicted in Figure 15-3.

The JavaScript used for this example is rather simple insofar as it uses functions that you've already seen throughout the book. First, it retrieves the *<p>* elements using the DOM's *getElementsByTagName()* method and stores them in a variable called *pElements*. Then it iterates over the *pElements* variable list using a *for* loop, changing each element's *style.font-Family* property to Arial.

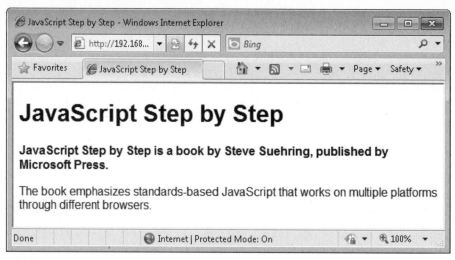

FIGURE 15-3 Using JavaScript to change the font of several elements at once.

Setting CSS Classes with JavaScript

In keeping with the development guideline to separate content and markup from style (the CSS) and behavior coding (JavaScript), an even better solution for changing styles of elements is to create a class in the CSS markup, and then, where necessary, apply that class using JavaScript rather than change specific attributes such as *font-weight* and *size* using JavaScript. This section shows how to both add and remove CSS classes from elements.

Recall that you create a CSS class like this:

```
.errorClass {
    font-weight: bold;
    border: 1px solid black;
}
```

You can apply that class through JavaScript using the *className* property, like this:

```
var tagLineElement = document.getElementById("tagline");  //retrieve the tagline element
tagLineElement.className += "errorClass";
```

Note the use of the += operator within this code. The operator causes the class to be *added* to any existing classes that the element may already belong to rather than *overwrite* classes that were already applied classes.

Removing a class from an element involves the *replace()* method and regular expressions. You retrieve the element as before, and then retrieve the list of classes that the element belongs to by using the *className* property. Finally, you replace the class name you want to remove using a regular expression:

```
var tagLineElement = document.getElementById("tagline");  //retrieve the tagline element
tagLineElement.className = tagLineElement.className.replace(/\berrorClass\b/,"");
```

This example removes the *errorClass* class name from the *className* property of the *tag
LineElement* with the help of the regular expression. The regular expression looks for a word
boundary (*b*), followed by the string *errorClass*, followed by another word boundary (*b*). It
replaces any match with an empty string ("").

Retrieving Element Styles with JavaScript

The existing styles applied to a given element are also accessible using JavaScript; however,
the method for retrieving the styles differs between Internet Explorer and other browsers.
For W3C-compliant browsers, you retrieve the styles using the *getComputedStyle()* method;
for Internet Explorer, you use the *currentStyle* array property. The style retrieved is the final
style applied, because it is the composite style calculated from all possible CSS locations,
including external style sheet files and all CSS styles applied within the document.

Listing 15-3 shows an example of retrieving the computed CSS *color* property of an element
with the ID of *heading*. In this example, the heading is an *<h1>* element:

```
<h1 style="font-family: arial; color: #0000FF;" id="heading">JavaScript Step by Step</h1>
```

In Listing 15-3, an *alert()* dialog box displays the result.

LISTING 15-3 Using JavaScript to retrieve a CSS *color* property.

```
var heading = document.getElementById("heading");
if (typeof heading.currentStyle != "undefined") {
    var curStyle = heading.currentStyle.color;
else if (typeof window.getComputedStyle != "undefined") {
    var curStyle =
        document.defaultView.getComputedStyle(heading,null).getPropertyValue("color");
}
alert(curStyle);
```

When you view through a web browser, you see an *alert()* dialog box, as shown in Figure 15-
4. The *getComputedStyle()* method accepts two parameters: the element to retrieve, and a
pseudo-element. In most cases, you use only the element itself, so you can ignore the second
parameter by setting it to null, as shown in the example.

FIGURE 15-4 The currently applied style for an element.

 Note Firefox returns *rgb(0, 0, 255)* for this same code to represent the *color* value.

Modifying Style Sheets with JavaScript

The examples given so far in this chapter show how to work with individual style elements through the *style* object. However, you might find that you want to alter the entire style applied to an element or elements—in other words, alter the style sheet as it applies to an element or class of elements. Unfortunately, doing this isn't quite as easy as the previously shown approaches for manipulating document styles.

The first hurdle is to determine whether the visitor's browser supports retrieval of the existing styles at all. You accomplished this by checking the *document.styleSheets* property, as follows:

```
if (typeof document.styleSheets != "undefined") {
    // The browser supports retrieval of style sheets.
}
```

The *document.styleSheets* array contains the styles applied to a document, listed in the order they're applied. This means that external style sheets linked within the document are set in the order in which they appear in the document, beginning with the index *0*. Consider this code:

```
<link rel="stylesheet" href="ex1.css" type="text/css" />
<link rel="stylesheet" href="ex2.css" type="text/css" />
```

These style sheets are indexed as *document.styleSheets[0]* and *document.styleSheets[1]*, respectively. Therefore, knowing the order in which style sheets appear in a document is important if you would like to retrieve the styles applied to a given element within the document.

After you determine whether the browser supports the retrieval of existing styles, you need to overcome the differences between Internet Explorer and W3C-compliant browsers.

Internet Explorer retrieves the rules applied by the given style sheet using the *rules* array, whereas W3C-compliant browsers retrieve the rules using the *cssRules* array. Just as you have to code around the differences between browsers in the event model, you must code around the differences between these browsers when dealing with style sheet retrieval. Suppose you have a style rule like this:

```
h1 { font-family: arial; }
```

Listing 15-4 shows an example of retrieving the first style sheet from a document.

LISTING 15-4 Retrieving the style sheet using JavaScript.

```
if (typeof document.styleSheets != "undefined") {
    var stylerules;
    if (typeof document.styleSheets[0].rules != "undefined") {
        stylerules = document.styleSheets[0].rules;
    } else {
        stylerules = document.styleSheets[0].cssRules;
    }
}
```

The following code, coupled with Listing 15-4, changes the font of each specified element within that CSS to a different font:

```
stylerules[0].style.fontFamily = "courier";
```

Changing *all* the selectors within a style sheet to one setting isn't common. Looping through the style sheet to look for a specific selector is usually more useful, as shown in Listing 15-5.

LISTING 15-5 Looping through style sheets to find an *<h1>* selector.

```
for (var i = 0; i < stylerules.length; i++) {
    if (stylerules[i].selectorText.toLowerCase() == "h1") {
        stylerules[i].style.fontFamily = "courier";
    }
}
```

Here's a more complete example of this functionality. Assume that you have a simple external CSS style called ex1.css for this example:

```
h1 { font-family: arial; }
```

Listing 15-6 shows the HTML page that uses the ex1.css style sheet and another called ex2.css.

LISTING 15-6 Changing an element style through the *styleSheets* array.

```
<!DOCTYPE HTML PUBLIC "-//W3C//DTD HTML 4.01//EN"
"http://www.w3.org/TR/html4/strict.dtd">
<html>
<head>
<title>JavaScript Step by Step</title>
<link rel="stylesheet" href="ex1.css" type="text/css" />
<link rel="stylesheet" href="ex2.css" type="text/css" />
<script type="text/javascript">
if (typeof document.styleSheets != "undefined") {
    var stylerules;
    if (typeof document.styleSheets[0].rules != "undefined") {
        stylerules = document.styleSheets[0].rules;
    } else {
        stylerules = document.styleSheets[0].cssRules;
    }

    for (var i = 0; i < stylerules.length; i++) {
        if (stylerules[i].selectorText.toLowerCase() == "h1") {
            stylerules[i].style.fontFamily = "courier";
        }
    }
}
</script>
</head>
<body>
<h1 id="heading">JavaScript Step by Step</h1>
<p id="tagline">JavaScript Step by Step is a book by Steve Suehring,
published by Microsoft Press.</p>
<p>The book emphasizes standards-based JavaScript that works on multiple
platforms through different browsers.</p>
</body>
</html>
```

When viewed in a web browser, the page shows a heading styled with the Courier font. This text was changed using the JavaScript inside the *for* loop in Listing 15-6. You can see the result in Figure 15-5.

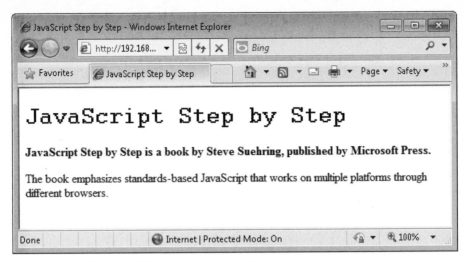

FIGURE 15-5 Using the *styleSheets* array to access the selector.

Exercises

1. Create a basic HTML document that uses a style sheet, either within the document itself or through an external file. Make sure the page has at least two *<p>* elements and one *<h1>* element. Give each of the elements ID attributes.

2. Use JavaScript to alter the style of one of the *<p>* elements, changing its *color* property to blue.

3. Use JavaScript to alter the style of all the *<p>* elements to change their visibility to hidden (refer to Table 15-1 for assistance on the property for visibility).

4. Use JavaScript to retrieve the current style for the *<p>* element's visibility, and display the current visibility setting using an *alert()* dialog box.

Chapter 16
JavaScript Error Handling

After reading this chapter, you'll be able to:

- Understand error handling using JavaScript methods: *try/catch* and *onerror.*

- Handle errors using *try/catch* statements.

- Use *try/catch/finally* statements.

- Handle the *onerror* event for window and image objects.

Introducing Two Ways to Handle Errors

This chapter looks at two primary, built-in ways of handling error conditions in JavaScript: *try/catch* and *onerror.* Many other languages, including Microsoft Visual Basic .NET and Microsoft Visual C#, also include *try/catch* to help you trap and handle error conditions. The *onerror* event allows you to perform an action when encountering an error.

Using *try/catch*

The *try* portion of the *try/catch* set of statements encapsulates a block of JavaScript. When the script executes, any exceptions that are thrown in the *try* block are caught by the *catch* statement. You can then handle the error within the JavaScript placed in the *catch* block. The code to do this follows this format:

```
try {
    // Execute some code
}
catch(errorObject) {
    //  Error handling code goes here
}
```

As the code within the *try* clause executes, any errors encountered cause processing to be immediately handed over to the *catch* clause. Listing 16-1 (in the file listing16-1.txt in the companion content) shows a simple example.

LISTING 16-1 A basic *try/catch* example.

```
try {
    var numField = document.forms[0]["num"];
    if (isNaN(numField.value)) {
        throw "it's not a number";
    }
}
catch(errorObject) {
    alert(errorObject);
}
```

When the value of *numField.value* is not a number, the *throw* statement throws a programmer-generated exception: the text *"it's not a number"*. The *catch* clause then executes, and in this case displays an *alert()* dialog box. Note the difference between a programmer-generated exception (*throw*) and an exception generated by the JavaScript run-time engine, such as a syntax error. A *try/catch* block won't catch syntax errors, so it does not provide protection against them.

When using a *catch* clause, it's common to perform multiple tasks, such as call another function to log an error, or handle a condition using a general, or generic, approach. Using *catch* is particularly helpful in problematic areas of code or in areas where the nature of the code can lead to errors (such as in code that processes user input).

In the following exercise, you build a web form similar to the form that you built in Chapter 15, "JavaScript and CSS." This time, in addition to providing visual feedback in the form's text field, you provide a bit of textual feedback.

Using *try/catch* with a web form

1. Using Microsoft Visual Studio, Eclipse, or another editor, edit the file number.htm in the Chapter16 sample files folder in the companion content.

2. Within the webpage, replace the TODO statement with the following code shown in boldface type (you can find this in the number.txt file in the companion content):

```
<!DOCTYPE HTML PUBLIC "-//W3C//DTD HTML 4.01//EN" "http://www.w3.org/TR/html4/
strict.dtd">
<html>
<head>
<title>Try/Catch</title>
<script type="text/javascript" src="ehandler.js"></script>
<script type="text/javascript" src="number.js"></script>
</head>
<body>
```

```
<form name="formexample" id="formexample" action="#">
<div id="citydiv">Enter a Number Between 1 and 100: <input id="num" name="num"> <span
id="feedback"> </span></div>
<div><input id="submit" type="submit"></div>
</form>
<script type="text/javascript">
var formEl = document.getElementsByTagName("form")[0];
EHandler.add(formEl,"submit", function(eventObj) { checkValid(eventObj); } );
</script>
</body>
</html>
```

3. Create a JavaScript source file called number.js. (This file is in the companion content.)

4. Convert the error handling code from Chapter 15 to the *try/catch* style, and match the content of this form. A *try/catch* statement isn't really required for the Chapter 15 code, but reworking it using *try/catch* illustrates how to use the statement. In the number.js file, enter the following code. (Although much of this code could be condensed into a single *if* statement, I wrote several *if* statements here because you will expand the code later in this exercise.)

```
function checkValid(eventObj) {
    try {
        var numField = document.forms[0]["num"];
        if (isNaN(numField.value)) {
            throw numField;
        }
        else if (numField.value > 100) {
            throw numField;
        }
        else if (numField.value < 1) {
            throw numField;
        }
        return true;
    }
    catch(errorObject) {
        errorObject.style.background = "#FF0000";
        if (eventObj.preventDefault) {
            eventObj.preventDefault();
        } else {
            window.event.returnValue = false;
        }
        return false;
    }
}
```

5. View the page in a web browser. You should see this window:

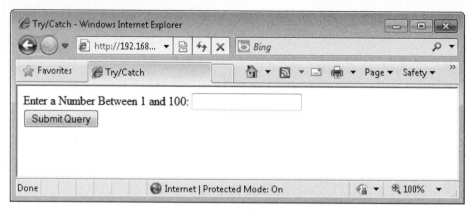

6. Test the functionality of the new *try/catch* clauses. Enter a number greater than 100 into the field (for example, **350**) and click Submit Query. You should see a page like this:

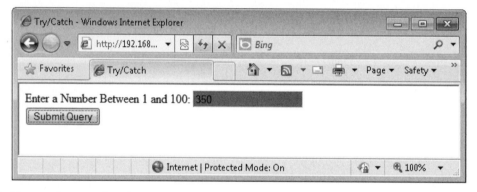

7. Type a phrase rather than a number, and click Submit Query again. The form field should remain red.

8. Type a number in the field that is less than 1, such as **-2**, and click Submit Query again. The field remains red.

9. Type the number **50** in the field, and click Submit Query again. This time, the form submits successfully, resulting in a blank form.

10. Modify the number.js file to add some textual feedback. The final number.js file should look like this:

```
function checkValid(eventObj) {
    try {
        var numField = document.forms[0]["num"];
        if (isNaN(numField.value)) {
            var err = new Array("It's not a number",numField);
            throw err;
```

```
            }
            else if (numField.value > 100) {
                var err = new Array("It's greater than 100",numField);
                throw err;
            }
            else if (numField.value < 1) {
                var err = new Array("It's less than 1",numField);
                throw err;
            }
            return true;
        }
        catch(errorObject) {
            var errorText = document.createTextNode(errorObject[0]);
            var feedback = document.getElementById("feedback");
            var newspan = document.createElement("span");
            newspan.appendChild(errorText);
            newspan.style.color = "#FF0000";
            newspan.style.fontWeight = "bold";
            newspan.setAttribute("id","feedback");
            var parent = feedback.parentNode;
            var newChild = parent.replaceChild(newspan,feedback);
            errorObject[1].style.background = "#FF0000";
            if (eventObj.preventDefault) {
                eventObj.preventDefault();
            } else {
                window.event.returnValue = false;
            }
            return false;
        }
    }
```

11. Refresh the page in the browser so that a new version of the JavaScript executes. You won't notice any visible changes compared with the first time you loaded the form.

12. Within the form, type **350** and click Submit Query. Now you see a page like the following, with textual feedback next to the form field:

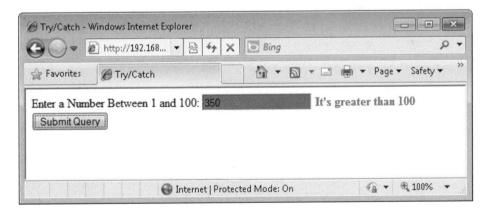

13. Type **-1** into the form, and click Submit Query again. You see this page:

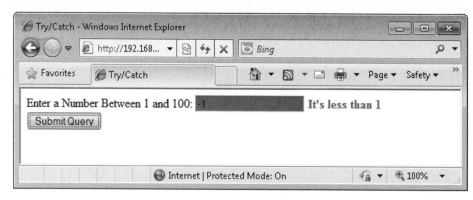

14. Type a text phrase into the form, and click Submit Query again. You see a page like this:

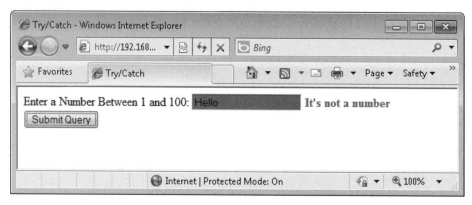

15. Type a valid number between 1 and 100 (for example, **50**) into the form, and click Submit Query. The form submits without an error.

This exercise used some of the approaches explained in earlier chapters to create a new element and place it into the document to provide feedback. The first portion of the exercise converted the web form from Chapter 15 so that it used the *try/catch* style and new content. The form in Chapter 15 asks the user to type a city name, whereas this form requests a specific range of numbers; in this way, the form demonstrates multiple conditions for feedback.

Each condition throws an error, with the *numField* object as its error object. Within the *catch* statement, the background color of *errorObject* changes to red, and the function returns *false* to indicate a failed, or invalid, form. The additional code uses an array to join both a textual error and the *form* object (*numField*). This *array* object is then thrown to the *catch* statement. Its first index (*0*) is the error text to display, and the second index (*1*) is the *numField* object, as shown here (pay particular attention to the code in boldface):

```
try {
    var numField = document.forms[0]["num"];
    if (isNaN(numField.value)) {
        var err = new Array("It's not a number",numField);
        throw err;
    }
    else if (numField.value > 100) {
        var err = new Array("It's greater than 100",numField);
        throw err;
    }
    else if (numField.value < 1) {
        var err = new Array("It's less than 1",numField);
        throw err;
    }
    else {
        return true;
    }
}
```

The *catch* statement performs several duties in this exercise. First, it retrieves the *<span>* element that will provide feedback to the user:

```
var feedback = document.getElementById("feedback");
```

Next, it creates a new text node by using the text of the error message found in the *errorObject*:

```
var errorText = document.createTextNode(errorObject[0]);
```

It then creates a new *span* element that will be put into the document later. This *span* element, known within the code as *newspan,* has the error text appended, and is styled with a red text color and boldface font so that it stands out. This new *span* element is given an ID of *feedback*, the same as the existing *span* element:

```
var newspan = document.createElement("span");
newspan.appendChild(errorText);
newspan.style.color = "#FF0000";
newspan.style.fontWeight = "bold";
newspan.setAttribute("id","feedback");
```

The code retrieves the *feedback* object's parent node, so it can use the *replaceChild()* method on the parent to replace the old *span* element with the new *span* element, as follows:

```
var parent = feedback.parentNode;
var newChild = parent.replaceChild(newspan,feedback);
```

The code then changes the background color of the form field to red:

```
errorObject[1].style.background = "#FF0000";
```

The final lines of the code, which you've seen in previous chapters, prevent the default form action, which causes the browser to stay on the same page rather than proceed to submit the form:

```
if (eventObj.preventDefault) {
    eventObj.preventDefault();
} else {
    window.event.returnValue = false;
}
return false;
```

> **Tip** Using *try/catch* statements as shown in this example helps to abstract the handling of exceptions within code. However, this approach does not prevent or provide assistance for syntax errors in the code.

Catching Multiple Exceptions

Certain browsers, including Firefox, enable you to handle multiple exceptions and multiple exception handlers easily. For example, consider this code:

```
if (isNaN(numField.value)) {
    throw "NotANumber";
}
else if (numField.value > 100) {
    throw "GreaterThan100";
}
else if (numField.value < 1) {
    throw "LessThan1";
}
```

The *catch* block looks like this:

```
catch(errorObject if errorObject == "NotANumber") {
    // Perform handling for NaN
}
catch(errorObject if errorObject == "GreaterThan100") {
    // Perform handling for > 100
}
catch(errorObject if errorObject == "LessThan1") {
    // Perform handling for < 1
}
catch(errorObject) {
    // Perform uncaught exception handling
}
```

In this code, each exception is caught and handled by its own exception handler block. If none of the exceptions occurs, the block falls through to the generic exception handler at the end of the *catch* block. Unfortunately, because Windows Internet Explorer doesn't support this functionality, it's of limited use.

And Finally…

An optional complementary statement in JavaScript, called *finally*, works with *try/catch*. The *finally* statement contains code that gets executed regardless of whether the *try* statement's code succeeded or the *catch* handler executed. Typically, you use a *finally* block to make sure that some code (such as cleanup code) executes every time.

Listing 16-2 (in the listing16-2.txt file in the companion content) shows the *checkValid()* function you saw in previous exercises in this chapter, but with the addition of a *finally* statement:

LISTING 16-2 Adding a *finally* statement onto the *checkValid()* function.

```
function checkValid(eventObj) {
    try {
        var numField = document.forms[0]["num"];
        if (isNaN(numField.value)) {
            var err = new Array("It's not a number",numField);
            throw err;
        }
        else if (numField.value > 100) {
            var err = new Array("It's greater than 100",numField);
            throw err;
        }
        else if (numField.value < 1) {
            var err = new Array("It's less than 1",numField);
            throw err;
        }
        return true;
    }
    catch(errorObject) {
        var errorText = document.createTextNode(errorObject[0]);
        var feedback = document.getElementById("feedback");
        var newspan = document.createElement("span");
        newspan.appendChild(errorText);
        newspan.style.color = "#FF0000";
        newspan.style.fontWeight = "bold";
        newspan.setAttribute("id","feedback");
        var parent = feedback.parentNode;
        var newChild = parent.replaceChild(newspan,feedback);
        errorObject[1].style.background = "#FF0000";
        if (eventObj.preventDefault) {
            eventObj.preventDefault();
        } else {
            window.event.returnValue = false;
        }
        return false;
    }
    finally {
        alert("This is called on both success and failure.");
    }
}
```

Using the *onerror* Event

You may see the *onerror* event used within programs to handle error events and conditions, but programmers are using it much less commonly now because they can handle errors in less obtrusive ways. The *onerror* event can be attached to the *window* and *image* objects.

Attaching *onerror* to the *window* Object

To use the *onerror* event, you assign it a function that gets called whenever a JavaScript error occurs. The *onerror* event can be helpful during development, though the use of tools like Firebug have reduced the need for it.

You attach the *onerror* event to the *window* object like this:

```
window.onerror = myErrorHandler;
```

The *myErrorHandler* variable refers to a user-defined function that handles the error condition. The JavaScript interpreter automatically sends three arguments to the error handler:

- A textual description of the error
- The Uniform Resource Locator (URL) where the error occurred
- The number of the line on which the error occurred

When an error handler function returns *true*, JavaScript won't handle the error itself; it assumes that the error has been taken care of by the error handler.

Listing 16-3 (in the companion content in the listing16-3.htm file) shows an example of JavaScript and a user-defined handler.

LISTING 16-3 An example of *onerror* in the *window* object.

```
<!DOCTYPE HTML PUBLIC "-//W3C//DTD HTML 4.01//EN" "http://www.w3.org/TR/html4/strict.
dtd">
<html>
<head>
<title>onerror</title>
</head>
<body>
<div id="mydiv">Hi</div>
<script type="text/javascript">
function init() {
    doSomething();
}
function errorHandler() {
    alert(arguments[0] + " on line " + arguments[2]);
    return true;
}
```

```
window.onload = init;
window.onerror = errorHandler;
</script>
</body>
</html>
```

When you load the code in Listing 16-3 into a web browser, you see an *alert()* dialog box like the one in Figure 16-1.

FIGURE 16-1 An error handler using the *onerror* event of the *window* object.

Listing 16-3 contains an intentionally undefined function within the *init()* function when the window loads. The JavaScript interpreter throws the error when it finds the undefined function, and because a user-defined function called *errorHandler* is assigned to the *onerror* event, the user-defined function gets called. The *errorHandler* function displays an *alert()* dialog box and returns *true* so that no further error handling occurs. The *alert()* dialog box displays the first and third indexes of the *arguments* array (*arguments[0]* and *arguments[2]*). The *arguments* array contains the three arguments sent to the error handler described earlier: the error message, the URL, and the line number of the error.

Avoid Handling Events Obtrusively

The example in Listing 16-3 handles a JavaScript error in a somewhat obtrusive manner: by using an *alert()* dialog box. Handling errors in the background whenever possible is a better practice than using an *alert* dialog box. If the page has a lot of errors, using *alert* dialog boxes quickly gets extremely annoying for visitors, who have to click through each one.

When you anticipate that an error might occur, you can code around that error and handle it to make the script degrade gracefully—for example, by substituting a different function, or by presenting a friendly error message.

Ignoring Errors

Rather than handle errors with extra error-handling code, you can choose to ignore them entirely. You accomplish this simply by returning *true* from the error handler. Whenever an error-handling function returns *true*, the browser behaves as though the error has been handled. So by returning *true*, you're essentially just telling the interpreter to ignore the error.

Take a look at the code in Listing 16-4. It's similar to the code in Listing 16-3; however, in Listing 16-4, the *errorHandler* function returns *true* (shown in boldface type). This means that when the undefined *doSomething()* function causes an error, that error is silently ignored. You can find the code for Listing 16-4 in the companion content in the listing16-4.htm file.

LISTING 16-4 Code that silently ignores an error.

```
<!DOCTYPE HTML PUBLIC "-//W3C//DTD HTML 4.01//EN" "http://www.w3.org/TR/html4/
strict.dtd">
<html>
<head>
<title>onerror</title>
</head>
<body>
<div id="mydiv">Hi</div>
<script type="text/javascript">
function init() {
    doSomething();
}
function errorHandler() {
    return true;
}

window.onload = init;
window.onerror = errorHandler;
</script>
</body>
</html>
```

You can see this behavior using Firefox with Firebug installed. First, load the code in Listing 16-4 as is. You won't see any errors noted. Then, comment the *return true;* statement from within the *errorHandler* function so that it looks like this:

```
function errorHandler() {
//    return true;
}
```

When you reload the page, you'll notice an error in the Firebug error console, as shown in Figure 16-2.

FIGURE 16-2 Commenting out the return value from the error handler causes a JavaScript error that can be viewed using Firebug.

Attaching *onerror* to the *image* Object

You can also attach an *onerror* event to *image* objects. When placed inline in the *<img>* tag, you can use these event handlers to handle images that aren't found. For example, Figure 16-3 shows a page with a missing image.

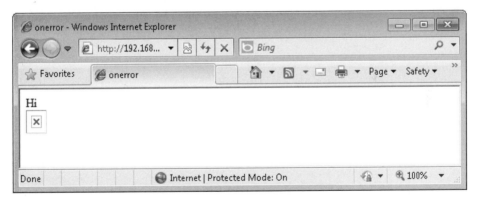

FIGURE 16-3 A missing image that can be avoided using JavaScript.

The code for this page is shown in Listing 16-5 (and is in the companion content in the listing16-5.htm file).

LISTING 16-5 A page with a missing image.

```
<!DOCTYPE HTML PUBLIC "-//W3C//DTD HTML 4.01//EN" "http://www.w3.org/TR/html4/
strict.dtd">
<html>
<head>
<title>onerror</title>
</head>
<body>
<div id="mydiv">Hi</div>
<img src="notfound.png">
</body>
</html>
```

Now consider the code with an inline *onerror* handler. The *onerror* handler redirects the *<img>* element to an image that does exist. The content of the image isn't important in this case; the important point is that using the *onerror* handler in this way can help to prevent the common "Image Not Found" icon from appearing within your webpages. Listing 16-6 (in the companion content in the listing16-6.htm file) shows the new code.

LISTING 16-6 Adding an *onerror()* handler for the image.

```
<!DOCTYPE HTML PUBLIC "-//W3C//DTD HTML 4.01//EN" "http://www.w3.org/TR/html4/
strict.dtd">
<html>
<head>
<title>onerror</title>
</head>
<body>
<div id="mydiv">Hi</div>
<img src="notfound.png" onerror="this.src='logo.png'; return true;">
</body>
</html>
```

When you load this page into a web browser, the page won't find the notfound.png image; however, in its place, the browser retrieves and displays an image called logo.png, shown in Figure 16-4.

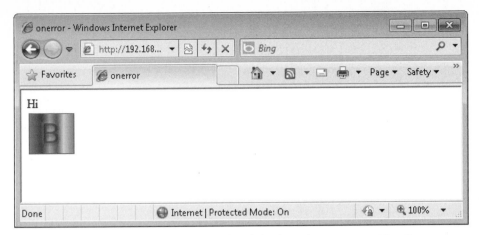

FIGURE 16-4 The missing image has been replaced, thanks to the *onerror* event handler.

Exercises

1. Use an *onerror* event handler attached to the *window* object to handle errors when a function is undefined. Note that you can use the code in Listing 16-3 as a basis for your new code, but the error handler should present the error in a friendlier way than by using an *alert()*.

2. Build a web form and use a *try/catch* block to catch the case when a city entered into a text field is not *"Stockholm"*. Provide visual feedback that the city was incorrect.

3. Build a web form and use a *try/catch/finally* block to catch a case when a number is greater than 100. Be sure that visitors are thanked every time that they use the form, no matter what they enter (either valid or invalid values).

Part IV
AJAX and Server-Side Integration

Chapter 17
JavaScript and XML

After reading this chapter, you'll be able to:

- Examine the functions for opening an Extensible Markup Language (XML) document by using JavaScript.

- Display an XML document as a Hypertext Markup Language (HTML) table.

- View a Microsoft Office Excel 2007 XML spreadsheet by using JavaScript.

Using XML with JavaScript

XML is a language consisting almost completely of user-defined tags. Because the user-defined tags make XML extremely customizable, XML is frequently used as a file format for exchanging data. An important consideration for JavaScript programmers is that XML is the *X* in the acronym AJAX (Asynchronous JavaScript and XML). AJAX has become a very popular method for creating interactive web applications. You learn more about AJAX in the next two chapters: Chapter 19, "A Touch of AJAX," and Chapter 20, "A Bit Deeper into AJAX."

XML is an open standard defined by the World Wide Web Consortium (W3C) and is currently in its fourth edition. This section looks briefly at XML as it pertains to JavaScript. You can find more information about XML on the XML Working Group's website at *http://www.w3.org /XML/Core/,* or on Microsoft's website at *http://msdn.microsoft.com/xml/.*

Looking at an Example XML Document

XML documents consist of elements within a document structure. These elements have syntax rules of their own, including that they need a start tag and an end tag. To the web programmer, the look of a document (defined in the text between tags) might be familiar. Here's an example XML document, also provided in the books.xml file in the Chapter17 folder in the companion content:

```
<books>
<book>
    <title>MySQL Bible</title>
    <author>Steve Suehring</author>
    <isbn>9780764549328</isbn>
    <publisher>Wiley Publishing Inc.</publisher>
</book>
<book>
    <title>JavaScript Step by Step</title>
    <author>Steve Suehring</author>
```

```
    <isbn>9780735624498</isbn>
    <publisher>Microsoft Press</publisher>
</book>
</books>
```

The structure of the document as a whole needs to meet certain criteria to qualify as a well-formed document. As you can see in the example, each element has its own start tag followed by a corresponding end tag. Elements also can be nested within each other. Many of these rules are similar to HTML rules.

XML documents can contain attributes as well, so the following is also valid:

```
<?xml version="1.0"?>
<book title="JavaScript Step by Step" author="Steve Suehring" isbn="9780735624498"
publisher="Microsoft Press" />
```

Loading an XML Document with JavaScript

You can load and manipulate XML documents using JavaScript. This section looks at doing just that.

Importing the Document

You can import an XML document using one of two approaches, depending on the browsers you're supporting. For newer browsers, including Chrome, Firefox, and later versions of Windows Internet Explorer, you can use the *XMLHTTPRequest()* object, whereas older versions of Internet Explorer use the *ActiveXObject* object. The following code loads the books.xml document in a cross-browser manner:

```
if (window.XMLHttpRequest) {
    var httpObj = new XMLHttpRequest();
} else {
    var httpObj = new ActiveXObject("Microsoft.XMLHTTP");
}
httpObj.open("GET","books.xml",false);
httpObj.send();
var xmlDocument = httpObj.responseXML;
```

Displaying the Document

Often, XML data can best be visualized in a table or spreadsheet format. Figure 17-1 shows the books.xml file in Excel 2007.

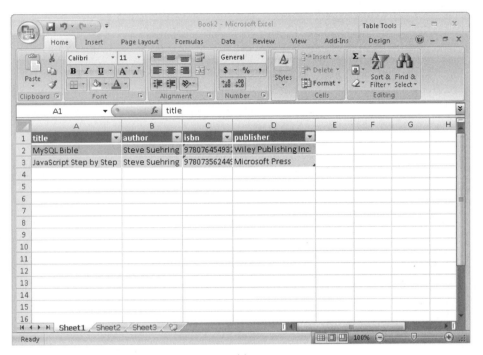

FIGURE 17-1 An XML file represented in a spreadsheet.

An HTML table is helpful for representing in a browser the same data shown in Figure 17-1. In large part, displaying XML data using JavaScript requires some knowledge of the Document Object Model (DOM), but no other special functions or methods beyond those needed to load the document itself, which you already learned about.

The next example creates a function called *displayData()* that displays information in a tabular manner.

The *readyState* Property

Previous versions of this book used the *readyState* property to determine when the XML document was loaded. The *readyState* property is an integer that holds one of five values indicating the current state of the document request being processed. Table 17-1 shows the values and corresponding descriptions of *readyState*.

TABLE 17-1 The *readyState* Property

Value	Description
0	Uninitialized. Open but has yet to be called.
1	Open. Initialized but not yet sent.
2	Sent. The request has been sent.
3	Receiving. The response is actively being received.
4	Loaded. The response has been fully received.

You learn more about the *readyState* property and the *onreadystatechange* event in Chapter 18, "JavaScript Applications."

Displaying the nodes and child nodes within an XML document requires iterating through the document's levels and building the output document. The next function shown does that by iterating through a hierarchical XML document to display that document's data in an HTML table. This code continues the example shown already, where a variable called *xmlDocument* is created and loaded with an XML document called books.xml:

```
function displayData(xmlDocument) {
    var xmlEl = xmlDocument.getElementsByTagName("book");
    var table = document.createElement("table");
    table.border = "1";
    var tbody = document.createElement("tbody");

    // Append the body to the table
    table.appendChild(tbody);

    // Create the table cells for the new row
    for (i = 0; i < xmlEl.length; i++) {
        var row = document.createElement("tr");
        // Create the row/td elements
        for (j = 0; j < xmlEl[i].childNodes.length; j++) {
            // Skip it if the type is not 1
            if (xmlEl[i].childNodes[j].nodeType != 1) {
                continue;
            }

            // Insert the actual text/data from the XML document.
            var td = document.createElement("td");
            var xmlData =
                document.createTextNode(xmlEl[i].childNodes[j].firstChild.nodeValue);
```

```
            td.appendChild(xmlData);
            row.appendChild(td);
        }
        tbody.appendChild(row);
    }
    document.getElementById("xmldata").appendChild(table);
}
```

To put all the code together into a webpage, you attach to an event the functions that load
and display the XML file. Listing 17-1 (included in the listing17-1.html file in the companion
content) creates a new function called *getXML* and attaches it to the *window* object's *load*
event. The code that attaches the event is in boldface type.

LISTING 17-1 Displaying XML data in an HTML table.

```html
<!DOCTYPE HTML PUBLIC "-//W3C//DTD HTML 4.01//EN" "http://www.w3.org/TR/html4/
strict.dtd">
<html>
<head>
<title>Books</title>
<script type="text/javascript" src="ehandler.js"></script>
</head>
<body id="mainBody">
<div id="xmldata"></div>
<script type="text/javascript">

function displayData(xmlDocument) {
    var xmlEl = xmlDocument.getElementsByTagName("book");
    var table = document.createElement("table");
    table.border = "1";
    var tbody = document.createElement("tbody");

    // Append the body to the table
    table.appendChild(tbody);

    // Create table row
    for (i = 0; i < xmlEl.length; i++) {
        var row = document.createElement("tr");
        // Create the row/td elements
        for (j = 0; j < xmlEl[i].childNodes.length; j++) {
            // Skip it if the type is not 1
            if (xmlEl[i].childNodes[j].nodeType != 1) {
                continue;
            }

            // Insert the actual text/data from the XML document.
            var td = document.createElement("td");
            var xmlData =
                document.createTextNode(xmlEl[i].childNodes[j].firstChild.nodeValue);
            td.appendChild(xmlData);
            row.appendChild(td);
        }
        tbody.appendChild(row);
```

```
        }
        document.getElementById("xmldata").appendChild(table);
    }

    function getXML() {
        if (window.XMLHttpRequest) {
            var httpObj = new XMLHttpRequest();
        } else {
            var httpObj = new ActiveXObject("Microsoft.XMLHTTP");
        }
        httpObj.open("GET","books.xml",false);
        httpObj.send();
        var xmlDocument = httpObj.responseXML;
        displayData(xmlDocument);
    }

    var mainBody = document.getElementById("mainBody");
    EHandler.add(mainBody, "load", function() { getXML(); });

</script>
</body>
</html>
```

When viewed through a web browser, the table displays the data much like a spreadsheet would, as shown in Figure 17-2.

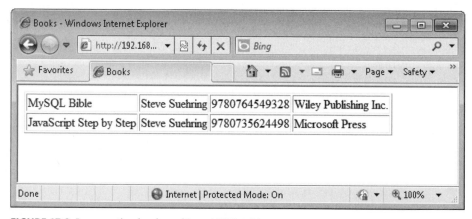

FIGURE 17-2 Representing books.xml in an HTML table.

Examining the code from Listing 17-1 reveals a large *for* loop that walks through the XML hierarchy, building table rows as it goes. One item to note is that the loop looks only for *Element* nodes within the XML document by using this bit of code:

```
// Skip it if the type is not 1
if (xmlEl[i].childNodes[j].nodeType != 1) {
    continue;
}
```

The *nodeType* of *1* represents an *XML Element* node. If the type of node currently being examined in the loop is not an element, the code moves to the next part of the document.

One issue you may notice in the display in Figure 17-2 is that no column headings exist. Adding column headings requires adding some code. The next procedure shows you how.

Adding column headings from an XML document

1. Using Microsoft Visual Studio, Eclipse, or another editor, edit the file books.htm in the Chapter17 sample files folder, which you can find in the companion content. (At this point in the procedure, when viewed through a web browser, books.htm should resemble Figure 17-2.)

2. Within books.htm, add the following code shown in boldface type to the *displayData()* method (in the companion content in books.txt), replacing the TODO comment:

```
<!DOCTYPE HTML PUBLIC "-//W3C//DTD HTML 4.01//EN" "http://www.w3.org/TR/html4/
strict.dtd">
<html>
<head>
<title>Books</title>
<script type="text/javascript" src="ehandler.js"></script>
</head>
<body id="mainBody">
<div id="xmldata"></div>
<script type="text/javascript">

function displayData(xmlDocument) {
    var xmlEl = xmlDocument.getElementsByTagName("book");
    var table = document.createElement("table");
    table.border = "1";
    var tbody = document.createElement("tbody");

    // Append the body to the table
    table.appendChild(tbody);
    var row = document.createElement("tr");

    for (colHead = 0; colHead < xmlEl[0].childNodes.length; colHead++) {
        if (xmlEl[0].childNodes[colHead].nodeType != 1) {
            continue;
        }
        var tableHead = document.createElement("th");
        var colName = document.createTextNode(xmlEl[0].childNodes[colHead].nodeName);
        tableHead.appendChild(colName);
        row.appendChild(tableHead);
    }

    // Append the row to the body
```

```
            tbody.appendChild(row);

        // Create table row
        for (i = 0; i < xmlEl.length; i++) {
            var row = document.createElement("tr");
            // Create the row/td elements
            for (j = 0; j < xmlEl[i].childNodes.length; j++) {
                // Skip it if the type is not 1
                if (xmlEl[i].childNodes[j].nodeType != 1) {
                    continue;
                }

                // Insert the actual text/data from the XML document.
                var td = document.createElement("td");
                var xmlData =
                    document.createTextNode(xmlEl[i].childNodes[j].firstChild.nodeValue);
                td.appendChild(xmlData);
                row.appendChild(td);
            }
            tbody.appendChild(row);
        }
        document.getElementById("xmldata").appendChild(table);
    }
    function getXML() {

        if (window.XMLHttpRequest) {
            var httpObj = new XMLHttpRequest();
        } else {
            var httpObj = new ActiveXObject("Microsoft.XMLHTTP");
        }
        httpObj.open("GET","books.xml",false);
        httpObj.send();
        var xmlDocument = httpObj.responseXML;
        displayData(xmlDocument);

    }

    var mainBody = document.getElementById("mainBody");
    EHandler.add(mainBody, "load", function() { getXML(); });


    </script>
    </body>
    </html>
```

3. View the page in a web browser. It should look like this:

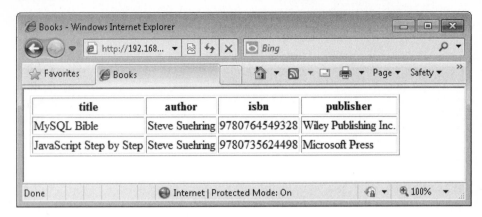

Working with XML Data from Excel 2007

Excel 2007 has several features that make working with XML data rather easy. Both importing and exporting XML data is possible with Excel. In fact, when exporting data from Excel, Excel adds nothing proprietary to the XML document. Here's what the books.xml file looks like when exported from Excel 2007 (included in the companion content as newbooks.xml):

```
<?xml version="1.0" encoding="UTF-8" standalone="yes"?>
<books xmlns:xsi="http://www.w3.org/2001/XMLSchema-instance">
        <book>
                <title>MySQL Bible</title>
                <author>Steve Suehring</author>
                <isbn>9780764549328</isbn>
                <publisher>Wiley Publishing Inc.</publisher>
        </book>
        <book>
                <title>JavaScript Step by Step</title>
                <author>Steve Suehring</author>
                <isbn>9780735624498</isbn>
                <publisher>Microsoft Press</publisher>
        </book>
</books>
```

Because Excel 2007 is XML-friendly, the *displayData()* function already examined in this chapter works with XML data exported from Excel 2007 without modification. For developers who have worked with proprietary formats in the past, this comes as a welcome surprise.

A Preview of Things to Come

Though XML is indeed the X in the AJAX acronym, there's much more to AJAX than just JavaScript and XML. AJAX can work with data types other than XML, and in Chapter 19, you work with AJAX, building upon the brief foundation introduced in this chapter.

In Chapter 20, you examine the integration of JavaScript, AJAX, and Cascading Style Sheets (CSS) that allows you to present data retrieved with JavaScript.

Exercises

1. Use the code from the book display exercise in this chapter to display the table after a link is clicked rather than when the page loads.

2. Use the code from the book display exercise in this chapter to display the table, but use the DOM to alternate the colors for each row so that every other row has a gray background. Hint: #*aaabba* is the hexadecimal representation of this gray color.

Chapter 18
JavaScript Applications

After reading this chapter, you'll be able to:

■ Understand the components that go into a JavaScript-based application.

Components of JavaScript Applications

Building a browser-based application with the sophisticated look and feel of a desktop application frequently involves using JavaScript. Such an application has some of the same features and responsiveness of a desktop application, as though it were sitting on the local computer rather than operating through a web browser.

This brief chapter provides an overview of the components that constitute an application based on JavaScript. The goal is to help you understand the underlying architecture and some of the complexity necessary to create this type of application at the enterprise level.

The Big Three: Display, Behavior, Data

Three primary components exist in a web application:

■ **Display**   The look and feel of the page.

■ **Behavior**   What the application interface does, that is, what happens when the user clicks an element on the page or otherwise interacts with the page.

■ **Data**   The server component that contains the data and performs the actions, the results of which appear on the page.

JavaScript code typically handles the first two components in the preceding list—display and behavior—to affect the interface or react when a user performs an action on a page. JavaScript works with the data returned from the server as well, but usually only does so to alter the display in some manner. For example, a call to a web service that returns the current temperature or sky condition might use JavaScript to change an icon when the weather is sunny. The following sections examine each of these three elements in a little more detail.

Display: Page Layout

The webpage display encompasses the page layout and anything related to the look and feel of the page and site, including the color scheme, images, styling of menus (whether they have rounded corners or square ones, and so on), the placement of buttons and content, font colors, and use of images. JavaScript can affect all these items, as you've seen in previous chapters on Cascading Style Sheets (CSS) and form validation. These elements are the primary focus of web design and receive the most attention from users, and you should consider these elements when determining requirements for your site.

Behaviors: Controlling What Happens When

One of the most important factors in determining the user experience is also one of the most often overlooked elements of a web application design: the behavior of the application interface, which controls what happens when users interact with a given element. Consider these two simple scenarios:

- When a visitor clicks the Submit button on a web form, does that Submit button stay active or become disabled?

- When an input text field gains focus, should it change color or be highlighted?

Even these minor behaviors can greatly enhance the user experience when designed properly. However, when working through a design of a site, these behaviors are also frequently forgotten, ignored, or discounted in favor of the look and feel or raw design of the site.

Data: Consume, Display, and Validate

JavaScript, at least its use as far as this book is concerned, doesn't interact directly with a database or server. Obviously, JavaScript does so through Asynchronous JavaScript and XML (AJAX) and through web services, but those processes require server-side code to return data back to the calling JavaScript.

Like the display portion of the site, the back-end server-side data components should receive a fair share of attention when you design a web application. From database design to programming the business logic, this back-end coding needs careful attention.

JavaScript and Web Interfaces

Programmers use JavaScript to create front ends that provide a quality user experience. Microsoft Bing Maps (formerly Live Search Maps) is an example of a web application that relies heavily on JavaScript. Figure 18-1 shows an example of Microsoft Bing Maps, which you can find at *http://www.bing.com/maps/*.

FIGURE 18-1 The Bing Maps interface uses JavaScript to provide good interactivity.

Users can drag the map display around in much the same way they would when interacting with a desktop application. The map is composed of tiles at various resolutions. When a user drags the map, the browser sends several HTTP requests to the Virtual Earth web server requesting additional tiles that the browser then quickly displays.

The Bing search engine also uses a type-ahead search similar to that of other search engines like Google. If you begin typing in the main text box on *http://www.bing.com*, the browser immediately sends an HTTP request to the server to find similar searches, as shown in Figure 18-2.

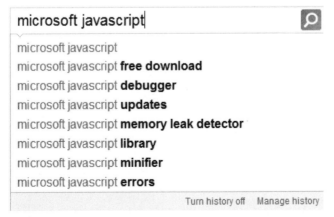

FIGURE 18-2 The type-ahead search capability uses JavaScript to obtain a matching search list from the server.

All of these elements from the Bing search engine use JavaScript. Countless other web interfaces rely on JavaScript to enhance the user experience by controlling the behavior layer of the page. The remainder of this book starts you on the path toward building this type of application with JavaScript. Chapter 19, "A Touch of AJAX," and Chapter 20, "A Bit Deeper into AJAX," show how to build a simple type-ahead search interface using JavaScript. They also introduce AJAX and show examples of working with data to build applications. Chapter 21, "An Introduction to JavaScript Libraries and Frameworks," and Chapter 22, "An Introduction to jQuery," introduce JavaScript libraries, concentrating on jQuery, which you can use to simplify many of the tasks related to writing complex JavaScript applications.

Chapter 19
A Touch of AJAX

After reading this chapter, you'll be able to:

- Understand the basics of the Asynchronous JavaScript and XML (AJAX) programming paradigm.

- Understand the difference between synchronous and asynchronous AJAX calls.

- Use AJAX to retrieve data.

- Use AJAX with different Hypertext Transfer Protocol (HTTP) methods to retrieve responses from a server.

Introduction to AJAX

AJAX describes the programming paradigm that combines JavaScript and a web server. Developers use AJAX to create highly interactive web applications such as Microsoft Virtual Earth.

Without AJAX, a web application might make the visitor wait while a response is gathered from the web server. An AJAX-based application sends requests from the web browser to the web server in the background (asynchronously) while the visitor is using the application. This makes the application feel much more responsive to the user.

In an AJAX application, JavaScript processes the response and presents the data to users. When combined with Cascading Style Sheets (CSS) and a good layout, an AJAX application provides excellent usability and the portability that only a web application can.

As complex as some AJAX applications may seem, the actual process of sending a request and handling the response are not terribly complicated. This chapter explores how you can send requests and receive responses using a fundamental AJAX object: *XMLHttpRequest*.

One central concept in AJAX is that you call server-side applications to return data. In this chapter, I give you a brief overview of how to create such an application using both ASP.NET and PHP. (PHP is a recursive acronym for PHP Hypertext Preprocessor.) If you need additional assistance in creating the server-side portion of an AJAX application, you can get help from several sources.

If you're creating a server-side application using Microsoft technologies, the Microsoft Developer Network provides a great resource with many tutorials and an introductory article on AJAX (*http://msdn.microsoft.com/en-us/magazine/cc163363.aspx*). Microsoft Press also publishes several excellent books on building applications for the web. One such title is *Microsoft ASP.NET 3.5 Step By Step* (Microsoft Press, 2008). For others, look at *http://www.microsoft.com/mspress* for more information.

If you're developing a server-side application using other technologies such as the LAMP (Linux, Apache, MySQL, Perl/PHP/Python) stack, searching the web for tutorials is likely the easiest way to get up to speed quickly on development on the platform. The book *Learning Perl* (O'Reilly, 2005) is a great resource for learning the basics of the Perl programming language.

> **Note** If you like my writing style, I wrote *Beginning Perl Web Development* (Apress, 2005), which focuses on using Perl to work with web applications.

PHP's main website (*http://www.php.net*) is a good place to start for information on PHP, and for Python, take a look at the Python website (*http://www.python.org*).

The *XMLHttpRequest* Object

The *XMLHttpRequest* object is central to building an AJAX application. Although implementations of JavaScript differ, the ECMAScript and the World Wide Web Consortium (W3C) have standardized many aspects of it except the *XMLHttpRequest* object, which has never been subject to a standardization process. Even so, since the release of Windows Internet Explorer 7, you use the *XMLHttpRequest* object in the same way across all major browsers.

Microsoft first implemented the *XMLHttpRequest* object in Microsoft Internet Explorer 5.0. If a visitor is using a browser version earlier than that, applications using *XMLHttpRequest* won't work. In Internet Explorer versions prior to version 7, the *XMLHttpRequest* object was instantiated as an *ActiveXObject* object, but other browsers implemented the XMLHttpRequest object as a JavaScript object built into the browser. This means that if your applications need to work with versions of Internet Explorer earlier than version 7, you need to instantiate the *XMLHttpRequest* object for those browsers in a different way, as I show you later in the chapter. The next section, "Instantiating the *XMLHttpRequest* Object," shows how you can test for the existence of *XMLHttpRequest* and how to instantiate it in all versions of Internet Explorer.

Instantiating the *XMLHttpRequest* Object

Internet Explorer 7 and later versions, and all other major browsers that support *XMLHttpRequest*, instantiate the *XMLHttpRequest* object in the same way:

```
var req = new XMLHttpRequest();
```

For Internet Explorer versions earlier than version 7, you must instantiate an *ActiveXObject* instead. However, the way you do this varies depending on the version of the XMLHTTP library installed on the client. Therefore, you need to do a bit of code juggling to instantiate an *XMLHttpRequest* object in these earlier versions of Internet Explorer.

The code in Listing 19-1 is a cross-browser function that instantiates an *XMLHttpRequest* object across multiple browsers.

LISTING 19-1 Instantiating an *XMLHttpRequest* object across browsers.

```
function readyAJAX() {
    try {
        return new XMLHttpRequest();
    } catch(e) {
        try {
            return new ActiveXObject("Msxml2.XMLHTTP");
        } catch(e) {
            try {
                return new ActiveXObject("Microsoft.XMLHTTP");
            } catch(e) {
                return "A newer browser is needed.";
            }
        }
    }
}
```

The function in Listing 19-1 uses multiple levels of *try/catch* blocks to instantiate an *XMLHttpRequest,* regardless of whether the visitor is using Internet Explorer or another browser. If the native call to *XMLHttpRequest* fails, that means that the visitor is using an Internet Explorer browser older than version 7. In such a case, the error is caught and one of the methods for instantiating *XMLHttpRequest* that is based on *ActiveXObject* is tried. If none of these methods succeed, the likely reason is that the browser is too old to support *XMLHttpRequest.*

The article "About Native XMLHTTP" on MSDN describes some of the version history and security nuances of the XMLHttpRequest object in Internet Explorer. This article can be found at http://msdn2.microsoft.com/en-us/library/ms537505.aspx.

You call the *readyAJAX()* function shown in Listing 19-1 like this:

```
var requestObj = readyAJAX();
```

The *requestObj* variable now contains the *XMLHttpRequest* object returned by the function, or, if the function couldn't create the object, the *requestObj* variable contains the string *"A newer browser is needed."*

Sending an AJAX Request

With a newly created *XMLHttpRequest* object in hand, you can send requests to the web server and get responses. To send the request, you use a combination of the *open()* and *send()* methods of the *XMLHttpRequest* object.

There are two fundamentally different ways to send AJAX requests: synchronously and asynchronously. When sent in a synchronous manner, the requesting code simply waits for the response—a process called *blocking*. So, for a synchronous request, the requesting code will block, effectively preventing further processing or execution of other JavaScript while the script waits for the response from the web server. This process has obvious disadvantages when the request or response gets lost in transit or is just slow. With asynchronous requests, the requesting code doesn't block. Instead, the caller can check the request status to discover when the request has completed. You see more about asynchronous requests later in this chapter; it's easier to work with synchronous requests first.

Before you can send a request, you have to build it. To do that, you use the *open* method, which has three arguments: the request method (*GET*, *POST*, *HEAD*, or others), the Uniform Resource Locator (URL) to which the request will be sent, and a Boolean *true* or *false*, indicating whether you want to send the request asynchronously or synchronously, respectively.

Assuming that your request object has been retrieved using the *readyAJAX()* function and placed into a variable named *requestObj*, a typical asynchronous call to the *open* method might look like this:

```
var url = "http://www.braingia.org/getdata.php";
requestObj.open("GET", url, true);
```

That same call, sent synchronously, looks like this:

```
var url = "http://www.braingia.org/getdata.php";
requestObj.open("GET", url, false);
```

You actually send the request with the *send* method, as follows:

```
requestObj.send();
```

Note If the parameters sent with the request have any special characters, such as spaces or other characters reserved by the URI RFC, you must first escape those characters using the % notation. This is discussed further in RFC 3986, which you can find at *ftp://ftp.rfc-editor.org/in-notes/rfc3986.txt*. You can also find more information at *http://msdn2.microsoft.com/en-us/library/aa226544(sql.80).aspx*.

How the Web Works in 500 Words or Fewer

The Hypertext Transfer Protocol (HTTP) is the language of the web. HTTP is currently defined by RFC 2616 and describes a protocol for exchanging information by using requests from clients and responses from servers.

Requests from clients such as web browsers contain a specific set of headers that define the method used for retrieval, the object to be retrieved, and the protocol version to be used. Other headers contain the web server host name, languages requested, the name of the browser, and other information that the client deems relevant to the request.

Here's a basic HTTP version 1.1 request that shows only the most important of these headers:

```
GET / HTTP/1.1
Host: www.braingia.org
```

This request specifies the *GET* method to retrieve the document located at the */* (root) directory location using HTTP version 1.1. The second line, commonly called the *Host* header, is the URL *http://www.braingia.org*. This header tells the web server which website is being requested. Several different methods can be used in a request; the three most common are *GET*, *POST*, and *HEAD*. The client and server also exchange HTTP cookies as part of the headers. Cookies are sent in the request, and others might be received in the response.

When the web server for *http://www.braingia.org* receives a request like this, the web server sends response headers that indicate how it has handled the request. In this case, the web server sends response headers similar to these:

```
HTTP/1.1 200 OK
Date: Sat, 12 Mar 2011 01:04:34 GMT
Server: Apache/1.3.33 (Debian GNU/Linux) mod_perl/1.29 PHP/4.3.10-22
Transfer-Encoding: chunked
Content-Type: text/html; charset=iso-8859-1
```

The requested document follows the response headers. The first and most important header indicates the status of the response. In the example, the response is *200*, which is synonymous with OK. Other common responses include *404* (which indicates that the requested document was not found), *302* (which indicates a redirect), and *500* (which indicates that a server error occurred).

Understanding these basics of HTTP is important for understanding how to build AJAX requests and how to troubleshoot those requests when things go wrong. You can find more information about HTTP, including the various response codes, in RFC 2616 at *ftp://ftp.rfc-editor.org/in-notes/rfc2616.txt*.

Processing an AJAX Response

It's easier to work with the response when the request is sent synchronously, because the script's execution stops while awaiting the response. The *requestObj* variable provides helpful methods for processing a response, including giving access to the status codes and text of the status sent from the server. Regardless of whether the request is synchronous or asynchronous, you should evaluate the status code to ensure that the response was successful (usually indicated by a status of *200*).

The *responseText* method contains the text of the response as received from the web server.

For example, assume a server application returns the sum of two numbers. Calling the application to add the numbers 2 and 56 looks like this:

```
http://www.braingia.org/addtwo.php?num1=2&num2=56
```

Here's a synchronous call and response retrieval:

```
requestObj.open("GET", "http://www.braingia.org/addtwo.php?num1=2&num2=56", false);
requestObj.send();
if (requestObj.status == 200) {
    alert(requestObj.responseText);
} else {
    alert(requestObj.statusText);
}
```

In this example, assume that the *requestObj* was created using the *readyAJAX()* function that you saw earlier. The preceding code then calls the *open* method using a *GET* request to the specified URL (*http://www.braingia.org/addtwo.php?num1=2&num2=56*). The request is sent synchronously because the last argument to the *open* method is *false*. Next, the code calls the *send* method, which actually sends the request to the web server.

When the client receives the response from the web server, it calls the status method to check the status value. If the response code is *200*, indicating success, the code displays the *responseText*, which holds the response from the server. If the response status code is anything other than *200*, the code displays the status text.

Processing an asynchronous response is a bit more complex. When a request is sent asynchronously, script execution continues. Therefore, it is unpredictable when the script will be notified that the response has been received. To know the response status, you can use the *onreadystatechange* event to trigger code that checks the event's *readyState* property to determine the state of the request/response cycle. Recall from Chapter 17, "JavaScript and XML," that the *readyState* property has five states, as shown in Table 19-1.

TABLE 19-1 Values for the *readyState* Property

Value	Description
0	Uninitialized. Open but has yet to be called.
1	Open. Initialized but not yet sent.
2	Sent. The request has been sent.
3	Receiving. The response is actively being received.
4	Loaded. The response has been fully received.

For practical purposes, the only state that matters to the JavaScript and AJAX programmer is state *4*—Loaded. Attempting to process a response that has a *readyState* value other than *4* results in an error.

You typically use an anonymous function to handle the *onreadystatechange* event for asynchronous AJAX calls. The function checks to see whether the *readyState* property has reached *4*, and then checks to ensure that the status is 200, indicating success. The code follows this format:

```
requestObj.onreadystatechange = function() {
    if (requestObj.readyState == 4) {
        if (requestObj.status == 200) {
            alert(requestObj.responseText);
        } else {
            alert(requestObj.statusText);
        }
    }
}
```

In this next exercise, you create an *XMLHttpRequest* object and send a request to a web server to retrieve a book title based on its ISBN. You need a web server and web server code to print the response, because requests sent using *XMLHttpRequest* are subject to the JavaScript same-origin policy.

The *same-origin policy* requires that requests go only to servers within the same domain from which the calling script was loaded. In other words, because I'm executing the script in this exercise directly from my web server at *http://www.braingia.org*, my script is able to call that server and retrieve a response. If you tried to call a URL on another web server, however, the same-origin policy would prevent the script from retrieving the response.

> **Note** One way to get around the same-origin security feature is to use an HTTP proxy or to write the server-side program so that it sends a request on behalf of the calling program; however, learning how to do that is beyond the scope of this book.

For the upcoming exercise, the script or program running on the server needs to return the phrase *"JavaScript Step by Step"* when it receives a *GET* request with a name/value argument with the following value:

isbn=9780735624498

For example, at its most basic, the server-side program could look like this when implemented inside an Active Server Pages (ASP) page based on VBScript:

```
<%
dim isbn
isbn=Request.QueryString("isbn")
If isbn<>"" Then
    If isbn=="9780735624498" Then
        Response.Write("JavaScript Step by Step")
    End If
End If
%>
```

A functionally similar program looks like this if written in PHP:

```
<?php

$isbn = $_GET['isbn'];

if (! $isbn) {
    print "That request was not understood.";
} else if ($isbn == "9780735624498") {
    print "JavaScript Step by Step";
}

?>
```

In the following exercise, the URL to which the request will be sent is predefined, but you must replace that URL with the URL where your server-side program is located. Because of the same-origin policy, the server-side program needs to be within the same domain as the page that calls it.

Sending and receiving with *XMLHttpRequest*

1. Create your server-side program to return the book title when it receives the *isbn* argument shown earlier. You can do this in your choice of languages. (If you need to, look at the two examples shown earlier.)

2. Using Microsoft Visual Studio, Eclipse, or another editor, edit the file isbn.htm in the Chapter19 sample files folder (in the companion content).

3. Within the webpage, replacing the TODO comment with the following code shown in boldface (in the isbn.txt file in the companion content). Be sure to replace the *url* variable with the appropriate URL for your server-side program:

```
<!DOCTYPE HTML PUBLIC "-//W3C//DTD HTML 4.01//EN"
"http://www.w3.org/TR/html4/strict.dtd">
<html>
<head>
<title>ISBN</title>
```

```
</head>
<body>
<div id="data"></div>
<script type="text/javascript">
function readyAJAX() {
    try {
        return new XMLHttpRequest();
    } catch(e) {
        try {
            return new ActiveXObject("Msxml2.XMLHTTP");
        } catch(e) {
            try {
                return new ActiveXObject("Microsoft.XMLHTTP");
            } catch(e) {
                return "A newer browser is needed.";
            }
        }
    }
}
var requestObj = readyAJAX();
var url = "http://www.braingia.org/isbn.php?isbn=9780735624498";
requestObj.open("GET",url,true);
requestObj.send();
requestObj.onreadystatechange = function() {
    if (requestObj.readyState == 4) {
        if (requestObj.status == 200) {
            alert(requestObj.responseText);
        } else {
            alert(requestObj.statusText);
        }
    }
}
</script>
</body>
</html>
```

4. Save and view the page in a web browser. You should receive an alert like the one shown here:

Congratulations! You've now processed your first *XMLHttpRequest*.

Processing XML Responses

The AJAX examples you've seen so far have all used plain Hypertext Markup Language (HTML) and text responses from the web server, so you could retrieve them using the *XMLHttpRequest* object's *responseText* method. However, server applications can also return XML responses, which you can process natively using the *responseXML* method.

Earlier in this chapter, the sidebar titled "Describing How the Web Works in 500 Words or Fewer" discussed an example web server response. The server response contained this *Content-Type* header:

```
Content-Type: text/html; charset=iso-8859-1
```

To retrieve a response using the *responseXML* method, the web server needs to send a *Content-Type* of *text/xml* or *application/xml* like this:

```
Content-Type: application/xml
```

When the *XMLHttpRequest* object receives native XML as the response, you can use Document Object Model (DOM) methods to process the response.

The *responseXML* method has been somewhat quirky historically, and using it can result in unexpected behavior, depending on the browser and operating system. In addition, *responseXML* isn't as widely supported as other JavaScript methods. Using *responseXML* means combining the *XMLHttpRequest* techniques already seen in this chapter with the XML parsing techniques described in Chapter 17. For example, consider this XML document (call it book.xml):

```
<?xml version="1.0" encoding="ISO-8859-1"?>
<book>
  <title>JavaScript Step by Step</title>
  <isbn>9780735624498</isbn>
</book>
```

Combining the *XMLHttpRequest* object and XML parsing leads to the following code, which retrieves and displays the ISBN from the book.xml document:

```
var requestObj = readyAJAX();
var url = "http://www.braingia.org/book.xml";
requestObj.open("GET",url,false);
requestObj.send();
if (requestObj.status == 200) {
    var xmldocument = requestObj.responseXML;
    alert(xmldocument.getElementsByTagName("isbn")[0].childNodes[0].nodeValue);
} else {
    alert(requestObj.statusText);
}
```

When the request completes successfully, *requestObj.responseXML* contains the requested XML document (book.xml). The *xmldocument.getElementsByTagName("isbn")* code retrieves an array of the *<isbn>* tags in the document. There's only one of those in this document; the *[0]* indicates the first one. The *.childNodes[0]* portion of the code retrieves the first child node from that *<isbn>* tag. In this case, that's the text node, which contains the ISBN number. Finally, the *.nodeValue* portion of the code retrieves the value of that text node, the ISBN itself, which the preceding code displays with an *alert* call.

Working with JSON

JavaScript Object Notation (JSON) is a way to pass data as native JavaScript objects and arrays, rather than encode data within XML (or HTML) responses. JSON is a more efficient way to pass data from server to client. Parsing XML using the DOM is more complex and thus slower, whereas parsing JSON-encoded data is done directly in JavaScript.

Recall the book.xml document from an earlier example in this chapter. That same data in JSON looks like this:

```
{
"book":
    {
    "title": "JavaScript Step by Step",
    "isbn": "9780735624498"
    }
}
```

Retrieving an individual element is somewhat easier with JSON than with XML. You use the JavaScript *eval()* function to parse the JSON-formatted response. For example, here's the code to retrieve and display the book title:

```
var requestObj = readyAJAX();
var url = "http://www.braingia.org/json.php";
requestObj.open("GET",url,false);
requestObj.send();
if (requestObj.status == 200) {
    var xmldocument = eval('(' + requestObj.responseText + ')');
    alert(xmldocument.book.title);
} else {
    alert(requestObj.statusText);
}
```

Using JSON carries an inherent security risk, because it uses the *eval()* function to parse the response. The *eval()* function essentially executes the JavaScript code received, so if that code were malicious, it would execute in the context of the application being run. It is your responsibility to ensure that the data your application is using with JSON is clean and free of malicious code that could cause problems when executed using *eval()*.

Using a JavaScript framework such as jQuery alleviates much of this concern, as does the addition of native JSON into ECMA-262 version 5. You learn how to use jQuery and how to use it for processing JSON in Chapter 22, "An Introduction to jQuery."

Processing Headers

The *HTTP HEAD* method returns just the response headers from the server, rather than the headers and the body in the way the *GET* method does. The *HEAD* method is sometimes helpful for determining whether a given resource has been updated or changed.

One frequently-sent HTTP header is *Expires*, which indicates when the client should request a refreshed copy of a document rather than read it from the client's cache. If the server sends the *Expires* header, the *HEAD* method is an efficient way to view and parse the *Expires* header because the *HEAD* method retrieves only the response header rather than the entire body of the requested resource.

To request only the response headers from a server, whether using a *HEAD* request or any other type of request such as *GET* or *POST*, use the *getAllResponseHeaders()* method of the *XMLHttpRequest* object, as follows:

```
requestObj.getAllResponseHeaders();
```

For example, Listing 19-2 shows how to retrieve the response headers from the default page of my website.

LISTING 19-2 Retrieving headers.

```
<!DOCTYPE HTML PUBLIC "-//W3C//DTD HTML 4.01//EN"
"http://www.w3.org/TR/html4/strict.dtd">
<html>
<head>
<title>Response Headers</title>
</head>
<body>
<div id="data"></div>
<script type="text/javascript">
function readyAJAX() {
    try {
        return new XMLHttpRequest();
    } catch(e) {
        try {
            return new ActiveXObject("Msxml2.XMLHTTP");
        } catch(e) {
            try {
                return new ActiveXObject("Microsoft.XMLHTTP");
            } catch(e) {
                return "A newer browser is needed.";
            }
        }
```

```
        }
    }
}
var requestObj = readyAJAX();
var url = "http://www.braingia.org/";
requestObj.open("HEAD",url,true);
requestObj.send();
requestObj.onreadystatechange = function() {
    if (requestObj.readyState == 4) {
        if (requestObj.status == 200) {
            alert(requestObj.getAllResponseHeaders());
        } else {
            alert(requestObj.statusText);
        }
    }
}
</script>
</body>
</html>
```

Troubleshooting The same-origin policy that you came across during the exercise earlier in the chapter applies equally to the *HEAD* method in Listing 19-2. When writing Listing 19-2, I forgot about the same-origin policy and originally set the *url* variable to *http://www.microsoft.com/*, thinking I'd get that site's default page. However, upon receiving an error, I realized the problem and changed the *url* variable to match the domain on which the script was running (my site). You are likely to encounter the same problem. Remember to change the *url* variable to your server of origin when attempting to run the code in Listing 19-2.

Using the *POST* Method

Up to this point, the examples you've seen have used the *GET* and *HEAD* methods to retrieve data from the server. To submit queries through HTTP, you often use the *POST* method. Using the *POST* method with *XMLHttpRequest* is a bit more complex than using either the *GET* or *HEAD* methods. However, the *POST* method offers two specific advantages over the *GET* method. First, parameters you send with a *POST* request are contained in the body of the request rather than in the URL, as they are with the *GET* method, and therefore are less likely to be seen by the casual observer trying to find ways into your application. Second, the *POST* method supports larger requests. Some servers limit the amount or size of a *GET* request to a certain number of characters, and although those servers might also limit the size of a *POST* request, the limitation for *POST* requests is almost always much greater.

The HTTP *POST* method requires an additional header to be set within the request. You set that additional header with the *setRequestHeader()* method:

```
requestObj.setRequestHeader(header, value);
```

For example, to set the *Content-Type* header for a web form, as you would do for a *POST* request, you could write:

```
requestObj.setRequestHeader("Content-type", "application/x-www-form-urlencoded");
```

When you saw the AJAX requests sent earlier using the *GET* method, the URL included the parameters or *name/value* pairs for the application, like so:

```
http://www.braingia.org/books/javascriptsbs/isbn.php?isbn=9780735624498
```

In the preceding example, the *isbn* parameter has the value *9780735624498*. However, when working with *POST* requests, the URL contains only the document or resource requested— it doesn't contain any parameters. Therefore, you must send the parameters as part of the *send()* method.

Listing 19-3 presents an AJAX request using the *POST* method, shown in boldface type. It uses two parameters—see whether you can spot them.

LISTING 19-3 Constructing a *POST* request.

```
<!DOCTYPE HTML PUBLIC "-//W3C//DTD HTML 4.01//EN"
"http://www.w3.org/TR/html4/strict.dtd">
<html>
<head>
<title>Post</title>
</head>
<body>
<div id="xmldata"></div>
<script type="text/javascript">
function readyAJAX() {
    try {
        return new XMLHttpRequest();
    } catch(e) {
        try {
            return new ActiveXObject("Msxml2.XMLHTTP");
        } catch(e) {
            try {
                return new ActiveXObject("Microsoft.XMLHTTP");
            } catch(e) {
                return "A newer browser is needed.";
            }
        }
    }
}
```

```
var requestObj = readyAJAX();
var url = "http://www.braingia.org/books/javascriptsbs/post.php";
var params = "num1=2&num2=2";
requestObj.open("POST",url,true);
requestObj.setRequestHeader("Content-type", "application/x-www-form-urlencoded");
requestObj.send(params);
requestObj.onreadystatechange = function() {
    if (requestObj.readyState == 4) {
        if (requestObj.status == 200) {
            alert(requestObj.responseText);
        } else {
            alert(requestObj.statusText);
        }
    }
}
</script>
</body>
</html>
```

Listing 19-3 creates two parameters placed into a variable called *params*:

```
var params = "num1=2&num2=2";
```

After constructing the request object (*requestObj*), the parameters are passed as an argument to the *send()* method:

```
requestObj.send(params);
```

Case Study: Live Searching and Updating

There are many examples of type-ahead, or predictive, searching using JavaScript, such as the one shown in Chapter 18, "JavaScript Applications." One example is a form that searches for email addresses that have been either whitelisted or blacklisted through a spam filter.

The whitelist/blacklist search uses AJAX to import an XML file and provides results based on input from the administrator. You can easily adapt this application to provide live search results or live bookmarks. Chapter 20, "A Bit Deeper into AJAX," uses a portion of that application from Chapter 18 to create a live search form, and the next section introduces an adaptation of the application to create a live searchable bookmark feed using XML.

I frequently find it necessary to access web browser bookmarks from multiple computers. With that in mind, here's an AJAX application that provides a Bookmarks page. The page manages the bookmarks using an XML file that resides in a central location. The code retrieves the file and builds a web page that extracts the bookmarks and provides a search interface.

The bookmark application is shown in Figure 19-1. Granted, it's showing only 3 bookmarks, but the application works the same with 3 bookmarks or 300, and providing just a few makes demonstrating bookmarks easier.

FIGURE 19-1 A view of the live bookmark application.

The search box works by narrowing down the list of viewed bookmarks as a user types text into the text box. For example, typing the letter **m** into the text box immediately changes the pages so that it shows only those bookmarks that begin with the letter *m,* as depicted in Figure 19-2.

FIGURE 19-2 Typing the letter **m** narrows down the displayed bookmarks to those beginning with *m.*

Typing more—for example, typing **i** to make the characters **mi**—continues to narrow down the available bookmarks, as shown in Figure 19-3.

FIGURE 19-3 Adding additional characters to further narrow down the results.

When a user deletes the text from the text box, the Bookmarks page changes back to its default (shown in Figure 19-1).

Here's the XML for this application (see the file bookmark.xml in the companion content):

```xml
<?xml version="1.0" encoding="UTF-8" standalone="yes"?>
<bookmarks xmlns:xsi="http://www.w3.org/2001/XMLSchema-instance">
        <bookmark>
                <title>Steve Suehring's Home Page</title>
                <url>http://www.braingia.org/</url>
        </bookmark>
        <bookmark>
                <title>MSDN</title>
                <url>http://msdn.microsoft.com/</url>
        </bookmark>
        <bookmark>
                <title>Microsoft Press</title>
                <url>http://www.microsoft.com/mspress</url>
        </bookmark>
</bookmarks>
```

The application, along with the webpage, is shown here and in the bookmark.htm file (in the companion content):

```html
<!DOCTYPE HTML PUBLIC "-//W3C//DTD HTML 4.01//EN"
"http://www.w3.org/TR/html4/strict.dtd">
<html>
<head>
<title>Search</title>
</head>
<body>
<form name="nameform" id="nameform" action="" method="post">
Bookmark Search: <input id="textname" type="text" name="textname">
</form>
<div id="data"></div>
<script type="text/javascript" src="ehandler.js"></script>
<script type="text/javascript">
```

```javascript
function textSearch() {
    var textName = document.getElementById("textname");
    var dataNode = document.getElementById("data");
    while (dataNode.hasChildNodes()) {
        dataNode.removeChild(dataNode.firstChild);
    }
    listName(textName.value);
}


function readyAJAX() {
    try {
        return new XMLHttpRequest();
    } catch(e) {
        try {
            return new ActiveXObject("Msxml2.XMLHTTP");
        } catch(e) {
            try {
                return new ActiveXObject("Microsoft.XMLHTTP");
            } catch(e) {
                return "A newer browser is needed.";
            }
        }
    }
}
function listName(text) {
    var xmlEl = AJAXresponse.getElementsByTagName("bookmark");
    elLength = xmlEl.length;
    for (i = 0; i < elLength; i++) {
        var div = document.createElement("div");
        // Create the row elements
        for (j = 0; j < xmlEl[i].childNodes.length; j++) {
            // Skip it if the type is not 1
            if (xmlEl[i].childNodes[j].nodeType != 1) {
                continue;
            }
            var url = new RegExp("http");
            if (! xmlEl[i].childNodes[j].firstChild.nodeValue.match(url)) {
                var pattern = "^" + text;
                var title = xmlEl[i].childNodes[j].firstChild.nodeValue;
                var nameRegexp = new RegExp(pattern, "i");
                var existDiv = document.getElementById(title);
                if (! existDiv) {
                    if (title.match(nameRegexp)) {
                        var anchor = document.createElement("a");
                        var xmlData =
                        document.createTextNode(xmlEl[i].childNodes[j].firstChild.nodeValue);

                        var urls = AJAXresponse.getElementsByTagName("url");
                        anchor.setAttribute("href", urls[i].firstChild.nodeValue);
                        anchor.appendChild(xmlData);
                        div.appendChild(anchor);
                    }
                }
            }
        }
    }
```

```
            document.getElementById("data").appendChild(div);
        }
    }

    var requestObj = readyAJAX();
    var url = "http://www.braingia.org/books/javascriptsbs/bookmark.xml";
    requestObj.open("GET",url,true);
    requestObj.send();
    var AJAXresponse;
    requestObj.onreadystatechange = function() {
        if (requestObj.readyState == 4) {
            if (requestObj.status == 200) {
                AJAXresponse = requestObj.responseXML;
                listName("");
            } else {
                alert(requestObj.statusText);
            }
        }
    }
    var textEl = document.getElementById("textname");
    EHandler.add(textEl,"keyup", function() { textSearch(); } );

</script>
</body>
</html>
```

The JavaScript portion of the code is broken into several functions, which I discuss shortly. First, the code brings in the event handler script ehandler.js, which you encountered in Chapter 11, "JavaScript Events and the Browser":

```
<script type="text/javascript" src="ehandler.js"></script>
```

The HTML for the page consists of only a few lines. Here's the web form:

```
<form name="nameform" id="nameform" action="" method="post">
Bookmark Search: <input id="textname" type="text" name="textname">
</form>
```

And here's the *div* that will hold the bookmarks:

```
<div id="data"></div>
```

The JavaScript portion of the code declares several functions and executes the following code within the main block. This code is largely the same as the code you've seen throughout this chapter already: It uses the *readyAJAX()* function and sends an AJAX request for a bookmark XML file to the server. When the response is received, the code calls the *listName()* function.

In addition to the AJAX code, an event handler is attached to the web form's text box. The event to be handled is *keyup*, which detects when a key is pressed and released within the text box. The code looks like this:

```
var requestObj = readyAJAX();
```

```
var url = "http://www.braingia.org/books/javascriptsbs/bookmark.xml";
requestObj.open("GET",url,true);
requestObj.send();
var AJAXresponse;
requestObj.onreadystatechange = function() {
    if (requestObj.readyState == 4) {
        if (requestObj.status == 200) {
            AJAXresponse = requestObj.responseXML;
            listName("");
        } else {
            alert(requestObj.statusText);
        }
    }
}

var textEl = document.getElementById("textname");
EHandler.add(textEl,"keyup", function() { textSearch(); } );
```

The event handler that handles key presses in the search form resides in two functions: *text Search* and *listName*. The *textSearch* function is responsible for removing bookmarks from the list. It calls the *listName()* function.

```
function textSearch() {
    var textName = document.getElementById("textname");
    var dataNode = document.getElementById("data");
    while (dataNode.hasChildNodes()) {
        dataNode.removeChild(dataNode.firstChild);
    }
    listName(textName.value);
}
```

Finally, the *listName()* function contains the code to display only those bookmarks that at least partially match the text that's been typed into the text box. If no text is in the text box, it shows all the bookmarks:

```
function listName(text) {
    var xmlEl = AJAXresponse.getElementsByTagName("bookmark");
    elLength = xmlEl.length;
    for (i = 0; i < elLength; i++) {
        var div = document.createElement("div");
        // Create the row elements
        for (j = 0; j < xmlEl[i].childNodes.length; j++) {
            // Skip it if the type is not 1
            if (xmlEl[i].childNodes[j].nodeType != 1) {
                continue;
            }
            var url = new RegExp("http");
            if (! xmlEl[i].childNodes[j].firstChild.nodeValue.match(url)) {
                var pattern = "^" + text;
                var title = xmlEl[i].childNodes[j].firstChild.nodeValue;
                var nameRegexp = new RegExp(pattern, "i");
                var existDiv = document.getElementById(title);
                if (! existDiv) {
                    if (title.match(nameRegexp)) {
```

```
                    var anchor = document.createElement("a");
                    var xmlData =
                    document.createTextNode(xmlEl[i].childNodes[j].firstChild.nodeValue);
                    var urls = AJAXresponse.getElementsByTagName("url");
                    anchor.setAttribute("href", urls[i].firstChild.nodeValue);
                    anchor.appendChild(xmlData);
                    div.appendChild(anchor);
                }
            }
        }
    }
    document.getElementById("data").appendChild(div);
    }
}
```

Exercises

1. Which of the HTTP request methods covered in this chapter is the most secure? Why?

2. Describe the differences among an *XMLHttpRequest* request/response using HTML, XML, and JSON.

3. Construct a server-side program to return the sum of two numbers that the program receives as parameters. Call the program using an asynchronous *XMLHttpRequest* object.

Chapter 20
A Bit Deeper into AJAX

After reading this chapter, you'll be able to:

- Understand how Asynchronous JavaScript and XML (AJAX) and Cascading Style Sheets (CSS) can be used together.

- Understand more about the relationship between the Document Object Model (DOM), AJAX, and CSS.

- Use AJAX and CSS to create and style a Hypertext Markup Language (HTML) table with Extensible Markup Language (XML) data.

- Create an AJAX-based drop-down text box using CSS.

In the previous chapter, you saw how to use the *XMLHttpRequest* object to send, receive, and process requests, and ultimately how to create an AJAX application. In this chapter, you see how to use CSS to display data retrieved with AJAX.

The relationship between JavaScript and CSS was covered in Chapter 15, "JavaScript and CSS." In that chapter, you learned that you can change document styles programmatically using JavaScript. In Chapter 17, "JavaScript and XML," you learned how to display XML data as an HTML table. And in Chapter 19, "A Touch of AJAX," you saw how to create a live, searchable bookmarks webpage using some CSS and a lot of the DOM. This chapter shows how you can use CSS to style the table from Chapter 17 and expand and retool the bookmark application from Chapter 19, again with the help of CSS and JavaScript.

Along the way, I hope to convey that AJAX is really pretty easy to use. Retrieving and parsing the information using *XMLHttpRequest* is the simple part—it's what you do with that data that matters. That's why CSS and the DOM matter! AJAX is where you bring together all the JavaScript that you've learned throughout this book to create larger applications.

Creating an HTML Table with XML and CSS

Chapter 17 presented an example that retrieved XML and used its data as part of an HTML table, as depicted in Figure 20-1. The code to create that table was developed in Chapter 17 and expanded to show not only the data but also the column headings. The result of the code at the end of Chapter 17 was as follows:

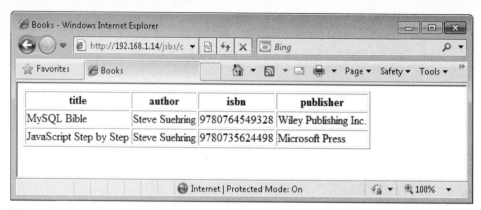

FIGURE 20-1 Displaying XML data in an HTML table.

The code from Chapter 17 uses XML methods to obtain the data directly. The next exercise converts the code to retrieve the XML using *XMLHttpRequest*. Like the exercise in Chapter 19, the following exercise requires the XML file to be stored on a web server.

Using *XMLHttpRequest* to retrieve and display XML data

1. Use the books.xml file that you created in Chapter 17, or—if you didn't create one or didn't save the file—create a file now called books.xml with the following data (you can get it from the books.xml file in the companion content). Place this file on the same web server as the HTML file that you will create in the next step.

```
<books>
<book>
    <title>JavaScript Step by Step</title>
    <author>Steve Suehring</author>
    <isbn>9780735624498</isbn>
    <publisher>Microsoft Press</publisher>
</book>
<book>
    <title>MySQL Bible</title>
    <author>Steve Suehring</author>
    <isbn>9780764549328</isbn>
    <publisher>Wiley Publishing Inc.</publisher>
</book>
</books>
```

2. Using Microsoft Visual Studio, Eclipse, or another editor, edit the file ajaxbooks.htm in the Chapter20 sample files folder (in the companion content).

3. Within ajaxbooks.htm, add the following code shown in boldface type (and in the ajaxbooks.txt file in the companion content), replacing the TODO comments. Be sure to replace the Uniform Resource Locator (URL) placeholder *YOUR SERVER HERE* with the correct URL for your web server. Note that you're changing only the function definition and the first line of the *displayData()* function from the original version in Chapter 18.

```
<!DOCTYPE HTML PUBLIC "-//W3C//DTD HTML 4.01//EN" "http://www.w3.org/TR/html4/strict.
dtd">
<html>
<head>
<title>Booksx</title>
</head>
<body>
<div id="xmldata"></div>
<script type="text/javascript">

function readyAJAX() {
    try {
        return new XMLHttpRequest();
    } catch(e) {
        try {
            return new ActiveXObject('Msxml2.XMLHTTP');
        } catch(e) {
            try {
                return new ActiveXObject('Microsoft.XMLHTTP');
            } catch(e) {
                return "A newer browser is needed.";
            }
        }
    }
}

var requestObj = readyAJAX();
var url = "http://YOUR SERVER HERE/books.xml";
requestObj.open("GET",url,true);
requestObj.send();
var AJAXresponse;
requestObj.onreadystatechange = function() {
    if (requestObj.readyState == 4) {
        if (requestObj.status == 200) {
            AJAXresponse = requestObj.responseXML;
            displayData(AJAXresponse);
        } else {
            alert(requestObj.statusText);
        }
    }
}

function displayData(response) {
    var xmlEl = response.getElementsByTagName("book");
    var table = document.createElement("table");
    table.border = "1";
    var tbody = document.createElement("tbody");

    // Append the body to the table
    table.appendChild(tbody);
    var row = document.createElement("tr");

    // Append the row to the body
    tbody.appendChild(row);

    for (colHead = 0; colHead < xmlEl[0].childNodes.length; colHead++) {
```

```
            if (xmlEl[0].childNodes[colHead].nodeType != 1) {
                continue;
            }
            var tableHead = document.createElement("th");
            var colName = document.createTextNode(xmlEl[0].childNodes[colHead].nodeName);
            tableHead.appendChild(colName);
            row.appendChild(tableHead);
        }
        tbody.appendChild(row);

        // Create table row
        for (i = 0; i < xmlEl.length; i++) {
            var row = document.createElement("tr");
            // Create the row/td elements
            for (j = 0; j < xmlEl[i].childNodes.length; j++) {
                // Skip it if the type is not 1
                if (xmlEl[i].childNodes[j].nodeType != 1) {
                    continue;
                }

                // Insert the actual text/data from the XML document.
                var td = document.createElement("td");
                var xmlData =
                    document.createTextNode(xmlEl[i].childNodes[j].firstChild.nodeValue);
                td.appendChild(xmlData);
                row.appendChild(td);
            }
            tbody.appendChild(row);
        }
        document.getElementById("xmldata").appendChild(table);
    }

</script>
</body>
</html>
```

4. View the page in a web browser. You see a page like this:

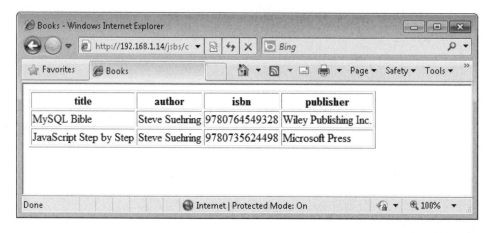

This exercise combined code from each of the last two chapters to show how to retrieve and display XML data with the *xmlHttpRequest* object associated with AJAX applications. Although the original XML application shown in Chapter 18 was converted to use *xmlHttp Request*, the table it displays is still rather ugly. This is where CSS styling comes into play.

Styling the Table with CSS

The main function that displays the table in the previous exercise is the *displayData()* function. Within this function, you can apply CSS styles to make the table look more like one you'd see in a modern web application.

> **Note** The approach to working with styles in this chapter makes changes to the style attributes directly within the JavaScript, but you should understand that this approach is offered for educational purposes only; it's not preferred in real-world code because it can make troubleshooting why a certain style attribute is applied to a given element difficult, because information can change both in CSS and in the JavaScript code. Another way to work with CSS, shown in Chapter 22, "An Introduction to jQuery," applies style changes by altering the CSS styles applied to HTML elements. This is the preferred way to work with CSS in JavaScript, because it keeps a separation between display (CSS) and behavior (JavaScript code).

Changing Style Attributes with JavaScript

One of the first tasks to accomplish is to remove the border by removing the following line from near the top of the *displayData()* function:

```
table.border = "1";
```

Within the *displayData()* function are two primary loops: one to display the column headings and one to display the data itself. The first loop displays the column headings, and looks like this:

```
for (colHead = 0; colHead < xmlEl[0].childNodes.length; colHead++) {
    if (xmlEl[0].childNodes[colHead].nodeType != 1) {
        continue;
    }
    var tableHead = document.createElement("th");
    var colName = document.createTextNode(xmlEl[0].childNodes[colHead].nodeName);
    tableHead.appendChild(colName);
    row.appendChild(tableHead);
}
tbody.appendChild(row);
```

The second loop, which displays the actual data, looks like this:

```
for (i = 0; i < xmlEl.length; i++) {
```

```
    var row = document.createElement("tr");
    // Create the row/td elements
    for (j = 0; j < xmlEl[i].childNodes.length; j++) {
        // Skip it if the type is not 1
        if (xmlEl[i].childNodes[j].nodeType != 1) {
            continue;
        }
        // Insert the actual text/data from the XML document.
        var td = document.createElement("td");
        var xmlData = document.createTextNode(xmlEl[i].childNodes[j].firstChild.nodeValue);
        td.appendChild(xmlData);
        row.appendChild(td);
    }
    tbody.appendChild(row);
}
```

Most of the changes made to the table's display will be made within these loops. I highlight the changes as they're made.

Another item you might want to change is the font. (I've always been partial to the Arial font myself.) You do this using the *fontFamily* style property in JavaScript. This change must be made within each of the loops to style all the text in the table with the Arial font. After adding that code, the loops now look like this (note the two new lines in boldface):

```
for (colHead = 0; colHead < xmlEl[0].childNodes.length; colHead++) {
    if (xmlEl[0].childNodes[colHead].nodeType != 1) {
        continue;
    }
    var tableHead = document.createElement("th");
    var colName = document.createTextNode(xmlEl[0].childNodes[colHead].nodeName);
    tableHead.style.fontFamily = "Arial";
    tableHead.appendChild(colName);
    row.appendChild(tableHead);
}
tbody.appendChild(row);

for (i = 0; i < xmlEl.length; i++) {
    var row = document.createElement("tr");
    // Create the row/td elements
    for (j = 0; j < xmlEl[i].childNodes.length; j++) {
        // Skip it if the type is not 1
        if (xmlEl[i].childNodes[j].nodeType != 1) {
            continue;
        }

        // Insert the actual text/data from the XML document.
        var td = document.createElement("td");
        var xmlData = document.createTextNode(xmlEl[i].childNodes[j].firstChild.nodeValue);
        td.style.fontFamily = "Arial";
        td.appendChild(xmlData);
        row.appendChild(td);
    }
    tbody.appendChild(row);
}
```

The results of these changes and the removal of the table border yields a table that looks like the one shown in Figure 20-2.

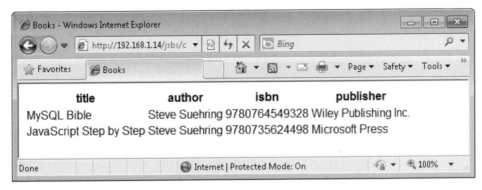

FIGURE 20-2 Beginning to style the table with CSS.

Some color would certainly help make the table more readable, especially if several or even several hundred or more rows of data were shown. Alternating the colors so that every other row is a slightly different shade, and changing the table heading to an entirely different color, might also help readability. Here's what the two loops look like after adding some *backgroundColor* style properties. Again, the changes are in boldface.

```
for (colHead = 0; colHead < xmlEl[0].childNodes.length; colHead++) {
    if (xmlEl[0].childNodes[colHead].nodeType != 1) {
        continue;
    }
    var tableHead = document.createElement("th");
    var colName = document.createTextNode(xmlEl[0].childNodes[colHead].nodeName);
    tableHead.style.fontFamily = "Arial";
    tableHead.style.backgroundColor = "#aaabba";
    tableHead.appendChild(colName);
    row.appendChild(tableHead);
}
tbody.appendChild(row);

for (i = 0; i < xmlEl.length; i++) {
    var row = document.createElement("tr");
    // Create the row/td elements
    for (j = 0; j < xmlEl[i].childNodes.length; j++) {
        // Skip it if the type is not 1
        if (xmlEl[i].childNodes[j].nodeType != 1) {
            continue;
        }

        // Insert the actual text/data from the XML document.
        var td = document.createElement("td");
        var xmlData = document.createTextNode(xmlEl[i].childNodes[j].firstChild.nodeValue);
        if (i % 2) {
            td.style.backgroundColor = "#aaabba";
        }
```

```
        td.style.fontFamily = "Arial";
        td.appendChild(xmlData);
        row.appendChild(td);
    }
    tbody.appendChild(row);
}
```

This code uses the modulo operator (%) to shade every other row of the table data with the light gray background. There are only two data rows in this table, so only the second row gets the gray shading. Figure 20-3 shows the results after adding the color. You can find the finished version of this page in the CompletedCode directory in the Chapter20 sample code for this book.

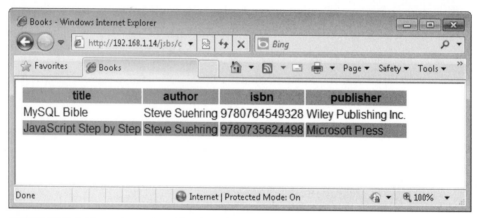

FIGURE 20-3 Adding color to the table using CSS.

Creating a Dynamic Drop-Down Box

You can use a variation of the bookmark application shown in Chapter 19 to create a live drop-down box for any type of textual list data. Sometimes this is known as a *suggest-as-you-type* drop-down box, because as you type, the user interface shows commonly entered values in a drop-down box below the text box, making it easier for users to complete their entries. Google Suggest is one such application.

Another implementation of this same principle is a drop-down box that shows common items (such as U.S. states) as the visitor types. The key to this variation is that the subset of data that can be retrieved to quickly populate the live drop-down box is manageable. For example, it's possible to retrieve a subset of states from a list of the 50 U.S. states as a visitor is typing a query into a text box. In contrast, if you were working with 1,000,000 database records, retrieving a subset would probably not be possible within a time that still appears responsive to the end user. As another example, you might use an application like this in a business to retrieve a list of employees for a company directory.

Here's a demonstration of this application. Using the *xmlHttpRequest* object, the application retrieves a list of the 50 states. When a user enters the letter **w**, the application retrieves all the states that begin with that letter, as shown in Figure 20-4.

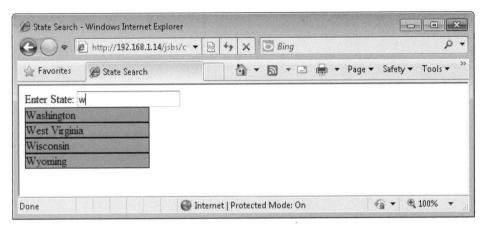

FIGURE 20-4 Retrieving a list of states that begin with the letter *w*.

Moving the mouse over the various states changes the states' background color, as shown in Figure 20-5, where I moved the mouse over Wisconsin (the mouse pointer is not visible in this screenshot).

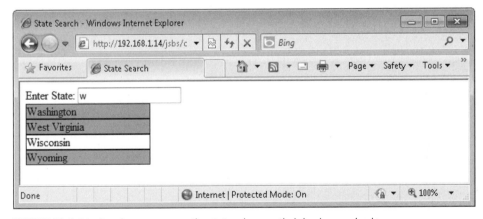

FIGURE 20-5 Moving the mouse over the states changes their background color.

Finally, clicking one of the state names causes that name to get copied into the text box. The result of this action is shown in Figure 20-6. From here, the form might be submitted, taking whatever action is appropriate for the application based on the input.

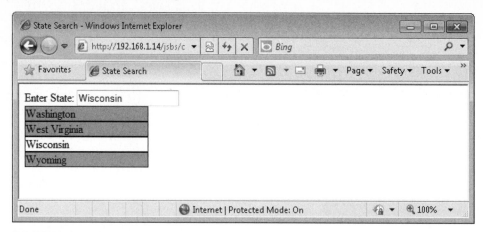

FIGURE 20-6 Moving a state into the text box.

This code works the same way as the bookmark application code from Chapter 19, insofar as the visitor can continue to type to narrow down, or focus, the search to a specific selection. Consider the case where the visitor typed the letter **n**. Doing so would reveal the eight states that begin with the letter *n*. Typing more—for example, typing the word **new**—would narrow that search down to four states, and typing more letters would narrow the results even more.

The code for this application is shown in Listing 20-1.

LISTING 20-1 A search application.

```
<!DOCTYPE HTML PUBLIC "-//W3C//DTD HTML 4.01//EN" "http://www.w3.org/TR/html4/
strict.dtd">
<html>
<head>
<title>State Search</title>
<script type="text/javascript" src="ehandler.js"></script>
</head>
<body>
<form name="nameform" id="nameform" action="" method="post">
Enter State: <input id="textname" type="text" name="textname">
</form>
<div id="data"></div>
<script type="text/javascript">

function textSearch() {
    var textName = document.getElementById("textname");
    var dataNode = document.getElementById("data");
    while (dataNode.hasChildNodes()) {
        dataNode.removeChild(dataNode.firstChild);
    }
    if (textName.value != "") {
        listName(textName.value);
    }
```

```
}

function readyAJAX() {
    try {
        return new XMLHttpRequest();
    } catch(e) {
        try {
            return new ActiveXObject('Msxml2.XMLHTTP');
        } catch(e) {
            try {
                return new ActiveXObject('Microsoft.XMLHTTP');
            } catch(e) {
                return "A newer browser is needed.";
            }
        }
    }
}

function listName(text) {
    var nameList = AJAXresponse.split(",");
    var pattern = "^" + text;
    var nameRegexp = new RegExp(pattern, "i");
    for (var i = 0; i < nameList.length; i++) {
        var existDiv = document.getElementById(nameList[i]);
        if (! existDiv) {
            if (nameList[i].match(nameRegexp)) {
                var displayDiv = document.getElementById("data");
                var newDiv = document.createElement("div");
                if (window.attachEvent) {
                    newDiv.attachEvent("onclick",function(e) {
                        document.forms["nameform"].textname.value =
                            e.srcElement.firstChild.nodeValue;});
                    newDiv.attachEvent("onmouseover",function(e) {
                        e.srcElement.style.background = "#FFFFFF"; });
                    newDiv.attachEvent("onmouseout",function(e) {
                        e.srcElement.style.background = "#aaabba"; });
                } else {
                    newDiv.addEventListener("click",function () {
                        document.forms["nameform"].textname.value =
                            this.firstChild.nodeValue; },false);
                    newDiv.addEventListener("mouseover",function() {
                        this.style.background = "#FFFFFF"; },false);
                    newDiv.addEventListener("mouseout",function() {
                        this.style.background = "#aaabba"; },false);
                }
                newDiv.setAttribute("id",nameList[i]);
                newDiv.style.background = "#aaabba";
                newDiv.style.color = "#000000";
                newDiv.style.border = "solid 1px";
                newDiv.style.display = "block";
                newDiv.style.width = "175px";
                newDiv.appendChild(document.createTextNode(nameList[i]));
                displayDiv.appendChild(newDiv);
            }
```

```
                }
            }
        }

        var requestObj = readyAJAX();
        var url = "http://YOUR SERVER HERE/statelist.php";
        requestObj.open("GET",url,true);
        requestObj.send();
        var AJAXresponse;
        requestObj.onreadystatechange = function() {
            if (requestObj.readyState == 4) {
                if (requestObj.status == 200) {
                    AJAXresponse = requestObj.responseText;
                } else {
                    alert(requestObj.statusText);
                }
            }
        }

        var textEl = document.getElementById("textname");
        EHandler.add(textEl,"keyup", function() { textSearch(); } );

    </script>
    </body>
    </html>
```

You already saw most of the code in Listing 20-1 in other places throughout this book, but I explain it again briefly here.

The code retrieves the list of states by calling an external server-based file, *statelist.php*. This file returns a simple comma-separated list of states, like this:

Alabama,Alaska,Arizona,California,Colorado,Delaware,Florida,Georgia, ...

The file splits this state list along the comma delimiter and puts the names into an array called *nameList*, like this:

```
var nameList = AJAXresponse.split(",");
```

In the code are some additions to applications you saw in the last two chapters, to create small clickable CSS-styled drop-down boxes. That code went into the *listName()* function that you saw in Chapter 19. The code applies event listeners and CSS styles to these HTML *DIV* elements in the *listName* function, shown here with the additional code in boldface:

```
function listName(text) {
    var nameList = AJAXresponse.split(",");
    var pattern = "^" + text;
    var nameRegexp = new RegExp(pattern, "i");
    for (var i = 0; i < nameList.length; i++) {
        var existDiv = document.getElementById(nameList[i]);
```

```
        if (! existDiv) {
            if (nameList[i].match(nameRegexp)) {
                var displayDiv = document.getElementById("data");
                var newDiv = document.createElement("div");
                if (window.attachEvent) {
                    newDiv.attachEvent("onclick",function(e) {
                        document.forms["nameform"].textname.value =
                            e.srcElement.firstChild.nodeValue;});
                    newDiv.attachEvent("onmouseover",function(e) {
                        e.srcElement.style.background = "#FFFFFF"; });
                    newDiv.attachEvent("onmouseout",function(e) {
                        e.srcElement.style.background = "#aaabba"; });
                } else {
                    newDiv.addEventListener("click",function () {
                        document.forms["nameform"].textname.value =
                            this.firstChild.nodeValue; },false);
                    newDiv.addEventListener("mouseover",function() {
                        this.style.background = "#FFFFFF"; },false);
                    newDiv.addEventListener("mouseout",function() {
                        this.style.background = "#aaabba"; },false);
                }
                newDiv.setAttribute("id",nameList[i]);
                newDiv.style.background = "#aaabba";
                newDiv.style.color = "#000000";
                newDiv.style.border = "solid 1px";
                newDiv.style.display = "block";
                newDiv.style.width = "175px";
                newDiv.appendChild(document.createTextNode(nameList[i]));
                displayDiv.appendChild(newDiv);
            }
        }
    }
}
```

Accepting Input from the User and AJAX

The next logical step in developing AJAX applications is to accept input from the user and do something with that input. Building an AJAX application is all about providing a highly inter-active application based on user actions. Unfortunately, to do justice to this subject, I would need to delve into the creation of server-side applications that would handle that input, and that is beyond the scope of this beginner-level book, which focuses primarily on JavaScript. With some luck, I'll write another book on intermediate JavaScript or building JavaScript applications that will show both the JavaScript and the server aspects of AJAX.

But I hope that even with this limited coverage, I've been able to convey that the building of AJAX applications is really nothing more than providing friendly, interactive ways for visitors to use applications, and that a large part of this task involves the design around the JavaScript, not the *XMLHttpRequest* alone. The *XMLHttpRequest* object is merely a carrier, or delivery mechanism, for getting data into the program. The layer on which *XMLHttpRequest* operates is well below the presentation layer upon which the page is built. Therefore, users never see the *XMLHttpRequest* processing in the background; they see only the design that you create on the front end of the application.

The remaining two chapters of this book build on everything you've done so far, but they will do so with the help of the jQuery JavaScript library.

Exercises

1. Create a *submit* event handler for the state example shown in this chapter such that the state submitted is displayed back to the user when she or he submits the form.

2. Create an application that uses *XMLHttpRequest* to return a list of names (such as an employee directory). You can use either plaintext or XML for the source data.

Part V
jQuery

Chapter 21

An Introduction to JavaScript Libraries and Frameworks

After reading this chapter, you'll be able to:

- Understand the role of JavaScript programming libraries and frameworks.

- Understand how to define your own library.

- Understand the role of third-party JavaScript libraries and frameworks and how to find more information about them.

Understanding Programming Libraries

In programming terms, a *library* is a grouping of code that provides common or additional functionality. Typically, libraries consist of one or more files that expose objects and functions. Within a program, a developer includes or calls the library to use these additional objects and functions. In this way, JavaScript libraries and frameworks are useful because they offload the maintenance and development of additional and enhanced functions. They help make common programming tasks easier and can also aid in smoothing out the differences and nuances in cross-browser development.

This chapter explores libraries in JavaScript, including the process of defining your own library, and takes a look at some of the more popular JavaScript libraries and frameworks available.

Defining Your Own JavaScript Library

Developers working in any language find themselves performing common functions repeatedly in many of their coding tasks, so creating a personal library, or grouping, of common functions that you can use in future projects is helpful.

The event handler script developed in Chapter 11, ehandler.js, shows how to create a library by creating a namespace for it:

```
var EHandler = {};
```

Within that namespace, the *EHandler* library adds two functions. Here's the first one:

```
EHandler.add = ...
```

And here's the second:

```
EHandler.remove = ...
```

Although short, *EHandler* is a true library. As you can see, libraries don't have to be large to be useful. You've seen numerous examples of using *EHandler* earlier in this book. With the *EHandler* library concept in mind, in this next example, you create your own library.

Creating a library

1. Using Microsoft Visual Studio, Eclipse, or the editor of your choice, open the library.js file, which you can find in the Chapter21 folder of this book's companion content.

2. Within library.js, add the following code (replacing the TODO comment) to create a namespace, and then add a function:

   ```
   var MyLibrary = {};


   MyLibrary.sendAlert = function(mesg, elm) {
           alert(mesg);
   };
   ```

3. Save the file and close it.

4. Open the file librarypage.htm. Within librarypage.htm, add the boldface code shown here (to replace of the TODO comment):

   ```
   <!DOCTYPE HTML PUBLIC "-//W3C//DTD HTML 4.01//EN" "http://www.w3.org/TR/html4/strict.
   dtd">
   <html>
   <head>
   <title>A Basic Example</title>
   <script type="text/javascript" src="library.js"></script>
   </head>
   <body>
   <script type="text/javascript">
   MyLibrary.sendAlert("hello, this is the message");
   </script>
   </body>
   </html>
   ```

5. Load the page librarypage.htm in a web browser. You should receive an alert like this:

> **Troubleshooting** If you don't receive an alert like the one just shown, be sure you have specified the path to the library.js file correctly. The example shown in the preceding librarypage.htm code assumes that the JavaScript file library.js is in the same directory as the HTML file.

Take care when defining and using your own libraries so that you don't overlap or collide with existing functions and reserved words from the ECMA-262 specification. Additionally, if you use an external library or framework such as jQuery or YUI, you need to make sure that your library doesn't collide with the naming conventions used for those.

Looking at Popular JavaScript Libraries and Frameworks

There are numerous publicly available libraries and frameworks for JavaScript. Their goal is to take difficult tasks and make them easier for programmers developing JavaScript-centric web applications.

Web developers spend a great deal of time trying to make pages look and act the same way across browsers. A significant advantage to using many JavaScript libraries or frameworks is that they remove the cross-browser compatibility headaches. All the popular JavaScript libraries and frameworks include code to make their respective functions work across all the browsers they support.

jQuery

jQuery provides a rich feature set, powerful options, extensibility, and excellent community support. Using jQuery, which is contained in a single JavaScript file, you can add effects to your web pages, enhance usability, and make processing of data with AJAX easier. Additionally, Microsoft ships jQuery with Visual Studio 2010. Chapter 22, "An Introduction to jQuery," and Chapter 23, "jQuery Effects and Plug-Ins," examine jQuery in greater detail. You can find more information about jQuery at *http://jquery.com*.

Yahoo! User Interface

Yahoo! User Interface (YUI) provides both JavaScript and Cascading Style Sheets (CSS), which simplifies developing web applications. Like jQuery, YUI includes features for enhancing usability and improving the web application. As an added bonus, YUI's documentation is excellent. You can find more information about YUI at *http://developer.yahoo.com/yui/*.

MooTools

MooTools is a very small, highly optimized library for JavaScript. MooTools differs from YUI and jQuery because it concentrates on optimizing JavaScript processing, whereas YUI and jQuery focus on effects, CSS, and direct user-experience interactions. That's definitely not to say that MooTools doesn't have effects—MooTools also offers many of the same effects (such as an accordion and a slider) that you find in YUI and jQuery. MooTools is recommended for intermediate to advanced JavaScript programmers and is available from *http://mootools.net/*.

Other Libraries

There are numerous other libraries and frameworks available for JavaScript—too many to cover, or even mention in this book. As a starting point, see *http://en.wikipedia.org /wiki/Comparison_of_JavaScript_frameworks* to find out more information about JavaScript frameworks.

Exercises

1. Examine each of the libraries and frameworks shown in this chapter. Which do you think is easiest for the new JavaScript programmer to learn? Why?

2. Create your own JavaScript library with an external JavaScript file. Include that file in an HTML page and call it.

Chapter 22
An Introduction to jQuery

After reading this chapter, you'll be able to:

- Understand how to include jQuery in your HTML.

- Understand important jQuery concepts and syntax.

- Use jQuery with your webpages.

jQuery Primer

jQuery is a popular and easy-to-use JavaScript framework. jQuery makes difficult JavaScript tasks easy, often by taking the pain out of cross-browser JavaScript.

The entire jQuery library consists of only a single JavaScript file, which simplifies its inclusion in your JavaScript. jQuery syntax is also easy to learn; it uses a simple namespace and consistent functionality. Used together with the jQuery User Interface (UI) add-on (covered in Chapter 23, "jQuery Effects and Plug-Ins"), you can create powerful, highly interactive web applications.

This chapter provides an introduction to jQuery, including how to download and use it in your JavaScript.

Using jQuery

You can obtain jQuery from *http://www.jquery.com/*. In this section, you'll see how to download jQuery and integrate it into a webpage.

The Two jQuery Downloads

On the jQuery home page, two downloads are available: a production version and a development version. Unless you're planning to develop jQuery plug-ins, or need to look at the internals of jQuery, you should download and use the minified production version.

As another viable option, especially for working through this chapter, you could use a content delivery network (CDN) to access a hosted version of jQuery. Google hosts jQuery and other libraries through its API website. This means that you can include jQuery in your webpages and JavaScript programs without having to host the file locally on your server. See *http://code.google.com/apis/libraries/devguide.html* for more information.

> **Note** For almost all scenarios in which you are working with jQuery, I recommend downloading and hosting the jQuery file locally. Using the local version can be faster and more reliable than using the CDN version. For example, if you use a CDN-hosted version and the CDN server goes down, anything on your site that uses the library won't work! However, for development tasks in this chapter, using a CDN-hosted file is perfectly acceptable.

Performing the exercises and following along in this chapter requires that you have jQuery downloaded to your local development computer or are connected to it from a CDN.

Including jQuery

You include jQuery in a webpage in the same manner as you would any other external JavaScript file—with a *<script>* tag pointing to the source file. Consider the code in Listing 22-1.

LISTING 22-1 Including jQuery in a webpage.

```
<!DOCTYPE HTML PUBLIC  "-//W3C//DTD HTML 4.01//EN"  "http://www.w3.org/TR/html4/
strict.dtd">
<html>
<head>
<title>Adding jQuery</title>
<script type="text/javascript" src="jquery-1.4.3.min.js"></script>
</head>
<body>
</body>
</html>
```

Now that you have jQuery downloaded or referenced from a CDN site, and you've looked at the preceding example showing how to include jQuery in a file, it's time to move into learning jQuery syntax.

> **Important** Version 1.4.3 is the latest as of this writing. However, that version will almost certainly be different by the time you read this, so you'll need to change the *src* attribute appropriately for the version of the jQuery script that you download.

Basic jQuery Syntax

When you include the jQuery library in a page, jQuery adds a function called *jquery()*. You might think that you'd make all calls to jQuery functions through this *jquery()* function interface, but there's a shortcut to the *jquery()* function: *$()*. Rather than typing **jquery** each time, you access the jQuery library using a dollar sign followed by parentheses, as shown in the examples in Table 22-1.

TABLE 22-1 A Few jQuery Selectors

Syntax	Description
$("a")	All *<a>* elements in the document.
$(document)	The entire document, frequently used to access the *ready()* function shown later in this chapter.
$("#elementID")	The element identified by ID *elementID*.
$(".className")	The element or elements that have the *className* class.

You see more selectors and related functions later in this chapter.

Like JavaScript code, jQuery statements should end with a semi-colon. It is also worth noting that you can use either single or double quotation marks as selectors within jQuery. For example, both of these statements are equally valid:

```
$("a")
```

```
$('a')
```

When you see examples of jQuery usage in the real world (not that this book isn't in the real world), both single and double quotation marks are used. Examples throughout this chapter use a mix of the two to get you familiar with seeing both cases; however, in your real-world programming, it's best to choose one style and stick with it.

Connecting jQuery to the Load Event

One of the most common ways to work with jQuery is by connecting to elements during the *load* (or *onload*) event of the page. (This chapter discusses events and functions in more detail later.) In jQuery, you do this through the *.ready()* utility function of the document element.

Recall from the brief example shown in the previous section that jQuery accesses elements with the *$()* syntax. Keeping that in mind, you can access the document element like this:

```
$(document)
```

And you can then access the *ready()* function like this:

```
$(document).ready()
```

The following exercise requires that you either have jQuery downloaded to your local development computer or that you use a CDN. The example shows version 1.4.3 of jQuery, but this version number will likely be different when you perform the exercise.

Using *Document Ready*

1. Using Microsoft Visual Studio, Eclipse, or another editor, edit the file docready.html in the Chapter22 sample files folder (in the companion content).

2. Within that file, add the following code shown in boldface in place of the TODO comment:

```
<!DOCTYPE HTML PUBLIC "-//W3C//DTD HTML 4.01//EN"
"http://www.w3.org/TR/html4/strict.dtd">
<html>
<head>
<title>Document Ready</title>
<script type="text/javascript" src="jquery-1.4.3.min.js"></script>
</head>
<body>
<script type="text/javascript">
$(document).ready(alert('hi'));
</script>
</body>
</html>
```

3. Save the file and view the page in a web browser. You'll see an alert like this one:

The code in this step-by-step exercise combines jQuery through the *$(document).ready()* function and also regular, plain old JavaScript, represented by the *alert()* function in this example. This mixture of jQuery and JavaScript is an important concept to understand: you use jQuery to supplement normal JavaScript. jQuery makes many of the difficult and sometimes mundane tasks easy—so easy, in fact, that you can spend your time building features rather than worrying about cross-browser nuances.

The *$(document).ready()* function removes the need for you to use the browser's *load* event or to insert a function call into the *load* event. With *$(document).ready()*, all the elements of the Document Object Model (DOM) are available before the *.ready()* function.

> **Tip** The *$(document).ready()* function is central to much of the programming that you do with jQuery.

Using Selectors

Selectors are key to working with jQuery and the DOM. You use *selectors* to identify and group the elements on which a jQuery function is executed. As shown in Table 22-1, you use selectors to gather all the elements of a certain tag, of a certain ID, or with a certain class applied to them. You can also use selectors in much more powerful ways, such as to select a specified number of elements; or to select only elements with a particular ancestry, for example, only those *<p>* tags that follow a *<div>* tag. This section introduces selectors in more detail.

Tip *Selectors* and the way they work in jQuery are based on selectors in CSS. If you are comfortable with using them in CSS (discussed in Chapter 15, "JavaScript and CSS"), you will feel right at home with this model.

Selecting Elements by ID

The example in Table 22-1 showed the general syntax for selecting an element by its ID attribute:

```
$("#elementID")
```

For example, consider this bit of HTML:

```
<a href="#" id="linkOne">Link</a>
```

With normal JavaScript, you access this element like so:

```
getElementById("linkOne")
```

With jQuery, you access the element using this:

```
$("#linkOne")
```

Selecting Elements by Class

You select elements by class by prefixing a dot (.) to the class name. The syntax is this:

```
$(".className")
```

For example, here's a div with a class applied:

```
<div class="specialClass">
```

You would access that element through jQuery like this:

```
$(".specialClass")
```

Bear in mind that you might not be accessing a single element; the class selector accesses *all* elements for which the specified class is applied. In other words, if several elements in the page have the *"specialClass"* class applied, jQuery accesses all of them using the *$(".special-Class")* selector. You see more on this later when working with functions that iterate through each element retrieved with such a selector.

Selecting Elements by Type

You can also use selectors to access elements by type, such as all *<div>* elements, all *<a>* elements, and so on. For example, you would access all *<div>* elements in a document like this:

```
$('div')
```

Similarly, to access all the *<a>* elements, you would write:

```
$('a')
```

Using a type selector provides access to all the elements of the specified type on a page. Like the class selector, type selectors can return multiple elements.

Selecting Elements by Hierarchy

As mentioned earlier, you can select elements by their position in relation to other elements on the page. For example, to select all the *<a>* elements that are within <div> elements, you use this syntax:

```
$("div a")
```

You can get more specific than that as well. For example, if you want all the anchors that followed only a specific div, you combine the type selector with the ID selector syntax. Consider this HTML:

```
<div id="leftNav">
<a href="link1.html">Link 1</a>
<a href="link2.html">Link 2</a>
</div>
```

Here's the jQuery selector syntax to retrieve the two anchor elements within the *leftNav* div:

```
$("#leftNav a")
```

More generically, if you want only the direct descendants of an element, use the greater-than sign:

```
$("div > p")
```

This syntax yields all the *<p>* elements that are direct descendents of a div but does not include any *<p>* elements within the selected *<p>* elements.

You can also choose the *n*th child in a set with the *:nth-child()* selector. This example chooses the third child:

```
$("p:nth-child(3)")
```

Several other hierarchical selectors exist. You can find more in the jQuery selector reference documentation at http://api.jquery.com/category/selectors/.

Selecting Elements by Position

As you've seen, the selectors in jQuery are greedy. For example, the *$('a')* syntax selects all anchor tags. jQuery offers several ways to select more specific elements within a group. One such method is to use the *first* and *last* selectors. The following code selects the first *<p>* within the page:

```
$("p:first")
```

Likewise, the last element is selected like this:

```
$("p:last")
```

You can also select elements by their direct position. As another example, consider this HTML:

```
<p>First P</p>
<p>Second P</p>
<p>Third P</p>
```

To select the second *<p>* element, you use this syntax:

```
$("p")[1]
```

Note that the array index begins with *0* for this type of selector, so the first element is index *0*, the second is index *1*, and so on. Using this syntax is a little dangerous because it relies on the strict positioning of the elements within the hierarchy. If someone adds another *<p>* tag to the page before the element you're trying to select, the addition causes the array index to change, so the selector chooses the wrong element. When possible, it's better to use an ID selector to choose an individual or specific element than to rely on an element's position.

An alternative way of selecting by index is to use the *:eq* syntax. For example, to choose the third paragraph, you could write:

```
$("p:eq(3)")
```

Finally, another sometimes useful set of positional selectors are *even* and *odd*, which select every other element in a set:

```
$("p:even")
```

The *even* and *odd* selectors are quite helpful when working with tabular data to alternate row colors. Listing 22-2 shows an example that uses the *odd* selector to differentiate the background color of alternating rows in a table.

> **Note** The code from Listing 22-2 uses two items that haven't yet been formally introduced: a user-defined function and the *.css()* function. Don't worry about that now. You examine each of these items in more detail later in the chapter.

LISTING 22-2 Tabular data and jQuery.

```
<!DOCTYPE HTML PUBLIC "-//W3C//DTD HTML 4.01//EN"  "http://www.w3.org/TR/html4/strict.
dtd">
<html>
<head>
<title>Table Test</title>
<script type="text/javascript" src="jquery-1.4.2.min.js"></script>
</head>
<body>
<table>
  <tr>
    <td>Row 1 Column 1 of the table</td>
    <td>Row 1 Column 2 of the table</td>
  </tr>
  <tr>
    <td>Row 2 Column 1 of the table</td>
    <td>Row 2 Column 2 of the table</td>
  </tr>
  <tr>
    <td>Row 3 Column 1 of the table</td>
    <td>Row 3 Column 2 of the table</td>
  </tr>
  <tr>
    <td>Row 4 Column 1 of the table</td>
    <td>Row 4 Column 2 of the table</td>
  </tr>
  <tr>
    <td>Row 5 Column 1 of the table</td>
    <td>Row 5 Column 2 of the table</td>
  </tr>
  <tr>
    <td>Row 6 Column 1 of the table</td>
    <td>Row 6 Column 2 of the table</td>
  </tr>
</table>
```

```
<script type="text/javascript">
$(document).ready(function() {
    $('tr:odd').css("background-color", "#abacab");
});
</script>

</body>
</html>
```

This main portion of this code is contained in the JavaScript section within the body of the HTML:

```
$(document).ready(function() {
    $('tr:odd').css("background-color", "#abacab");
});
```

The code uses the *$(document).ready()* function along with the *:odd* selector to set the background color to hexadecimal *#abacab*—a light gray color. Figure 22-1 shows an example of the output.

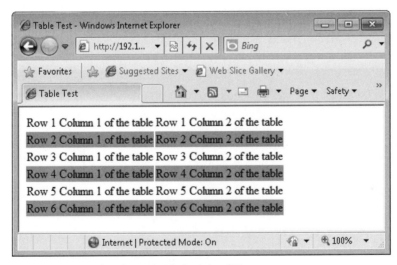

FIGURE 22-1 A table colorized with the help of jQuery.

You've seen some of the most common positional selectors, but there are many more positional selectors available. Refer to http://api.jquery.com/category/selectors/ *for more information.*

Selecting Elements by Attribute

As you might suspect from the class selector you've already seen, jQuery lets you select elements that merely contain an attribute or those that contain an attribute with a specific value. For example, to select all images that have an *alt* attribute, you write this:

```
$("img[alt]")
```

Selecting only images that have an *alt* attribute set to a certain value looks like this:

```
$("img[alt='alternate text']")
```

The preceding code selects an image only if the alt text is the word *alternate text*. Note the use of alternating single and double quotation marks within this example. The selector is wrapped in double quotation marks whereas the internal *alt* attribute selector is wrapped in single quotation marks, but the examples could just as easily have been in the reverse, single quotation marks used on the *img* selector and double quotation marks used on the *alt* attribute selector:

```
$('img[alt="alternate text"]')
```

You could also use the same quotation mark scheme for both, but if you do that, you need to escape the internal quotation marks, as follows:

```
$("img[alt=\"alternate text\"]")
```

It's important to note that this type of selector expects an exact match. In this example, the *alt* attribute needs to be the string *"alternate text"*. Any variation of that, such as *"alternate text 2"* or *" alternate text "* would not match.

jQuery includes wildcard selectors that don't require an exact match on attributes. Consider the examples in Table 22-2.

TABLE 22-2 Attribute Selector Matching

Syntax	Description
attribute=value*	Selects elements that contain the attribute for which the attribute value contains the specified value as a substring.
attribute~=value	Selects elements that contain the attribute for which the attribute value contains the specified value as a whole word.
attribute!=value	Selects elements that either do not contain the attribute or for which the attribute value does not match the specified value.
attribute$=value	Selects elements that contain the specified attribute for which the attribute's value ends with the specified string.
attribute^=value	Selects elements that contain the attribute for which the attribute's value begins with the specified string.

Selecting Form Elements

jQuery contains native selectors related to web forms. Table 22-3 lists some of these selectors, some of which are used in remainder of this chapter.

TABLE 22-3 Form-related Selectors

Selector	Description
:checkbox	Selects all check boxes
:checked	Selects all elements that are checked, such as check boxes
:input	Selects all input elements on a page
:password	Selects all password inputs
:radio	Selects all radio button inputs
:reset	Selects all input types of reset
:selected	Selects all elements that are currently selected
:submit	Selects all input types of *submit*
:text	Selects all input types of text

More Selectors

There are many more selectors in jQuery, such as those that select all hidden elements (*:hidden*) or all visible elements (*:visible*) as well as enabled elements, disabled elements, and others. See *http://api.jquery.com/category/selectors/* for a complete and up-to-date list of selectors in jQuery.

> **Tip** Rather than devising a complex and fragile selector syntax to get at a certain element, refer to the jQuery selector reference (*http://api.jquery.com/category/selectors/*) to see whether someone has already solved the selector problem.

Functions

So far, you've seen a lot of examples that select elements with jQuery, but only a couple of examples that show what you can do with those elements after selecting them. jQuery uses functions to perform actions on selected elements. Functions can be built-in to jQuery or user-defined. You almost always end up using both at the same time.

Traversing the DOM

The nature of programming on the web using JavaScript and now jQuery frequently requires looping or iterating through several elements—for example, the *.each()* function takes a list of selected elements and iterates over each of them, doing something (or nothing) to each as it loops through the list. jQuery contains numerous functions for looping and iterating. This process is known in jQuery parlance as *traversing*. You can find more information about the traversing-related functions at *http://api.jquery.com/category/traversing/*.

When using traversal functions, you almost always do so with the help of a user-defined wrapper function along with the *$(this)* selector. Like the *this* keyword in object-oriented programming, the *$(this)* selector refers to the current object—in this case, the item currently being traversed.

An example might be useful here. The following HTML builds a standings page for a fictitious volleyball league:

```
<!DOCTYPE HTML PUBLIC "-//W3C//DTD HTML 4.01//EN"  "http://www.w3.org/TR/html4/strict.dtd">
<html>
<head>
<title>Iteration Test</title>
<script type="text/javascript" src="jquery-1.4.2.min.js"></script>
</head>
<body>
<table>
  <th>Team Name</th>
  <th>W-L Record</th>
  <th>Win Percentage</th>
  <tr>
    <td>Team 1</td>
    <td>12-8</td>
    <td class="percentage">.600</td>
  </tr>
  <tr>
    <td>Team 5</td>
    <td>11-9</td>
    <td class="percentage">.550</td>
  </tr>
  <tr>
    <td>Team 4</td>
    <td>10-10</td>
    <td class="percentage">.500</td>
  </tr>
  <tr>
    <td>Team 2</td>
    <td>9-11</td>
    <td class="percentage">.450</td>
  </tr>
  <tr>
    <td>Team 6</td>
    <td>6-14</td>
    <td class="percentage">.300</td>
```

```
    </tr>
    <tr>
      <td>Team 3</td>
      <td>2-18</td>
      <td class="percentage">.100</td>
    </tr>
</table>
<script type="text/javascript">
$(document).ready(function() {
    $('tr:odd').css("background-color", "#abacab");
});
</script>

</body>
</html>
```

When viewed in a web browser, the page looks like Figure 22-2.

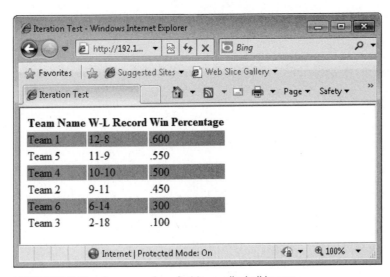

FIGURE 22-2 Standings page for a fictitious volleyball league.

This example iterates through all the elements that contain a *class* attribute matching *percentage*—a *class* that's applied to the cells in the Win/Loss Percentage column in the table. For any team whose Win/Loss percentage is at or above .500 (meaning they've won at least half of their games), this example applies a boldface font to their field. You can accomplish this with the following jQuery code, added just below the other jQuery code already in the page:

```
$('.percentage').each(function() {
    if ($(this).text() >= .5) {
        $(this).css('font-weight', 'bold');
    }
});
```

This code uses a selector to gather all the elements that have the *percentage* class applied to them. It then accesses each of these elements using the *.each()* function in jQuery. Within the *.each()* function, a user-defined function performs a conditional to determine whether the value in the *Win Percentage* column is greater than or equal to .5. If it is, the code calls the *.css()* function to add a *font-weight* property set to *bold* for that element. After adding this code to the page, the result looks like Listing 22-3.

LISTING 22-3 Adding jQuery to the volleyball league page.

```html
<!DOCTYPE HTML PUBLIC "-//W3C//DTD HTML 4.01//EN"  "http://www.w3.org/TR/html4/strict.
dtd">
<html>
<head>
<title>Iteration Test</title>
<script type="text/javascript" src="jquery-1.4.2.min.js"></script>
</head>
<body>
<table>
  <th>Team Name</th>
  <th>W-L Record</th>
  <th>Win Percentage</th>
  <tr>
    <td>Team 1</td>
    <td>12-8</td>
    <td class="percentage">.600</td>
  </tr>
  <tr>
    <td>Team 5</td>
    <td>11-9</td>
    <td class="percentage">.550</td>
  </tr>
  <tr>
    <td>Team 4</td>
    <td>10-10</td>
    <td class="percentage">.500</td>
  </tr>
  <tr>
    <td>Team 2</td>
    <td>9-11</td>
    <td class="percentage">.450</td>
  </tr>
  <tr>
    <td>Team 6</td>
    <td>6-14</td>
    <td class="percentage">.300</td>
  </tr>
  <tr>
    <td>Team 3</td>
    <td>2-18</td>
    <td class="percentage">.100</td>
  </tr>
</table>
```

```
<script type="text/javascript">
$(document).ready(function() {
    $('tr:odd').css("background-color", "#abacab");
    $('.percentage').each(function() {
        if ($(this).text() >= .5) {
            $(this).css('font-weight', 'bold');
        }
    });
});
</script>

</body>
</html>
```

When you view this page in a browser, you see that the Win Percentage column is now bold-face for those teams who have won at least half of their games, as depicted in Figure 22-3.

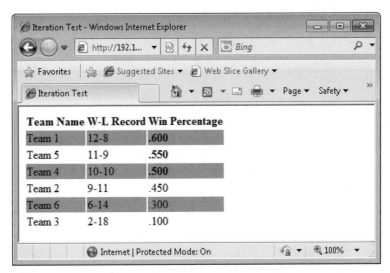

FIGURE 22-3 The Win Percentage column is now boldface with the help of jQuery.

Looking at the output from Figure 22-3, you see that it would be even nicer to apply the boldface font weight to the entire table row rather than to just the Win Percentage column. Doing that might seem difficult, because logically the code is already past that HTML table row by the time the test is applied to find out the win percentage. Fortunately, jQuery has a function that can help: the *.parent()* function. (Actually, there are several ways to accomplish this. The *.parent()* function is just one way.)

Applying the *parent()* function essentially moves up the DOM tree to find the *<tr>* tag that encloses this particular *<td>* element. By applying the CSS style change to the *<tr>* element, you can make the entire row boldface. The new code looks like this, with the change high-lighted in boldface:

```
$('.percentage').each(function() {
    if ($(this).text() >= .5) {
        $(this).parent().css('font-weight', 'bold');
    }
});
```

When added to the code from Listing 22-3, the output becomes similar to that in Figure 22-4.

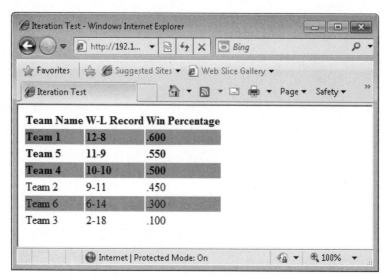

Team Name	W-L Record	Win Percentage
Team 1	12-8	.600
Team 5	11-9	.550
Team 4	10-10	.500
Team 2	9-11	.450
Team 6	6-14	.300
Team 3	2-18	.100

FIGURE 22-4 Applying CSS style at the table row level.

Note This revised code is available in the listing22-4.html file in the companion content.

The use of the *.parent()* function introduces a new concept called chaining. *Chaining* is a powerful construct in jQuery because it enables additional levels of selection as well as multilevel application of functions. In this example, the *$(this)* selector is chained to the *.parent()* function, which further selects the parent of *$(this)*. Only then does the code execute the *.css()* function.

With the power of chaining comes a bit of danger. It's quite possible to chain your way into difficult-to-read and difficult-to-maintain code. In addition, chaining can create fragile code when the elements in a chained selector change. Chaining is powerful—and I recommend using it when possible—but not at the expense of readability or maintainability.

The examples shown so far in the chapter have all accessed and changed the CSS directly, using JavaScript. As stated in Chapter 15, changing the style or presentational aspects of a webpage through JavaScript is not recommended. It's better practice to apply or remove styles through CSS rather than change attributes directly. Several methods exist to work with CSS style classes using jQuery, including *.hasClass()*, *.addClass()*, *.removeClass()*, and *.toggle-Class()*. See *http://api.jquery.com/category/css/* for more information about working with classes by using these and other functions.

Working with Attributes

In addition to the class-related attribute functions, jQuery has functions to work with attributes of the DOM. The most generic of these is the *.attr()* function, although others, such as *.html()* and *.val()*, are useful as well. This section looks at the *.attr()* function, saving *.html()*, *.val()*, and others for a later section.

You use the *.attr()* function to both retrieve and set attributes. For example, you can both retrieve and set an image's *alt* attribute using this syntax:

```
// Get the alt attribute:
$("#myImageID").attr("alt")
// Set the alt attribute:
$("#myImageID").attr("alt", "new text")
```

> **Note** Retrieving the value of the element before setting it is unnecessary.

Changing Text and HTML

You can completely rewrite a page using functions such as *.text()*, and *.val()*. Of course, just because it's possible doesn't mean it's a good idea. However, you sometimes find that you need to rewrite portions of HTML within a page or change text or values.

The *.html()* function retrieves or changes the entire HTML within a selected element. For example, consider this HTML:

```
<div id="myDiv">Here is a div, it's quite nice</div>
```

And here's the jQuery:

```
$("#myDiv").html('<span class="redStyle">This is the new content of the div</span>');
```

The outcome of this bit of jQuery is that the *<div>* identified by *myDiv* would now contain a *<span>* element with new text in it, as shown in the code example. This is a rather simplistic example, but imagine if *<div>* contained an entire content section. Using jQuery, you can essentially rewrite that entire section, HTML and all.

Like the *.html()* function, the *text()* function supports both retrieval and setting of the text within a selected element. Unlike HTML, the *.text()* function changes only the text, so it's not possible to alter the HTML within the selected element.

```
<div id="myDiv">Here is a div, it's quite nice</div>
$("#myDiv").text('This is the new content of the div');
```

In the preceding example, only the text changed; the code didn't add a span or apply styling.

Inserting Elements

You can easily use jQuery to add elements to a page. Two primary functions for doing this are the *:after()* and *:before()* functions. As their names suggest, they add elements either after or before a selected element, respectively.

For example, here's that div again:

```
<div id="myDiv">Here is a div, it's quite nice</div>
```

And here's some jQuery that inserts another div before it:

```
$("#myDiv").before("<div>This is a new div</div>");
```

The *:after()* function works in a similar fashion:

```
$("#myDiv").after("<div>This is a new div, it appears after myDiv</div>");
```

When run, the page containing this code would have three *<div>* elements:

```
<div>This is a new div</div>
<div id="myDiv">Here is a div, it's quite nice</div>
<div>This is a new div, it appears after myDiv</div>
```

The examples shown insert additional *<div>* elements—but of course you could use any valid element within these functions.

Callback Functions

Sometimes you need to run a function when another function or part of a function completes, a construct called a *callback function*. A callback function executes after its parent function completes. jQuery uses of callback functions heavily, especially in AJAX. You already saw an example of a callback function when iterating using the *.each()* function.

For more information about callback functions, see
http://docs.jquery.com/Tutorials:How_jQuery_Works.

You see examples of callback functions used throughout the remainder of this chapter. For those of you who are beginner or intermediate JavaScript programmers, it's important that you don't *over* think callback functions. They're merely a grouping of code that gets called within another function.

Events

You've now seen several examples of selectors and scratched the surface of functions in jQuery. The final piece of your initial look at jQuery involves events. Just like the event handling you already saw in JavaScript, jQuery enables your programs to respond to mouse clicks, form submissions, keystrokes, and more. Unlike JavaScript, cross-browser event handling in jQuery is quite easy. jQuery thrives in a cross-browser environment. This is especially true in event handling, which saves you the hassle of trying to figure out how each browser will respond to certain functions.

Binding and Unbinding

The .*bind()* function connects an event handler to an event, such as a mouse click:

```
.bind(event, data, handler)
```

In this instance, *event* is the event to which you want to respond, *data* is an optional object containing additional data to be passed into the event handler, and *handler* is the function that you want to run in response to this event.

For example:

```
<a href="/link1.html" id="myLink">A link</a>
$("#myLink").bind("click", function() {
alert("clicked the link");
});
```

The result of this code is that after the *click* event is captured for the anchor tag, the page displays an alert. Notice that this example didn't use the optional *data* parameter within the call to .*bind()*.

You can bind the following events with the .*bind()* function:

- beforeunload
- blur
- change
- click
- dblclick
- error
- focus
- focusin
- focusout

- hover
- keydown
- keypress
- keyup
- load
- mousedown
- mouseenter
- mouseleave
- mousemove

- mouseout
- mouseover
- mouseup
- resize
- scroll
- select
- submit
- toggle
- unload

In previous chapters, you captured events using the ehandler.js script developed in Chapter 11, "JavaScript Events and the Browser." The ehandler.js script provided a somewhat cross-browser–capable generic event handler. That's essentially what jQuery's .bind() function is doing. The difference is that jQuery's .bind() function is much better at cross-browser event handling and much more powerful than the ehandler.js script.

Although you can use .bind() for event handling, jQuery also provides shortcut functions that perform the same way as .bind(). Instead of writing .bind("click", function())... you can simply write .click(function()).... For example, you could rewrite the earlier .bind() example as:

```
$("#myLink").click(function() {
alert("clicked the link");
});
```

Not only can you respond to events such as clicking a link, but you can also trigger events. For example, consider the code in Listing 22-5:

LISTING 22-5 Responding to events.

```
<!DOCTYPE HTML PUBLIC "-//W3C//DTD HTML 4.01//EN"
"http://www.w3.org/TR/html4/strict.dtd">
<html>
<head>
<title>Trigger Test</title>
<script type="text/javascript" src="jquery-1.4.2.min.js"></script>
</head>
<body>
<div id="myDiv">
Here is some text.<br>
It goes inside this div<br>
</div>
<p>
<a id="braingiaLink" href="http://www.braingia.org">Steve Suehring</a>
</p>
<script type="text/javascript">
$(document).ready(function() {

$('#braingiaLink').click(function() {
    alert("hello");
    return true;
});

$('#myDiv').click(function() {
    $('#braingiaLink').click();
});

});
</script>

</body>
</html>
```

When this page is loaded into a web browser, clicking anywhere within the <div> triggers the click event for the anchor as if you had clicked the anchor itself.

To stop responding to events, you can unbind them using the .unbind() function, which accepts two arguments:

```
.unbind(event, function)
```

The *event* argument is the event you want to stop responding to, whereas the *function* argument is the function currently bound to the event.

 Note You can bind multiple event handlers to the same event by calling *.bind()* multiple times for that event.

Mouse Events and Hover

You already saw how to bind and handle the *click* event in the preceding examples, but you can also work with mouse events such as *mouseover* and *mouseout*. One fun thing to do is to make items disappear when a user moves the mouse over them (although doing so can lead to user frustration, so you shouldn't use it on a live site). Listing 22-6 shows some code that makes an anchor disappear when the mouse moves over its containing paragraph.

LISTING 22-6 Working with mouse events.

```
<!DOCTYPE HTML PUBLIC "-//W3C//DTD HTML 4.01//EN"
"http://www.w3.org/TR/html4/strict.dtd">
<html>
<head>
<title>Trigger Test</title>
<script type="text/javascript" src="jquery-1.4.2.min.js"></script>
<style type="text/css">
#braingiaLink {
    border: solid 1px black;
    padding: 3px;
}
#wrapperP {
    padding: 50px;
}
</style>
</head>
<body>
<div id="myDiv">
Here is some text.<br>
It goes inside this div<br>
</div>
<p id="wrapperP">
<a id="braingiaLink" href="http://www.braingia.org">Steve Suehring</a>
</p>
```

```
<script type="text/javascript">
$(document).ready(function() {
$('#braingiaLink').click(function() {
    alert("hello");
    return true;
});

$('#myDiv').click(function() {
    $('#braingiaLink').click();
});

$('#wrapperP').mouseover(function() {
    $('#braingiaLink').hide();
});

$('#wrapperP').mouseout(function() {
    $('#braingiaLink').show();
});

});
</script>

</body>
</html>
```

The keys to this code are the *.mouseover()* and *.mouseout()* event handlers, which in turn use two additional jQuery functions, *.hide()* and *.show()*. The *.mouseover()* and *.mouseout()* events are connected to the paragraph with ID *wrapperP*. When the mouse enters this paragraph, the anchor identified by *braingiaLink* disappears, only to reappear when the mouse leaves the paragraph area. It's worth noting that the link can still be activated using keyboard navigation. Always keep in mind that there's more than one way around a webpage.

jQuery also has a *.hover()* function that performs much like the *.mouseover()* and *.mouseout()* events. See *http://api.jquery.com/hover/* for more information about the *.hover()* function.

Many More Event Handlers

As the list earlier shows, there are numerous other event handlers in jQuery—too many to cover in a single introductory chapter on jQuery. I recommend the excellent documentation on jQuery events available at *http://api.jquery.com/category/events/*.

AJAX and jQuery

The previous two chapters showed how to write and use AJAX. As you might expect after reading the previous sections of this chapter, jQuery has its own methods for working with AJAX. And just like many other JavaScript-related tasks, jQuery makes using AJAX easier, too. This section shows how to use AJAX with jQuery.

jQuery offers several functions for working with data from and sending data to a server. Among these are the *.load()* function, the *.post()* function, and the *.get()* function. jQuery also includes a specific AJAX function, aptly titled *.ajax()*.

Using the *.ajax()* function, you can set several parameters, including which HTTP method the call should use (*GET* or *POST*), the timeout, and what to do when an error occurs (as well as when the code succeeds, of course).

> **More Information** See *http://api.jquery.com/jQuery.ajax/* for a full list of the available parameters for use with the *ajax()* function.

The basic syntax of the *ajax()* function is:

```
$.ajax({
    parameter: value
});
```

You can pass a number of *parameter: value* pairs to the *.ajax()* function, but you typically specify the method, the URL, and a callback function. It's also quite common to specify the data type to be returned, whether to cache the response, the data to be passed to the server, and what to do when an error occurs.

> **Note** The *.ajaxSetup()* function lets you set defaults for AJAX-related parameters, such as for caching, methods, and error handling, among others.

Here's a real-world example of the *.ajax()* function in action:

```
$.ajax({
    url:  "testajax.aspx",
    success:  function(data) {
        alert("Successful load");
    }
});
```

jQuery also includes a function called *.getJSON()* that performs the same essential function as the other AJAX-related functions, but it works specifically with JSON-encoded data from the server. The *.getJSON()* function is the equivalent of calling the *.ajax()* function with the additional parameter *dataType: 'json'*.

For example, consider this JSON-encoded list of a few states:

```
["Wisconsin","California","Colorado","Illinois","Minnesota","Oregon","Washington","New
York","New Jersey","Nevada","Alabama","Tennessee","Iowa","Michigan"]
```

For this example, assume that the JSON-encoded data is returned when the file json.php is called on the local server. The following use of the *.ajax()* function retrieves the data and calls a function named *showStates* when successful:

```
$.ajax({
    type: "GET",
    url: "json.php",
    dataType: "json",
    success: showStates
});
```

The function *showStates* creates a list and adds it to a form's *<select>* drop-down box.

Using AJAX with jQuery

To complete this step-by-step exercise, you need to have a file called json.php available in the same directory as the file you'll use in this exercise (a json.php file is included with the book's companion content). Like the examples from the previous chapters on AJAX, the json.php file must reside in the same domain as the file that's making the AJAX request.

1. Edit the file ajax.html file (also included with this book's companion content) using your editor of choice.

2. Within the file, place the code shown in boldface (and in ajax.txt, in the companion content), replacing the TODO comment:

```
<!DOCTYPE HTML PUBLIC "-//W3C//DTD HTML 4.01//EN"  "http://www.w3.org/TR/html4/strict.
dtd">
<html>
<head>
<title>AJAX Test</title>
<script type="text/javascript" src="jquery-1.4.2.min.js"></script>
```

```
</head>
<body>
<div id="states">
</div>
<script type="text/javascript">
$(document).ready(function() {

$.ajax({
    type: "GET",
    url: "json.php",
    dataType: "json",
    success: showStates
});

function showStates(data,status) {
    $.each(data, function(item) {;
        $("#states").append("<div>" + data[item] + "</div>");
    });
}


});
</script>
</body>
</html>
```

3. Save the file and view it in a web browser. You see a list of states, like the one shown here:

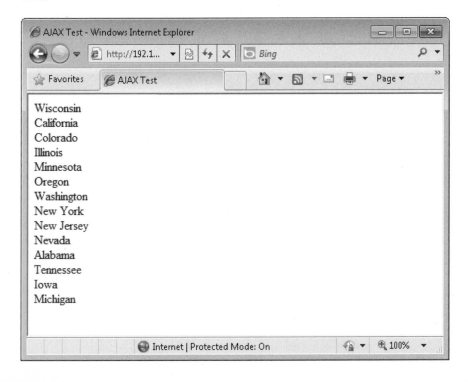

AJAX Errors and Timeouts

The *.ajax()* function lets you handle errors and timeouts gracefully. In addition to the success handler, you can specify an error handler with the *error* parameter. The value of the *error* parameter is usually a callback function. Here's an example, with the newly added error parameter in boldface:

```
$.ajax({
    type: "GET",
    url: "json.php",
    dataType: "json",
    success: successFunction,
    error:  errorFunction
});
```

The callback function used for error handling (*errorFunction* in the previous code example) receives three arguments: the *XMLHTTPRequest* object; a string representing the error encountered; and an exception object, if an exception occurred. Therefore, an error handler function should accept these three arguments and then do something with the results. This example shows an alert:

```
function errorFunction(xhr, statusMessage, exceptionObj) {
    alert("An error was encountered " + statusMessage);
}
```

You may find it necessary to set a timeout for an AJAX request. You can set a generic AJAX timeout value through the default *$.ajaxSetup*, but you can also specify a timeout value for any individual call using the *timeout* parameter. Here's an example:

```
$.ajax({
    type: "GET",
    url: "json.php",
    dataType: "json",
    success: successFunction,
    error:  errorFunction,
    timeout: 5000
});
```

It's important to realize that the timeout is in milliseconds. Therefore, the example shown sets the timeout at 5 seconds.

Sending Data to the Server

You not only need to receive data from a server in an AJAX call, but also to send data to a server and receive a response. You use the *data* parameter to the *.ajax()* function for this, sending data using either *GET* or *POST*.

You can format the data as ampersand-separated *key=value* pairs (*key1=value1&key2=value2*) or as mapped pairs *{key1: value1, key2: value2}*. The example here uses the *key=value* option, also known as the *query string option*.

This example calls a server-side program titled statefull.php, which, given a two-letter state abbreviation, returns the full name of the state.

```
$.ajax({
    type: "POST",
    url: "statefull.php",
    dataType: "json",
    success: successFunction,
    data: "state=WI"
});
```

Other Important Options

There are numerous options to the *.ajax()* function. You've seen how to use many of them already, but I'd like to highlight two more options:

- *async*
- *cache*

The *async* option, which is set to *true* by default, informs the script whether it should wait (and block further input in the browser) while the AJAX transaction is sent, received, and processed. When set to *true*, the AJAX transaction is done asynchronously, so it does not block.

The *cache* setting, which defaults to *true* in most instances, controls whether jQuery will cache the AJAX transaction. This is useful when the data being received doesn't change often, because *caching* speeds up the transaction, but caching can cause problems when your application is using older cached data that has changed on the server. I've found it helpful to set this option to *false* so that the response is not cached, especially in cases where you encounter problems when data is apparently not refreshing.

More jQuery

You've seen only a small portion of what jQuery can do. As you learn more about JavaScript and how it can help activate your websites, consider using jQuery or another JavaScript library to help you with those development efforts.

For more jQuery learning and reference material, see the resources at http://www.jquery.com.

Exercises

1. Using the code in ajax.html (from the exercise titled "Using Ajax with jQuery") as a base, add a CSS style to make the background color of the state's individual <div> turn blue when the mouse hovers over one of the states in the list. Hint: There are multiple ways to do this.

2. Create a server-side program to return data when you pass in parameters using the $.ajax() function. Process this data somehow, using an alert or writing to the page. For instance, you could implement a server-side program to return the sum of two numbers or, like the example shown, return the full state name if the program receives the state's abbreviation.

Chapter 23
jQuery Effects and Plug-Ins

After reading this chapter, you'll be able to:

- Understand and use native jQuery effects.
- Understand jQuery UI.
- Use jQuery UI.

Core Features for Enhancing Usability

Effects and usability enhancements such as dragging and dropping, fading elements in and out, and sliding elements are easy to implement with the help of jQuery. And if those features aren't enough to make you love the product, jQuery is extensible and has a healthy community supporting it.

Among the features the jQuery community contributes are plug-ins. jQuery plug-ins provide additional functionality not included in the core jQuery package. You can obtain more information about plug-ins and a list of those currently available at the jQuery Plugins website: *http://plugins.jquery.com/*.

This chapter provides an overview of some effects included in the jQuery core product as well as in jQuery UI.

Native Effects

As mentioned in the introduction to this chapter, jQuery includes several functions that can enhance the usability of a web application, such as showing and hiding elements, and fading elements in and out. This section examines a few of the native effects included with jQuery. It's worth noting that as of this writing, jQuery and jQuery UI are being updated to work with Windows Internet Explorer 9, so some of the examples shown in this chapter don't work with the current beta of Internet Explorer 9. However, there's a great chance that by the time you read this chapter, jQuery and jQuery UI will be updated and Internet Explorer 9 released.

Show, Hide, and Toggle

The *.show()* and *.hide()* functions show and hide elements of a page, respectively. These functions set the Cascading Style Sheets (CSS) *display* property. To hide an element, you set the *display* property to *none*. Note that setting *display* to *none* does not remove the element from the DOM, so you can still show the element using the *.show()* function. Listing 23-1 provides an example of the *.hide()* function.

LISTING 23-1 Hiding an element.

```
<!DOCTYPE HTML PUBLIC "-//W3C//DTD HTML 4.01//EN"
"http://www.w3.org/TR/html4/strict.dtd">
<html>
<head>
<title>Hide</title>
<script type="text/javascript" src="jquery-1.4.2.min.js"></script>
<style type="text/css">
.removeBtn {
    color: #0000CC;
}
</style>
</head>
<body>
<ul>
<li id="option1">Option 1 <span class="removeBtn" id="remove1">(x)</span></li>
<li id="option2">Option 2 <span class="removeBtn" id="remove2">(x)</span></li>
<li id="option3">Option 3 <span class="removeBtn" id="remove3">(x)</span></li>
<li id="option4">Option 4 <span class="removeBtn" id="remove4">(x)</span></li>
</ul>
<script type="text/javascript">
$(document).ready(function() {

$('#option1').click(function() {
    $('#option1').hide();
});
$('#option2').click(function() {
    $('#option2').hide();
});
$('#option3').click(function() {
    $('#option3').hide();
});
$('#option4').click(function() {
    $('#option4').hide();
});

});
</script>

</body>
</html>
```

Unfortunately, the example in Listing 23-1 is poorly optimized because it requires adding handling for each element individually. (You wouldn't expect to see this type of programming in a live production program; however, it's useful for illustrative purposes.) A better solution is to handle the options by using their functions. Listing 23-2 shows a better way to accomplish the same functionality by using jQuery and without the hardcoded options.

LISTING 23-2 Hiding an element, improved with jQuery.

```
<!DOCTYPE HTML PUBLIC "-//W3C//DTD HTML 4.01//EN"
"http://www.w3.org/TR/html4/strict.dtd">
<html>
<head>
<title>Hide</title>
<script type="text/javascript" src="jquery-1.4.2.min.js"></script>
<style type="text/css">
.removeBtn {
    color: #0000CC;
}
</style>
</head>
<body>
<ul>
<li id="option1">Option 1 <span class="removeBtn" id="remove1">(x)</span></li>
<li id="option2">Option 2 <span class="removeBtn" id="remove2">(x)</span></li>
<li id="option3">Option 3 <span class="removeBtn" id="remove3">(x)</span></li>
<li id="option4">Option 4 <span class="removeBtn" id="remove4">(x)</span></li>
</ul>
<script type="text/javascript">
$(document).ready(function() {

$('.removeBtn').each(function(elm) {
    $(this).click(function() {
        $(this).parent().hide();
    });
});

});
</script>

</body>
</html>
```

The only change in the code in Listing 23-2 is within the JavaScript:

```
$('.removeBtn').each(function() {
    $(this).click(function() {
        $(this).parent().hide();
    });
});
```

This JavaScript applies a function to each element with the *removeBtn* class, which sets the *click* event on that element. It calls the *.hide()* function, but because when the event fires, *$(this)* refers to the *removeBtn* element (in this case, the *<span>* element), you need to walk up the hierarchy to find the parent node, which in this case is the *<li>*.

The *.toggle()* function shows or hides an element based on its current state. For example, when an element is currently visible, calling *.toggle()* hides it. Likewise, when an element is hidden, the element becomes visible when you call *.toggle()*.

All three functions, *.show()*, *.hide()*, and *.toggle()*, accept two arguments: a duration and a call-back function. Notice in the code from Listings 23-1 and 23-2, when the element is hidden, it disappears instantaneously. Adding a duration to the *.hide()* function causes the element to disappear at that specified rate. Like other functions in jQuery, you specify the duration in milliseconds. Alternatively, you can use the strings *"fast"* and *"slow"*, which represent 200 and 600 milliseconds, respectively.

The callback function performs an action after the showing or hiding of the element is complete. One possible use of the callback is to display an Undo button after hiding an element, to enable users to reshow the element that they just hid.

Adding a duration

1. Using an editor such as Microsoft Visual Studio, Eclipse, or a text editor, open the file duration.html, which you can find in the Chapter23 folder in this book's companion content.

2. Within the file, add the following code shown in boldface:

```
<!DOCTYPE HTML PUBLIC "-//W3C//DTD HTML 4.01//EN"
"http://www.w3.org/TR/html4/strict.dtd">
<html>
<head>
<title>Hide</title>
<script type="text/javascript" src="jquery-1.4.2.min.js"></script>
<style type="text/css">
.removeBtn {
    color: #0000CC;
}
</style>
</head>
<body>
<ul>
<li id="option1">Option 1 <span class="removeBtn" id="remove1">(x)</span></li>
<li id="option2">Option 2 <span class="removeBtn" id="remove2">(x)</span></li>
<li id="option3">Option 3 <span class="removeBtn" id="remove3">(x)</span></li>
<li id="option4">Option 4 <span class="removeBtn" id="remove4">(x)</span></li>
</ul>
<script type="text/javascript">
$(document).ready(function() {

$('.removeBtn').each(function(elm) {
    $(this).click(function() {
        $(this).parent().hide(500);
    });
});

});
</script>

</body>
</html>
```

3. Save the file and view the page in a web browser. You see a page similar to this:

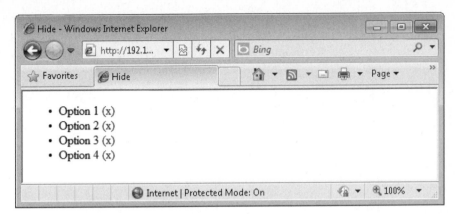

4. Now click the *(x)* next to any of the elements. The element disappears from the page, and you see a page like this:

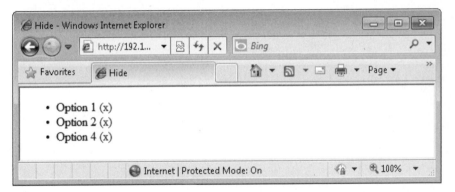

5. If you're using a browser with a debugger, such as Firefox with Firebug, you can right-click one of the other options and choose Inspect Element to see that the *display* property has been set to *none* on the hidden element.

Fade In and Fade Out

Adding a duration to the *.show()*, *.hide()*, and *.toggle()* functions changes their opacity until they're visible or hidden. Similar functionality is available through the *.fadeIn()* and *.fadeOut()* functions. See *http://api.jquery.com/category/effects/fading/* for more information about these as well as the *.fadeTo()* function.

Sliding

Another method for setting the *display* property to *none* is available through the *.slideUp()* and *.slideDown()* functions. These functions create a slide effect that makes the element appear to move before disappearing, or to move before appearing. Use the *.slideUp()* function to make an element disappear and *.slideDown()* to make it reappear.

Changing the base code that you saw earlier in this chapter so that it uses *.slideUp()* instead of *hide* looks like this:

```
$('.removeBtn').each(function(elm) {
    $(this).click(function() {
        $(this).parent().slideUp();
    });
});
```

> **Note** Don't be confused into thinking that you have a choice of which way to slide the elements—up or down—based on the names of the functions. The *.slideUp()* function always makes elements disappear, whereas *.slideDown()* always makes them appear.

jQuery UI

jQuery UI is built on top of the jQuery core and provides extended functionality tied to the user interface. Several components in jQuery UI provide specific widgets or actions, including a date chooser, an accordion function, and autocomplete. This section examines some of the jQuery UI widgets.

> **More Information** See *http://jqueryui.com/* for more information about all the available widgets with jQuery UI.

Using jQuery UI

jQuery UI requires you to include a separate JavaScript file in your code. You can obtain this file from *http://jqueryui.com/,* where you can download the full stable release or build a custom download with only the components that you need for your site. This chapter uses the full release of jQuery UI, but for most sites, I recommend that you customize the jQuery UI download to your individual needs, including only those specific components necessary for the effects on your site.

The jQuery UI download is a zip file containing both the jQuery core and jQuery UI code along with CSS files related to jQuery UI. You need to unzip this file into a location where it is available for the web server, such as the *httpdocs* or *public_html* directory. In essence, the files need to be in the same place as the rest of the JavaScript and HTML that you've been working with throughout this book.

> **Note** Using the jQuery UI functions may have accessibility implications unless you provide an alternative means to perform the same functionality.

Drag and Drop

jQuery UI includes functions for moving elements by dragging and dropping, called *.draggable()* and *.droppable()*, respectively. Calling *.draggable()* lets users use the mouse to move an element around the page. Consider the code in Listing 23-3.

LISTING 23-3 The *.draggable()* function in action.

```
<!DOCTYPE HTML PUBLIC "-//W3C//DTD HTML 4.01//EN"
"http://www.w3.org/TR/html4/strict.dtd">
<html>
<head>
<title>Drag</title>
<script type="text/javascript" src="jquery-1.4.2.min.js"></script>
<script type="text/javascript" src="js/jquery-ui-1.8.4.custom.min.js"></script>
<style type="text/css">
#container span {
    border: solid 1px black;
    padding: 3px;
}
</style>
</head>
<body>
<div id="container">
<span>Drag me around</span>
</div>
<script type="text/javascript">
$(document).ready(function() {

$('#container > span').draggable();

});
</script>

</body>
</html>
```

This code establishes a *<p>* element that is then able to be dragged with the call to the *.draggable()* function:

```
$('#container > span').draggable();
```

> **Note** The code in Listing 23-3 assumes that you have jQuery downloaded already and that the jQuery UI files are downloaded to your current working directory—the same directory where the HTML for Listing 23-3 resides. The jQuery UI code is then loaded from a js/ subdirectory.

Try the code from Listing 23-3 in a browser. You'll see that it's possible to click and drag the element around.

You can use the *.droppable()* function in conjunction with *.draggable()* to create a target for a dragged element, to enable someone to use a drag-and-drop operation to work with items visually on the screen. Listing 23-4 expands on the *.draggable()* example from Listing 23-3 to provide a *<div>* as a droppable target:

LISTING 23-4 The *.droppable()* function in action.

```
<!DOCTYPE HTML PUBLIC "-//W3C//DTD HTML 4.01//EN"
"http://www.w3.org/TR/html4/strict.dtd">
<html>
<head>
<title>Drop</title>
<script type="text/javascript" src="jquery-1.4.2.min.js"></script>
<script type="text/javascript" src="js/jquery-ui-1.8.4.custom.min.js"></script>
<style type="text/css">
#container span {
    border: solid 1px black;
    padding: 3px;
}
#targetContainer {
    height: 200px;
    width: 200px;
    border: solid 1px black;
    background-color: #abacab;
    margin: 50px;
}
</style>
</head>
<body>
<div id="container">
<span>Drag me and drop me</span>
</div>
<div id="targetContainer">
</div>
<script type="text/javascript">
$(document).ready(function() {

$('#container > span').draggable();
```

```
$('#targetContainer').droppable({
    drop: function(event,ui) {
        alert("Dropped Element: " + ui.draggable.text());
    }
});

});
</script>

</body>
</html>
```

The key to this code is the use of the *.droppable()* function set on the *<div>* with ID *targetContainer*:

```
$('#targetContainer').droppable({
    drop: function(event,ui) {
        alert("Dropped Element: " + ui.draggable.text());
    }
});
```

The *.droppable()* function handles several events, enabling you to respond when an item is dragged over the top of the droppable element (*over*), is moved out of the droppable element (*out*), when an element is dropped in (*drop*, shown in the example), and when a valid *draggable* element is picked up or let go of (*activate* and *deactivate*). See *http://jqueryui.com /demos/droppable/* for examples of these events.

Accordion

Creating an accordion effect, where options appear to roll up and down into each other, is possible using jQuery UI. The key to getting an accordion working properly is using well-formed HTML along with a layout that lends itself to being in an accordion. A good candidate for an accordion is a group of similar items or options.

Listing 23-5 shows the HTML and JavaScript to create a simple accordion.

LISTING 23-5 A jQuery accordion.

```
<!DOCTYPE HTML PUBLIC "-//W3C//DTD HTML 4.01//EN"
"http://www.w3.org/TR/html4/strict.dtd">
<html>
<head>
<title>Accordion</title>
<script type="text/javascript" src="jquery-1.4.2.min.js"></script>
<script type="text/javascript" src="js/jquery-ui-1.8.4.custom.min.js"></script>
<style type="text/css">
#container {
    border: solid 1px black;
    padding: 3px;
}
.optionHead {
    border: solid 1px black;
    background-color: #abacab;
}
.optionDiv {
    border-bottom: dotted 1px black;
}
</style>
</head>
<body>
<div id="container">
<h3 class="optionHead">Option 1</h3>
<div class="optionDiv" id="option1">
<p>Text of option 1</p>
</div>
<h3 class="optionHead">Option 2</h3>
<div class="optionDiv" id="option2">
<p>Text of option 2</p>
</div>
<h3 class="optionHead">Option 3</h3>
<div class="optionDiv" id="option3">
<p>Text of option 3</p>
</div>
</div>
<script type="text/javascript">
$(document).ready(function() {

$('#container').accordion();

});
</script>

</body>
</html>
```

Loading the code in Listing 23-5 into a web browser results in a page similar to that shown in Figure 23-1.

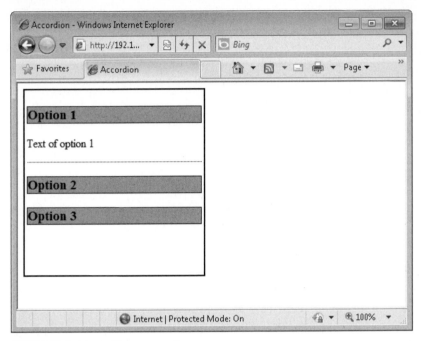

FIGURE 23-1 A basic jQuery accordion.

When using a jQuery accordion, you'll notice that the first option is always expanded on page load. Depending on the needs of the layout and how the accordion is being used, you may find that you need to have a different option expanded on page load, or have all the options collapsed on load. The *.accordion()* function includes several options that control its behavior. The *active* option, when used in conjunction with *collapsible* set to *true*, starts the accordion in a collapsed state or with a certain option selected.

In this next step-by-step exercise, you use an accordion within a webpage and set a default state for the accordion.

Setting default state for an accordion

1. Open the file accordion.html using your editor such as Microsoft Visual Studio or Eclipse. (You can find this file in the companion content.)

2. Within accordion.html, add the following code shown in boldface:

```html
<!DOCTYPE HTML PUBLIC "-//W3C//DTD HTML 4.01//EN"
"http://www.w3.org/TR/html4/strict.dtd">
<html>
<head>
<title>Accordion</title>
<script type="text/javascript" src="jquery-1.4.2.min.js"></script>
<script type="text/javascript" src="js/jquery-ui-1.8.4.custom.min.js"></script>
<style type="text/css">
#container {
    border: solid 1px black;
    padding: 3px;
}
.optionHead {
    border: solid 1px black;
    background-color: #abacab;
}
.optionDiv {
    border-bottom: dotted 1px black;
}
</style>
</head>
<body>
<div id="container">
<h3 class="optionHead">Option 1</h3>
<div class="optionDiv" id="option1">
<p>Text of option 1</p>
</div>
<h3 class="optionHead">Option 2</h3>
<div class="optionDiv" id="option2">
<p>Text of option 2</p>
</div>
<h3 class="optionHead">Option 3</h3>
<div class="optionDiv" id="option3">
<p>Text of option 2</p>
</div>
</div>
<script type="text/javascript">
$(document).ready(function() {

$('#container').accordion({
    collapsible: true,
    active: false
});

});
</script>

</body>
</html>
```

3. Save the file and view the page in a browser. Notice that the accordion is started in a collapsed form, as shown here:

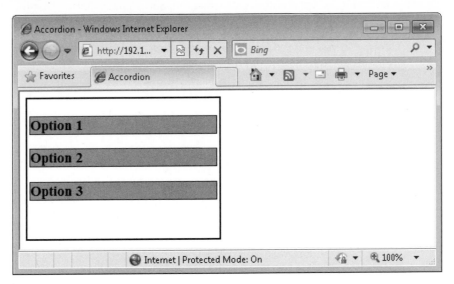

4. Change the active option to *2* instead of *false*. The code should look like this:

```
$('#container').accordion({
    collapsible: true,
    active: 2
});
```

5. Reload the page in your browser. Notice that the third option on the screen appears expanded. This occurs because the index begins with *0*, thus making the first option (seen as Option 1 on the screen) really index *0*.

See http://jqueryui.com/demos/accordion/ *for additional information about the available options and events with the accordion widget.*

More jQuery UI

There is much, much more to jQuery UI than part of a chapter in one book can cover, such as sophisticated CSS theme capabilities that let you choose color schemes for the effects and widgets used through jQuery UI. Entire books have been written on jQuery UI alone. See *http://jqueryui.com/themeroller/* for information about CSS themes and jQuery UI. Additionally, see *http://jqueryui.com* for more information and tutorials on jQuery UI.

Exercises

1. Using the code from Listing 23-2 as a base, add a link or button that restores all the options using .*show()* function.

2. Using what you learned from this and previous chapters, create a jQuery accordion that includes dynamically created options loaded through AJAX.

Appendix

Answer Key to Exercises

This appendix shows the answers and explanations for the exercises that have appeared throughout the book. In many cases, there is more than one way to solve a problem. Therefore, unless the question specified a particular way to solve the problem, any working implementation is acceptable. It's also expected that your function names could differ from the ones in this appendix.

Chapter 1

1. False. Although JavaScript is indeed defined by a standards body, ECMA International, it is not supported on all web browsers. And the support that does exist varies (sometimes widely) among browsers.

2. False. There are many reasons why a visitor to your website might have JavaScript disabled. The browser they're using might not support it, they might have special software installed that doesn't support it, or they simply might have JavaScript disabled as a personal preference. You should strive to make your site work without JavaScript, or at least have it fail gracefully for those visitors who don't have JavaScript enabled.

3. A typical JavaScript definition block looks like this:

```
<script type="text/javascript">
// JavaScript code goes here
</script>
```

4. False. The version of JavaScript isn't placed within the DOCTYPE definition. In fact, it's quite uncommon to declare the version of JavaScript being used at all.

5. True. JavaScript code can appear in both the head and the body of a Hypertext Markup Language (HTML) document.

Chapter 2

1. The code of mysecondpage.htm looks similar to this, though yours may differ slightly (and of course will contain your name instead of mine!):

```
<!DOCTYPE HTML PUBLIC "-//W3C//DTD HTML 4.01//EN"
"http://www.w3.org/TR/html4/strict.dtd">
<html>
<head>
<title>My Second Page</title>
<script type="text/javascript">
alert("Steve Suehring");
</script>
</head>
<body>
<p>My Second Page</p>
</body>
</html>
```

2. Here's the new code, with the changes shown in bold type:

```
<!DOCTYPE HTML PUBLIC "-//W3C//DTD HTML 4.01//EN"
"http://www.w3.org/TR/html4/strict.dtd">
<html>
<head>
<title>My Second Page</title>
<script type="text/javascript">
function callAlert() {
    alert("Steve Suehring");
}
</script>
</head>
<body>
<script type="text/javascript">
callAlert();
</script>
<p>My Second Page</p>
</body>
</html>
```

3. I created a file called 3.htm and a file called 3.js, which are shown below. (The reference in 3.htm to 3.js is shown in boldface type.)

3.js:

```
function callAlert() {
    alert("Steve Suehring");
}
```

3.htm:

```
<!DOCTYPE HTML PUBLIC "-//W3C//DTD HTML 4.01//EN"
"http://www.w3.org/TR/html4/strict.dtd">
<html>
```

```
<head>
<title>My Second Page</title>
<script type="text/javascript" src="3.js"> </script>
</head>
<body>
<script type="text/javascript">
callAlert();
</script>
<p>My Second Page</p>
</body>
</html>
```

Chapter 3

1. The valid statements are a, b, c, and d. The only invalid statement is e, because it uses a reserved word, *case,* as a variable name.

2. False. Not all JavaScript statements require a semicolon at the end. In fact, semicolons are usually optional.

3. The *orderTotal* variable is changed after the visitor is alerted to how many of each item were ordered, but before the value is returned from the function. The lesson here is that you must be careful not to alter the value or contents of variables unexpectedly. The visitor is expecting to order a certain quantity, but the code clearly changes that quantity after telling the visitor how many he or she ordered!

Chapter 4

1. Variable declarations:

   ```
   var first = 120;

   var second = "5150";

   var third = "Two Hundred Thirty";
   ```

2. Array (your values will probably be different, but the data types and syntax are the important part):

   ```
   var newArray = new Array(10, 20, 30, "first string", "second string");
   ```

3. Escaped string:

   ```
   alert("Steve's response was \"Cool!\"");
   ```

4. This exercise is for the reader to follow. There is no right or wrong answer.

Chapter 5

1. Alerts (your values will probably be different, but the data types and syntax are the important part.):

```
var num1 = 1;
var num2 = 1;
var num3 = 19;
var fourthvar = "84";
var name1 = "Jakob";
var name2 = "Edward";
alert(num1 + num2);
alert(num3 + fourthvar);
alert(name1 + name2);
```

2. Postfix:

```
var theNum = 1;
alert(theNum);
alert(theNum++);
alert(theNum);
```

   Prefix:

```
var theNum = 1;
alert(theNum);
alert(++theNum);
alert(theNum);
```

3. Code:

```
var num1 = 1;
var num2 = 1;
var num3 = 19;
var fourthvar = "84";
var name1 = "Jakob";
var name2 = "Edward";
alert(typeof num1);
alert(typeof num2);
alert(typeof num3);
alert(typeof fourthvar);
alert(typeof name1);
alert(typeof name2);
```

   This should result in three alerts with the word *number* followed by three others with the word *string*.

4. False. Unary operators appear fairly often in JavaScript, especially within *for* loops that increment a variable using the ++ postfix operator.

5. False. Even though saving a few bytes is helpful, especially for web applications, it's almost always preferable to spend those same few bytes making the code readable and maintainable. This is largely a matter for your style and coding standards, however. In a later chapter, you are introduced to jQuery. That library's typical "minimized" version is an example of taking the byte saving to an extreme.

Chapter 6

1. Replace *YOUR NAME* in the following code with the appropriate content:

```
var inputName = prompt("Please enter your name:");
switch(inputName) {
    case "YOUR NAME":
        alert("Welcome " + inputName);
        break;
    case "Steve":
        alert("Go Away");
        break;
    default:
        alert("Please Come Back Later " + inputName);
}
```

2. Here's the code:

```
var temp = prompt("Please enter the current temperature");
if (temp > 100) {
    alert("Please cool down");
} else if (temp < 20) {
    alert("Better warm up");
}
```

   Note that it would also be a good idea to provide a default action in case the temperature is between 20 and 100!

3. This exercise is actually impossible to accomplish as specified. Because ternary operators expect a single test condition and Exercise 2 required two conditions, a ternary operator cannot be used to accomplish exactly the same task. The following code creates an alert that tells the visitor to cool down when the temperature is above 100 and to warm up when the temperature is less than or equal to 100:

```
var temp = prompt("Please enter the current temperature");
temp > 100 ? alert("Please cool down") : alert("Better warm up");
```

4. Here's the code:

```
for (var i = 1; i < 101; i++) {
    if (i == 99) {
        alert("The number is " + i);
    }
}
```

   Note that because the variable *i* began counting at 1 (as was called for in the exercise), the counter needs to go to 101 to meet the requirement of counting from 1 to 100.

5. Here's the code:

```
var i = 1;
while (i < 101) {
    if (i == 99) {
        alert("The number is " + i);
```

```
    }
    i++;
}
```

Note the placement of the postfix increment of the *i* variable within the loop. You could also use *i=i+1*, but the postfix operator is preferred.

Chapter 7

1. It's important to note that this code uses the *isNaN* function to check whether the input was a number. This is a best practice that may not always be obvious. Another way to accomplish the ultimate return value here is to use *return theNumber++;* as the final return, rather than as shown. Here's the code:

```
<head>
    <title>Chapter 7 Exercise 1</title>
<script type = "text/javascript" >
function incrementNum(theNumber) {
    if (isNaN(theNumber)) {
        alert("Sorry, " + theNumber + " isn't a number.");
        return;
    }
    return theNumber + 1;
}
</script>
</head>
<body>
<script type = "text/javascript" >
alert(incrementNum(3));
</script>
</body>
```

2. Here's the code:

```
function addNums(firstNum,secondNum) {
    if ((isNaN(firstNum)) || (isNaN(secondNum))) {
        alert("Sorry, both arguments must be numbers.");
        return;
    }
    else if (firstNum > secondNum) {
        alert(firstNum + " is greater than " + secondNum);
    }
    else {
        return firstNum + secondNum;
    }
}
```

3. This exercise is meant to show variable scoping problems. Note how the value of the *result* variable changes outside the function—even though the change is made only within the function. The two locations for alerts are shown in boldface in the following code:

```
function addNumbers() {
    firstNum = 4;
    secondNum = 8;
    result = firstNum + secondNum;
    return result;
}
result = 0;
alert(result);
result = addNumbers();
alert(result);
```

4. Here's the code:

```
<head>
<title>Chapter 7 Exercise 4</title>
<script type="text/javascript">
var stars = ["Polaris","Aldebaran","Deneb","Vega","Altair","Dubhe","Regulus"];
var constells = ["Ursa Minor","Taurus","Cygnus","Lyra","Aquila","Ursa Major","Leo"];

function searchStars(star) {
    var starLength = stars.length;
    for (var i = 0; i < starLength; i++) {
        if (stars[i] == star) {
            return constells[i];
        }
    }
    return star + " Not Found.";
}
</script>
</head>
<body>
<script type = "text/javascript" >
var inputStar = prompt("Enter star name: ");
alert(searchStars(inputStar));
</script>
<p>Stars</p>
</body>
```

Chapter 8

1. Here's the code:

```
var star = ["Polaris", "Deneb", "Vega", "Altair"];
var starLength = star.length;
for (var i = 0; i < starLength; i++) {
    alert(star[i]);
}
```

2. Here's one way:

```
function Song(artist,length,title) {
    this.artist = artist;
    this.length = length;
    this.title = title;
```

```
}

song1 = new Song("First Artist","3:30","First Song Title");
song2 = new Song("Second Artist","4:11","Second Song Title");
song3 = new Song("Third Artist","2:12","Third Song Title");
```

3. Assuming you are using the code given in the exercise, this code in the body would concatenate all the names into one long string, as follows:

```
var names = new Array;
for (var propt in star) {
    names += propt;
}
alert(names);
```

The code to comma-delimit the names would look like this:

```
var names = new Array;
for (var propt in star) {
    if (names != "") {
        names += "," + propt;
    } else {
        names = propt;
    }
}
alert(names);
```

Chapter 9

1. Here's the code:

```
if (screen.availHeight < 768) {
    alert("Available Height: " + screen.availHeight);
}
if (screen.availWidth < 1024) {
    alert("Available Width: " + screen.availWidth);
}
```

2. The full code is shown here, including the code from the exercise. The additional code for this exercise is shown in boldface. Note the use of the *unescape()* function to remove the URL–encoded *%20* (space) character from the country name. This is necessary because the country name *"Great Britain"* specified in this exercise must be URL-escaped for *HTTP GET* requests.

```
<!DOCTYPE HTML PUBLIC "-//W3C//DTD HTML 4.01//EN"
"http://www.w3.org/TR/html4/strict.dtd">
<html>
<head>
    <title>Location, Location, Location</title>

</head>
```

```
<body>
    <script type="text/javascript">
            var body = document.getElementsByTagName("body")[0];
            for (var prop in location) {
                var elem = document.createElement("p");
                var text = document.createTextNode(prop + ": " + location[prop]);
                elem.appendChild(text);
                body.appendChild(elem);
            }
            if (location.search) {
                var querystring = location.search.substring(1);
                var splits = querystring.split('&');
                for (var i = 0; i < splits.length; i++) {
                    var splitpair = splits[i].split('=');
                    var elem = document.createElement("p");
                    var text = document.createTextNode(splitpair[0] + ": " + splitpair[1]);
                    if (splitpair[0] == "country") {
                        switch(unescape(splitpair[1])) {
                            case "Brazil":
                                alert("Obrigado");
                                break;
                            case "Great Britain":
                                alert("Thank You");
                                break;
                        }
                    }
                    elem.appendChild(text);
                    body.appendChild(elem);
                }
            }
    </script>
</body>
</html>
```

3. This exercise doesn't have an answer in the answer key. You can install the User Agent Switcher to complete the exercise.

Chapter 10

1. Here's the code:

```
var newelement = document.createElement("p");
newelement.setAttribute("id","pelement");
document.body.appendChild(newelement);
newelement.appendChild(document.createTextNode("This is a paragraph, albeit a short
one."));
var anchorelem = document.createElement("a");
anchorelem.setAttribute("id","aelement");
anchorelem.setAttribute("href","http://www.braingia.org/");
document.body.appendChild(anchorelem);
anchorelem.appendChild(document.createTextNode("Go To Steve Suehring's Web Site."));
```

2. Here's the code:

```
// create the initial elements (if you use an existing HTML file, you won't
need to do this)
var newelement = document.createElement("p");
newelement.setAttribute("id","pelement");
document.body.appendChild(newelement);
newelement.appendChild(document.createTextNode("This is a paragraph, albeit a
short one."));
var anchorelem = document.createElement("a");
anchorelem.setAttribute("id","aelement");
anchorelem.setAttribute("href","http://www.braingia.org/");
document.body.appendChild(anchorelem);
anchorelem.appendChild(document.createTextNode("Click Here"));

// make the change
var existingp = document.getElementById("pelement");
existingp.firstChild.nodeValue="This is the new text.";
var newanchor = document.getElementById("aelement");
newanchor.setAttribute("href","http://www.microsoft.com/");
```

3. Here's the code:

```
<head>
<title>Chapter 10 Exercises</title>
</script>
</head>
<body>
<div id="thetable"></div>
<script type = "text/javascript" >
var table = document.createElement("table");
table.border = "1";
var tbody = document.createElement("tbody");

// Append the body to the table
table.appendChild(tbody);
var row = document.createElement("tr");

// Create table row
for (i = 1; i < 3; i++) {
    var row = document.createElement("tr");
    // Create the row/td elements
    for (j = 1; j < 3; j++) {
        // Insert the actual text/data from the XML document.
        var td = document.createElement("td");
        var data = document.createTextNode("Hello - I'm Row " + i + ", Column " + j);
        td.appendChild(data);
        row.appendChild(td);
    }
    tbody.appendChild(row);
}
document.getElementById("thetable").appendChild(table);
</script>
</body>
```

Chapter 11

1. Here's the code:

```
<!DOCTYPE HTML PUBLIC "-//W3C//DTD HTML 4.01//EN"
"http://www.w3.org/TR/html4/strict.dtd">
<html>
<head>
<title>Onclick</title>
<script type="text/javascript">
function handleclick() {
    alert("You Clicked Here");
    return false;
}

</script>
</head>
<body>
<p><a href="#" onclick="return handleclick();">Click Here</a></p>
</body>
</html>
```

2. Here's the code:

```
<!DOCTYPE HTML PUBLIC "-//W3C//DTD HTML 4.01//EN"
"http://www.w3.org/TR/html4/strict.dtd">
<html>
<head>
<title>Onclick</title>
<script type="text/javascript" src="ehandler.js"></script>
<script type="text/javascript">
function handleclick() {
    alert("You Clicked Here");
    return false;
}
</script>
</head>
<body>
<p><a href="#" id="clickMe">Click Here</a></p>
<script type="text/javascript">
var aLink = document.getElementById("clickMe");
EHandler.add(aLink, "click", function() { handleclick(); });
</script>
</body>
</html>
```

3. No JavaScript is necessary for this exercise. The HTML code looks as follows:

```
<!DOCTYPE HTML PUBLIC "-//W3C//DTD HTML 4.01//EN"
"http://www.w3.org/TR/html4/strict.dtd">
<html>
<head>
<title>New Tab</title>
</head>
<body>
```

```
<p><a target="Microsoft" href="http://www.microsoft.com" id="mslink">Go To Microsoft
</a></p>
</body>
</html>
```

Chapter 12

1. A variation on an example in the chapter:

```
<!DOCTYPE HTML PUBLIC "-//W3C//DTD HTML 4.01//EN"
"http://www.w3.org/TR/html4/strict.dtd">
<html>
<head>
<title>Hello Cookie</title>
<script type = "text/javascript">
var cookName = "cookie1";
var cookVal = "testvalue";
var date = new Date();
date.setTime(date.getTime()+86400000); // one day, in milliseconds
var expireDate = date.toGMTString();
var myCookie = cookName + "=" + cookVal + ";expires=" + expireDate;
document.cookie = myCookie;
</script>
</head>
<body>
<p>Hello</p>
</body>
</html>
```

2. This code is basically the same as the code in Exercise 1, with the changed lines shown in boldface:

```
<!DOCTYPE HTML PUBLIC "-//W3C//DTD HTML 4.01//EN"
"http://www.w3.org/TR/html4/strict.dtd">
<html>
<head>
<title>Hello Cookie</title>
<script type = "text/javascript">
var cookName = "cookie2";
var cookVal = "testvalue";
var date = new Date();
date.setTime(date.getTime()+86400000); // one day, in millseconds
var expireDate = date.toGMTString();
var myCookie = cookName + "=" + cookVal + ";expires=" + expireDate + ";secure";
document.cookie = myCookie;
</script>
</head>
<body>
<p>Hello</p>
</body>
</html>
```

3. Unless you're using a Secure Sockets Layer (SSL) connection, you won't be able to read a cookie with the *secure* flag set.

4. In Exercise 1, I set a cookie named *cookie1*; therefore, that's the only one I want to display for this exercise. The code is:

```
<!DOCTYPE HTML PUBLIC "-//W3C//DTD HTML 4.01//EN"
"http://www.w3.org/TR/html4/strict.dtd">
<html>
<head>
<title>Reading Cookie</title>
<script type = "text/javascript">
var incCookies = document.cookie.split(";");
for (var c = 0; c < incCookies.length; c++) {
    var splitCookies = incCookies[c].split("=");
    if (splitCookies[0] == "cookie1") {
        alert(incCookies[c]);
    }
}
</script>
</head>
<body>
<p>Hello</p>
</body>
</html>
```

Chapter 13

1. See Listing 13-2 in Chapter 13 for an example of this exercise.

2. See Listing 13-2 in this chapter for an example of preloading images. You would apply that same code logic to the image map that you make for this exercise.

Chapter 14

1. See the section titled "Working with Select Boxes" in Chapter 11 for an example solution for this exercise.

2. Based on the pizza.htm example, the *<head>* portion of code now looks like this, with the additions shown in boldface:

```
<head>
    <title>Pizza</title>
    <script type = "text/javascript">

    function prepza() {
        var checkboxes = document.forms["pizzaform"].toppingcheck.length;
        var crusttype = document.forms["pizzaform"].crust;
        var size = document.forms["pizzaform"].size;
        var crustlength = crusttype.length;
        var sizelength = crusttype.length;
        var newelement = document.createElement("p");
        newelement.setAttribute("id","orderheading");
        document.body.appendChild(newelement);
```

```
newelement.appendChild(document.createTextNode("This pizza will have:"));

for (var c = 0; c < crustlength; c++) {
    if (crusttype[c].checked) {
        var newelement = document.createElement("p");
        newelement.setAttribute("id","crustelement" + i);
        document.body.appendChild(newelement);
        newelement.appendChild(document.createTextNode(
            crusttype[c].value + " Crust"));
    }
}

for (var s = 0; s < sizelength; s++) {
    if (size[s].checked) {
        var newelement = document.createElement("p");
        newelement.setAttribute("id","sizeelement" + i);
        document.body.appendChild(newelement);
        newelement.appendChild(document.createTextNode(size[s].value + " Size"));
    }
}

for (var i = 0; i < checkboxes; i++) {
    if (document.forms["pizzaform"].toppingcheck[i].checked) {
        var newelement = document.createElement("p");
        newelement.setAttribute("id","newelement" + i);
        document.body.appendChild(newelement);
        newelement.appendChild(document.createTextNode(
            document.forms["pizzaform"].toppingcheck[i].value));
    }
}
}
</script>
</head>
```

The HTML follows. This particular solution uses a three-column table, though that's not technically required for this answer to be correct—that is just one way to do it. The additions are again shown in boldface:

```
<form id="pizzaform" action="#">
<table>
<tr><td>Toppings</td><td>Crust</td><td>Size</td></tr>
<tr>
<td><input type="checkbox" id="topping1" value="Sausage" name="toppingcheck"
/>Sausage</td>
<td><input type="radio" name="crust" value="Regular" checked="checked" id="radio1"
/>Regular</td>
<td><input type="radio" name="size" value="Small" checked="checked" id="radiosize1"
/>Small</td>
</tr>
<tr>
<td><input type="checkbox" id="topping2" value="Pepperoni" name="toppingcheck"
/>Pepperoni</td>
<td><input type="radio" name="crust" value="Deep Dish" id="radio2" />Deep Dish</td>
<td><input type="radio" name="size" value="Medium" id="radiosize2" />Medium</td>
</tr>
```

```
<tr>
<td><input type="checkbox" id="topping3" value="Ham" name="toppingcheck" />Ham</td>
<td><input type="radio" name="crust" value="Thin" id="radio3" />Thin</td>
<td><input type="radio" name="size" value="Large" id="radiosize3" />Large</td>
</tr>
<tr>
<td><input type="checkbox" id="topping4" value="Green Peppers" name="toppingcheck"
/>Green Peppers</td>
<td></td>
<td></td>
</tr>
<tr>
<td><input type="checkbox" id="topping5" value="Mushrooms" name="toppingcheck"
/>Mushrooms</td>
<td></td>
<td></td>
</tr>
<tr>
<td><input type="checkbox" id="topping6" value="Onions" name="toppingcheck" />Onions
</td>
<td></td>
<td></td>
</tr>
<tr>
<td><input type="checkbox" id="topping7" value="Pineapple"
name="toppingcheck">Pineapple</td>
<td></td>
<td></td>
</tr>
</table>
<p><input type="submit" id="prepBtn" name="prepBtn" value="Prep Pizza"></p>
</form>
```

3. Add the following code to the *<head>* portion of the pizza application from the previous exercise:

```
function flip(pizzatype) {
    if (pizzatype == "veggiespecial") {
        document.getElementById("peppers").checked = "true";
        document.getElementById("onions").checked = "true";
        document.getElementById("mushrooms").checked = "true";
    } else if (pizzatype == "meatspecial") {
        document.getElementById("sausage").checked = "true";
        document.getElementById("pepperoni").checked = "true";
        document.getElementById("ham").checked = "true";
    } else if (pizzatype == "hawaiian") {
        document.getElementById("ham").checked = "true";
        document.getElementById("pineapple").checked = "true";
    }
}
```

Use the following HTML form. (Note the addition of the three buttons and the change to each ingredient's *id* attribute.)

```html
<form id="pizzaform" action="#">
<p>
<input type="button" id="veggiespecial" name="veggiespecial" value="Veggie Special" />
<input type="button" id="meatspecial" name="meatspecial" value="Meat Special" />
<input type="button" id="hawaiian" name="hawaiian" value="Hawaiian" />
</p>
<table>
<tr><td>Toppings</td><td>Crust</td><td>Size</td></tr>
<tr>
<td><input type="checkbox" id="sausage" value="Sausage" name="toppingcheck"
/>Sausage</td>
<td><input type="radio" name="crust" value="Regular" checked="checked" id="radio1"
/>Regular</td>
<td><input type="radio" name="size" value="Small" checked="checked" id="radiosize1"
/>Small</td>
</tr>
<tr>
<td><input type="checkbox" id="pepperoni" value="Pepperoni" name="toppingcheck"
/>Pepperoni</td>
<td><input type="radio" name="crust" value="Deep Dish" id="radio2" />Deep Dish</td>
<td><input type="radio" name="size" value="Medium" id="radiosize2" />Medium</td>
</tr>
<tr>
<td><input type="checkbox" id="ham" value="Ham" name="toppingcheck" />Ham</td>
<td><input type="radio" name="crust" value="Thin" id="radio3" />Thin</td>
<td><input type="radio" name="size" value="Large" id="radiosize3" />Large</td>
</tr>
<tr>
<td><input type="checkbox" id="peppers" value="Green Peppers" name="toppingcheck"
/>Green Peppers</td>
<td></td>
<td></td>
</tr>
<tr>
<td><input type="checkbox" id="mushrooms" value="Mushrooms" name="toppingcheck"
/>Mushrooms</td>
<td></td>
<td></td>
</tr>
<tr>
<td><input type="checkbox" id="onions" value="Onions" name="toppingcheck" />Onions</
td>
<td></td>
<td></td>
</tr>
<tr>
<td><input type="checkbox" id="pineapple" value="Pineapple" name="toppingcheck"
/>Pineapple</td>
<td></td>
<td></td>
</tr>
</table>
<p><input type="submit" id="prepBtn" name="prepBtn" value="Prep Pizza"
onclick="prepza();" /></p>
</form>
```

Add handlers to the JavaScript section found within the *<body>* of the page:

```
var veggieBtn = document.getElementById("veggiespecial");
EHandler.add(veggieBtn,"click",function() { flip("veggiespecial"); });
var meatBtn = document.getElementById("meatspecial");
EHandler.add(meatBtn,"click",function() { flip("meatspecial"); });
var hawaiiBtn = document.getElementById("hawaiispecial");
EHandler.add(hawaiiBtn,"click",function() { flip("hawaiian"); });
```

Chapter 15

1. Here's an example page; there are many ways to complete this exercise correctly:

```
<!DOCTYPE HTML PUBLIC "-//W3C//DTD HTML 4.01//EN"
"http://www.w3.org/TR/html4/strict.dtd">
<html>
<head>
<title>CSS</title>
<link href="exercise1.css" rel="stylesheet" type="text/css">
</head>
<body>
<h1 id="h1element">The Title</h1>
<p id="firstelement">The first element.</p>
<p id="secondelement">The second element.</p>
</body>
</html>
```

Here is the stylesheet exercise1.css:

```
#h1element {
background-color: #abacab;
}

#firstelement {
color: red;
}

#secondelement {
    color: blue;
}
```

2. This code changes the element named *firstelement* so that its font color is blue:

```
<script type="text/javascript">
var element1 = document.getElementById("firstelement");
element1.style.color = "#0000FF";
</script>
```

3. This code hides all the *<p>* elements using the Cascading Style Sheets (CSS) *visibility* property:

```
<script type="text/javascript">
var pelements = document.getElementsByTagName("p");
var pelmLength = pelements.length;
```

```
    for (var i = 0; i < pelmLength; i++) {
        pelements[i].style.visibility = "hidden";
    }
</script>
```

4. This code shows the visibility setting both before and after it has been set within the script. When you run the code, notice that the alert is empty before the property is set.

```
<script type="text/javascript">
var pelements = document.getElementsByTagName("p");
var pelmLength = pelements.length;
for (var i = 0; i < pelmLength; i++) {
    alert(pelements[i].style.visibility);
    pelements[i].style.visibility = "hidden";
    alert(pelements[i].style.visibility);
}
</script>
```

Chapter 16

1. Listing 16-3 in Chapter 16 provides a solution for this exercise.

2. An alert provides visual feedback, and that works as a solution to this problem. You can find better ways to provide visual feedback in the solution to Exercise 5 in Chapter 15, shown previously, which used a new element. Here's the basic solution to this problem:

```
<!DOCTYPE HTML PUBLIC "-//W3C//DTD HTML 4.01//EN"
"http://www.w3.org/TR/html4/strict.dtd">
<html>
<head>
<title>Try/Catch</title>
<script type="text/javascript">
</script>
</head>
<body>
<form name="formexample" id="formexample" action="#">
<div id="citydiv">Enter a City: <input id="city" name="city"></div>
<div><input id="submit" type="submit"></div>
</form>
<script type="text/javascript">
function checkValid() {
    try {
        var cityField = document.forms[0]["city"];
        if (cityField.value != "Stockholm") {
            throw "It's not Stockholm";
        }
    }
    catch(errorObject) {
        alert(errorObject);
    }
}
```

```
function init() {
    document.forms[0].onsubmit = function() { return checkValid() };
}
window.onload = init;
</script>
</body>
</html>
```

3. This is one method for accomplishing this exercise. Other methods exist, including using the ehandler.js script:

```
<!DOCTYPE HTML PUBLIC "-//W3C//DTD HTML 4.01//EN"
"http://www.w3.org/TR/html4/strict.dtd">
<html>
<head>
<title>Try/Catch</title>
<script type="text/javascript">
</script>
</head>
<body>
<form name="formexample" id="formexample" action="#">
<div id="citydiv">Enter a Number Between 1 and 100: <input id="num" name="num"></div>
<div><input id="submit" type="submit"></div>
</form>
<script type="text/javascript">
function checkValid() {
    try {
        var numField = document.forms[0]["num"];
        if (isNaN(numField.value)) {
            throw "it's not a number";
        }
        if ((numField.value > 100) || (numField.value < 1)) {
            numField.style.background = "#FF0000";
            return false;
        }
        else {
            numField.style.background = "#FFFFFF";
            return true;
        }
    }
    catch(errorObject) {
        alert(errorObject);
    }
    finally {
        alert("Thank you for playing.");
    }
}
function init() {
    document.forms[0].onsubmit = function() { return checkValid() };
}
window.onload = init;
</script>
</body>
</html>
```

Chapter 17

1. This solution requires the books.htm and books.xml files that are used within Chapter 17. This solution changes only books.htm. The few changes to this file are highlighted in boldface.

```
<!DOCTYPE HTML PUBLIC "-//W3C//DTD HTML 4.01//EN"
"http://www.w3.org/TR/html4/strict.dtd">
<html>
<head>
<script type="text/javascript" src="ehandler.js"></script>
<title>Books</title>
</head>
<body>
<div id="xmldata"></div>
<p><a href="#" id="displaytable">Display Table</a></p>
<script type="text/javascript">

function displayData() {
    var xmlEl = docObj.getElementsByTagName("book");
    var table = document.createElement("table");
    table.border = "1";
    var tbody = document.createElement("tbody");

    // Append the body to the table
    table.appendChild(tbody);
    var row = document.createElement("tr");

    for (colHead = 0; colHead < xmlEl[0].childNodes.length; colHead++) {
        if (xmlEl[0].childNodes[colHead].nodeType != 1) {
            continue;
        }
        var tableHead = document.createElement("th");
        var colName = document.createTextNode(xmlEl[0].childNodes[colHead].nodeName);
        tableHead.appendChild(colName);
        row.appendChild(tableHead);
    }
    tbody.appendChild(row);


    // Create table row
    for (i = 0; i < xmlEl.length; i++) {
        var row = document.createElement("tr");
        // Create the row/td elements
        for (j = 0; j < xmlEl[i].childNodes.length; j++) {
            // Skip it if the type is not 1
            if (xmlEl[i].childNodes[j].nodeType != 1) {
                continue;
            }

            // Insert the actual text/data from the XML document.
            var td = document.createElement("td");
            var xmlData = document.createTextNode(xmlEl[i].childNodes[j].firstChild.
nodeValue);
```

```
            td.appendChild(xmlData);
            row.appendChild(td);
        }
        tbody.appendChild(row);
    }
    document.getElementById("xmldata").appendChild(table);
}

function getXML()
{
    tablelink.style.visibility = "hidden";
    if (typeof document.implementation.createDocument != "undefined")
    {
        docObj = document.implementation.createDocument("", "", null);
        docObj.onload = displayData;
    }
    else if (window.ActiveXObject)
    {
        docObj = new ActiveXObject("Microsoft.XMLDOM");
        docObj.onreadystatechange = function () {
            if (docObj.readyState == 4) displayData()
        };
    }
    docObj.load("books.xml");
}
var tablelink = document.getElementById("displaytable");
EHandler.add("tablelink","click",function() { getXML(); });
</script>
</body>
</html>
```

Bonus: The following code adds a *"Display Table"* link, and then, when the table is displayed, it adds a *"Hide Table"* link. This wasn't part of the exercise.

```
<!DOCTYPE HTML PUBLIC "-//W3C//DTD HTML 4.01//EN"
"http://www.w3.org/TR/html4/strict.dtd">
<html>
<head>
<script type="text/javascript" src="ehandler.js"></script>
<title>Books</title>
</head>
<body>
<div id="xmldata"></div>
<p><a href="#" id="displaytable">Display Table</a></p>
<script type="text/javascript">

function displayData() {
    var xmlEl = docObj.getElementsByTagName("book");
    var table = document.createElement("table");
    table.setAttribute("id","bookstable");
    table.border = "1";
    var tbody = document.createElement("tbody");

    // Append the body to the table
    table.appendChild(tbody);
```

```
        var row = document.createElement("tr");

        for (colHead = 0; colHead < xmlEl[0].childNodes.length; colHead++) {
            if (xmlEl[0].childNodes[colHead].nodeType != 1) {
                continue;
            }
            var tableHead = document.createElement("th");
            var colName = document.createTextNode(xmlEl[0].childNodes[colHead].nodeName);
            tableHead.appendChild(colName);
            row.appendChild(tableHead);
        }
        tbody.appendChild(row);


        // Create table row
        for (i = 0; i < xmlEl.length; i++) {
            var row = document.createElement("tr");
            // Create the row/td elements
            for (j = 0; j < xmlEl[i].childNodes.length; j++) {
                // Skip it if the type is not 1
                if (xmlEl[i].childNodes[j].nodeType != 1) {
                    continue;
                }

                // Insert the actual text/data from the XML document.
                var td = document.createElement("td");
                var xmlData = document.createTextNode(xmlEl[i].childNodes[j].firstChild.
nodeValue);
                td.appendChild(xmlData);
                row.appendChild(td);
            }
            tbody.appendChild(row);
        }
        var tableanchor = document.createElement("a");
        var tableanchortext = document.createTextNode("Hide Table");
        tableanchor.setAttribute("id","hidetable");
        tableanchor.setAttribute("href","#");
        tableanchor.appendChild(tableanchortext);
        if (typeof window.addEventListener != "undefined") {
            tableanchor.addEventListener("click",hideTable,false);
        } else {
            tableanchor.attachEvent("onclick",hideTable);
        }
        document.getElementById("xmldata").appendChild(tableanchor);
        document.getElementById("xmldata").appendChild(table);
}

function hideTable() {
    var bookstable = document.getElementById("bookstable");
    bookstable.style.display = "none";
    tablelink.style.display = "";
    var tableanchor = document.getElementById("hidetable");
    tableanchor.style.display = "none";
}
```

```
function getXML()
{
    tablelink.style.display = "none";
    if (typeof document.implementation.createDocument != "undefined")
    {
        docObj = document.implementation.createDocument("", "", null);
        docObj.onload = displayData;
    }
    else if (window.ActiveXObject)
    {
        docObj = new ActiveXObject("Microsoft.XMLDOM");
        docObj.onreadystatechange = function () {
            if (docObj.readyState == 4) displayData()
        };
    }
    docObj.load("books.xml");
}

var tablelink = document.getElementById("displaytable");
EHandler.add("tablelink","click",function() { getXML(); });

</script>
</body>
</html>
```

2. This solution requires the books.xml file as well. Most of the code is the same as the final books.htm code in Chapter 17, with the differences shown in boldface:

```
<!DOCTYPE HTML PUBLIC "-//W3C//DTD HTML 4.01//EN"
"http://www.w3.org/TR/html4/strict.dtd">
<html>
<head>
<title>Books</title>
</head>
<body>
<div id="xmldata"></div>
<script type="text/javascript">

window.onload = getXML;

function displayData() {
    var xmlEl = docObj.getElementsByTagName("book");
    var table = document.createElement("table");
    table.border = "1";
    var tbody = document.createElement("tbody");

    // Append the body to the table
    table.appendChild(tbody);
    var row = document.createElement("tr");

    for (colHead = 0; colHead < xmlEl[0].childNodes.length; colHead++) {
        if (xmlEl[0].childNodes[colHead].nodeType != 1) {
            continue;
        }
        var tableHead = document.createElement("th");
```

```
            var colName = document.createTextNode(xmlEl[0].childNodes[colHead].nodeName);
            tableHead.appendChild(colName);
            row.appendChild(tableHead);
        }
        tbody.appendChild(row);


        // Create table row
        for (i = 0; i < xmlEl.length; i++) {
            var row = document.createElement("tr");
            // Create the row/td elements
            for (j = 0; j < xmlEl[i].childNodes.length; j++) {
                // Skip it if the type is not 1
                if (xmlEl[i].childNodes[j].nodeType != 1) {
                    continue;
                }

                // Insert the actual text/data from the XML document.
                var td = document.createElement("td");
                if (i % 2) {
                    td.style.background = "#aaabba";
                }
                var xmlData = document.createTextNode(xmlEl[i].childNodes[j].firstChild.
nodeValue);
                td.appendChild(xmlData);
                row.appendChild(td);
            }
            tbody.appendChild(row);
        }
        document.getElementById("xmldata").appendChild(table);
    }

    function getXML()
    {
        if (typeof document.implementation.createDocument != "undefined")
        {
            docObj = document.implementation.createDocument("", "", null);
            docObj.onload = displayData;
        }
        else if (window.ActiveXObject)
        {
            docObj = new ActiveXObject("Microsoft.XMLDOM");
            docObj.onreadystatechange = function () {
                if (docObj.readyState == 4) displayData()
            };
        }
        docObj.load("books.xml");
    }

</script>
</body>
</html>
```

Chapter 18

There are no exercises for Chapter 18.

Chapter 19

1. None of the Hypertext Transfer Protocol (HTTP) methods discussed in the chapter offer more security than any of the others. Only the addition of Secure Sockets Layer (SSL) provides a layer of security on top of the HTTP methods. It should be noted that using the *POST* method does not hide the input data, and only the *POST* method should be used with SSL because the *GET* method places the parameters directly on the URL, where they could be seen regardless of SSL.

2. Responses using standard HTML are retrieved with the *responseText* method and can contain just about anything that could be obtained through HTTP. Extensible Markup Language (XML) responses must be obtained with the *responseXML* method and must be served as an XML content type by the server. JavaScript Object Notation (JSON) responses are JavaScript responses; therefore, they offer some performance advantages over the other methods.

3. This solution was discussed in the chapter itself, but here is the asynchronous call (replace *YOUR SERVER* appropriately for your environment):

```
<!DOCTYPE HTML PUBLIC "-//W3C//DTD HTML 4.01//EN"
"http://www.w3.org/TR/html4/strict.dtd">
<html>
<head>
<title>Async</title>
</head>
<body>
<div id="xmldata"></div>
<script type="text/javascript">
function readyAJAX() {
try {
    return new XMLHttpRequest();
} catch(e) {
    try {
        return new ActiveXObject('Msxml2.XMLHTTP');
    } catch(e) {
        try {
            return new ActiveXObject('Microsoft.XMLHTTP');
        } catch(e) {
            return "A newer browser is needed.";
        }
    }
}
}
var requestObj = readyAJAX();
var url ="http://YOUR SERVER/sum.php?num1=2&num2=2";
```

```
requestObj.open("GET",url,true);
requestObj.send();
requestObj.onreadystatechange = function() {
    if (requestObj.readyState == 4) {
        if (requestObj.status == 200) {
            alert(requestObj.responseText);
        } else {
            alert(requestObj.statusText);
        }
    }
}
</script>
</body>
</html>
```

The file sum.php is a woefully small and inadequately secured server-side program in PHP that looks like this:

```
<?php
print $_GET['num1'] + $_GET['num2'];
?>
```

Chapter 20

1. This solution uses Listing 19-1 and requires the addition of a submit button to the form. The form now looks like this:

```
<form name="nameform" id="nameform" action="" method="GET">
Enter State: <input id="textname" type="text" name="textname">
<input type="submit" name="submit" id="statesubmit">
</form>
```

Aside from including ehandler.js, an event handler and new function are all that's required for this solution. These are added within the existing JavaScript.

```
var formSubmit = document.getElementById("nameform");
EHandler.add("formSubmit","submit",function() { showstate(); });

function showstate() {
    alert(document.forms[0].textname.value);
}
```

2. This solution is a variation of the previous solution and others shown in Chapter 19. The server-side program will need to return the comma-delimited list of people for the company directory, much as the state example returned a list of U.S. states.

Chapter 21

1. Both jQuery and MooTools offers a small learning curve, though PrototypeJS is also fairly easy to learn. Dojo doesn't aim for the beginner-level JavaScript programmer, and I've encountered more than one developer confused by YUI, even though it has extensive documentation. However, everyone learns differently, so I'd recommend trying each one yourself rather than taking my word for it!

2. The exercise in this chapter provides an example of creating your own library and including it in a page.

Chapter 22

1. One method for achieving this is using the *.hover()* function together with the *.css()* function to change the background color. That happens within the *showStates* function. Here is the altered *showStates* function from ajax.html:

```
function showStates(data,status) {
    $.each(data, function(item) {
        $("#states").append("<div>" + data[item] + "</div>");
        $('#states').children().hover(
            function() {
                $(this).css('background-color','blue');
            },
            function() {
                $(this).css('background-color','');
            }
        );
    });
}
```

2. Here is the server-side code written in PHP. This code returns *"Wisconsin"* when the abbreviation *WI* is passed in:

```
<?php


$stateAbbrev = trim($_POST['state']);
if ($stateAbbrev == "WI") {
        print json_encode("Wisconsin");
}


?>
```

3. Here is the HTML, JavaScript, and jQuery to produce output based on the AJAX call:

```
<!DOCTYPE HTML PUBLIC "-//W3C//DTD HTML 4.01//EN"
  "http://www.w3.org/TR/html4/strict.dtd">
<html>
<head>
<title>AJAX Data Test</title>
<script type="text/javascript" src="jquery-1.4.2.min.js"></script>
</head>
<body>
<div id="state">
</div>
<script type="text/javascript">
$(document).ready(function() {

$.ajax({
        type: "POST",
        url: "statefull.php",
        dataType: "json",
        success: showStateFull,
        data: "state=WI"
});

function showStateFull(data,status) {
        $("#state").text(data);
}


});
</script>

</body>
</html>
```

Chapter 23

1. You can add functionality to show all options in multiple ways. This example adds an anchor element with an ID of *showAll*. That ID is then tied to a function in the jQuery /JavaScript code. The function loops through each of the option items and, if the display property for an option is set to *none*, the code executes the *.show()* function for it. Another—and arguably better—option would be to add a class called *hidden* to the *<li>* element when the *.hide()* function is originally executed. Then, finding the hidden element would be much easier, because you could just search for any *<li>* elements that are hidden within the *<ul>* tag. There's also a way to do this with the *jQuery :hidden* selector; however, I've encountered a few difficulties in getting the *:hidden* selector to work in a cross-browser manner, which is why I chose to show the other approaches for accomplishing this task. Regardless, here's the code:

```
<!DOCTYPE HTML PUBLIC "-//W3C//DTD HTML 4.01//EN"
  "http://www.w3.org/TR/html4/strict.dtd">
```

```
<html>
<head>
<title>Hide</title>
<script type="text/javascript" src="jquery-1.4.2.min.js"></script>
<style type="text/css">
.removeBtn {
    color: #0000CC;
}
</style>
</head>
<body>
<ul>
<li id="option1">Option 1 <span class="removeBtn" id="remove1">(x)</span></li>
<li id="option2">Option 2 <span class="removeBtn" id="remove2">(x)</span></li>
<li id="option3">Option 3 <span class="removeBtn" id="remove3">(x)</span></li>
<li id="option4">Option 4 <span class="removeBtn" id="remove4">(x)</span></li>
</ul>
<a href="" id="showAll">Show All</a>
<script type="text/javascript">
$(document).ready(function() {

    $('.removeBtn').each(function(elm) {
        $(this).click(function() {
            $(this).parent().hide();
        });
    });

    $('#showAll').click(function() {
        $('.removeBtn').each(function(elm) {
            if ($(this).parent().attr("display","none")) {
                $(this).parent().show();
            }
        });
    });

});
</script>

</body>
</html>
```

2. The key to this exercise is the use of the *async* option in jQuery's *.ajax()* function. Without *async*, the *.accordion()* function tends to fire prior to the options for the accordion being received and processed by AJAX. This code sample uses a JSON call to retrieve the list of states used in Chapter 22. This list is then placed into the accordion. The code sets *async* to *false* within the call to *.ajax()* and then adds a bit of processing to the *showStates* function from Chapter 22. Otherwise, this is a variation of the accordion example from Chapter 23.

```
<!DOCTYPE HTML PUBLIC "-//W3C//DTD HTML 4.01//EN"
  "http://www.w3.org/TR/html4/strict.dtd">
<html>
<head>
<title>Accordion</title>
```

```
<script type="text/javascript" src="jquery-1.4.2.min.js"></script>
<script type="text/javascript" src="js/jquery-ui-1.8.4.custom.min.js"></script>
<style type="text/css">
#container {
    width: 350px;
    height: 700px;
    border: solid 2px black;
    padding: 3px;
}
.optionHead {
    border: solid 1px black;
    background-color: #abacab;
}
.optionDiv {
    border-bottom: dotted 1px black;
}
</style>
</head>
<body>
<div id="container">
</div>
<script type="text/javascript">
$(document).ready(function() {

    $.ajax({
            type: "GET",
            url: "json.php",
            dataType: "json",
            success: showStates,
            async: false
    });

    function showStates(data,status) {
            $.each(data, function(item) {;
                $("#container").append(
                    "<h3 class=\"optionHead\">" +
                        data[item] +
                        "</h3>" +
                        "<div class=\"optionDiv\">" +
                        "Option text goes here</div>");
            });
    }

    $('#container').accordion({
        collapsible: true,
        active: false
    });

});
</script>

</body>
</html>
```

Index

Symbols

$(document).ready() function (jQuery), 390, 395
$ (dollar sign) character in regular expressions, 92
$(this) selector (jQuery), 398
+ addition operators, 99–100
& (ampersand) character
  as bitwise operator, 101
  in XHTML, 8
/* and */ multiline comments, beginning
    and ending, 51
\ (backslash)
  character in regular expressions, 92
/body tags
  placement of JavaScript within, 7
(^) (caret) character
  as bitwise operator, 101
  in regular expressions, 92
{ } (curly braces)
  creating objects with, 72
  in if statement, 52
/ (division) operator, 100
. (dot) notation, 68
. (dot sign)
  character in regular expressions, 92
  operator, accessing methods, 155
" " (double quotes)
  escaping, 67–68
  in jQuery statements, 389
  strings enclosed in, 66
  to designate JavaScript file in Notepad, 45
== equality tests, 102–103
! (exclamation point)
  operator (unary), 106, 107
/ (forward slashes), delineating regular expressions, 131
> (greater than) operator, 104
>= (greater than or equal to) operator, 104
/head tags
  placement of JavaScript within, 7
.js file extensions
  changing name of file, 29
  defining JavaScript using, 54
  designating file extension in Notepad, 45
  reasons for using, 30, 39
<< (left arrows) as bitwise operator, 101
< (less than)
  operator, 104
  sign in XHTML, 8
<= (less than or equal to) operator, 104
.load() function (jQuery), 409
- (minus sign)
  operator (unary), 106, 107

subtraction operator, 99
% modulo operator, 101, 374
* multiplication operator, 100
{n, } characters in regular expressions, 92
.NET Common Language Runtime, 97
{n,m} characters in regular expressions, 92
/nonscript tags, 232
( ) (parentheses)
  characters in regular expressions, 92
  evoking functions with empty, 152–153
% (percent sign)
  modulo operator, 101
| (pipe) as bitwise operator, 101
+ (plus sign)
  additive operators, 99–100
  character in regular expressions, 92
  operator (unary), 106, 107
++ (plus signs) operator (unary), 106–107
? (question mark)
  character in regular expressions, 92
  operator in if/else constructs, 131
>> (right arrows) as bitwise operator, 101
>>> (right arrows) as bitwise operator, 101
// single-line comments, 51
' ' (single quotes)
  escaping, 67–68
  in jQuery statements, 389
  strings enclosed in, 66
/ (slash) characters
  division operator, 100
  in closing tag, 7
/ slash characters
  in comments, 51
[ ] (square brackets)
  character in regular expressions, 92
  in implicit array constructor, 171
* (star sign)
  character in regular expressions, 92
  multiplication operator, 100
- subtraction operator, 99
(~) tilde
  character as bitwise operator, 101
  operator (unary), 107
_ (underscore character)
  using in variables, 74

A

abs.x() function, 66
accordion effects, creating in jQuery UI, 423–426
ActiveXObjects, instantiating, 347
addClass() method, 403

459

H

I

About the Author

Steve Suehring is a technology architect who's written about programming, security, network and system administration, operating systems, and other topics for several industry publications. He speaks at conferences and user groups and has served as an editor for a popular technology magazine.